Public Health and the Poverty of Reforms

Public Health and the Poverty of Reforms

The South Asian Predicament

Editors

Imrana Qadeer
Kasturi Sen
K.R. Nayar

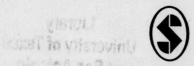

Sage Publications
New Delhi • Thousand Oaks • London

First published in 2001 by

Sage Publications India Pvt Ltd
M-32 Market, Greater Kailash I
New Delhi 110 048

Sage Publications Inc
2455 Teller Road
Thousand Oaks, California 91320

Sage Publications Ltd
6 Bonhill Street
London EC2A 4PU

Published by Tejeshwar Singh for Sage Publications India Pvt Ltd, typeset in 10 pt. Bruce Old Style by Siva Math Setters, Chennai, and printed at Chaman Enterprises, Delhi.

Library of Congress Cataloging-in-Publication Data
Public health and the poverty of reforms: the South Asian predicament/ edited by Imrana Qadeer, Kasturi Sen, K.R. Nayar.
p. cm.
Includes bibliographical references.
1. Public health—South Asia. 2. Health care reform—South Asia. 3. Structural adjustment(Economic policy)—South Asia. 4. Primary health care—South Asia. I. Qadeer, Imrana, 1941– II. Sen, Kasturi, 1956– III. Nayar, K.R., 1955–

RA541.S64 P82 362.1′0954—dc21 2001 00-051557

ISBN: 0-7619-9518-8 (US-Hb)
81-7036-988-6 (India-Hb)

Sage Production Team: Shweta Vachani, O.P. Bhasin, and Santosh Rawat

Dedicated to a collective vision of public health that evolves around human dignity, rights, and needs.

Contents

List of Tables

List of Figures

List of Abbreviations

ADB	Asian Development Bank
AMD	Army Medical Division of Her Majesty's Service
AMOPOP	assistant medical officers per 10,000 population
API	annual parasite index
ARI	acute respiratory infections
ASMRs	age-specific mortality rates
AVSS	Association for Voluntary Surgical Sterilization
BHU	basic health unit
BI	bacillary index
BL	borderline lepromatous leprosy
BMI	Body Mass Index
BSP	Bhilai Steel Plant
BT	borderline tuberculoid
CHIP	Contraceptive and Health Innovations Project
CHW	community health worker
CIP	central issue price
CLG	consumption loan or grant
CMCH	Christian Medical College and Hospital
CMM	Chattisgarh Mukti Morcha
CMSS	Chhattisgarh Mines Shramik Sangh
CPI	Consumer Price Index
CPIAL	consumer price index for agricultural laborers
CRPS	Center for Research on Population and Security
CV	coefficient of variation
DALYs	disability adjusted life years
DB	decentralized budgeting
DDC	district development councils
DDHS	Divisional Director Health Service
DOTS	directly observed treatment short course
DPA	district political authorities
DPDHS	Deputy Provincial Director of Health Services
DTC	district TB centers
DTH	delayed type hypersensitivity
DTO	district TB officer
DTP	District Tuberculosis Program
DTPE	district TB program efficiency

EFF	extended fund facility
EMU	European Monetary Union
EPI	expanded program for immunization
ESAF	extended structural adjustment facility
EU	European Union
FDT	fixed duration therapy
FHB	family health bureau
FHI	Family Health International
FI	fertility indicator
FP	family planning
FPP	Family Planning Program
FYP	Five Year Plan
GDP	gross domestic product
GNP	gross national product
GRI	annual average growth rate, 1982–87
GRII	annual average growth rate, 1987–96
HAPP	Health and Population Program
HD	Hanson's disease
HDI	human development index
HLA	histocompatibility complex—class II antigens
HSR	health sector reforms
ICPD	International Conference on Population and Development
IDA	International Development Agency
IFFH	International Federation for Family Health
IMF	International Monetary Fund
IMR	infant mortality rates
IMS	Indian Medical Service
IRDP	Integrated Rural Development Program
IUCD	intra-uterine contraceptive device
LL	lepromatous leprosy
MB leprosy	multi-bacillary leprosy
MCH	maternal and child health services
MDT	multi-drug therapy
MHC	major histocompatibility complex
MNC	Multinational Company/Corporation
MO	medical officer
MOH	Ministry of Health
MOPOP	medical officers per 10,000 population
MPH	Medical and Public Health

NAM	Non-Aligned Movement
NCAER	National Council for Applied Economic Research
NCH	The New Civil Hospital
NGO	non-governmental organization
NHS	National Health Services
NLCP	National Leprosy Control Program
NNMR	neo-natal mortality rate
NPC	National Planning Committee
NPH	new public health
NSSO	National Sample Survey Organization
NTP	National Tuberculosis Program
OECD	Organization for Economic Cooperation and Development
ORS	oral rehydration solution
PB leprosy	pauci-bacillary leprosy
PCFPD	Population Control and Family Planning Division
PCI	per capita income
PDHS	Provincial Director of Health Services
PFWS	Plantation Family Welfare Supervisors
PHC	primary health care/center
PHD	provincial health department
PHI	peripheral health institutions
PHM	public health midwives
PHMPOP	public health midwives per 3,000 population
PID	pelvic inflammatory diseases
PRI	panchayati raj institutions
QALYs	quality adjusted life years
RCH	reproductive and child health
RHC	rural health center
RNTCP	Revised National Tuberculosis Program
RPC	regional plantation companies
RSE	real per capita expenditure on social services
SAL	structural adjustment loan
SAP	structural adjustment programs/policies
SC/ST	scheduled caste/scheduled tribes
SCC	short-course chemotherapy
SCTPR	social time preference rate
SDD	Social Development Division

SDP	State Domestic Product
SET	survey, education, and treatment
SIDA	Swedish International Development Agency
SMC	Surat Municipal Corporation
SPHC	Selective Primary Health Care
SRS	sample registration survey
STD	sexually transmitted disease
TB	tuberculosis
TBAs	traditional birth attendants
TE	efficiency of treatment
THC	thana health complex
TRC	Tuberculosis Research Center
TRUST	Plantation, Housing and Social Welfare Trust
UNDP	United Nations Development Program
UNFPA	United Nations Fund for Population Activities
UNICEF	United National Children's Fund
USAID	United States Agency for International Development
VHAI	Voluntary Health Association of India
WB	World Bank
WHO	World Health Organization
WPI	wholesale price index
YLDs	Years of Life Disabled

Preface

The impact of two decades of Structural Adjustment Policies in African and Latin American countries has been extensively studied. Hence, the negative consequences of the health sector reforms, which were part of the Structural Adjustment Programs, and their implications for the poor are well known in these countries. In South Asia, however, the reforms were implemented much later and their nature was so varied that, to begin with, the interpretations of the structural shifts were very different in each of these countries. The first phase of structural reforms that introduced the concept of devolution and decentralization in Sri Lanka, the opening up of medical care to non-governmental and private sectors in India, the increase in health care investments in Bangladesh, all projected a diverse picture initially. The shared negative consequences began to emerge only when the thrust of the reforms—creation of a medical market and minimizing costs of public services—became visible and when subsequent cuts in the welfare sector started impinging upon its growth.

In most parts of the South Asian region, the reform process in the health sector had begun in the eighties itself. However, the continuing expansion of public sector infrastructure for certain services such as family planning and the official commitment to primary health care on paper actually created an illusion of change for the better. That is why, despite acceptance of Structural Adjustment Policies in the nineties, the talk of a "safety net" was sufficient to lull the policy watchers into believing that there would be no drastic impact on the social sector. It took a series of epidemics such as malaria, cholera, gastroenteritis, kala azar, hepatitis and encephalitis, and finally the plague epidemic of 1994, to shake this confidence. It is only then that the criticism of "reforms" received some space and attention. Some rethinking also followed on the part of a few governments. For example, India retreated from introducing cuts as drastic as those introduced in the year 1992–93. Notwithstanding these developments, the perception among administrators about the need and value of Structural Adjustment Programs did not change. Hence, there was barely any effort to assess the implications of the prescribed structural changes. The reforms continued even after the public health disasters, although at a slower pace.

The Structural Adjustment Programs held far-reaching implications for the vulnerable sections for two reasons. First, it was well accepted in official circles that the brunt of the negative effects—be it shrinking job opportunities or rising prices—were to be borne by the poor sections. Second, the cuts in investments in the welfare sector too were to affect the poor the most. For a long time now the association between ill-health/disease and poverty has been well-recognized by researchers and policy-makers. It was, therefore, not too difficult to foresee/anticipate that the dwindling food security systems and other negative effects referred to above were going to have a significant impact on the health status of the affected population. Changes, such as the gradual dismantling of public sector health institutions, their receding resource base, introduction of user fee in public hospitals, and opening up of medical care to the private sector, meant that the interests of the poor would not be safeguarded any more. On the contrary, their problems were to increase. Through all this the so-called "safety net" was nowhere to be seen.

Although it was difficult to discriminate between the influence of each of the above factors, the importance of recording some of these early shifts and analyzing their possible implications for public health was evident. To initiate this process, a series of seminars were organized by the faculty of the Centre of Social Medicine and Community Health, Jawaharlal Nehru University, New Delhi. The objective was to share common concerns and research findings with other scholars from the South Asian and other countries. In the process, a group of concerned scholars, public health practitioners, administrators, policy-makers, clinicians, and activists gathered to assess the situation in their respective countries and to compare them with other countries.

This book is the outcome of one such seminar held in September 1997 to explore the impact of Structural Adjustment Policies on primary health care in South Asia. It attempts to bring together multiple dimensions of public health, ranging from its conceptual and theoretical basis, history, and political economy to its contemporary practical dimensions such as financing, service delivery, planning processes, organizational issues, and therapeutic aspects. It contrasts the South Asian experience with that of the European countries and points out the differences in implementation of reforms in their respective historical and socio-economic contexts. This helps to place reforms in South Asia in a global context and in highlighting the stark contradictions of its contents in these two parts of the world. Intertwined within these dimensions are accounts of the lives and experiences of the common people living in small towns, slums of metropolitan cities, and the rural hinterland. The perceptions of these people, the conditions of their lives, and their struggles to improve the same, provide the vantage point from where the book looks at the future. Contributors from a range of disciplines document the contemporary shifts and their background. Though India, given its size and internal variation, inevitably occupies considerable space in this, Bangladesh, Sri Lanka, and Pakistan add significantly to the regional dimension.

For those who argue that the health sector reforms alone will solve the crisis in public health in the region and claim that there is no need for pessimism regarding its consequences, this book provides sufficient evidence and a basis for rethinking. Then there are those who seek "hard evidence" before they are even willing to consider the possibility of any tragic consequences of the reforms. The contents of this book indicate that the reform package may not necessarily ensure health for the people. In fact, as the final draft goes to the press, substantive evidence has emerged from the Indian National Sample Registration Scheme of not just stagnation in the decline in infant mortality rates (IMR) in different states, but of a definite increase in them. In some major states of India, such as Kerala, Karnataka, Gujarat, Maharashtra, Andhra Pradesh, Punjab, as well as Madhya Pradesh, Orissa, and Assam, the IMR in 1998 has risen above the levels recorded in 1996 and 1997. This is the first statistical pointer and an indication of much worse that is to come. Must we wait to be hit by more "hard evidence" or should we begin to think of how the negative aspects of reforms can be arrested and contained?

This is the question that the book raises in the domain of public health. It has been compiled with the conviction that it is far better and far more important to ask the right questions and strive for approximate answers than to unquestioningly accept certain methodologies in pursuit of the perfectly objective answer and therefore limit the question itself.

Silverman, an eminent American pediatrician, has observed that enormous resources are spent to provide unlimited intensive treatment for marginally viable newborns, yet social security and resource inputs to improve living conditions of overwhelmed families who must care for the fragile survivors are meager (Silverman 1998). This is no accident; it is a reality that reflects the tensions and imbalances between available knowledge and possible action for public health. Often accumulated evidence regarding the limits of technology remains unheeded or the insights available from social sciences remain unutilized by public health experts. This book addresses these challenges thrown up by the politics of knowledge itself. We earnestly hope that it will be read by specialists and non-specialists alike and would bridge the gap which often blocks creative criticism and that it will spark off a refreshing debate on the vital, yet rarely asked question: reforms for whom and for what?

Reference

Silverman, W.A. (1998): *Where's the Evidence? Debates in Modern Medicine*. New York: Oxford University Press.

Acknowledgements

We acknowledge the sincere efforts of all the participants and express our deep appreciation for their enthusiasm and active participation. The process of bringing out this book has given rise to a nascent group that is convinced of the need for creating a South Asian alternative to the present reform package, an alternative that is rooted in the regional context. Despite the frequent power breakdowns, slow internet connections, and frequently dead telephone lines, the members of the group have managed to keep in touch and develop ideas. This book, hopefully, is the beginning of an effort at sharing ideas, research, and experiences in the region, and to learn from our strengths and weaknesses.

We also acknowledge the support extended by the European Commission in this endeavor. It not only provided the financial assistance for organizational purposes, but the participation of its specialists also contributed to the substantive debate. We value very much the Commission's unconditional support to this project and the encouragement provided to the spirit of freedom of inquiry and exchange of ideas.

The research staff and the students of the Centre of Social Medicine and Community Health were an integral part of this process in many ways and they helped at different points in different ways. We would specially like to thank Indira Chakravarthi who diligently took care of the numerous tasks, big and small, that go into the making of a book. Her help in bringing out this book was invaluable.

Introduction

When the countries of South Asia freed themselves from the grip of colonial rule to reshape their destinies, they adopted a two-pronged strategy toward development. One component was the use of structural reforms at the social level. These included land reforms, protective legislation for the vulnerable religious and caste groups, provision of education for all, and building of infrastructures to provide basic services such as public health (including medical care), transport, electricity, housing, and drinking water. The other component was the promotion and use of technology to increase the outputs in all areas of primary, secondary, and tertiary production. These two legs of developmental strategy were used in different combinations by various countries depending upon their specific context and political formation.

The task was enormous—rooted as it was in extreme poverty, backwardness (social and economic), and inequitable social structures. Governmental efforts were largely guided by the ruling elite of each of the South Asian countries, with a measure of caution towards drastic reforms, acceptance of a slow evolutionary process, and a high degree of dependence on international professional and technical support. Equally unavoidable, therefore, was their dependence (however limited to begin with) on international financial aid. These independent nations thus began to carve out their own histories within a broadly liberal-welfarist development framework.

After the first oil crisis of 1973, the international market started putting pressure on the Third World countries by restricting entry of their goods and introducing restrictive monetary policies. The falling price of goods and the consequent fall in export taxes and revenues and, therefore, national economic growth were detrimental to the already vulnerable economies. The rising real interest rates added to this squeeze in the late seventies. The first to fall were the nations of Latin America, followed by those of Africa. The South Asian countries were not far behind. Their external debt burden continued to rise, as did their acceptance of the debt management strategies of the eighties. In 1997, the total external debt of the developing countries was US$ 2,173 billion and of the South Asian region US$ 150 billion. Of this India accounted for US$ 94 billion (HDC 1999). India's external debt in end-September 1999 stood at US$ 98.87 billion (Government of India 2000).

This crisis threw the South Asian experiment with autonomy out of gear and the countries of the region accepted the terms of the International Monetary Fund (IMF) and World Bank (WB) for "reconstruction and development." Their governments saw the support of these institutions as the only option to prevent the line of credit from drying up. From creating politically and economically independent, self-sufficient, and less inequitable societies, their central concern shifted to foreign exchange reserves and creditworthiness. The monetary crisis thus cloaked the basic questions pertaining to the use of loans and the nature of control over the recipient nation's economy. For instance, it was already well known that the inefficiencies and inherent problems of these "soft states" had led to the siphoning off of not just the aid money and loans, but of all national resources to a small set of beneficiaries. Equally, these states had systems that exhibited differing sensitivities to the needs of the majority and to the professed national priorities. Sub-regions like Sri Lanka and the State of Kerala in India had managed to acquire a Human Development Index (HDI) comparable with the developed countries, while others lagged behind in varying degrees. Refusing to deal with the structural issues underlying these inequities, the governments of these regions approached the IMF and WB for support and sustenance.

There were two basic responses to this official acceptance of Structural Adjustment Policies (SAP). One lauded the step as bold, desirable, and necessary for South Asia's successful entry into the twenty-first century and its globalized modernity. The other saw it as a step backward in the region's effort at independence, self-sufficiency, and building a less iniquitous society. Both viewpoints accepted the innumerable problems of the present system of governance, but with a difference. While the former believed in promoting private initiatives and removing the bottlenecks of government rules, the latter asserted the importance of regulatory mechanisms of the state, which required reform not rejection. This second view not only upheld the primacy of the state in protecting the interests of the under-privileged in the process of development, but also put at center-stage the unfinished task of social and structural reforms initiated during the early phases of national reconstruction. On the other hand, the proponents of SAP placed their faith in the process of globalization, mechanisms of free market, and international cooperation. They argued that only these would encourage the "quality" and "efficiency" of technological growth, which was the basis for long-term economic growth and development.

Over time the evidence for this debate accumulated from a wide range of developed and under-developed countries, which were forced to accept the uniform model of the so-called "reforms." Interestingly, the very use of the word "reforms" was misleading because in recent social memory rooted in historical experience, reforms meant measures for the welfare of the majority of the people. The World Bank and IMF took advantage of this social perception and never made it explicit for whom their "reforms" were meant! It was argued that in the long run the poor would benefit even if they carried the burden of reforms on their shoulders initially. Reforms were projected as the only answer to the problems of the Third World countries. Therefore, this was an inevitability that had to be tackled with security nets. The justification for the World Bank reforms was provided by highlighting the existing state structures and failures of the promises made by the nation-states, such as democratic governance, individual rights and choices, and efficient and participatory local self-government. The inefficiencies of the governments, particularly of the Third World, thus became a key justification for the rolling back of the states. Other than a handful of dissenters, the elite and the nascent middle classes of these countries, aspiring towards international standards, vociferously supported the "reforms." The supporters of the reforms argued that there were not enough resources to invest in public provision and that the only way forward was to privatize as the quality of public services could never be improved. This was to only further distort access and enhance existing inequities in the provision of health services, despite the fact that their non-affordability remains to be proven.

Given the long history of political, cultural, and intellectual colonization, winning over the ruling classes was easy. The dismantling of existing structures and institutions was initiated with their full consent and collaboration. For example, in 1992, the World Bank took the liberty of planning the health sector for India (World Bank 1992). In 1993, it produced the *World*

Development Report on health, which was its blueprint for planning for health in the Third World. Instead of critiquing and pointing out the deficiencies, these reports were used by the majority of politicians, technocrats, and bureaucrats as guidelines for transforming national-level plans. As a result, not only was the onslaught of reforms unscientific and insensitive to democratic processes, but also callous and arrogant. The methodologies that evolved in the process were high-handed and manipulative. For instance, tools such as Disability Adjusted Life Years (DALYs) were invented to replace those based on years of public health experience (Barker and Green 1996); data were distorted to accommodate vertical programs such as AIDS (Priya 1994) and DOTS (Banerjee 1996). Evaluation of new strategies was not only conceptually and methodologically flawed (Qadeer 1995) but was often avoided—as in the case of higher efficiency claims for private sector hospitals, which were never actually evaluated for coverage as well as effectiveness (Baru 1997). In addition, it helped to always look at achievements and to never address the implications—such as the side-effects of technology-based interventions (Richter 1993) or the structural changes involved in opening up public sector hospitals to private investment (Evans 1997). The fact that the state had all through protected private practitioners and legitimized their use of and negative influence on public sector health services, made privatization in health care even easier.

In spite of almost two decades of pressurizing and cajoling, the international monetary forces could not succeed in satisfactorily transforming the structures of the poorer nations. All the talk of "safety nets" notwithstanding, the general experience was that the social sectors were the first to collapse generating a dangerous degree of inequity. To cope with this threat, international organizations with a philanthropic image, such as WHO, were mobilized to talk of equity. Equity in health through mobilization of multiple agencies such as NGOs, the private sector, and the public sector became the popular slogan, with the public sector being projected as a mere partner (Rafei 1997). This sanitization of equity was a veil to hide the relentless aggression of international funding agencies to break the backs of the fragile South Asian nations.

Although this veil of "reforms" has been so obviously swept aside, the World Bank has still succeeded in pushing the health services in South Asia to the brink! This is a reality that has to be faced by all those who are responsible for public health, particularly the academicians, the policy-makers, and the providers of services. Their role may be critical if the region is to save itself from repeating the mistakes of others. If their middle class or elite backgrounds have created the illusion that their privileges are exclusive, then the case of Britain should be a lesson, where the rising costs of health care and failures of protective insurance systems have severely struck at these classes (Pollock, Brannigen, and Liss 1995). As has been recently suggested by some public health scholars, the benefits of current reforms may soon become a mirage for all unless the historical gains made by the state-supported health sector for the population at large are acknowledged and defended.

The evidence accumulating from across the globe, from regions varying in socio-economic conditions, levels of achievements in welfare, and the time when SAPs were introduced, provides an excellent opportunity to build a case for alternative strategies. The varied richness of this evidence helps construct probabilities for future and possibilities for avoiding disasters. There is a clear need for a comprehensive evaluation of SAP and health sector reforms and their implications for health. Even the most committed proponents of market mechanism and competition agree that any strategy can go wrong if not properly monitored and evaluated. Walking through the corridors of power in Southern nations with money-bags, forcing vulnerable and weak states to agree to conditionalities may be easy, but it may not necessarily deliver the projected results.

Instead of generating more and stable markets, the SAP reforms have sown the seeds of social conflict and discontent. The rolling back of the state has enhanced inequalities by marginalizing the poor and increasing accumulation and consumption by the rich. The growing social tensions, an outcome of increasing isolation and rejection of the poor, are inevitable. The shrinking social sectors have denied basic amenities and access to vast numbers of the under-privileged. This may become a prescription for economic and political instability. Witness the looting of vegetable markets in Patna (India) after the price hike of onions in November 1998, the beating up of the urban affairs minister in Surat (India) during the 1998 Assembly elections' campaign after an epidemic, and the mass suicides of the peasants in Andhra Pradesh in 1998 when the cotton crops failed due to failure of rains and pest infestation, and total neglect by the state which was pursuing its policy of cuts in subsidies and dismantling its infrastructures.

This book is an attempt to look at the health sector in South Asia in a global context. It moves away from the prevailing neoclassical framework of analysis of health sector reforms to look at the health sector through epidemiological, health, and social sciences, rooted in alternative theoretical moorings. It uses a perspective wherein the health sector moves beyond the context of markets, medical technologies, and overpopulation and takes into account social processes born out of conflicting and complementary economic, political, social, and cultural realities. The focus is on complexities and processes and on unraveling the internal and external linkages of the health sector in order to draw attention to the challenges of health planning in South Asia. By examining different layers of dynamics, key variables, priorities, and ideological underpinnings, the authors try to explore the depth and spread of influence of SAP on the health sector and the people. They also highlight the need to grasp differences within the region in order to avoid simplistic solutions. These differences are set against the background of a shared historical experience of colonialism.

All the South Asian countries have developed a variety of infrastructure, basic production systems, social and political institutions, class structures and conflicts, and patterns of social sector development. While Sri Lanka invested the most in its social sector and has demographic indicators and HDI comparable to the advanced countries, its slow economic growth over the sixties forced its terms of trade to deteriorate. Hence, restructuring of the social sector was introduced much earlier, even though reforms for stabilization were accepted only in the nineties. Its ethnic crises have added to the problems of slow economic growth.

In contrast, Bangladesh, the youngest of all the countries, with a military bureaucratic structure right from its inception in 1971, depended heavily on external aid. Its small middle class lives in "islands of private affluence in a stagnant ocean of public squalor" (Haq 1997). Only from 1980 did it start investing in its social sector in a visible fashion. Pakistan, on the other hand, has the highest Gross Domestic Product (GDP) and per capita income (PCI) in South Asia; yet in terms of literacy rates, demographic indicators and HDI, it fares poorly. The succession of military regimes have left it with poorly developed institutions, systems of public accountability, democratic governance, and social sectors. Though the proportion of population below the poverty line was only 28 percent in 1993, the proportion of illiterate women was 77 percent.

While Nepal is among the poorest of countries and its HDI and literacy rates are the lowest, it is interesting that over the last two decades inputs in education and health have improved and there are small pockets with better achievements in both. Its infrastructure, however, is very weak and despite the efforts of the monarchy to create a democratic and modernized Nepal, it has a long way to go. Compared to Nepal, Bhutan, though almost similar in condition, has better institutions and a smaller population with a comparatively higher economic growth rate since the eighties.

In contrast to these relatively smaller countries, India presents a picture of diversity wherein each province has a unique experience. As a country though, while its GDP is less than that of Pakistan and the proportion of population below the poverty line much higher, its social sector indicators are comparatively better (though still poor). Economic growth is not creating enough jobs nor is it adequately linked to human lives through increasing investments in education and health. On the one hand, there are provinces like Kerala with lower growth rates but higher levels of social indicators and on the other hand, there is Haryana where the latter are lower despite better economic achievements.

Given these variations in the region the impact of SAP cannot be uniform. It is bound to be influenced by the nature and structure of the health sector, the economy as a whole, political mobilization, presence of participating and democratic institutions, and international influences. In the region as a whole, the social basis of health and the importance of an equitous and balanced socio-economic development is well recognized (WHO 1992). Even though the nature and the limitations of the past and present models for development are not the central concerns of this book, yet the role of inter-sectoral linkages and economic and social sector planning for health are highlighted. The book has six sections, starting with the political economy of health services, followed by concepts and evidence related to public health, shifts in health programs and health financing, decentralization in health care, practitioner's views, and micro-level studies. Each section covers a range of issues as discussed in the overview to each section.

The South Asian experience of the health sector reinforces the criticism of SAP by those who argue that structural adjustments may be necessary but the kind of adjustments being posed as inevitable is certainly debatable (Patnaik 1994). It highlights a number of measures that may help to save the situation, such as:

1. The urgent need for saving public sector health services from being completely distorted in order to earn a few dollars through soft loans that help achieve a favorable balance of payments. It is worthwhile noting that according to the WB itself, such aid, though only a minor proportion of the total investment in health sector (2 percent), is in fact a major influence on the health sector planning process (World Bank 1992);
2. strengthening the social sector and saving it from the clutches of the market which is known to be inadequate in resolving issues of distribution and equity in health services (Rice 1997);
3. state control over market mechanisms to ensure provision of services at a reasonable price and of acceptable quality; and
4. active intervention by the state to ensure health services to all, irrespective of their capacity to pay.

These measures remain an option against the increasing sphere of privatization in the arena of water supply, transportation, public health (including medical care), etc., where the increase in costs following privatization is resulting in vast sections of the population being denied health care (Sen and Koivusalo 1998).

The sections as well as the chapters in each section are diverse as they deal with the inherent complexities of the health systems of various countries and their varying conditions. Though not easy to handle, this diversity is the basis of a comprehensive vision of the regional problems and their global context. Views and analyses of people working at different levels and for different purposes generate myriad inter-disciplinary insights that lend strength to building alternatives. This coming together of a group of public health scholars, health economists, policy-makers, health administrators, practicing physicians, and political activists is the beginning of an effort to consolidate evidence from South Asia and assimilate it with the rapidly accumulating global evidence. Together they may become a corrective instrument for health planning in South Asia, which at present is a mere cost-saving exercise rather than a process of creating conditions that promote the well-being of populations.

References

Banerjee, D. (1996): *Serious Implications of the World Bank's Revised National Tuberculosis Control Programme for India.* New Delhi: Nucleus for Health Policies and Programmes.

Barker, C., and **Green, A.** (1996): Opening the debate on DALYs. *Health Policy and Planning,* 11(2):179–83.

Baru, R. (1997): *Private Health Care in India: Social Characteristics and Trends.* New Delhi: Sage Publications.

Evans, R.G. (1997): Going for the Gold: The Redistributive Agenda behind Market-based Health Care Reform. *Journal of Health Policy, Politics and Law,* 22(2):422–65.

Government of India (2000): *Economic Survey 1999–2000.* New Delhi: Economic Division, Ministry of Finance.

Haq, M. (1997): *Human Development in South Asia.* Published for the HDC Centre. New Delhi: Oxford University Press.

Human Development Centre (1999): *Human Development in South Asia: The Crisis of Governance.* London: Oxford University Press.

Patnaik, P. (1994): Notes on the Political Economy of Structural Adjustment. *Social Scientist,* 22(9–12):14–19.

Pollock, A.M., Brannigen, M., and **Liss, P.E.** (1995): Rationing Health Care: From Needs to Markets? Paper one: The Politics of Destruction: Rationing in the UK Health Care Market. *Health Care Analysis,* 3:299–314.

Priya, R. (1994): AIDS: Public Health and the Panic Reaction. *National Medical Journal of India,* Pt 1, 7(5):235–40; Pt 2, 7(6):288–91.

Qadeer, I. (1995): Primary Health Care: A Paradise Lost. *IASSI Quarterly,* 14(1 & 2):1–20.

Rafei, U.M. (1997): *Partnerships: A New Health Vision.* New Delhi: WHO.

Rice, T. (1997): Can Markets Give Us the Health System We Want? *Journal of Health Policy and Law,* 22(2):383–426.

Richter, J. (1993): *Vaccination against Pregnancy: Miracle or Menace.* The Netherlands: Health Action International.

Sen, K., and **Koivusalo, M.** (1998): Health Care Reforms and Developing Countries—A Critical Overview. *International Journal of Health Planning and Management*, 113:199–215.

WHO (1992): *The WHO Collaboration in Health Developments in South-East Asia 1948–1988*. Regional Publication No. 19. Geneva: WHO.

World Bank (1992): *Health Sector Financing—Coping with Adjustment Opportunities for Reforms*. Report No. 10859-IN.

Part I

The Political Economy of Health and Development

This section deals with the interrelationship between politics, economics, and development of health systems in the South Asia region, an issue that has been marginalized in much of contemporary social analysis and policy-making. It reflects the concern over the deliberate neglect of historical forces in policy debates and analyzes the macro-linkages in the national and international domains. The predominance of the neo-classical economic paradigm in health policy and the politics of aid in the region are explored. The six papers in this section reveal a diversity of experience and highlight the common origins of the current state of health services. Interestingly, the European experience of health sector reforms reinforces the shared experience as well as highlights important structural differences in the implementation of reforms. This is reflected by lesser disruption of the public sector health system in Europe as compared to South Asia; however, the focus on individual care and the biomedical approach remains.

The first paper by Banerji traces the evolution of health services in India within the political historiography of the region. He locates the current reforms in the disparate nature of health services and powerful policy interests of international capital that prevailed upon the political, bureaucratic, and professional elite of the region. Bennett offers a stringent critique of the Structural Adjustment Policies in Pakistan. She argues that the costs of the failure to lift the economy out of recession are being borne disproportionately and unjustly by the poor in Pakistan. Akhtar illustrates an extreme case of verticalization of health services in Bangladesh, where family planning, the most powerful and well-funded program, subsumes all other programs. She argues that the draconian population control measures perpetuated by economic dependency are unsustainable. All three papers emphasize the need for an autonomous and people-centered development in the health sector.

The other three papers of this section look at the experience of liberalization in regions where the tradition of basic services was strong before health sector reforms were introduced. Hettiarachchi traces the transitions in the health sector in the tea plantations in Sri Lanka. Even though only this sector has been privatized, it is indicative of the possible implications of wider health sector reforms. There is concern about the deterioration in health and social services for plantation workers, as reflected by substantial differences in the health indices of these workers compared to the rest of the population. Koivusalo offers a detailed account of health sector reforms in Europe, their global imperatives, and their impact in the OECD countries, particularly in Finland. Given the relatively agricultural and rural background and the centrality of equity in its social policies, Finland offers an interesting comparison for South Asia. Koivusalo also examines the growing disquiet in Europe over the social costs of the reforms and the largely negative experiences in terms of cost savings. De Bruycker's paper examines the ethical moorings of the current paradigms in health systems development and research, and explores the implications of these for equity. All three papers point towards the negative consequences of decontextualized reforms.

1

Landmarks in the Development of Health Services in India

Debabar Banerji

Introduction

The main theme of this paper is to place issues concerning health and health services in India within the South Asian context.* There continue to be numerous serious problems in the field of health and health services in this region. Over the years, particularly in the recent past, there has been a tendency among some responsible international organizations and aid agencies to paint the conditions prevailing in this region in colors which are darker than those warranted by available evidence. Their database is often dubious, their analyzes superficial and highly skewed, and above all, they are patently ahistorical in arriving at their conclusions. However, an enormous amount of work has been undertaken by scholars in this region in studying health and health services in a broader context. This has involved incorporating important political, historical, socio-cultural, epidemiological, and other such dimensions in the analysis of health systems.

First and foremost, analysis of health services must be located in the socio-cultural, ecological, economic, and political settings of the countries of this region. This requires definition and analyzes of highly complex systems, where a large number of factors are in continuous interaction. In addition, the epidemiological aspects of the myriad health problems prevailing in different parts of the region need to be considered together with the structure of

*A fuller version of this paper, entitled "Landmarks in the Development of Health Services in the Countries of South Asia", which was prepared for the conference, deals with the political economy of SAPs and health for the whole region, and has been published by Nucleus of Health Policies and Programs in New Delhi.

service provision in the realms of medical care, preventive, promotive, and rehabilitative service institutions. Finally, the human resource implications of running the institutions, health information systems, and evaluation and research organizations will require consideration. Researchers will need to project the above in a temporal perspective to gain understanding of historical evolution and context. Together, these form the main components of the complex system to be understood in terms of the different countries and specific regions in South Asia.

In the context of South Asia, time span has crucial meaning, beginning with India's independence in 1947. The year 1971 marks yet another dividing line, when East Pakistan became Bangladesh. While Nepal has always been an independent kingdom, the British colony of Ceylon also attained political freedom during this time. During the pre-1947 period, developments in India were almost synonymous with those of South Asia. Nepal and Ceylon, which formed a very small fraction of the population of the region, were also deeply influenced by events in pre-1947 India.

In the Indian subcontinent, independence was associated with the partition of the country and the political cost of witnessing extensive communal riots accompanied by the massive migration of frightened people seeking refuge. Millions crossed borders. Both India and Pakistan had to suffer major upheavals, which affected all aspects of the lives of the people, from personal tragedies and losses to ill effects upon health status and access to any kind of services. Bangladesh also had to suffer additional birth pangs when the erstwhile East Pakistan became a sovereign state. Thus, based on a common history of deprivation during colonial rule, present day India, Bangladesh, and Pakistan have charted out their own paths for health service development over the past five decades. Despite the common past, the historical markers are of considerable significance because they indicate the beginnings of profound and rapid changes in the countries of the region in every field, which include differences in levels of health service provision and of health status among the population. More recently, the imposition of the Structural Adjustment Programs in all the countries (World Bank 1992, 1993) have in turn had far-reaching consequences for health service development.

Developments in the Pre-1947 Period

The British conquest of India in the mid-eighteenth century was the culmination of its efforts to get more favorable conditions for exploitation of the country and its people for imperialistic aims. Induction of Western medicine in India has been one of the components of the domination by Western civilization. The two features of this process were: first, the military formed the conduit for the induction. This is quite the reverse of what happened in the Western countries themselves. Second, Western medicine was imposed on a pre-existing system of indigenous health practices which different strata of the society had developed over the millennia. It was almost "automatic" that those who played an important role in perpetuating the unjust colonial rule enjoyed the advantage of having access to Western medical services. Reciprocally, the exploited masses were kept out.

The rapid growth of the colonial organization for the governance of the country led to the formation of a cadre of medical personnel called the Indian Medical Service (IMS). The IMS has played a key role in the making of the health services in the Indian region. In the course of their service in the IMS, the Indian officers were properly socialized and sanitized so that they became the Brown Englishmen. Commenting on this aspect in relation to the medical education in 1929, B.C. Roy made some pertinent observations on the overwhelming dominance of the IMS in the health services. These observations reflect the understandable frustration and anger among those Indian physicians who had acquired high qualifications but were denied access to a large number of key posts in the government simply because they did not join the IMS.

However, this should not obscure some very positive outcomes. The establishment of three medical colleges in Calcutta, Bombay, and Madras in 1835 was an important landmark in the history of health services in the country. These medical colleges followed the guidelines laid down by the General Medical Council of Great Britain. Perhaps no other country outside the Western world could match India in this regard. Incidentally, the first medical college in China was established in Peking, by the United Missionaries, as late as in 1925 (Grant 1963). Interestingly, the nursing profession was established in India at an early stage.

Florence Nightingale took personal interest in developing the profession in the country.

The deep interest of the colonial rulers in developing health services for their employees can be understood from the scraps of epidemiological data that have been culled out of the archives. For instance, it is stated that in the mid-nineteenth century as many as 69 out of every 1,000 soldiers sent from Britain died of various diseases during the first year of their arrival (Ramasubban 1982). This led to the setting up of cantonments and civil lines exclusively for the rulers and their army, where sanitary practices like protected water supply, and proper disposal of wastes, were adopted. Spectacular discoveries in the West in the medical sciences, leading to the development of chemo-therapeutic drugs and vaccines, provided the motive force for the development of health services for the ruling classes. The outbreak of a massive epidemic of plague towards the end of the century reinforced this trend. A large number of research and training institutes were set up to strengthen the health organization. A comparative study of that time of the developments in India with those in other parts of the world outside Europe and USA will show that it was way ahead of them in terms of laying firm foundations for health service development.

Meanwhile, the state of health of the "subalterns" and their access to health services was materially different from that of the rulers. The colonial exploitation in the form of ruthless extortion of revenues added substantially to their already miserable conditions. This made them much more vulnerable to diseases of various kinds and to famines and epidemics. At the very time when the disease load became heavier, these "forgotten people" were also fast losing access to the various mechanisms for coping with the problems, which they had developed over the centuries. This was so because the elite of the society, who had earlier been enriching the indigenous systems of medicine, had now transferred their loyalty to the Western system.

On the eve of independence, medical services were scattered and highly inadequate, not only in number but in the kind of medical care they delivered. Rural populations, in particular, were starved of services. Some of India's most eminent medical professionals, such as Dr. B.C. Roy, Dr. A.R. Ansari, Dr. Khan Saheb, Hakim Ajmal Khan, Dr. Jeevraj Mehta, and Dr. N.M. Jaisoorya, occupied leadership positions in the national struggle. Inspired by the welfare state movement in the United Kingdom and the socialized health services in the Soviet Union, they demanded a more egalitarian health service system and made this demand an important plank in the anti-colonial struggle. Dr. B.C. Roy's presidential address at the All India Medical Conference at Lahore in 1929 presents many important facets of the health services during the movement (Roy 1982). Another remarkable feature of the movement for health services was the initiative taken by prominent persons in different parts of this vast country to start a large variety of institutions on a voluntary basis.

An important feature of health policies, plans, and programs in India is that they originated during the national movement against colonial rule. The National Planning Committee (NPC) of the Indian National Congress was set up in 1938. The then president of the Congress, Subhas Chandra Bose, nominated Jawaharlal Nehru as the chairman of the committee. This committee set up a subcommittee on national health (Sokhey Committee) which made an incisive appraisal of the health situation and health services in the country and recommended measures for their improvement (NPC 1948). Although the Health Survey and Development Committee, generally known as the Bhore Committee, was set up by the British colonial authorities (1943), it was greatly influenced by the aspirations of the national movement (Government of India 1946). In fact, several of its influential members had been in the forefront of the struggle for independence. The impact of the committee is clearly seen in the shaping of health services in independent India. The report, to this day, is regarded as an authoritative document, not only because of its distinguished authorship, but also because many of its proposals and recommendations continue to be pertinent and valid even today.

The guiding principles adopted by the Bhore Committee were: (*i*) no individual should be denied adequate medical care because of inability to pay for it; (*ii*) the health services should provide, when fully developed, all the consultant, laboratory, and institutional facilities necessary for proper diagnosis and treatment; (*iii*) the health program must, from the beginning, lay special emphasis on preventive work; (*iv*) medical relief and preventive health care must be urgently provided as soon as possible to the vast rural population of the country; (*v*) the health services should be located as close to the people as possible to ensure maximum benefit to the communities served; (*vi*) the active cooperation of the people must be secured in the development of the health programs. The idea must be inculcated that, ultimately, the health of the individual is his own responsibility; and (*vii*) health development must be entrusted to the ministers of health who enjoy the confidence of the people and are able to secure their cooperation.

It is most essential to keep in mind the conditions prevailing at the time of the end of colonial rule in India in 1947. It was already densely populated and poverty-stricken, which meant a very heavy load of diseases of various kinds. This vicious cycle had been at the root of, and is reinforced by the rapid growth of the population. The population of India in the 1951 Census was 350 million; it is now one billion—an addition of 650 million. This is a colossal problem of human ecology, which gravely affects the health status of the people.

Health Service Development after Independence

Although the class interests of India's new rulers came to the fore after independence, yet they had to adopt an egalitarian stance given the democratic urges kindled among the masses and their own egalitarian convictions. This impelled them to take such actions in health and other fields, in the first two decades of independence, which placed the country very high among the newly sovereign countries. An example is that of ensuring protection and promotion of health and nutrition of the people by placing it in the Directive Principles for the State Policy in the Constitution of India (Basu 1970). The motive force generated by the leadership's commitment and the experience gained by the health administrators from their work in the IMS, enabled them to give concrete shape to the political vision of the rulers. This led to some far-reaching developments in the health services. I term this period as the Golden Two Decades of Public Health in India. Some of the landmarks requiring a mention are: vertical programs, primary health centers, social orientation of medical education, indigenous systems of medicine, Family Planning/Welfare Program, water supply and sanitation, nutrition, Minimum Needs Program, the Multi-Purpose Workers' Scheme, the Community Health Volunteers (Guide) Scheme, and the Statement of National Policy.

The political vision to establish a comprehensive health service system in the aftermath of independence was unfortunately short-lived. However, despite this fact, a number of achievements or success stories are worth mentioning. These include the mass BCG campaign of the fifties (Banerji 1993), the National Malaria Eradication Program of the period 1958–63 (Borker 1960), and the setting up of the National Tuberculosis Institute and the National Institute of Health Administration and Education to train physicians to inculcate managerial, epidemiological, social, and political capabilities.

Over the next three decades, there was a sharp decline in the quality of health services in the country. The major forces contributing to this decline were:

- Obsessive preoccupation with the Family Planning Program at the cost of serious neglect of the health service needs of the people, particularly the poor.
- The imposition of so-called "international initiatives in health," during the last two decades, by a formidable combination of "development aid" agencies of many Western countries and international organizations.
- The considerable involvement of Western countries in shaping social (including health), economic, and political policies of the country in the form of pressures for privatization in the Structural Adjustment Program (SAP) from the late eighties onwards.

The year 1967 marked the beginning of a steep decline in the health services, culminating in the present state of its serious "sickness." An all-out effort to push forward the Family Planning Program at all costs had a devastating impact on the wider provision of health services. The political leadership permitted bureaucrats to make the people "targets" of their own "democratic" government. Owing to the overriding priority given to the family planning program, plan allocations for it jumped a phenomenal 10,000 fold—from Rs 6.5 million in the

First Plan (1950–55) to Rs 65,000 million in the Eighth Plan (1991–95).

The declaration of self-reliance by the world at Alma-Ata (WHO 1978) brought swift and sharp responses from the major world powers, who were opposed to the principles of sharing power and the distribution of resources, and especially to moving away from a bio-medical model of health. There was, in this author's view, a swift invention of the idea of "Selective Primary Health Care" (Walsh and Warren 1979) to nip the Alma-Ata Declaration in the bud. This led to the utilization of the very same WHO and United Nations Children's Fund (UNICEF) for the implementation of a virtual barrage of specific and vertical programs selected by them. These included universal programs for immunization, oral rehydration and other child survival strategies, and social marketing of contraceptives.

Clearly, these programs were antithetical to the Alma-Ata Declaration. Considerable damage was inflicted upon the provision of comprehensive health services by according overriding priority to a single vertical program over the former. Not only were the vertical programs technocentric, they were imposed on the people from above, their cost-effectiveness was not demonstrated; and worst of all, they made developing countries dependent upon the North for funds, supply of vaccines, and other logistic support (Banerji 1990). Despite the considerable weaknesses of these programs, in terms of their economic, administrative, and epidemiological sustainability in countries such as India, they were pushed through for political and ideological reasons rather than out of consideration for the real need for comprehensive programs.

The Private Sector and the Structural Adjustment Program

The failure to support public sector personnel to perform their duties in the skeleton comprehensive programs inevitably created a very big "market" for the private sector. This was an increasing burden on the poor who were at the receiving end in this scheme of things. Two recent nationwide surveys (NSSO 1992; NCAER 1992) on the pattern of utilization of medical institutions reveal that expenditure for getting treatment for diseases was the second most common cause for rural indebtedness (after dowry) among these impoverished people.

India is being exhorted by the international banks to reduce public expenditure in health through increasing privatization. It is conveniently forgotten that in Europe and Japan, the percentage of public expenditure in health is over 80 percent, while in India it is only 23 percent. Even in the USA it is over 50 percent (Sengupta 1994). A devastating blow was struck in the union budget after India submitted to the conditionalities laid down by the WB/IMF. There was a 20 percent reduction in the allocation for health services as compared to the previous year (World Bank 1992, 1993). This cut was made without accounting for inflation. Worse still, that cut was greater for programs critical to the poor—there was a 40 percent cut in the malaria program and a 20 percent cut in the program for eradication of tuberculosis (Sengupta 1994).

These cuts are a precursor to the further expansion of the private sector into health care and the continued marginalization of the public sector, while the poor in India and other South Asian countries continue to depend upon this very public sector for medical care. Given this state of affairs, concerned public health workers need to address the challenging issues in a strategic and coordinated manner with clear understanding of the interplay of historical forces that have led to the current situation. The following agenda for action could provide some guidelines for the subcontinent as a whole.

Agenda for Action

The prime movers for action to improve the situation must come from within the countries concerned. Even the common heritage shared by the countries cannot justify any "prefabricated" models: following what the international agencies call "global programs" is simply out of the question. Regional and international cooperation in health service development must be based on a solid foundation of endogenous public health. In all such activities it needs to be kept in mind that India provides rich data on how not to run certain programs.

Concerning the agenda for action for India, I would stress that adoption of a simplistic approach to such a complex system, as has been so often done in the past, is a prescription for disaster. What is needed is the adoption of inter-disciplinary research methodologies (Banerji 1997). By far, the most urgent and important measure will be to create political conditions which will impel the political leadership to initiate steps to undo the enormous damage that has been inflicted on the system. To respond to such political demands, the leadership will have to create conditions for some of the most competent people of the country to come together, in some or all the key institutions, to form "critical masses" to rejuvenate the training, research, and education activities of these institutions. Personnel trained in these institutions should be groomed to fill key positions in the top administration of the health services, both at the union and state levels. The current vertical programs should be integrated with the general health services, with a view to their ultimate transfer to the state health services. Similarly, the family planning department should be merged with the department of health at the union and state levels. The question of increased budgetary allocations is being deliberately left to the last because funding should be increased only after it is ensured that the system has become efficient enough to make effective use of funds that are already available.

Of the recommendations that will require extended time frames, top priority is to be assigned to the people. The response of the people to epidemiologically assessed health problems should be used to choose people-oriented technologies, which in turn will determine the organizational structures and management strategies. Efforts should be made, on a priority basis, to expand the capabilities of the panchayati raj and *nagarpalika* institutions so that they can take over the responsibilities for running the public health services. Another very crucial element of the prescription for improvement will be to ensure that the programs taken up for implementation are cost-effective. Programs for manpower development will have to conform to the requirements of the cost-effective, optimized systems. An associated priority area will be the development of a more appropriate health service cadre structure. Enforcement of ethical standards through the Medical Council of India and policy issues in the promotion of indigenous systems of medicine are other areas of concern.

For developing a mechanism for promoting regional cooperation for health service development, there are certain concepts, guiding principles, and social and political commitments which are of lasting value and which can be used within a wide range of variations in the countries of the Indian region. Many of them have been referred to in the foregoing account of the health service development in the pre- and post-1947 periods, including those mentioned in the reports of Sokhey and Bhore committees. A large number of them have been brought together in the comprehensive Alma-Ata Declaration. Columbia, which was the Chairman in the Fiftieth World Health Assembly (1995), deserves the gratitude of the developing countries for mobilizing the countries of the Non-Aligned Movement, and for bringing back to the center-stage the approach of primary health care. Among other issues, the resolution requests the international and multilateral institutions and agencies:

- To provide within their mandate, greater support and resources to facilitate health sector reforms in developing countries, that are designed to achieve equity in health care for their populations;
- to identify obstacles to "health for all" and to support and uphold the self-reliance of these countries in charting their own path in health and human development; and
- to implement the relevant conclusions of the summits and conferences of the United Nations system that address health problems and make recommendations in this field.

References

Banerji, D. (1988): New Public Health. *Journal of Sociological Studies*, 7: 160–67.

——— (1990): Crash of the Immunisation Programme: Consequences of a Totalitarian Approach. *International Journal of Health Services*, 20: 501–10.

——— (1993): A Social Science Approach to Strengthening India's National Tuberculosis Programme. *Indian Journal of Tuberculosis*, 40: 61–82.

——— (1997): India's Forgotten People and the Sickness of the Public Health Service System: A Prescription for the Malady: Summary-I. *Health for the Millions*, 23(3): 29–32.

Basu, D.D. (1970): *A Shorter Constitution of India*. Calcutta: S.C. Sarkar.

Borker, G. (1960): Health in Independent India. New Delhi: Ministry of Health.

Government of India (GOI) (1946): Health Survey and Development Committee (Bhore Committee) Report. Volume IV. Delhi: Manager of Publications.

Grant, J.B. (1963): International Organisation of Planning of Medical Care for the Community. In C. Seipp (ed.). *Health Care for the Community: Selected Papers by Dr. John Grant*. Baltimore: The Johns Hopkins University Press.

National Council for Applied Economic Research (1992): *Household Utilization of Medical Care*. New Delhi: NCAER.

National Planning Committee (1948): Sub-Committee on National Health (Sokhey Committee) Report. K.T. Shah (ed.). Bombay: Vora.

National Sample Survey Organisation (NSSO) (1992): Morbidity and Utilisation of Medical Services. NSSO 42nd Round. *Sarvekshana*, 15: S-134–S-556.

Ramasubban, R. (1982): Public Health and Medical Research in India: Their Origin, and the Impact of British Colonial Policy. Report no. 4. Stockholm: SAREC.

Roy, B.C. (1982): The Future of the Medical Profession in India. Reprint of the Presidential Address delivered at The All-India Medical Conference at Lahore in December 1929. *Journal of the Indian Medical Association*, 78(1 and 2): 24–30.

Sengupta, A. (1994): World Development Report: Implications for Infrastructure Development in Health Care and the Pharmaceutical Industry. *Social Scientist*, 22: 112–28.

Walsh, J.A., and **Warren, K.S.** (1979): Selective Primary Care: An Interim Strategy for Disease Control for Developing Countries. *New England Journal of Medicine*, 301: 967–74.

World Bank (1992): *Health Sector Financing: Coping with Adjustment Opportunities for Reform*. Washington: Population and Human Resources Operations Division.

——— (1993): *World Development Report: Investing in Health*. New York: Oxford University Press.

World Health Organization (WHO) (1978): *Primary Health Care: Report on the International Conference on Primary Health Care*. Alma-Ata, USSR. Geneva: WHO.

——— (1992): *A Call for New Public Health Action*. Geneva: WHO.

2

Structural Adjustment and the Poor in Pakistan

Jennifer Bennett

Structural Adjustment Programs (SAPs) are not simple instruments for rectifying macro-economic imbalances through the imposition of policies, such as currency devaluation, privatization, trade liberalization, and cuts in government spending, as proclaimed. They may be viewed instead as carefully engineered projects for generating social and economic transformation in the interests of the countries of the North. The main arbiters are the World Bank (WB) and the International Monetary Fund (IMF). Poor developing countries are usually given loans in the name of development. But the Third World countries are told that in order to pay off loans and be eligible for more, they must implement "structural adjustment" reforms, accompanied by conditionalities as set by the leaders based in the North. The vicious cycle never ends. Often the same conditionalities are imposed on every recipient country regardless of the kind of economic or social crises experienced or consideration of the context in which they are applied.

While the objectives for which Structural Adjustment Policies were their designed and implemented remain unsolved, their interminable adverse impacts on most developing countries include crippling declines in Third World economies, social degeneration, and rising unemployment and poverty, which pose serious challenges to human resource development and well-being. The period between 1989 and 1999 is marked by a series of debt crises, shrinking resources, structural changes, coupled with glaring socio-economic and environmental destruction in the developing world. Under the theme of "repay loans in order to be eligible for more loans," the total external debt of developing countries has increased from $100 billion in 1970 to $650 billion in 1980 and

$1,300 billion in 1990. In 1994, the ratio of the incomes of the richest 20 percent of the world to that of the poorest 20 percent was 78 to 1, up from 30 to 1 in 1960 (UNDP 1997).

The first Structural Adjustment Loan (SAL) was given in 1980 to Turkey, in the backdrop of appropriate "market oriented" policies. Since then, loans granted have been accompanied by SA reforms, which include reducing the role of the state in the economy, lowering barriers to imports, removing restrictions on foreign investment, eliminating subsidies for local industries, reducing spending for social welfare, cutting wages, devaluing the currency, and emphasizing production for export rather than for local consumption. Such conditionalities were made mandatory considering that many Third World countries ran into difficulties servicing the huge loans given in the seventies. Conditionalities, it was argued, were imposed to ensure debtors' abilities to continue paying debts beyond the short term. Unable to gain access to further private bank financing without the approval of the WB, many governments acceded to these conditionalities.

By the end of the decade, hundreds of SALs had been administered and a growing number of Third World economies came under the surveillance and control of the WB/IMF. Over time, the previous division of labor between the two institutions—the WB to promote growth and IMF to monitor financial restraint—also became indistinguishable. Both became the enforcers of the economic rollback strategy of the North. Under these institutions, 12 of the top 15 indebted countries had submitted to SAPs in 1985. These included Argentina, Mexico, and the Philippines—the top-priority debtors (Bello 1994). By 1990, more than 187 adjustment loans were provided to countries in Latin America, Asia, Africa, and Eastern Europe. Of the 47 countries in sub-Saharan Africa, 30 are currently undergoing WB/IMF adjustment programs (Gershman 1994). The real WB/IMF achievement came about in 1991 when India, the leader of the Non-Aligned Movement (NAM) and upholder of state-led nationalist development, agreed to restructure its economy in exchange for a SAL to enable servicing of debts to Western banks.

Human Condition under SAPs

While the economic problems that WB/IMF endeavored to lift remain intact, the impact of the conditionalities, such as drastic cuts in social expenditures, especially health and education, has been devastating. These conditionalities are contingent to the economic assault on the living standards of the poor by cutting consumer subsidies and raising producer prices for agricultural goods, charging user fees for social services such as health and education, all for regulating privatization to create incentives to attract foreign capital, and to allow the MNCs to flourish.

According to the UN Economic Commission for Africa, drastic cuts in social expenditures have led to a 50 percent decline in health expenditure and 25 percent decline in the education sector in most southern regions undergoing WB/IMF Structural Adjustment (Economic Commission for Africa 1989). Figures obtained from various annual publications of United Nations Children's Fund (UNICEF) show that at least six million children under the age of five have died each year, since 1982. About 1.3 billion people in the South now live in poverty, which is twice the number 10 years ago. This is as a result of plummeting wages, often to levels half as low as that at the beginning of the eighties (Haq 1997). Susan George reminds the world that

> every single month, from the outset of the debt crisis in 1982 until the end of 1990, debtor countries in the South remitted to their creditors in the North an average of $6.5 billion in interest payment alone. If payments of the principle are included, then debtor countries have paid creditors at a rate of almost $12.5 billion per month—as much as the entire Third World spends each month on health and education.

Despite these payments, these countries are about 61 percent more in debt than they were in 1982 (George 1994).

Pakistan's Saga of Social Development

In the last fifty years, Pakistan has managed to maintain a respectable average economic growth rate which exceeds 5 percent. Despite the economic development, human resource development has remained a much neglected factor in the process of economic development. Social expenditure from the late seventies oscillated between 2 and 3 percent and has stayed roughly constant since then (Government of Pakistan, Economic Survey, 1995–96), regardless of the needs of the rapidly growing population. However, as argued in the succeeding sections, the onset of SAPs in

Pakistan has led to further deterioration in human conditions as a consequence of misplaced priorities and market-oriented policies implemented to boost the development process and the economic situation of the country.

The military dictator, Zia-ul Haq (1977–88), first brought in the IMF in 1978–79 to tide over the fiscal and payments crises. Since then, some form of conditionality in return for loans has become a permanent feature of the country's economy. Chronologically, the spate of IMF Structural Adjustment Loans (SALs) offered and followed were: a Trust Fund Loan for the period 1979–80, a three-year Extended Fund Facility (EFF) from 1980–81 to 1982–83, SAL for the period 1983–84 which the government refused but accepted instead a series of sectoral loans for agriculture, industry, energy, and the financial sectors. Interestingly, the SAL offered in 1983–84 was refused because the country's foreign exchange reserves had recovered to over $2 billion (Banuri, Khan, and Mahmood 1997). This implies that given the opportunity and with political will, commitment, and domestic production of resources, self-sufficiency can be attained as opposed to total dependence on borrowed monies. Subsequently, structural adjustment agreements were signed for the periods 1987–88 to 1990–91 with the IMF, WB, and the Asian Development Bank, with the imposition of conditionalities. Pakistan signed a Stabilization Program with the IMF and an SAP with the WB, which, besides other conditionalities, called for substantial reduction in the budgetary deficit from 8.5 to 4.8 percent of the GDP over the next three years (Banuri et al. 1997). Since then, such agreements and conditionalities of budgetary cuts continue with the same institutions, with the endorsement of the succeeding regimes.

Not surprisingly, not only do the earlier economic crises for which SAPs were implemented persist, but the situation has worsened and is unlikely to be redeemed in the short or medium term. Estimates derived from various yearly *Pakistan Economic Surveys* indicate that the Gross National Product (GNP) of the country touched its lowest, i.e., 4.4 during 1989–90 to 1994–95; 1960 onward, the GNP of the country vacillated between 5.4 and 6.8, except during the period 1969–70 to 1974–75 when again it was 4.4 percent. No substantive improvements in removing the budgetary deficits (fiscal deficits and balance of payments) have taken place in spite of the conditionalities of reducing the overall GDP expenditures (development expenditure reduced from 6.8 percent in 1987–88 to 6.5 percent in 1990–91). On an average, the net current account deficit has remained above $1 billion which had, in effect, risen to 2.1 and 3.6 billion in 1990–91 and 1992–93, respectively. Conversely, unemployment, poverty, and widening disparities in income and resource distribution scaled up substantially. Unemployment, including underemployment, since the past few years has remained within the vicinity of 13 to 15 percent (Kemal 1995). More than 30 percent of the population now lives in absolute poverty, rising sharply from 20 percent in 1990 (Haq 1997), while inequality in income distribution has worsened from 5.5 to 7.8 percent during the period 1987–93 (Government of Pakistan, Economic Survey 1996–97).

During the Structural Adjustment Period of 1987–88 to 1990–91, the already thin slice of social expenditure was further trimmed from 3.4 percent in 1987–88 to 2.8 percent in 1990–91. It increased marginally from 2.8 percent in 1990–91 to 2.9 percent during the period 1991–92 to 1993–94. In 1994–95, the total social expenditure increased further to 3.1 percent and to 3.3 percent in 1996–97. This increase in the social expenditure is still low compared to that in 1987–88. Table 2.1 gives the GDP expenditure on social sectors with percentage allocation to education and health. It shows that the health sector fares even worse than the education sector. The percentage of the social expenditure on health did not exceed 1.0 percent during the entire structural adjustment period. In fact, this 1.0 percent (1987–88) declined to 0.7 percent in 1990–91. Thereafter, it has remained constant in spite of a slight increase in the overall social expenditure.

The increase in social expenditure came about as part of the overall increase in the GNP as well as the Social Action Program accompanying the SALs. This program was initiated for improving the social conditions of the masses and, perhaps, to mitigate the global criticism of the SAPs. Included as part of the Eighth Plan (1993–98), the Social Action Program became operational in 1993. The federal and provincial governments, with the cooperation of donors and the WB in the forefront, reallocated some of their public expenditures for key social services, namely, primary

Table 2.1
Expenditure on Education and Health as a Percentage of GDP

Year/Expenditure	*Education*	*Health*	*Total*
1987–88	2.4	1.0	3.4
1988–89	2.4	1.0	3.4
1989–90	2.2	0.9	3.1
1990–91	2.1	0.7	2.8
1991–92	2.2	0.7	2.9
1992–93	2.2	0.7	2.9
1993–94	2.2	0.7	2.9
1994–95	2.4	0.7	3.1
1995–96	2.4	0.7	3.1
1996–97	2.6	0.7	3.3

Source: Government of Pakistan, Economic Surveys 1994–95 and 1996–97.

education (for girls), basic health (rural areas), clean water, sanitation, and population planning. In economic terms, the actual increase in the social sector allocation can be termed as a mere compensation through an increase in user charges and imposing sales taxes for revenue enhancement, and supply response policies of increasing producer prices, all to comply with the WB/IMF conditionalities.

While the recent effort appears to be commendable, the Social Action Program suffers from inherent setbacks in terms of its impact and long-term sustainability. The basic problem with the program is that it relies solely on accelerated development funding without any obvious source of revenue for financing the downstream operation and maintenance expenditures. This specifically refers to the provision of recurring expenditures. In other words, schools and basic health centers are being constructed giving no due consideration to the ongoing need for teachers, books, doctors, nurses, medications *inter alia*. Many such programs were designed earlier; the reasons for their failures are self-explanatory. While designing new programs, the existing infrastructure has been totally ignored and there is no attempt to make it functional and optimize utilization. Thus, we have mushrooming construction of physical social infrastructure to tell the angry world that human welfare is not an ignored sector.

There exists a similar pattern of low priority to every other sector associated with human resource development. The reasons for this are demonstrated by past and present scenarios which reveal apathy, lack of political will and commitment, and unequal and biased utilization and distribution of resources in favor of monetary gains. Such macro-economic follies are exacerbated by negative forces which include mainly bad governance, and administrative and management systems. Together, these factors have had a devastating impact on the entire service delivery mechanism and its functional capacity. Although, some improvement in the overall health, nutrition, and education has been felt, the progress has been uneven. The poor still continue to suffer from sickness, malnutrition, and early death. Of greater significance is the fact that for years various governments have promoted health facilities which favor curative measures, while morbidity and mortality in the country are largely caused by preventable illnesses. The disease patterns are so obvious that no excuse seems fit for the governments' failure to rectify the lopsided service delivery system. Not to mention that, in the long run, catering to preventive diseases, would not only promote good health but would be much more cost-effective, cost-efficient, and environmentally conducive. The typical top-down approach of governments and donors seems to replicate itself, time and again, under different shapes, forms, and slogans to prove yet again the failures of these development models and waste of resources. One needs to be reminded of the success of Sri Lanka and the State of Kerala in achieving demographic results comparable to the developed world at GNPs lower than that of Pakistan. Crucial factors contributing to such successes were high minimum wages, land reforms, high literacy rates, and improved child survival through massive state-wide feeding programs for undernourished children.

The Health Scenario

Infant and child mortality rates are the basic indicators of health and the overall social development of the country. In Pakistan, infant and child mortality rates have declined over the past few years, but are still high even when compared to other South Asian countries, except Bhutan. Infant mortality rate (IMR) is as high as 95 per thousand live births, while child mortality stands at 137 per thousand live births (Haq 1997). The major contributors to child mortality are gastrointestinal, parasitic, immunizable, and respiratory diseases, and malnutrition, all of which are preventable. The high incidence of infective and parasitic diseases, malaria, and tuberculosis together with malnutrition result in 73 percent of the infant deaths alone (Irfan 1996). Where national coverage of immunization is claimed to be 80 percent, 75 percent of the children aged one or less are immunized against tuberculosis and only 53 percent against measles. Malaria has also cropped up as a major killer, claiming 70 percent of all adult and child deaths (Haq 1997) in spite of the fact that the Malaria Control Program was initiated as far back as 1974. More than 40 percent of the overall deaths and 60 percent of infant deaths result from diarrheal and other water-borne diseases caused by drinking unclean water. This is not surprising considering that only 50 percent of the total population has access to the so-called "safe drinking water," while only 33 percent are benefited with sanitation facilities (Haq 1997).

Moreover, under the conditionalities of the WB/IMF, rising unemployment, decrease in per capita income, and an increase in poverty form a concoction which debilitates the ability of the poor to improve their health. In the face of such realities, attempts, such as the Social Action Program will have a marginal impact unless health is made an integral part of the overall development of the country, which includes eradicating unemployment and poverty.

Health, Privatization, and Liberalization

More than 45 percent of the total population of Pakistan does not have access to basic health facilities. The existing national network of public health services is heavily skewed in favor of urban areas, while the majority of the population (approximately 65 percent) resides in rural areas. Consequently, facilities per population in the rural areas are extremely scarce compared to the urban areas. The population in relation to medical personnel works out to 1,773 persons per doctor and one nurse per 5,771 persons. In the rural areas, one rural health center with one health practitioner caters to a population of 203,109 (Government of Pakistan, Economic Survey 1994–95). The public sector consists of 830 hospitals, 4,250 dispensaries, 4,997 basic health units

(BHUs), 864 maternity and child centers (MCHs), 501 rural health centers (RHCs), and 260 tuberculosis (TB) centers. Proper functioning of rural centers is non-existent; more than 30 percent of the RHCs are completely shut down or are inoperative owing to the lack of resources and manpower (Government of Pakistan, Economic Survey 1996–97).

While inefficient and inadequate health services characterize every public hospital, it is mostly the rural and urban poor who bear the brunt. Often, it is the poor who have to wait in long queues as opposed to the relatively well off who either jump the queue or avail the attention of a specialized doctor by paying exorbitant fees in the private hospitals. Investment in public hospitals is negligible compared to the rapidly growing population. No new public hospitals are in sight. Instead, plans to privatize some government hospitals are underway, which when materialized would mean charging user fee for services that were earlier available free of charge. Moreover, private medical practice is being encouraged and is growing at the state level. Even doctors working in public hospitals are allowed private practice due to the supposedly unmet needs of the people. As a result, doctors in public hospitals have established flourishing businesses as they often refer patients to their private clinics. Also, unrestricted purchasing of medicines from the open markets has led to inflated price structures.

Major concessions have been granted to pharmaceutical firms. Reduction of price controls and tax relief have led to excessive profiteering and high cost of many essential drugs. Many medicines banned in the developed countries are available in the open market. The main objective of the state to promote economic growth and market efficiency raises serious questions about the claims of the government to improve health and make primary health care more affordable and accessible. These effects linked to the market-oriented economic reforms have further shrunk the purchasing capacity of the poor and threaten to deepen the disparities between the rich and the poor.

Lopsided Priorities: Focus on Family Planning

Population control measures are part of the WB/IMF conditionalities under SAP and a central theme of most donor agencies.

Greater focus on family planning (FP) is the projection of the old theory that growing population is the root cause of poverty. Instead of treating population control as a natural outcome of modern development, as in the Western industrialized countries, FP has been given disproportionately large attention. It eats into the meager health expenditure allocation and also sets back the process of strengthening the primary health care structure. FP programs were initiated in Pakistan as far back as the late fifties. Since then, billions of rupees have gone into the program without much success. The population of Pakistan continues to rise at an annual growth rate of over 3 percent (although the government figure suggests 2.9 percent) with a total fertility rate of around 6.0 percent (UNICEF 1996). These rates are amongst the highest when compared to many countries with lower GNPs. Even Bangladesh has managed to bring down its population growth rate to a level of 2.4 percent in the past one decade.

While emphasis is on contraceptive use, female morbidity is considered to be an outcome of high fertility and is generally ignored. While there is a need to improve maternal and child health through fertility control, reducing this complex reality by equating female health problems with reproductive health matters is a serious and a deliberate flaw in population planning. The main causes of morbidity and mortality lie in the lack of medical care, and poor living conditions which are susceptible to infectious and parasitic diseases. Statistics show that as high as 45 percent of women in their reproductive ages are anemic and 10 percent severely anemic. Lack of proper nutrition amongst children below the age of five takes the figure of anemics to 65 percent (National Institute of Health 1988). Maternal mortality rate also stands at 430 per 100,000 live births, which is as a result of malnutrition, lack of proper health care, knowledge and awareness, and medical attention at the time of delivery; only 35 percent of child delivery cases are handled by the so-called trained health personnel (Haq 1997).

Mere supply of contraceptives, with almost complete disregard of demand factors along with low socio-economic development, will have little impact on fertility. In a country where unemployment and poverty are widespread, where primary health care is deficient and unreliable, and does not reach the poor, where child mortality and morbidity are mostly caused by illnesses that can be prevented, and the survival of children remains uncertain, poor families can hardly be blamed for desiring a large number of children. To check population control, investing in human development capital is crucial. This includes adequate intersectoral inputs, such as housing, transport, drinking water supply, sanitation, and accessibility to health services.

Countervailing these Developments

The proponents of SAPs including its accomplices in the state insist that "free markets" will eventually foster development despite the glaring reality of stifling declines in Third World economies, rising poverty, and deteriorating human condition. What is needed to counter and reject such global designs and to de-link its effects is a strong and democratic, political and economic sovereignty of nations. Only then can the paradigm of people-centered development succeed, and ensure equitable growth and.distribution of resources across the entire spectra of the civil society. Strong democratic movements must come to the forefront with a slogan of self-reliant economic growth, and create conditions to pressurize governments to shift policy-emphasis from achieving efficiency and export-competitiveness to employment creation and alleviation of poverty. The national leaders have to be made accountable to the civil society rather than the neo-liberalists. The need for vigilance and informed pressure cannot be over-emphasized.

References

Banuri, T., Kemal, A.R., and **Mahmood, Moazam** (1997): The Policy Framework and Structural Adjustment. In Tariq Banuri, Shahrukh Rafi Khan, and Moazam Mahmood (eds.). *Just Development: Beyond Adjustment with a Human Face*. Karachi: Oxford University Press.

Bello, W. (1994): Global Economic Counterrevolution: How Northern Economic Warfare Devastates the South. In K. Danaher (ed.). *50 Years is Enough: The Case Against the World Bank and the International Monetary Fund.* Boston: South End Press.

Economic Commission for Africa (ECA) (1989): *The African Alternative Framework to Structural Adjustment Programmes for Socio-economic Recovery and Transformation (AAF-SAP)*. Addis Ababa.

George, S. (1994): The Debt Boomerang. In K. Danaher (ed.). *50 Years is Enough: The Case Against the World Bank and the International Monetary Fund.* Boston: South End Press, p. 29.

Gershman, J. (1994): The Free Trade Connection. In K. Danaher (ed.). *50 Years is Enough: The Case Against the World Bank and the International Monetary Fund.* Boston: South End Press.

Government of Pakistan (various years): *Economic Surveys*. Islamabad: Finance Division, Economic Adviser's Wing.

Haq, M. (1997): *Human Development Report in South Asia*. The Human Development Centre. Karachi: Oxford University Press.

Irfan, M. (1996): Mortality Trends and Patterns in Pakistan. *Asian Population Studies Series*, No. 75. Bangkok: ESCAP.

Kemal, A.R. (1995): Poverty and Growing Unemployment in Pakistan—Where and Why Pakistan Failed. In S. Ghayur (ed.). *South Asia Employment Generation and Poverty Alleviation*. Islamabad: Friedrich Ebert Stiftung/Pakistan Administrative Staff College.

National Institute of Health (1988): *National Nutrition Survey, 1985–87 Report*, Islamabad: Government of Pakistan, Nutrition Division.

UNICEF (1996): *The State of the World's Children, 1996*. New York: Oxford University Press.

United Nations Development Fund (UNDP) (1997): *Human Development Report*. New York: Oxford University Press.

Donor-driven Family Planning Services in Bangladesh: Impact on Women's Health

Farida Akhter

Introduction

The health and social sectors in Bangladesh are a product of a donor-driven development strategy led by the United States of America in the recent decade. East Pakistan had been an internal "colony" of West Pakistan. The agrarian surpluses of the former have been expropriated to meet the needs of industrial development of West Pakistan. A particular form of military-bureaucratic state structure and the powerful alliance between feudal, commercial, trade, military, and bureaucratic forces, more or less, can be seen as the consequence of a particular development strategy adopted in the post-colonial period. Interestingly, historians have failed to re-evaluate this aspect of history, partly because of the overwhelming dominance of the paradigm of "nationalism," and partly due to the lack of a tradition in historiography that emphasizes careful scrutiny and analysis of development plans that decide the fate of millions of people.

The struggle for political liberation and achievement of independence can be elusive. Political independence does not mean independence from the legacies of the past, or an improved capacity to chart and plan a future course distinctly different from the old path. This is evident in the case of Bangladesh. An examination of the health sector clearly underscores this point.

Since independence in 1971, almost every aspect of the social and economic development in Bangladesh has been part and parcel of international policies and plans. The newly independent country had to depend on the largesse of international donor agencies to reconstruct the war-damaged economy. Bangladesh won the war after nine months of continual fighting. Yet, on 16 December 1971, it had got rid only of the Pakistani generals occupying the country, and not the development policies which Bangladesh had inherited from its past. Today, Bangladesh continues to be dependent on international donors. The fact of independence becomes, in a sense, immaterial and irrelevant because of the carry-over of projects introduced by the donor agencies, particularly the World Bank, in the mid-sixties.

The two most important donor-driven policies inherited by Bangladesh from its predecessor East Pakistan were:

1. the introduction of the so-called green revolution (GR) technology; and
2. the modern contraceptive-based population control program.

The programs had taken off just before the liberation war. The newly-born country could abandon every other policy, except for these two. This, then, is the context of the relationship of health care to family planning.

The first path-breaking discussion on health, particularly primary health care (PHC) issues, was held much later, in 1978, when the Alma-Ata Declaration was drafted and endorsed the world over. It declared that health was a basic human right and that the pursuit of health was inseparable from the struggle for a more just and caring society. This declaration was too progressive and radical for many countries. The goal of Health for All by the Year 2000 is still one of the phrases used most commonly by the government and donor agencies, but has degenerated into a licence to do anything in the name of health. For Bangladesh, the Alma-Ata Declaration had little meaning.

The other important conferences were the World Population Conference (1974) held in Bucharest and the International Women's Conference (1975) held in Mexico. It was in these conferences that, by refusing to address the developmental issues raised by the Third World, the grave for the Alma-Ata Declaration was prepared even before it was born: health had already been sacrificed for other goals.

The contents of the Alma-Ata Declaration and the slogan of Health for All became popular among some non-governmental community-based groups; these organizations started implementing the principles of "primary health care" approach. However, developments such as the selective PHC, cost recovery, and taking over of the Third World health-care policy by the WB in the nineties (Werner 1994) turned around the policies. Primary health care lost its social and community dimensions and was reduced to a package of discrete services.

This chapter deals with the issue of the overwhelming dominance of population control policies over health care and its effect on women's health.

Policies and Programs for Population Control: Role of Donors

A Brief History

In 1952, the East Pakistan Family Planning Association (now known as the Bangladesh Family Planning Association [BFPA]) was formed with the objective of reducing population growth. This marks the beginning of the intervention by foreign agencies in fertility control. This association was funded mostly by foreign money, with nominal financial support from the government, under the First Five Year Plan of Pakistan, 1955–60. It was a low-intensity operation. Its achievement was "in informing the population of the possibility of family planning and its relation to food supply and national development. The population issue was brought into focus and generated some interest regarding the need for family planning" (ESCAP 1981).

As per the recommendations of a Population Council Mission which was sent to Pakistan in 1960, the government incorporated family planning as a regular component of the existing health services. A community development program known as Village-AID was entrusted with family planning related education and motivation work. This was later replaced by a public health research program which was set up with technical assistance from the University of California and financial support from the Ford Foundation. One of the objectives of this program was to assist in developing educational programs related to family planning (Akhter 1992: 5).

The government became involved in population control programs on a mass scale in the Third Five Year Plan (1965–70) period, and the depopulation strategy received maximum attention. A Family Planning Board was constituted with the Minister of

Health as its chairman, but kept separate from the existing health services. It was given maximum administrative and financial autonomy; this enabled the donor agencies to keep the program under their surveillance and control. For the first time, delivery of FP services and motivation work started in the rural areas, with paid female workers. Financial incentives were introduced for acceptors and recruiters for the use of intra-uterine devices and vasectomy. This indicates that acceptance was not voluntary and that efforts at motivation had failed.

Family planning activities virtually came to a standstill during the liberation-war of 1971, and during the post-war relief and rehabilitation work. However, important policy changes were made on the basis of previous experiences. These were:

1. abolition of the incentive-disincentive system;
2. introduction of oral contraceptives and tubectomy;
3. relaxation of abortion law; and
4. integration of the malaria program with the Ministry of Health and Family Planning.

Policies and Plans since Independence

After independence, the Government of Bangladesh started pursuing population and family planning programs with a new vigor. It had committed itself to population control since the formulation of the First Five Year Plan in 1973, largely because of heavy donor pressures (Akhter 1992: 98).

With each successive Five Year Plan (FYP), the importance accorded to "the gravity of the population problem" grew. Correspondingly, the emphasis placed on "population control" also increased. By the Third and Fourth FYP periods, population control had become "a compelling need...; leaving no option other than to invest all efforts to reduce drastically the population growth rate" (Akhter 1992: 99). A reflection of this is observed in the targets that were set for population control; they became progressively more ambitious/drastic (see Table 3.1).

It is seen that on the one hand, in the Second FYP, the concept of PHC was accepted as an integral part of socio-economic development, and on the other, the plan termed population-growth as the "number one problem" that has "frustrated the development efforts in Bangladesh." To achieve the targets for population control, it was decided in this plan-period to integrate maternal

Table 3.1
Goals for CBR Reduction and Couple Protection Rates (CPR)

	CBR[1] to be reduced from	*CPR[2] to be increased from*
First FYP	47/1,000 to 43/1,000	–
Second FYP	From above 43/1,000 to 31.6/1,000	14% to 37%
Third FYP	39/1,000 to 31/1,000	25% to 40%
Fourth FYP	TFR[3] to be reduced from 4.3 to 3.4	35.5% to 50%

Source: The First Five Year Plan (1973–78), Government of People's Republic of Bangladesh.
The Second Five Year Plan (1980–85), Government of People's Republic Bangladesh.
The Third Five Year Plan (1985–90), Government of People's Republic of Bangladesh.
The Fourth Five Year Plan (1990–95), Government of People's Republic of Bangladesh.

Note: [1] crude birth rate.
[2] couple protection rate.
[3] total fertility rate.

and child health services (MCH) with Family Planning Programs to enlist better community participation.

As far as the question of general health services is concerned, the emphasis across the four plan periods has been on infrastructure development for providing comprehensive and integrated health services, on increasing coverage of the services, on streamlining and strengthening services, on reducing rural-urban disparties, and on training and expansion. In the Fourth FYP, it was specifically mentioned that the private sector and non-governmental organizations will be encouraged to set up hospitals, clinics, pharmaceutical industries, and to help in the development of manpower.

In June 1979, the National Population Policy was enunciated. It aimed at reducing fertility, mainly by increasing the use of modern contraceptive methods. The basic approach was to meet the unmet demand for FP services, and to make specific efforts to improve the status of women. It took the form of a concerted program aimed at:

1. establishing, as close to the people as possible, an extensive network of facilities to provide FP-related services, including MCH services; and

2. promoting use of these facilities for the distribution of modern contraceptive devices, and to provide the necessary technical, managerial, and material support to maintain an acceptable quality of the services.

Replacement-level fertility emerged as a sectoral goal, though the time stipulated for its attainment has been repeatedly reviewed and revised. At the beginning of the project, the government set the year 2000 as the target date. The first two FYPs did not move in the direction specified in the following donor criteria:

- raising of CPR from 7.7 percent to around 25 percent; and
- lowering TFR from 7 to 5.8 between 1975 and 1985.

As a remedy, the interdependence between reduced fertility and increased child survival was suggested. A major outreach effort was planned in three areas of MCH:

1. reduction of diarrhea deaths through oral rehydration therapy;
2. Expanded Program for Immunization (EPI) of children below two years, and of pregnant woman; and
3. training of traditional birth attendants (TBAs) in safe-delivery practices.

In the First FYP period (1973–78) major organizational changes were also made. A Population Control and Family Planning Division (PCFPD) was formed in 1975 within the Ministry of Health and Population Control to coordinate the multi-sectoral program that had been initiated (Akhter 1992: 10, 11). This multi-sectoral program included eight ministries and divisions, working at integrating population related activities with the development programs of the government. Among these were: local government, rural development and co-operatives, education, science and technology, agriculture, women's affairs, and religious affairs.

This program was financed primarily by the World Bank and United Nations Fund for Population Activities (UNFPA), and was part of the overall development strategy of the World Bank in the Third World countries. Special emphasis was laid on enhancing the status of women and ensuring their involvement in development. For instance: Mothers' Clubs, sponsored by the World Bank, were formed at the union level to engage rural women of reproductive age in gainful economic activities and to help improve their status in the family. The aim was to register at least 20 acceptors annually for FP in each of the 760 Mothers' Clubs.

Non-governmental organizations (NGOs) funded by foreign agencies also played a key role in implementing population control policies. Their role intensified and the donors started depending on them to achieve their objectives. About 163 NGOs were engaged in FP activities. Of these, there were about 14 international NGOs working under agreement with the government. These had financial support from the United States Agency for International Development (USAID), the Ford Foundation, UNFPA, Pathfinder Fund, Asia Foundation, and the World Bank. The government also provided support from the PCFPD which had a committee comprising the World Bank and other donor agencies, for allocating funds to private organizations (Akhter 1992: 13).

The period from 1978 to 1985 can be termed as the phase of drastic intervention. Arguments such as "any measure is civilized to depopulate the country" were put forth in a vulgar and naked manner. A Two-Year Approach Plan (1978–80) was formulated, which was later integrated in the Second FYP. To achieve the objective of a "drastic decline" in the population, a shift from temporary to permanent methods of contraception was also affected. During the year 1980–81, more than 230,000 sterilizations were performed under the government's MCH–FP program, and the government envisaged an increase to 980,000 by 1985. Even the World Bank termed this target as ambitious, although it was happy with the enthusiasm of the government for drastic actions (Akhter 1992: 15).

Measures, such as integration of health and family planning services, introduction of various socio-legal measures and incentives/disincentives to encourage adoption of the small family norm (such as a bond-scheme), enlisting assistance of physicians in the private sector to provide family planning services, enhanced resource allocation for family planning, and hiring of religious leaders to reinterpret Islam in favor of family planning, were adopted to meet the targets.

Financing by Donor Agencies: WB, IDA, USAID

Despite the colonial structure of the health-services and its attendant limitations, the government looks upon health as a commitment to the people. Therefore, health care is financed through the revenue budget. This may be looked upon as the remnants of the anti-colonial spirit retained sporadically in the post-colonial state. In contrast, population control is entirely a donor-initiated and donor-funded project, and is therefore a commitment to the donors. This splitting of the commitment of the government to two constituencies—to health and to family planning—is a major political crisis for a Third World government.

The WB has been supporting several "population projects" in Bangladesh since 1975, by mobilizing the support of various countries of the North, such as Norway, Sweden, Canada, the U.K., Australia, Belgium, and Japan. In 1987, the initial co-financing arrangements were converted into a more structured "Population and Health Consortium." The IDA has been the leader of the consortium comprising the World Bank and its co-financiers, with WHO, UNFPA, and UNICEF as the executing agencies for a number of activities. The USAID and the Asian Development Bank (ADB) are not part of the consortium, but can attend its meetings as observers. The WB claims that the IDA has helped the Government of Bangladesh to mobilize substantial financial and technical support for family planning and health programs, and to coordinate donor assistance for this critical sector of the socio-economic development of the country. It has contributed significantly to the current consensus on the priority of population programs.

So far, nearly US$ 950.8 million have been spent on the four population and health projects of these agencies. For the Fifth Health and Population Program (HAPP-V), which was to commence in 1998, the World Bank and its co-financiers planned to commit around one billion dollars. The World Bank has shifted from its approach of uni-dimensional population control projects to multi-sectoral projects on health and population. This shift is reflected in the changing nomenclature of its projects, from "First Population Project" to "Second Population and Family Health Project" to finally "Health and Population Project."

The USAID is the single largest donor agency, which is also active in determining the policies and the direction to be adopted. It holds an independent position and is not part of the financial arrangements of the WB. It pays more than US$ 25 million annually for the FP program. Bangladesh is USAID's largest bilateral, population commitment in the world. USAID is quite happy with the performance of Bangladesh vis-à-vis its population control program. It committed US$ 210 million for the seven-year period (1997–2004) to the Population and Health Program.

USAID does not subscribe to the view that a functioning primary health care system or any social interventions are necessary for achieving population control targets. Direct delivery of contraceptive services has always been its priority. In fact, USAID has been aggressively promoting population control through imported contraceptive methods and even in conducting "forced" sterilization programs. The USAID believes in a vertical approach towards population control and feels that the population problems should be tackled as a crisis, as an epidemic; population control should be a single-focused objective. The need for MCH services is argued in a reverse way by USAID by saying that birth control is one of the most effective MCH interventions, i.e., health of the mother can be protected if she can be protected from childbearing. In other words, contraceptive acceptance is MCH. It is the suggestion of the USAID to the government that it should handle the problem by suspending the normal rules, by going outside the usual government procedures, and resorting to any and all socially acceptable measures which seem likely to work (USAID 1983).

Donor Needs: Integration of Health and FP Services and its Impact

The donor agencies interact directly with the Ministry of Health and Family Welfare. Thus, the priorities and decision of donor agencies are implemented through the highest decision-making body.

In 1980, a major change was effected at the organizational level, which was the "functional integration" of family planning and MCH services with primary health care at the *Upa-Zilla* level and below. The very proposal for integration was initially made by the WB, which had, by now, recognized the need for using some kind of health services to gain credibility for population control. According to the government, "this measure would permit FP, MCH and PHC services to be delivered in a co-ordinated and complementary manner at the grass-root level." The major objective of such integration was to improve the delivery of all three services, particularly of family planning (Government of Bangladesh 1983).

However, the reality is somewhat different. So far, the FP department produced only non-medical fieldworkers who were employed for the motivational aspects. Now more medical personnel were being recruited. This kind of integration allowed the use of the existing facilities and provided clinical support, personnel, and materials, which were needed for the delivery of the clinical methods of sterilization (Akhter 1992).

The 1984 Aid Group Meeting also clearly spelt out that this integration was essential for strengthening and promoting FP programs, and for "optimal use of the large cadre of health workers for delivery of priority services" (Government of Bangladesh 1984). Thus, in the garb of "integration," the infrastructure for general health services was appropriated for purposes of population control.

The two significant features of this "functional integration" of health and FP were:

1. Only the policy-making authority for the two divisions, namely health and family planning, is common through a common minister and secretary. The political and administrative culture of Bangladesh is such that it allows few individuals to remain in these policy-making positions long enough to become thoroughly familiar with the tasks.
2. It is restricted to the use of the human resources and infrastructure of the health services by the population control program. The latter has been allowed to retain its identity and independence. The planning, budgeting, administration, and management of logistics, training, and all other aspects of the population control program remain separate and independent of the health care delivery system.

The two divisions remain totally independent, organizationally, functionally, and even physically. This separation is to the extent that even on subjects of common concern, such as the maternal mortality rate, there is no shared policy for collection and/or sharing of data. At the district level too, the office of the civil surgeon (responsible for the health institutions such as the district hospital, thana health complexes and rural health centers) and that of the deputy director of family welfare (responsible for FP services at the thana level) have no formal contact with each other. They run independent offices and maintain independent contacts with their respective headquarters.

This lack of coordination and communication at the higher levels leads to a lot of confusion at the lower-levels through which actual functioning and implementation take place. The dual authority generates confusion, as well as resentment due to unequal resource allocations and extra pressures on the thana health complex (THC) and rural health center (RHC) staff. There is confusion and frustration among the field-level workers, who are burdened and pressurized from the top for fulfillment of FP targets, whereby they cannot provide the required health services to the people.

Main Features and Impact of Family Planning Program on the Health of Women

While the most important goal of population control and family planning is to reduce the TFR, and thereby the population growth rate, the design and practice is merely to increase the CPR. It is the contraceptive prevalence rate that is the barometer for measuring success or failure of the program. The other features of this contraceptive-based population program are:

1. The methods offered and the preference attached to particular methods do not leave much choice. The methods are: sterilization, intra-uterine devices, injectibles, oral pills, and condoms. Except for the last two, all the remaining methods are clinic-controlled. This thus centralizes the decision about the provision and withdrawal of the methods. The emphasis on the longer-term and clinic-based methods makes women dependent on the FP personnel. Traditional methods are not given importance or taken into account while compiling statistics or while setting targets. For example: The figure of 37 percent by 1995 for women using contraceptives is considered inadequate.[1] This is primarily because the policy-makers do not take into account: (*i*) the fact that some couples may be using some other method of contraception; and (*ii*) the existence of women-headed households, or of unmarried, widowed, and separated/divorced women.
2. Except for condoms and vasectomy (to a limited extent), all the methods are to be used by women. More than 80 percent

[1]Statistical figures for contraceptive methods are quoted from: MIS unit of Population Control and Family Planning Department, Government of People's Republic of Bangladesh.

of all the contraceptives offered to the couples are to be adopted by women.

3. It has been found that the majority of the total sterilizations were performed on women. In 1985, sterilizations accounted for 37 percent of the contraceptive mix, of which 31 percent consisted of female sterilization; only 6 percent were male. It was also found that majority of the sterilized women were poor and uneducated.
4. The field-level workers are trained to "motivate" women to accept contraceptives. However, they are not given full information regarding their side effects. Also, they are discouraged from bringing women suffering from side effects or adverse effects for treatment. The clinics do not have any programs or funds to treat women suffering from/with complications and problems. While this not only discredits the field-level worker amongst the local people, it also takes a heavy toll on the health of the women. UBINIG has taken up cases of many women who have developed problems/complications following use of contraceptives, such as that of Tohura and Selina. Selina had continuous bleeding and blurred vision after insertion of Norplant. It was only after much pleading by her and her husband that the FP personnel removed the implant. Tohura Begum had to pay with her life for the callousness and neglect that characterize the FP program. She died due to the side effects that she developed soon after she was injected with Depo-provera.
5. The field-level experience of the author shows that it is the poor Bangladeshi women, already suffering from poor health conditions and paucity of health services, who are the targets of the FP methods. In the ruthless pursuit of numbers and targets, no attention is paid to whether these women are physically fit for the methods adopted. The experiences of the author corroborate studies that demonstrate that anemic and malnourished women are highly vulnerable to complications (Mintzes et al. 1993).
6. The above issues of complications and side effects and the fitness of women assume grave significance given the obsession of the FP programs with targets and with "use-effectiveness" of contraceptives, i.e., while using a contraceptive there should be no pregnancy. The question of "safety" of the contraceptive is often not brought up. Further, even

though there is much rhetoric about maternal health and mortality, morbidity due to contraceptive usage is not given attention.

7. It is found that the MCH services are tied up with FP services and used as an inducement for women to accept contraceptives. Therefore, these MCH services are given mostly to potential FP clients, i.e., to women in the reproductive age group. That also consists only of ante- and post-natal care, immunization and a few other PHC services. A large number of women and their health problems are left unattended to. Further, this MCH approach does not take into account the illnesses of women that are unrelated to pregnancy and childbearing.
8. Internationally, the main problem of poor women is believed to be that of unwanted pregnancies. In recent times, therefore, the term "fertility decline" has been introduced, which carries positive connotations of addressing the needs of women, namely, decline in fertility will lead to decline in number of births, which means women are saved from morbidity and mortality. But this whole strategy, in reality and practice, is to do with targeting women for contraceptive usage and with controlling their bodies. This approach rests on the notion that women are breeders of unwanted populations. In FP vocabulary, women in the age group of 15–49 are merely "women in reproductive age." Their contributions in social, economic, cultural, and political spheres are never acknowledged. Even among women, it is the poor women who are targeted. This is inevitable since they are vulnerable to the economic incentives offered.

Population Control: An Encroachment on Health

The consensus of the Government of Bangladesh and donors "to provide adequate basic health care for the people of Bangladesh and to slow population growth" is neither new nor surprising. There has been no representative government over the past 25 years. The government has always expressed "political" commitment to drastic actions to reduce population growth. At the same time, it has been promising health for all since 1978. However, as we have seen above, these two goals are contradictory. The goal of slowing population growth has not much to do with providing adequate basic health care to the people; also, practical efforts to reduce population growth take away resources allocated for basic health care. The donors even go on to say that family planning means good health, i.e., contraceptive service delivery is a health service delivery. Therefore, the provision of basic health care services should not be linked to the goal of reducing population growth. This has proven to be wrong in the past and continues to be the same.

The basic concern of the World Bank is the "rapid population growth." Over the years, this concern has not changed although the formerly coercive language is now "softened" by phrases like reducing "unwanted fertility." The term "unwanted fertility" is as coercive as the population control measures based on a target-driven approach. This has always been a major criticism of health activists and feminists. They feel that in this strategy, women are forced to bear the burden of reducing population growth. It also labels as demographically "unwanted" those who are born out of social necessity, in a context where the survival of the family is dependent upon family labor and the survival of sons. It also does not guarantee that all health needs of clients will be taken care of. Moreover, the term "client" is based on the consumer orientation for certain "products," such as contraceptives and specific health services. Studies have already been conducted about "consumer preferences" for family planning services and this indicates a clear acknowledgement of the fact that FP services provided in the form of contraceptives are linked to the marketing of products produced by pharmaceutical companies. The client-centered reproductive health approach does not place responsibility on men.

Non-family planning measures proposed for reducing population growth include programs for delaying marriage by keeping girls at schools, thereby delaying childbearing. This project is a sham because it makes use of a basic human right of women, namely education, to achieve other goals. Girls must have access to education irrespective of potential changes in reproductive behavior. If education means "keeping girls in schools...leading to delay in marriage...leading to delay in initiation in childbearing," it ensures neither education nor reproductive rights for women. In fact, this is a gross violation of women's right to education because it implies that "something must be given in return," namely reduction in fertility.

The reproductive health approach which came into the population plans after the International Conference on Population and Development (ICPD) 1994 is also very interesting. It says clearly that it does not abandon the policy of family planning, but promotes more effective ways of accomplishing the objectives of the population policy and development policy. That is reproductive health, with the so-called client-centered approach that claims to provide users with informed choice and high quality family planning linked to maternal/child health care, etc., and merely has as its goal the reduction of population growth. This has been problematic in the past and will remain so if the goal does not change to provide effective health care facilities to the people, including women, children and men of all classes.

Though the definition of reproduction has become much wider than family planning, the general health care needs of women have not been ensured. We need to emphasize the various other diseases women suffer from besides maternal health problems. These are gastric and respiratory diseases, occupational health problems for working women, nutritional deficiencies, diseases caused by the use of pesticides and chemical fertilizers in food production, etc. The perspective of health care should be much broader in order to identify the causes of diseases rather than merely focus on the curative aspects.

References

Akhter, F. (1992): *Depopulating Bangladesh: Essays on the Politics of Fertility*. Bangladesh: Feminist Bookstore.

ESCAP (1981): Country Monograph Series No. 8. Thailand: ESCAP Population Division.

Government of Bangladesh (1983): Statement by Secretary, Ministry of Health and Population Control, Before Meeting of Local Consultation Group of Donors on Population Control. 12 September, Dhaka.

——— (1984): Population Control Program in Bangladesh: Status Paper for the Bangladesh Aid Group Meeting, Paris. Dhaka: Ministry of Health and Population Control, Planning Commission and External Resource Division.

Government of People's Republic of Bangladesh (various years): *The Five-Year Plans*. Dhaka: Planning Commission, Ministry of Finance and Planning.

Mintzes, B., Hardon, A., and Hanhart, J. (eds.) (1993): *Norplant: Under Her Skin*. The Netherlands: Eburen. p. 11.

USAID (1983): *An Emergency Plan for Population Control in Bangladesh—A Position Paper.*

Werner, D. (1994): The Life and Death of Primary Health Care. *Third World Resurgence,* No. 42/43, February–March.

4

Changes in Health Care Systems in Europe: Focus on Finland

Meri Koivusalo

Background

The idea of structural adjustment in the more affluent countries, such as in many of the European countries, may seem far-fetched when viewed from the context of developing countries. A closer look at the public sector reforms taking place in Europe reveals similarities with the structural adjustment and health sector reforms that have been implemented in developing countries and countries in transition. These changes may be related to the ideological domination of right-wing policies backed by neo-liberal economic prescriptions, all of which have altered the focus of policy action and understanding of the role of the state. However, the officially cited reasons include:

- the impact of globalization, and global pressures to cooperate and compete in new ways;
- consumer expectations; and
- the necessity to reduce the budget deficits.

The responses of the Organization for Economic Cooperation and Development (OECD) countries have been found to be remarkably similar in many aspects (see Table 4.1). The public sector reforms—and to a large extent health sector reforms—implemented to varying extents in Europe may, therefore, bear important messages for health systems development in other countries, even though the context differs to a substantial extent.

Two major international initiatives may be identified in the organization and financing of health care, "Health for All" and health care reforms. The World Health Organization (WHO) provided the intellectual background and legitimacy for the notion of Health for All. This program entailed implementing changes

Table 4.1
Common Features in Public Sector Responses in OECD Countries

- Decentralization of authority within governmental units, and devolution of responsibilities to lower levels of governments, for example municipalities.
- A re-examination of what the government should both do and pay for, what it should pay but not do, and what it should neither do nor pay for.
- Downsizing the public service, and privatization and corporatization of activities.
- Consideration of more cost-effective ways of delivering services, such as contracting out, market mechanisms, and user charges.
- Customer orientation, including explicit quality standards for public services.
- Benchmarking and measuring performance.
- Reforms designed to simplify regulation and reduce its costs.

Source: Anon 1996.

in the health care organization geared towards primary health care and decentralization, and some emphasis on health care financing. However, especially in the early days of the WHO, activities on health care financing or organization were opposed by some countries, such as the United States. Later, lack of resources for the issue ensured lack of action. In practice this meant that the vacuum that was created in research and study of health systems development was occupied by the OECD and the World Bank in the eighties. In the OECD, this was linked to a program of improvement in public management and public sector reform, and in the World Bank to the promotion of structural adjustment and public sector reforms.

This paper: (*i*) describes the elements of health care reforms and their role in public policies in many European countries; and (*ii*) looks at Finland as a case study. Despite the fact that Europe is substantially larger than the European Union, the chapter will deal predominantly with OECD countries and countries within the European Union.

Health Care Reforms

The term "health care reforms" tends to create a notion of bringing in positive change. It has been described as the process of improving the performance of existing systems and of assuring efficient and equitable responses to further changes. Some features and concerns of health care reforms are as shown in Table 4.2.

Table 4.2
Some Common Features and Concerns in Health Care Reforms

1. Organization of health care system

- Provider and purchaser split into health systems where health care is financed through general revenue and is provided by the government (Beveridge model)* in order to enhance possibilities to introduce more competitive elements in health systems.
- Introducing or enhancing contracting in health care systems or parts of it, e.g., in subcontracting cleaning or laboratory services.
- Primary providers and essential packages of health care.
- Preference on privatization of higher levels of care, especially tertiary care.
- Decentralization.
- Planned markets and managed competition.

2. Multiple actors and financing mechanisms

* Non-profit providers, active or passive enhancing of private actors and private insurance.
* Enhancing, actively or passively, the opting out from public services by those who can afford to pay for private services.
* Economic incentives in paying providers of health care.
* Hospital budgeting, guidelines in disease management, and pharmaceuticals.
* User charges and cost-sharing (e.g., pharmaceuticals, hospital stay).
* Insurance.
* Prioritization, outcome measurement, evaluation in QALYs (DALYs).

* Health systems where financing is in principle based on general taxation and provision through public service arrangements are often called Beveridge model health systems, according to the United Kingdom national health system.

A clear problem with these reforms is that the following issues have rarely been discussed:

1. How, why, by whom, and in what context are these changes being made?
2. The potential problems of prioritization, or incompatibilities involved with the fundamental aims of efficiency, equity, and effectiveness.

In general, there has been an emphasis on using competitive elements and cost-sharing in order to enhance efficiency and effectiveness, and thus reach a compromise on equity (equity has been considered predominantly as resulting from more effective allocation of resources and increased technical efficiency).

In the OECD countries, the competitive elements have been mostly dealt with in the context of the so-called planned or managed markets. The World Bank and the OECD may be seen as indirect promoters of competitive elements in health care in general, and of managed competition and planned markets in particular. The indirect influence of these institutions often trickles down through research, analyses, and networks of experts. Moran and Wood have seen the OECD as a facilitator, whose influence is derived from the power of the analyses which it sponsors, and the influence of the individuals and institutions in the networks it supports (Moran and Wood 1996). However, in the case of developing countries and countries in transition, the World Bank has clearly had direct influence on health sector policies.

In the OECD countries and Europe, the experiences of using market forces and competitive elements in health care have, in general, been rather dim, both in terms of costs and equity. In practice, the administrative costs, management costs, have tended to increase overall costs—even if savings would have been achieved in other fields—and competitive elements have remained scarce. The disillusionment within Europe and amongst the countries in transition was reflected in the 1996 Ljubljana conference. The Ljubljana declaration, while prescribing for more government steering than rowing, did, in essence, call for cautiousness in implementing changes toward increased use of private sector and market forces in health care (The Ljubljana Charter 1996). A similar approach can be perceived in the recent OECD discussion documents on health care organization (OECD 1995, 1996).

The disillusionment with markets is well reflected in the note by Evans:

> After several decades of experience, carefully reflected upon, in Europe, North America, and throughout the developed world, we can now be pretty sure that efficient, competitive markets for health care do not and cannot exist. Their advocates are selling powdered unicorn horn. So why are they getting a hearing? (Evans 1997a)

Such thinking is also to be found in New Zealand which has been a pioneer in introducing competitive elements but has changed its agenda and returned towards collaborative strategies as competitive markets in health care have actually increased the health care costs

(Malcolm 1997). Sweden and the United Kingdom have also reduced the competitive elements in contracting in favor of more cooperative models (Saltman 1997). It seems that in the OECD countries, both the approaches, namely public/private mix as well as competitive elements in health care organization, have not shown the promised returns. In comparison to the rest of the world, in Europe there seems to be a strong reliance on public services and with less enthusiasm for the ability of markets to solve the problems facing public services. In spite of the declining enthusiasm for market mechanisms, in many countries the reform process has changed the institutional environment in health care provision. There are sufficient grounds to believe that in the process of adjusting public sector services, the governments will continue to support further limits upon health care costs (see Table 4.1).

The experiences of competition and different forms of privatization have been dismal and it is well established that financing through cost-sharing by users is known to be the most regressive means of financing health care (Evans 1997a, 1997b; Maynard and Bloor 1995; Wagstaff and Doorslaer 1993). Yet, competition and markets continue to be advocated as they hold more opportunities for the private sector in health care and thus secure the interests of provider groups and industries. It is clear that the managed care industry will continue to seek global opportunities during the coming years, with specific reference to Europe, Latin America, and the Pacific rim (Academy for International Health Studies 1997). The global expansion of the managed care chains has also found support from international organizations such as the World Bank (Smith 1996).

When equity is considered, the principle of health care provision has been that health care should be provided according to the need and financed according to the ability to pay (Wagstaff and Doorslaer 1993). This view has also been shared broadly amongst the European countries. It is not only a measure of solidarity, but also a response to the actual realities in health care in many countries, where most of the health care costs are incurred by those severely ill. There is, therefore, a necessity to balance the risk and costs over a larger population. As long as the poor are more ill than the wealthy, shifting of health care finances from the public to the private will also result in unequal distribution impact and, in many cases, in costlier care in general (Evans 1997b).

Issues of Concern

In the European Union, the policies related to the European Monetary Union as well as emphasis on internal markets have repercussions in the health sector leading to tighter requirements for public budgets and predominance of private sector considerations. In the European Union, the subsidiarity principle sets social policies and health services as national issues. However, at times the subsidiarity principle may promote greater reliance on informal care and on non-governmental actors, when it is interpreted as suggesting that the government should act only when there are no other providers (Koski 1996; Ranjault 1992). While the non-profit actors have gained renewed attention in health and social policies, the question remains as to whether, and if so, to what extent, a transformation from non-profit to profit-seeking systems may take place in Europe.

The EU member countries have, to a large extent, transformed their health care system toward more competitive models, with respective changes in the players and potential future considerations over the extent to which competitive policies will become important in the realms of health care (Hamilton 1996). The more commercialized environment necessarily offers more chances to the old and new players in the health care industry—such as managed care chains and pharmaceutical and life sciences industries—which are becoming more involved in broader health care (Kanavos 1996). The purchaser-provider split in most countries of Europe and an increasing emphasis on contracting in the public sector can also open up further opportunities for more private providers to emerge in the delivery of services. While the size of the private sector in health is still limited in many European countries, they may be increasing in scope due to passive privatization and increasing use of contracting in service provision. Those countries which rely on social insurance-based models and/or those that have explicit contractual arrangements may offer the easiest avenues toward managed care, although, the prospects for managed care expansion in Europe have been considered limited (McKee et al. 1996).

Much of the health care prioritization exercise seems to be focused only on public sector activities, resulting in the definition of the "core" public services. This creates two-track services, a "full menu" in the private sector and a "restricted menu" in the public sector, and sends a clear message for those able to pay to seek additional private health care coverage. This also means that health care is no longer provided according to the need but according to the ability to pay. There are also concerns that the use of parameters like QALYs or DALYs, with their emphasis on outcome measures and clinical decision-making, may deflect the discussion toward prioritization in terms of treatment of diseases, or toward promoting values not necessarily shared by the broader public (Barker and Green 1996; Nord et al. 1995). The emphasis on cost-sharing by patients may also be seen as part of this process as one means to ensure that responsibilities are shared with consequent endorsement of user charges and their regressive distributional impacts. In addition, there seems to be an increasing emphasis on directing the publicly financed health services not only toward those groups which are in most need or can benefit more, but also depending on whether the persons could use private sector services or not. While orienting the services toward the poorest can be appreciated in the name of equity, the long-term consequences of these practices may easily lead toward growing disparity in the quality of public and private health care services.

There is also a tendency to define public health and preventive services as a public good which may be financed by public funds, and curative health care as a private good which may be financed by private funds. This creates new roles for the government as the provider of "public health and preventive services" and the subsidizer and guardian of contracted curative health services. While several strands may be detected in the current European discussion on public health, questions regarding the role of the state in public health and health services provision may be seen as one of major importance. There is a danger of re-definition of state responsibilities leading towards erosion of the social right to health services, with little more than rhetoric to promote the actual public health issues.

The current understanding of more state involvement in "steering" than in "rowing" in the provision of health services tends to leave open the question as to who will be rowing? Will they be local governments in decentralized systems, or profit-seeking or non-profit actors, or religious institutions, or in the case of informal care, predominantly women? The incremental changes in public sector development through, say, the creation of stronger transnational health care industries, may develop into a situation where governments and international institutions are not able to implement the steering and governance they would wish to undertake. It is clear that access to health care as a social right is undermined if care for those unable to pay becomes very basic or is provided more by charitable organizations.

It is important to note that the trends towards contracting and corporatization in health care—even when implemented under the public services umbrella—may actually pave the way towards an incremental change into a more pluralist model of health care provision resembling that of the United States. In the United States, health care provision and financing include strong private actors and a more competitive environment than in the European countries. Both health care costs and coverage are compromised and the organization of health care has been shown to be resistant to government steering, a phenomenon that has been attributed to the strong private actors in place (Mechanic 1995). Evidence on whether the managed care arrangements have led to a halt in the growth of absolute care costs is pending (Evans 1997b). There are increasing concerns over the lack of access, compromise made in terms of patient care and choice, and the fast change from non-profit providers to more commercial chains. High administrative and management costs have negated the savings from the decrease in costs of care and physicians' pay (Bond and Weismann 1997; Evans 1997b; Fuchs 1997; Gabel 1997). In spite of the very problematic experiences in the United States, the newly commercialized health care providers will, no doubt, seek markets elsewhere (Barer et al. 1995; Smith 1996).

Many European countries seem to have survived the eighties and the nineties with predominantly publicly funded services backed by the support and willingness of the population to maintain principles of equity and solidarity. This may, however, be compromised by other aims and policies resulting in diminished funds and changing institutional context in the health sector. For example, while there has been recent interest within the European Union, WHO, and the World Bank on the effects of broader policy measures on health, there is little research and analysis on the impact of trade agreements and policies on health and health care organization.

Changes in Health Care in Finland

The impact of the developments that have been described above has also been felt in Finland. Finland is a small, northern country with a population of about five million. It is one of the most rural OECD countries and has been going through a transition from a predominantly agricultural country toward a more urbanized Nordic welfare state. In the late eighties, Finland entered into a state of overheating of the economy and a subsequent economic crisis, with soaring unemployment. While the economic growth revived in the nineties, the unemployment figures have remained high at around 15 percent in the late nineties. This economic situation poses a persistent challenge to the country.

Equity has traditionally held a central place in Finnish social policies. There has also been decentralized sharing of responsibilities between the central government and the over 400 municipalities that have a long experience of local level governance. During the expansion of services, the major steps were linked to state subsidies, which enabled government guidance and ensured a degree of regional equity. The recession in the nineties rapidly raised the share of social expenditure due to the decrease in GDP and increases in unemployment, which led to cuts in public social spending. However, the crisis also showed the strength of the welfare state in practice.

In the eighties and nineties, the ideological grounds of the Finnish welfare state have also been debated and new forms of welfare have been sought. The Finnish social services could be said to largely resemble the so-called "Beveridge model," with universal public organization of services funded from general revenue. In Finland, primary health care and education have been provided for and funded partly by municipalities with their own revenue basis. On the other hand, the state subsidies have ensured substantial central involvement. This has been the focus of criticism with calls for greater municipal self-governance. While the number of non-governmental organizations is considerable, they are involved in service provision only to a limited extent, e.g., in services for special groups. The traditional criticism over Finnish welfare policies has been focused on the supposed creation of dependence, the loss of individual responsibility, as well as the apparent effects of taxation on enterprise. This argumentation, which has been influenced by international trends and advice, has increased during the eighties. In addition, the fiscal crisis of the state has brought to the fore the discussion on the future of the Finnish welfare state.

The Finnish welfare state has maintained public support, and public opinion is more in favor of public provision of services than for the alternatives in the market approaches that rely on private actors, non-governmental organizations, or informal care (Ervasti 1996; Uusitalo et al. 1995). The maintenance of the current universal and redistributive elements in health care and social welfare is, however, facing increasing pressures. The high unemployment rate has paved the way for arguments promoting more means-testing in social benefits as well as increased labor market flexibility. The incremental process of administrative changes and pressures also shows a tendency towards increasing private responsibility and publicly financed contracting (Ministry of Financial Affairs 1993). Market mechanisms and choice have been introduced through promotion of contracting and planned market models. User charges in primary health care have been introduced and raised during the nineties. In addition, there have been pressures to move towards a managerial and more market-oriented steering, both at the central and local administrative levels, including semi-privatizing public institutions into unincorporated state enterprises. The public-sector service project within the Ministry of Financial Affairs clearly discusses services production in the framework of consumer–citizen choice and managerialism, with stated support for market-based mechanisms in public services provision (Ministry of Financial Affairs 1993). Thus, the framework and pressures for reform have been introduced through the general public sector reform rather than a process originating from the Ministry of Social Affairs and Health, or specific problems in the health sector.

The suggested reforms have nevertheless faced difficulties in practice. The competitive elements in health sector have been hard to acquire and in practice are not feasible in small rural municipalities. In fact, during the recession de-privatization occurred to some extent as municipalities cut the costs of contracted services first. Municipal employees have played a crucial role in shouldering an increased workload while ensuring the quality of services. Weaker groups, such as alcoholics, mentally ill, and disabled people, were affected disproportionately more from the budgetary cuts in some municipalities (Kalland 1996). The lack of belief in market mechanisms and in privatization at municipal level has been based more on practical than ideological considerations (Lehto 1995), which may indicate that more contracting may be tried in the future, especially if it is supported by external finances. The municipal self-governance has, however, not necessarily improved equity issues, but instead brought new concerns. In the municipal level decision-making, the strong interest groups easily gain importance in the definition of social problems and policy orientations. In addition, the focus on decentralization and local self-governance may lead to increasing inequities between municipalities depending upon the potential for acquiring external funds (e.g., European Union) and the extent to which local income is available.

The emerging European Monetary Union poses additional challenges to the social policies. The conditionalities for joining the European Monetary Union have implications for countries with large public sectors to support. The EMU process has been seen to enhance the convergence of social policies within Europe (Kosonen 1994). The possible convergence of European social policies is problematic for Finland at three levels: universality, income redistribution, and the position of women. The share of women in the labor force is higher in Finland when compared with continental Europe, which has led to concerns about the ability of Finland to continue to maintain the women-friendly aspect in the context of a probable move toward the continental organization of social welfare. This would lean more on informal family structures and social security measures based on employment status. While the principle of subsidiarity limits the role of the EU in social policies, decisions on the economic sphere and the influence of structural funds and other policies will have implications for the organization and practice of Finnish social policies. In Finland, the subsidiarity principle has been interpreted not only as a principle dividing work between the EU and nation states, but also as a principle defining priorities with regard to social services, namely, what private persons, families, and groups can do should not be done by officials (Koski 1996). This interpretation would necessarily imply increasing individual responsibility and leaning on informal care, which is predominantly provided by women, thus indicating differential burden sharing by gender and undermining the current gender- sensitive policies of the state.

The Finnish experiences illustrate how public sector reforms orchestrated by the Ministry of Financial Affairs have shifted policies toward more market-oriented mechanisms, with the purchaser–provider split, contracting, and attempts to create a competitive environment in the purchasing decisions of municipal authorities. There have also been changes in the ability of the state to steer decentralization, and the introduction of cost-sharing with user charges, all of which follow the international doctrines of health care reforms. It may be expected that the pressures upon the Finnish health care system will grow due to European integration and convergence in social policies, steps that are expected to create pressures towards the continental (Bismarckian) model of social insurance.

Concluding Remarks

The European trends in health sector reforms illustrate major similarities when compared with the health care and public sector reforms implemented in other parts of the world. The experiences thus far highlight the importance of the public sector involvement as the crucial actor in health care financing as well as the problems of pluralism in health care provision. Market mechanisms and privatization have been found to be problematic in practice, especially in terms of their equity consequences. Yet, there are reasons to believe that incremental changes in the health sector may eventually lead to:

- the formation of private health care markets for those able to pay;
- greater government focus on public health and provision of services only to the poorest sections of society; and
- some contracting to the non-profit sector.

So far the northern European health systems have maintained their emphasis on universal access, but in practice there is growing pressure toward the creation of a two-tiered system in health. This is frequently expressed in terms of prioritization, and a definition of core services. The case study of Finland shows that the standard recipes have mainly been imposed through the Ministry of Financial Affairs resulting in health systems development and inter-sectoral action by default in the health sector.

The process of economic integration and transnational processes of policy-making may be a growing phenomena. Also, ideas about health systems development have always traveled around and most of the current functioning models are adaptations of those in other countries. The problem is that those marketed most aggressively are not always the ones with the best outcomes in terms of equity or cost-containment. An additional concern relates to the international scene in terms of the capacities, responsiveness, and policy-lines of the international organizations involved with health, as well as to the growing influence of trade and investment regimes in the guise of globalization. Globalization is often presented as a one-way track without any exit and it often offers very ideological arguments. It tends to right-size the government and shift the burden of risks and costs to individuals rather than to governments or employers. It is of crucial importance to demystify the ideological arguments presented in the garb of competitive necessities and discuss and analyze the implications of different international policy choices being thrust upon the public sector and ultimately upon the health and social security of people around the world. There is also a growing need for sharing of information and joint efforts by those committed to health, equity, social rights, and human dignity, to not only learn from the experiences of each other, but also to raise these issues and their significance in the international arena.

References

Academy for International Health Studies (1997): Homepage: http://www.aihs.com/summit/index/html.

Anon (1996): Professional Developments. OECD Symposium on the Future of Public Services. *Public Administration and Development* 16: 281–85.

Barer, M.L., Marmor, T.R., and **Morrison, E.M.** (1995): Health Care Reform in the United States: On the Road to Nowhere (Again). *Social Science and Medicine,* 41: 453–60.

Barker, C., and **Green, A.** (1996): Opening the Debate on DALYs. *Health Policy and Planning,* 11: 179–83.

Bond, P., and **Weissman, R.** (1997): The Costs of Mergers and Acquisitions in the US Health Care Sector. *International Journal of Health Services*, 27: 77–87.

Ervasti, H. (1996): *Research on Welfare Pluralism from the Legitimacy Viewpoint* (in Finnish). (Ervasti, H. Kenen vastuu? Tutkimuksia hyvinvointipluralismista legitimiteetin näkökulmasta). STAKES Research reports: 62. Helsinki.

Evans, R.E. (1997a): Health Care Reform: Who's Selling the Market and Why? *Journal of Public Health Medicine*, 19: 45–49.

——— (1997b): Going for the Gold: The Redistributive Agenda Behind Market-based Health Care Reform. *Journal of Politics, Policy and Law*, 22: 427–65.

Fuchs, V.R. (1997): Managed Care and Merger Mania. *Journal of American Medical Association*, 277: 920–21.

Gabel, J. (1997): Ten Ways HMOs have Changed during the 1990s. *Health Affairs*, 16: 134–45.

Hamilton, G.J. (1996): Competition and Solidarity in European Health Care Systems. *European Journal of Health Law*, 3: 323–29.

Kalland, M. (1996): Well Cut, Badly Sewn: The Recession and Services for Vulnerable Groups (in Finnish) (Kalland M. Hyvin leikattu, huonosti ommeltu. Erityisryhmien palveluihin kohdistuneet säästöt valtionosuusuudistuksen jälkeen. Sosiaali- ja terveysjärjestöjen yhteistyöyhdistys YTY ry). Edita: Helsinki.

Kanavos, P. (1996): Pharmaceutical Consolidation and Public Policy. *Eurohealth*, 2: 30–33.

Koski, H. (1996): The Citizen, the Municipality, the State. In Finnish. (Koski H. Kansalainen, kunta ja valtio. Sisäasiainministeriö). Edita: Helsinki.

Kosonen, P. (1994): European Integration: A Welfare State Perspective. Sociology of Law Series, No. 8. University of Helsinki.

Lehto, J. (1995): Direction of Change in Municipal Social and Welfare Services during the Recession (in Finnish) (Lehto J. Kunnallisten sosiaali- ja terveyspalvelujen muutossuunta 1990-luvun alun talouskriisin aikana. In Hänninen S., Iivari J., Lehto J. (eds.) Hallittu muutos sosiaali- ja terveydenhuollossa. Kunnallisen sosiaali- ja terveydenhuollon muutos ja muutoksen hallinta 1990-luvun alkuvuosina). STAKES Research reports: 182. Helsinki.

Malcolm, L. (1997): GP Budget Holding in New Zealand: Lessons for Britain and Elsewhere. *British Medical Journal*, 314: 1890–92.

Maynard, A., and **Bloor, K.** (1995): Health Care Reform: Informing Difficult Choices. *International Journal of Health Planning and Management*, 10: 247–64.

McKee, M., **Mossialos, E.**, and **Belcher, P.** (1996): The Influence of European Law on National Health Policy. *Journal of European Social Policy*, 6: 263–86.

Mechanic, D. (1995): Failure of Health Care Reform in the USA. *Journal of Health Services Research Policy*, Pre-launch issue, (October): 4–8.

Ministry of Financial Affairs (1993): Producing Service (in Finnish). Helsinki: Government of Finland.

Moran, M., and **Wood, B.** (1996) The Globalization of Health Care Policy. In P. Gummet (ed.). *Globalization and Public Policy*. Cheltenham, UK: Edward Elgar.

Nord, E., **Richardson, J.**, **Street, A.**, **Kuhse, H.**, and **Singer, P.** (1995): Who Cares about Cost? Does Economic Analysis Impose or Reflect Social Values? *Health Policy*, 34: 79–94.

OECD (1995): New Directions in Health Policy. *Health Policy Studies* No. 7, Paris: OECD.

——— (1996): Health Care Reform: The Will to Change. *Health Policy Studies* No. 8. Paris: OECD.

Ranjault, P. (1992): On the Principle of Subsidiarity. *Journal of European Social Policy*, 2: 49–52.

Saltman, R. (1997): Balancing State and Market in Health System Reform. *European Journal of Public Health*, 7: 119–20.

Smith, R. (1996): Global Competition in Health Care. *British Medical Journal*, 313: 764–65.

The Ljubljana Charter on Reforming Health Care (1996): *British Medical Journal*, 312: 1664–65.

Uusitalo, H., Konttinen, M., and **Staff, M.** (1995): *Review on Social Welfare and Health Services* (in Finnish) (H. Uusitalo et al.; Sosiaali- ja terveydenhuollon palvelukatsaus). STAKES Research reports: 173. Helsinki.

Wagstaff, A., and **Doorslaer, E.** (1993): Equity in the Finance and Delivery of Health Care: Concepts and Definitions. In E. van Doorslaer, A. Wagstaff, and F. Rutten (eds.). *Equity in the Finance and Delivery of Health Care. An International Perspective*. European Community Health Services Research Series, No. 8. Oxford: Oxford University Press.

5

Structural Adjustment Policies and Health in the Plantation Sector in Sri Lanka

Indira Hettiarachchi

Background

The creation of a formal plantation sector in Sri Lanka commenced in the colonial period, when there was a gradual change from a subsistence-based economy to a market-based one. Coffee was introduced as the first plantation crop in the thirties. The subsequent collapse of the coffee industry due to coffee blight led to its replacement by the more labor intensive tea industry and to the influx of south Indian migrant labor brought in as indentured labor by the British to Sri Lanka. Today the plantation sector has a population of nearly one million, comprising about 5 percent of the total population of Sri Lanka and has the largest workforce in the formal agricultural sector. This population is resident on about 500 state-owned estates leased to private management companies. The sector provides direct employment to nearly 310,000 workers, of whom 53 percent are females (Plantation Housing and Social Welfare Trust 1995).

During the colonial period, management and delivery of health care was the sole responsibility of the individual estate management which, in turn, was linked to the provisions of a Medical Wants Ordinance (MWO) enacted in 1912. The need to look after the workers who were mostly resident within the estates resulted in the development of a system of medical care which was mostly cure-oriented, and hence in the establishment of health institutions such as hospitals, maternity wards, and dispensaries within estates. This period was characterized by high morbidity and mortality as a result of ill ventilated and congested "line" type housing, poor sanitary conditions, very low literacy, and limited health care provisions on estates (Vidyasagara and Hettiarachchi 1994). In 1948, the policies adopted by the government to provide equal access to health services for all resulted in rapid improvement in the national health indicators. However, similar changes were not seen in the plantation sector, which continued to be owned by sterling and rupee companies.

Health Sector Reforms after Nationalization of Estates

In the mid-seventies, under the Land Reform Law, all foreign and company-owned estates as well as estates over a specific acreage owned by nationals were brought under state ownership and their management vested with two government corporations. The appalling health conditions that prevailed on the estates at the time of nationalization demanded effective measures to correct the situation.

In keeping with the government's health policy to provide the same quality of services to all sectors, a wide range of health and welfare interventions were initiated in the estates by the state and supported by donor agencies such as UNFPA and UNICEF. The Family Health Bureau (FHB) of the Ministry of Health was entrusted with planning and implementing national health programs on the estates. A Family Health/Family Planning Program covering 200 estates was implemented under a country agreement with UNFPA, signed in 1973. A medical officer in charge of the Estate Family Health Program was appointed to the FHB in 1973. This was followed by the creation of 10 posts of medical officers from the Ministry of Health, appointed to the periphery to be in charge of the Family Health Program in the estates. The program provided a total range of family health services through a network of estate polyclinics (Ministry of Health 1996a).

Maternal and child health services, the Expanded Program of Immunization (EPI), control of diarrheal diseases, family planning, and other preventive programs were introduced in the estate sector through this program. In addition, the health personnel needs of the estate sector were strengthened through the basic training of health personnel. In 1979, under an UNFPA project, the polyclinic network was expanded to cover an additional 200 estates. These interventions resulted in attracting more donor funds to improve housing, sanitation, provision of safe water, and childcare facilities on the estates.

The major strategies to strengthen estate health programs were:

- Orientation of estate management and estate health staff on the broader concepts of health and identifying their roles in delivery of health care.
- Human resource development for health.
- Strengthening of the health infrastructure through appropriate physical inputs. Substantial investments were made on construction of maternity homes, dispensaries, provision of ambulances, and equipment for EPI, maternal care, etc.
- A new category of welfare personnel, designated Plantation Family Welfare Supervisors (PFWSs) were recruited to the estate sector specifically to create health awareness among the community, promote family planning, and improve environmental sanitation and hygiene.
- The organization and planning of health services were strengthened by introducing a uniform health management information system.
- Closer linkages and dialogue were fostered with the Ministry of Health, particularly in the implementation of National Health Programs.

After nationalization, the two government estate agencies established an organized infrastructure for the development of social welfare programs on estates, both at central and regional levels. Separate Social Development Divisions (SDDs) at the central-level head offices and 14 regional offices were created in order to support, coordinate, and monitor the health and welfare programs conducted on the estates. A direct line of authority was established for coordinating and monitoring health programs on the estates by the head offices through the respective regional offices.

Another important change that took place at about the same period was that the estate schools, which were hitherto under the estate management, were brought under the purview of the Ministry of Education. In addition, the majority of estate workers of south Indian origin were conferred citizenship and voting rights.

Changes in the Management of the Estate Sector from the Eighties to the Present

During the latter part of the eighties, the tea industry suffered setbacks due to the rising cost of production and the general decline of tea prices in the world market. Stagnation in tea production as well as a decline in rubber production resulted in a drop in Sri Lanka's contribution in the world market. Among other factors, insufficient attention to human resource development and management practice contributed to poor performance, which became a major burden on the limited financial resources of the country.

Since the estate sector is a major contributor to the national economy and the GNP, its viability is vital to the stability of the sector and the national economy. Taking this into consideration, in the late eighties, the government introduced changes in the management of the estate sector with a view to improving efficiency and reducing losses. These changes resulted in creating confusion and uncertainty among the management and the staff, with ensuing detrimental effects on the plantation industry. Finally in 1992, in view of the financial losses incurred by the state-owned plantation corporations, and in keeping with the government policy of economic liberalization, the management of the estates was privatized, but ownership continued to remain with the government.

The main feature of the restructuring process was the formation of 23 government-owned Regional Plantation Companies (RPCs) each having 12 to 29 estates. With privatization, all staff including the health and welfare staff on the estates became employees of the RPCs. The management of these estates was entrusted to private companies for an initial period of five years in the belief that privatization would improve efficiency and lead to improved productivity and profits. According to the terms and conditions of privatization, the managing agents agreed to provide health and social welfare facilities to the workers and their families at least at the same level as existed at the time of takeover of the management of the estates.

The short-term management contracts did not result in the desired changes and therefore in 1995, the government initiated the sale of majority holdings to the private sector. By this step, managing agents were given "ownership" of the estates (for a lease period of 50 years) through competitive bidding in the share market, while the government retained ownership of the land and the remaining share of the estate holdings.

SAP and its Influence on Health in the Estate Sector

Health Management Structure

As a result of privatization, the SDDs ceased to function and instead a new independent organization, named the Plantation, Housing and Social Welfare Trust (TRUST), was created by the government under the Companies Act. The TRUST was an autonomous organization and did not have any administrative authority over the estate management, the estate health staff, or the management of health programs on the estates. The recurrent expenditure of the TRUST was funded through a levy paid by the companies. The operational structure of the TRUST was kept at a bare minimum. Scant attention was paid to the organizational feasibility and the functional effectiveness of such an organization in ensuring minimum standards of health on the estates. This resulted in disruption of the institutionalized health management structure that existed during the period of state management.

Expenditure on Health after Privatization

The consequences of these changes on the plantations in Sri Lanka have been far-reaching. The change in the attitude of the estate management toward health and social welfare following these reforms has been almost immediate. High priority has been given to minimize expenditure that would help cut down losses and/or increase short-term profitability of estates. With the emphasis directed at reducing expenditure, health and social welfare components have become prime targets. Expenditure on health and allied activities has been drastically reduced in most estates by the estate management.

A study carried out in 1995, on the annual cost of providing health care on the estates, revealed that on an average an estate spent between Rs 108.50 and Rs 139.40 (approx. US$ 2) per resident per year (Vidyasagara and Wijesekara 1995). In contrast, the national per capita annual expenditure on health was about Rs 582.00 revealed another study in the corresponding year (Ministry of Health 1996b). Nearly 65 percent of the health expenditure on the estates was on employing personnel for health

Table 5.1
Analysis of Direct Expenditure on Health Incurred by the Estate Management

Institutions	*Percentage of Annual Recurrent Expenditure*						
	Health-related & Support Personnel Cost	*Repair & Maintenance of Plant*	*Drugs & Supplies Misc. Items, Repairs & Maintenance of Equip.*	*Cost of Basic Amenities*	*Patient Diets*	*Patient Transport Cost*	*Training of Staff*
Estates with hospitals	67.7	0.8	5.0	2.5	5.5	18.5	0.1
Estates with maternity home-cum-dispensary	63.8	0.7	3.5	3.8	0.6	27.5	0.1
Estates with dispensary only	72.7	0.4	4.1	0.4	0.0	22.4	0.1

Source: Vidyasagara and Wijesekara 1995.

Table 5.2
Health and Welfare Staff Cadre 1992 and 1996

Designation	*1992*	*1996*
Registered/assistant medical officers	57	71
Estate medical assistants	125	101
Pharmacists/app. pharmacists	194	185
Midwives	322	273
Plantation family welfare supervisors	402	375
Creche attendants	1,576	1,474

Source: Ministry of Health 1992, 1996a.

and health-related activities. Less than 5 percent was spent on drugs and supplies, while costs incurred on repairs and maintenance of health facilities was less than 1 percent (see Table 5.1). Most of the drugs required were provided through a government grant to the estates, which was increased from Rs 2,000,000 to Rs 6,000,000 in 1995.

Fortunately, even after privatization, donor assistance and funds from the Ministry of Health have been made available to improve health infrastructure, procure essential drugs and equipment, provide in-service training for health and welfare staff, and also to improve housing, sanitation, and water supply for the workers and staff.

The private management has shown an increased tendency to depend on donor funds to effect even minor repairs to health buildings and equipment. In many instances, repairs to ambulances are not undertaken by the management. Patients are encouraged to use other estate vehicles, such as lorries, with little or no concern for patient comfort. New ambulances have not been provided to any of the estates by the estate management after privatization.

Health and Welfare Staff Cadre

Following privatization, a gradual decline in the numbers and quality of all categories of health and welfare staff has been observed (see Table 5.2).

This has been a result of, both non-availability of qualified personnel in the job market and lesser remuneration offered by the plantation sector as compared to the government sector. Reluctance to fill vacancies, suppressing existing cadre provisions, and recruiting lesser paid, unqualified staff is a very disturbing trend. In the past, when an estate was compelled to employ a partially qualified or unqualified person to provide health care due to the shortage of staff, measures were taken to ensure that he/she was supervised by a qualified medical assistant. In contrast, after privatization, it has been observed that in certain instances even unqualified staff are given charge of other estates (Vidyasagara and Wijesekara 1995). The close relationship that prevailed between the estate management and health staff has also deteriorated resulting in low motivation of the staff and reduced commitment.

Health Service Delivery

Prior to privatization of estates, pregnant mothers were given paid leave and transport by the estate management (when needed) to attend antenatal clinics that were held regularly on fixed days of the month. After privatization, this practice has been changed by some companies without giving due consideration to the importance of ensuring that all pregnant mothers attend antenatal clinics. In some estates, the clinic days have been changed without giving adequate notice and are most often held on Sundays which is a non-working day. These changes imposed by the management with regard to conducting antenatal clinics are liable to result in a decline in the utilization of services and the quality of care provided at these clinics.

The Expanded Program on Immunization, which was one of the most successful programs implemented on the estates, also suffered a setback soon after privatization. However, it was possible to correct this situation early through the intervention of the TRUST with funding from UNICEF.

Impact of Privatization on Health Indicators

Despite some of the aforesaid adverse developments, a major deterioration of the vital health statistics has not yet been observed, even though some indicators such as infant mortality rate (IMR) and maternal mortality rate (MMR) have stagnated when compared to national averages (see Table 5.3).

Probably, this could be due to the fact that estate health programs and services referred to earlier have continued to receive reasonable assistance and patronage from donor agencies and the

Table 5.3
Vital Statistics of Sri Lanka and Estate Sector
(1974–96)

Indicator	*Estate Sector*			*Sri Lanka*		
	1974	*1992*	*1996*	*1974*	*1992*	*1996**
Crude birth rate[1]	27.3	18.3	15.8	27.5	20.1	18.6
Crude death rate[1]	18.6	6.0	7.0	9.0	5.6	6.5
Infant mortality rate[2]	144.0	27.9	26.2	51.2	18.2	16.5
Maternal mortality rate[3]	22.0	12.0	16.0	19.0	2.0	2.4**

Source: Ministry of Health 1996.
Notes: [1] per 1,000 population
[2] per 1,000 live births
[3] per 10,000 live births
*provisional
**for 1995

Ministry of Health, and are closely monitored and coordinated by the TRUST. Deworming campaigns, health volunteer programs, and anemia control measures are implemented on the estates with donor funds, which have contributed to maintaining the health gains achieved in the estate sector.

In the recent years, much emphasis has been paid by the TRUST to create self-reliance among the estate resident workers through community participation and social mobilization. These interventions have resulted in positive behavioral changes, as seen by an increase in institutional births with a resultant decline in still births, perinatal and neonatal deaths.

Health-related Inputs

In addition to the direct health interventions, other health-related inputs channeled to the estates would have contributed to maintaining the health status of the estate community. Over the past two decades, donor assistance had been provided to the estate sector to implement social welfare projects and improve availability of water, sanitation, and living conditions.

Experience has shown that the welfarist approach is not sustainable in the long term, and highlights the need for active participation of the recipients at all stages of implementation of investment projects. The strategies introduced to increase community participation after the privatization of estates has led to the mobilization of the plantation community to build houses and latrines on a self-help basis. They were able to obtain loans from state banks to improve their living conditions. It is estimated that at the completion of the present donor-funded investment program, a coverage of nearly 70 percent and 40 percent will be achieved for water and sanitation respectively.

Minimizing the Consequences of Privatization on Health

Long-term consequences of privatization on the health of the plantation workers would probably surface in the future unless measures are taken to prevent such a situation. It is important to maintain the viability of the industry and safeguard the health of the human resource on the estates. Given the current trend of total privatization of the estates, a greater degree of involvement by the Ministry of Health, particularly in areas of training, provision of health personnel, and technical support, becomes crucial.

Following the granting of citizenship to estate workers of Indian origin, the Medical Wants Ordinance has become obsolete. The uncertainty that prevails within the recently privatized milieu makes it imperative that the roles and responsibilities of the respective actors in the provision of health care to the estate community are clearly defined. In this context, an Estate Health Act has been recently drafted which intends to provide a legal framework to safeguard the interests of the estate community.

The government has also embarked on a program to gradually integrate the health services on the estates with the national system. The open economic policies adopted by the government have provided increased access to information, a greater degree of mobility, and less dependence of the plantation community on the management. This has gradually transformed them into a group that is now interested in participating in the development process. The privatization strategy should be made use of to achieve and foster long-term benefits rather than short-term gains, while attempting to maintain the gains that have already been achieved, specially in the health sector.

References

Ministry of Health (1992): Overview on Health in the Plantation Sector. Consultative Workshop on Estate Health. Colombo: Family Health Bureau.

——— (1996a): Annual Health Bulletin. Colombo.

——— (1996b): Annual Health Bulletin, Annual Health Returns (Estate Sector). Colombo.

Plantation Housing and Social Welfare Trust (1995): Health Bulletin of the Estate Sector, 1992–94. Colombo.

Vidyasagara, N.W., and **Hettiarachchi, I.** (1994): Perspective Plan for Health Development in the Plantation Sector. Plantation Housing and Social Welfare Trust. Colombo.

Vidyasagara, N.W., and **Wijesekera, D.C.** (1995): A Study to Identify Actual Costs Incurred in the Provision of Health Care on Estates. Plantation Housing and Social Welfare Trust. Colombo.

6

Dilemmas for Research in Primary Health Care in the Era of Reforms

Marc De Bruycker

Health as a Common Good

Good health is an invaluable asset for the well-being of individuals and nations. Therefore, some of the key indicators for the measurement of development have been health-related. Access to appropriate food, shelter, education, and a productive social, cultural, or spiritual life have remained the pillars of health and well-being (Gish 1983). These pillars have been differently shaped and sized, but vast inequalities among individuals, communities, nations, and regions have been observed. These have been variously described, maintained, introduced, or abolished through agreement, enforcement, negotiation, or neglect, through peace and through war. Today these same "realities" persist.

Historically, the quality of life and the acquisition of good health for individuals and for populations were not necessarily solely due to medical care or dependent only on medical technology. Since the dawn of mankind, the wish to influence health and to repair or prevent disease has occupied people's minds and has created multiple environments where a variety of medical professions could flourish, often without regulation. Taking advantage of the explosive progress in science and technology, medical sciences have taken huge strides into the Golden Century of Medicine. Europe has played a major role in the development of tools to control disease with many advances in vaccine, drug, and surgical technology. And this technology has found eager exporters and importers. Among these developments was the birth of tropical medicine

(Cook 1997). Initially it served humanitarian needs, but rapidly also started serving political, economic, and religious interests. These have often reinforced certain international inequalities.

The post-war, cold war, and de-colonization period offered several decades of unprecedented socio-economic growth in Europe, the US, and Japan. This was coupled with an increase in political awareness and the establishment of democratic movements in many other countries. Gradually, European citizens began to enjoy broader access to health care and prevention packages through heavily state-subsidized and organized health services available to the population at large. According to OECD, the 15 EU member states spend today between 5 and 10 percent of their GDP on health care of which 60 to 95 percent is government-supported. The institutional capacity (public and private) to offer, organize, study, and regulate "health provision" has grown enormously in Europe. Nevertheless, certain inequalities in access and quality of care have remained insufficiently addressed. In contrast to what has been achieved in Europe, the situation in developing countries has not evolved as was hoped for some decades ago.

Triggered by the "energy-crisis" of the seventies and the inability of most developing countries, particularly Africa, to maintain the level and quality of infrastructures including health services, education, and transport, which were put in place prior to the seventies, global interdependency was suddenly on the agenda. In a climate of crisis, theories about development changed and were no longer concentrated on physical growth and industrial progression. The belief that as the economy flourished the poorer groups would also benefit was rapidly eroded. In many sectors, there was increasing intolerance of the large differences between the poor and the rich, and an increasing awareness that health is an integral part of development. New trends emerged, for example: community involvement and comprehensive, integrated, decentralized, and continuous care (Kasongo Project Team 1984; Sawhny 1994; Walt and Vaughan 1982) was championed while isolated vertical family planning was attacked (Banerji 1978). The inadequacies of multiple vertical programs as a strategy for sustainable health care were revealed. Some developing countries had more than 10 separate and largely autonomous vertical programs, and at the same time had to cope with health problems for which there were no services (Smith and Bryant 1988).

It appeared difficult to adjust between two options: a potentially scientifically valid top-down technical intervention which may have to be imposed on groups of people and a bottom-up approach of responding to demands, although not always considered rational, of people seeking health care. The challenge to marry needs and demands in a context of self-reliance was brought to the agenda.

And Then There was Health for All

Health for All by the year 2000 was a global strategy based on the primary health care approach and was adopted by the World Health Assembly in 1977 and then by the Alma-Ata conference in 1978. It has provided, mainly under the auspices of the WHO, a revised health policy framework in the last two decades and has generated a wealth of publications. Sadly, many of these have paid lip service to the idea of PHC or Health for All, and real conviction, in terms of attempts to implement the concept, has been weak.

The rare attempts to implement Health for All as a new and broader concept of health, health care, and health research, seem to have been hampered by the predominant focus on developing countries and has had the effect of alienating economically advanced countries. Also, the relative absence of a debate on primary health care in the European or US context is a missed opportunity for timely positive change in the industrialized countries. This may be understood as a symptom of a somewhat different attitude toward "poor" developing countries. Interventions have been "short-lived," sometimes "cheap," sometimes expensive, but mostly opportunistic, and often inappropriate, and have failed to address the underlying problems. In reality, health service development has hardly been considered as a political process.

Often, there was a dislocation between general objectives and the ways and means in which health-related operations were organized. Donor-led or donor-initiated interventions in developing countries often established village health workers without the essential support of secondary referral services. On the other hand, the continued blind belief in the building of tertiary hospitals eroded the credibility of many actors in the field, both nationally and internationally.

The inter-sectorial (Hammad 1986), systemic (Nitayarumphong and Mercenier 1992), and long-term character of the approach, the awareness of context-dependency—health care as a socio-economic (Banerji 1986; Barraclough 1991), political (Navarro 1984; Qadeer 1994), and cultural (Walt and Rifkin 1990) issue, as well as a medical one—has received too little attention and study. Lessons from history have not been learned. One of the most notable of the early statements of the need for integrated and comprehensive approaches to health services and manpower development was the Bhore Report in India in 1946.

The Gap between Words and Acts

"PHC seemed to be all things to all men" (Muhondwa 1986). Although there has been an active change of "labels," there has been little change of "structures." Health services were renamed PHC in some countries without any changes being made to their structures or organization. There was reluctance to re-formulate or implement policies and planning processes for redistributing existing resources (Olle-Goig 1993). PHC programs were converted (in)effectively into vertical programs. PHC was captured by market principles; community participation became a means (instrumental, tactical) instead of an end (Vuori 1984). In the framework of the PHC concept, community financing should not be a mere instrument for generating additional resources, but should rather serve more political objectives, regardless of the level of government funding. It should make people responsible for more rational health-care utilization and involve them in the management of their services. There were many other elements that formed part of what might now be considered a global deception: economic support was inadequate and well-motivated but unprepared, underpaid, unsupported health workers or health personnel were reluctant to accept change (Hellberg and Makela 1994). Hospital care was effectively abandoned from the PHC context partly as a natural reaction against the heritage of elitist urban-based teaching hospitals (Van Lerberghe, de Béthune, and De Breuwere 1997). In reality, a substantial shift of resources from tertiary toward secondary referral hospitals serving health centers was rarely made. Hospital care now urgently needs to be reconsidered in its proper role.

Integrated programs were "sold to" and approved by planning, finance, and health ministries in developing countries as more cost-effective approaches to organization of health services. At the time, however, considerable expansion of the health-services infrastructure was still required in many countries to provide adequate population coverage. This led to considerable concern later as the extension of more services to a larger number of people brought requests for even higher budget allocations rather than the expected savings. Nonetheless, there were examples of sustained successes, but these were rare on the scale of developing countries (Morley, Rhode, and Williams 1983).

After 1978, world economic conditions worsened. Resources for the Health for All program decreased, world income distribution decreased, inequalities increased, and management capacity was questioned. In most places, particularly in Africa, the needed transition to the PHC approach did not take place (Kiljunen 1994).

Health Sector Reform—Crisis Management

Facing a situation of conflict between economic and human development, balancing health needs with the economically attainable, the socially acceptable, the medically possible, and the malleable public demand, new proposals or "interim" strategies were formulated.

Some quickly assumed that comprehensive PHC was beyond the reach of most developing countries, so selective primary health care (SPHC) was "invented" (Walsh and Warren 1982). This shift, although criticized (Tarimo 1988; Unger and Killingsworth 1986), reopened the door for further top-down strategies, disease-oriented, technocratic approaches that denied the necessity for community participation. As such, the SPHC approach called for no change in the status quo with regard to established health systems and local community power structures.

In addition, the "enforced" application of the standard economic reform strategies of the International Monetary Fund/World Bank gradually became routine in many developing countries. Reduction in the budget deficit through a combination of cuts in public enterprise deficits, rationalization in public sector employment, trade liberalization, phased removal of subsidies, and devaluation of the local currency has had a severe impact on the way essential public goods such as health and education were handled. Privatization, liberalization, and "free markets" became the dominant slogans from which the already weakened health sector could not escape.

What was considered by neo-liberal economic theory as a solution for halting economic decline, Structural Adjustment Policies with conditions imposed by the "donors" became perceived by others as instruments leading to decline in terms of health and social capital, particularly in developing countries (Logie and Woodroffe 1993; Patnaik 1994).

At the same time, in many industrially advanced countries, overproduction of expensive medical technology was stimulated, partly through selective private insurance schemes to which only the better-off subscribed. This pushed and stimulated wider demand and often over-consumption of largely subsidized medical care and technology, leading to increasing costs for the community but further benefits predominantly for the "service" providers and upper-income citizens. Within this situation of relative prosperity in the EU, but with the "Maastricht convergence criteria" in mind, the phenomenon of increasing healthcare costs with "diminishing returns" in health benefits for the population as a whole has become a focus of concern and debate in most EU countries. There seems to have been a growing tendency to support the shifting of health financing from public to private sources. This mindset has weighted heavily on the current relations with developing countries with respect to their health policies. The urgent question for today, however, is to what extent decisions or selective measures applied in Europe or elsewhere are applicable in or transferable to developing countries where in many cases and in contrast with the situation in Europe, basic public health measures or access to essential qualitative health care are hardly available or are predominantly limited to upper-income citizens. The respective roles of the state and the market in health care are put on the political agenda but often without clear social objectives and without sufficient reflection, analysis, or evaluation either in the "North" or in the "South". The contexts in which people operate are incomparably uneven and unequal in most terms (political, socio-economic, and cultural). Too often, health sector reform has become driven by and confined to financial or economic concerns, while medical care, hospitals, nursing homes, and related insurance systems have become attractive options for the profit-making multinational private business. The means have become an end.

Recently, within the UN organizations, the terms of the debate regarding health have been dictated by the WB rather than the WHO which is now trying to "catch up" (Frenk et al. 1997; Godlee 1997).

Public Health and Public Interest

Room for Scientists

Since the *World Development Report: Investing in Health* (World Bank 1993), the debate on public health, or on public interest considerations has became dominated by economic aspects, with a focus which is disease and risk-factor specific (Kenna 1996), leading to a fragmented picture of health.

The health needs were re-evaluated through sophisticated calculations in terms of burdens (Murray and Lopez 1996) and financial costs. Unfortunately, health needs were dissected disease by disease and with the assumed present and future cost-effectiveness of single interventions expressed in "best buys" or compilations of disability adjusted life years (DALYs). This emphasis was translated into a research agenda with the help of the same authors through the report of an "ad hoc" committee on health research (WHO 1996). The results of this exercise confirmed, both our state-of-the-art knowledge of the epidemiology of specific diseases and the continuing importance of bio-medical research. In the report, references to work based on PHC principles and earlier and current thinking were practically omitted. Some priorities for what was called research relating to health policy, households, and populations received regrettably little attention. This clearly leaves room for further questioning and highlights the need for better insight and knowledge of health-related policy issues.

The most important commodity for sustainable development is knowledge. If one wishes to safeguard the future and to increase knowledge, more needs to be invested in research now (De Bruycker and Hagan 1996). Moreover, research supported by the public sector has a mandate to serve public interests. Health research that should serve public health interests is a house with many interconnected rooms and derives its utility and justification from the comfort and harmony afforded to its inhabitants and neighbors by continuous maintenance and renovation of its essential components, including the surroundings in which it is built. More is needed than knowing what should be studied. Knowledge needs to be assessed also in terms of its relationship to ideology and power. There are the compelling questions like, what and whose values or whose development it will serve (?), how the problem may or should be studied (?) and perhaps more importantly, who is performing the research, who is or should be involved and who owns the questions and the results?

Regardless of whether they are dealing with basic or classical bio-medical or health-systems research, researchers will have to respond to those prerequisites and accept to be part of a learning society to which they are accountable.

The development of a culture of science and research is everyone's responsibility. The European Commission's mandate and strength lie in its ability to harness expertise at a supranational level within Europe and in forging relations with developing countries, thus adding a European dimension to complement the existing bilateral regional and national interactions. It would be naïve to consider that any scientific interaction can take place in a vacuum, insulated from other aspects of life. The mechanism to implement the EU policy of scientific cooperation in health research gives consideration to the societal aspects of science. In other words, there must be an expectation that the scientific work will, at some time, bring tangible benefits for the country where research is conducted and for society as a whole. The European Commission Research and Technological Development (ECRTD) Program on Scientific and Technological Cooperation with Developing Countries (INCO-DC), seeks to provide such an environment for partnerships. In establishing these partnerships, the principles considered to be most important are:

- The first is the scientific aspect. It is essential that the process of science is of a high quality and respected on its own merits and rules. What matters is that science flourishes in a variety of socio-economic and cultural environments, where all critical questions can be aired.
- The second principle is that the work supported by the commission must be aimed at addressing the major health

problems faced by developing countries. New practices and technologies have to take account of the context in which they may be applied and the health benefits of their application must be clearly established. Public-health concepts should be a common platform for all health research.

- The third important aspect is that health-research partnerships cannot be established without strong equitable partners. What is needed for both EU and developing countries is a prolonged intensive investment and other support to ensure mutual capacity and capability strengthening. In other words, sharing of knowledge and skills is a key component of equitable partnerships. This will be achieved only through the political will and the economic commitment of the countries themselves, supported by other national and international sources. Fortunately, the need for this support has been recognized by the European Union through its economic and development cooperation policy and has been reiterated in a recent council resolution.

The EC is not interested in providing strictly preconceived "European" solutions to problems of development. A dialogue and collaboration between equally respected partners from a diversity of backgrounds is a prerequisite for further progress in finding solutions for global development. There is an acute awareness that the complex problems of development cannot be contained within national or regional boundaries; they affect all societies. The aim is to find a common path to achieving improvements in development bringing together scientists across the globe who will address the problems as an integrated unit, each bringing their own expertise and experience to bear on the problem at hand. If this is done in the right way, the goal of learning to learn will be achieved. A culture of learning, in which scientific methodology becomes an intrinsic part of society, will be established. Hypotheses will be tested and development programs modified in the light of the results; things will not be left to chance.

References

Banerji, D. (1978): *Health and Family Planning Services in India: An Epidemiological, Socio-cultural and Political Analysis and a Perspective.* New Delhi: Lok Paksh.

Banerji, D. (1986): *Social Sciences and Health Service Development in India: Sociology of Formation of an Alternative Paradigm*. New Delhi: Lok Paksh.

Barraclough, S. (1991): *An End to Hunger? The Social Origins of Food Strategies*. London: Zed Books.

Cook, C.G. (1997): Debate: Tropical Medicine as a Formal Discipline is Dead and Should be Buried. *Transactions of the Royal Society of Tropical Medicine and Hygiene*, 91: 372–75.

De Bruycker, M., and **Hagan, P.** (1996): Partnership between Europe and Developing Countries in Health Research. *Tropical Medicine and International Health*, Oct (1): 553–57.

Frenk, J., Sepiilveda, J., Gourez-Dantes, O., McGuinness, M.J., and **Knaul, F.** (1997): The Future of World Health: The New World Order and International Health. *British Medical Journal*, 314: 1404–10.

Gish, O. (1983): Progress since Alma-Ata: Health with Equity. *People*, 10(2): 3–5.

Godlee, F. (1997): WHO Reform and Global Health. *British Medical Journal*, 314: 1359–60.

Hammad, A.E. (1986): Inter-sectoral Co-operation in Primary Health Care. *World Health*, March: 3–5.

Hellberg, H., and **Makela, H.** (1994): Health for All or for Some Only? In K.S. Lankinen, S. Bergstrom, P. Helena Makela, and K. Peltoma (eds.). *Health and Disease in Developing Countries*. London: Macmillan Press, 461–68.

Kasongo Project Team (1984): Primary Health Care for less than a Dollar a Year. *World Health Forum*, 5: 211–15.

Kenna, O. (1996): Fragmenting Health Care: The World Bank Prescription for Africa. *Alternatives*, 21: 211–35.

Kiljunen, K. (1994): World Economy and Developing Countries. In K.S. Lankinen, S. Bergstrom, P. Helena Makela, and K. Peltoma (eds.). *Health and Disease in Developing Countries*. London: Macmillan Press, 13–18.

Logie, D.E., and **Woodroffe, J.** (1993): Structural Adjustment: The Wrong Prescription for Africa? *British Medical Journal*, 307: 41.

Morley, D., Rhode, J.E., and **Williams, G.** (eds.) (1983): *Practising Health for All*. Oxford: Oxford University Press.

Muhondwa, E.P. (1986): Rural Development and Primary Health Care in Less Developed Countries. *Social Science and Medicine*, 22(11): 1247–56.

Murray, C.J.L., and **Lopez, A.D.** (eds.) (1996): *The Global Burden of Disease*. A Comprehensive Assessment of Mortality and Disability from Diseases, Injuries and Risk Factors in 1990 and Projected to 2020. *Global Burden of Disease and Injury Series*, Vol. I. Cambridge, Massachusetts: Harvard School of Public Health on behalf of the WHO and the World Bank.

Navarro, V. (1984): A Critique of the Ideological and Political Positions of the Willy Brandt Report and the WHO Alma-Ata Declaration. *Social Science and Medicine*, 18(6): 467–74.

Nitayarumphong, S., and **Mercenier, P.** (1992): Ayutthaya Research Project: Thailand Experiences on Health Research. Life Sciences and Technologies for Developing Countries. Area "Health." Methodology and Relevance of Health Systems Research. Research Reports. Contractholders Meeting 8, 9 and 10 April, Paris, France. Commission of the European Communities, DGXII.

Olle-Goig, J.E. (1993): The Year 2000: Health for All and Power for a Few? (letter) *Medecina Clinica*, 100(2): 76–77.

Patnaik, P. (1994): Notes on the Political Economy of Structural Adjustment. *Social Scientist*, 22(9–12): 4–17.

Qadeer, I. (1994): The World Development Report 1993: The Brave New World of PHC. *Social Scientist*, 22(9–12): 27–39.

Sawhny, A. (1994): Women's Empowerment and Health Experiences from Rajasthan. *Social Scientist*, 22(9–12): 137–46.

Smith, D.L., and **Bryant, J.H.** (1988): Building the Infrastructure for Primary Health Care: An Overview of Vertical and Integrated Approaches. *Social Science and Medicine*, 26(9): 909–17.

Tarimo, E. (1988): Is PHC a More Cost-effective Strategy to Improving Health Status than Selective Control of Specific Diseases of Public Health Importance? Ten Years of Alma-Ata Declaration: Tanzania's Experiences. Proceedings of the 7th Annual Scientific Conference, Arusha, 8–11 November. Tanzania Public Health Association, 7–21.

Unger, J.P., and **Killingsworth, K.R.** (1986): Selective Primary Health Care: A Critical Review of Methods and Results. In: *Social Science and Medicine*, 22(10): 1001–13.

Van Lerberghe, W., de Béthune, X., and **V. De Brouwere** (1997): Hospitals in Sub-Saharan Africa: Why We Need More of What Does Not Work as it Should. *Tropical Medicine and International Health*, 2(8): 799–808.

Vuori, H. (1984): Community Participation in Primary Health Care—A Means or an End? (unpublished). Presented at the WFPHA IV International Congress, Tel Aviv, 19–24 February, p. 18.

Walsh, J.A., and **Warren, K.S.** (1982): Selective Primary Health Care: An Interim Strategy for Disease Control in Developing Countries. *New England Journal of Medicine*, 301(18): 967–74.

Walt, G., and **Vaughan, P.** (1982): Primary Health Care Approach: How Did it Evolve? *Tropical Doctor*, 12(4Pt 1): 145–47.

Walt, G., and **Rifkin, G.** (1990): The Political Context of Primary Health Care. In P. Streefland, and J. Chabot (eds.). *Implementing Primary Health Care: Experiences Since Alma-Ata*. Amsterdam: Royal Tropical Institute, 13–20.

World Bank (1993): *World Development Report: Investing in Health*. Washington: World Bank.

World Health Organization (1996): *Investing in Health Research and Development*. Report of the Ad hoc Committee on Health Research Relating to Future Intervention Options. Geneva: WHO.

Part II

Concepts and Evidence

At no other point in time since the Second World War has the universalist premise of primary health care been so far removed from the lives of people in the developing world than now. It has been systematically eroded by a technocentric model, embodied in health sector reforms based primarily on profit than on distributive justice. The assumed consensus on the supremacy of this model parallels the transformation in the meaning of the term "reform," which has been dislocated from the progressive roots that laid the foundations of the welfare state. The class-based compulsions of the state led to the non-implementation of a progressive agenda and the questioning of its own ideals. The welfare perspective was then increasingly challenged by a view of health care that is selective, interventionist, and heavily dependent on cost-effectiveness. At the heart of this debate on reforms and health is the dissonance between the current neo-liberal paradigm and the volume of historical evidence on the most effective approaches to public health services. This section attempts to disentangle the myriad distortions embodied in ideas such as "efficiency" and "effectiveness" and unravels the mystification created by this new aggressive advocacy for change. The chapters provide a multi-dimensional critique of current thinking in public health policy, incorporating a range of intellectual, historical, and empirical evidence.

The first chapter by Imrana Qadeer emphasizes the historical tension between science as practiced and the requirements of objectivity. It argues that power balances determine the patterns in the conceptual growth of sciences, as is evident in the paradigmatic shifts in public health. Kasturi Sen provides an overview of the global process of reforms. She shows that the advocates of reforms have ignored the mounting empirical evidence on the problems with the cost-benefit model in health services. It is being imposed with a heavy hand as part of debt-restructuring, despite lack of evaluation of its impact. Ritu Priya offers a critical appraisal of the methodology underlying the calculation of Disability Adjusted Life Years (DALYs). She argues that despite its intrinsic attractiveness to those who seek quantitative comparative models, the concept is unscientific.

The last two chapters present substantive evidence that question the wisdom of current reforms. Exploring the links between nutrition and infection, Shiela Zurbrigg illustrates the demographic and bio-medical biases in the debate. The explanations of the decline in mortality have been singularly overshadowed by the assumed role of medical sciences. Zurbrigg meticulously reveals the place of hunger and starvation in this debate. Lalita Chakravarty reinforces Zurbrigg's argument through her rigorous study of the four millet producing states of India between 1970 and 1993. She links evidence of biological stress (high mortality rate) to economic indicators over the period and proposes a consistent relationship between them. The evidence put forward by these researchers is umambiguous and deserves the close attention of the policy-makers.

7

Impact of Structural Adjustment Programs on Concepts in Public Health

Imrana Qadeer

The history of the dynamic between medical sciences and society reveals a strange contradiction. In the field of public health, for instance, a discovery as seminal as the germ was used to rationalize the linear approach to causality in germ theory instead of being allowed to resonate with the multi-causal thinking in classical public health. Similarly, specialization developed in medicine not because knowledge had matured to demand it, but because a few practitioners acquired the social power to call themselves specialists (McKeown 1971). In other words, the dominating social processes that shape and direct knowledge may well introduce distortions into the "pure" academic concepts they use.

Knowledge, as it grows, deeply influences the thinking processes of those who have access to it. People strive constantly to improve their lot: some with formal knowledge and some without it, but perhaps with greater wisdom. The former may pursue knowledge with the assumption that it is objective and universal, or they may choose to acknowledge their biases. Either way they claim to seek answers for society as a whole to establish certain ways of thinking. In this chapter, we propose to examine the impact of Structural Adjustment Policies on thinking in public health. We argue that of the various interpretations of public health, the Indian subcontinent is being pushed into choosing a restrictive paradigm, which offers apparently sophisticated methodologies for the collective good without actually helping the good to materialize. The first part examines the evolution of the concept of primary health care and the intellectual efforts to undermine it. The second and the third parts explore the linkages between the political interests of the state and its public policies and the implications for popular and professional perceptions of public health. The last section examines the alternatives that are now being offered.

I

In the evolution of science over the twentieth century there have been major shifts in perspectives. Science has questioned its own objectivity and emphasized the linkages, interdependence, complexities, and conflicts implicit in a systemic view of things. Interdisciplinary methodologies have provided a broader comprehension of reality. From the closed systems of the black box variety new notions of open systems emerged, in which technological, economic, social, and political forces met, interacted, and transformed each other to constitute a whole.

While these shifts were considered path-breaking in the realm of knowledge, experimentation in the arena of public health policy took place largely in those countries where major political shifts had taken place. These experiments contributed to the emergence of the concept of primary health care which reflected a paradigm shift. A shift from the bio-medical model to one that looks at human beings as groups of individuals affected by their total environment, yet having a hand in their own healing processes.

It is important to emphasize that PHC is not just a descriptive term denoting the first level of health care. It is a comprehensive view of health that emerges from the most critical conceptual advances of twentieth-century public health. Unlike the technocentric approaches that derive from the bio-medical sciences—such as the linear campaigns against smallpox and malaria—the PHC approach confronts complex socio-economic, political, and technological relationships. It offers an approach that is open to the possibilities of conflict and change, striving to nurture cooperation rather than control. For implementing the PHC approach in specific regions, open systems analyses, with interdisciplinary inputs are as basic as the political commitment of local governments.

Within this framework, the emphasis of PHC is on:

1. equity in health care;
2. need-based, socially acceptable services with full participation of people;

3. state responsibility for incorporating PHC into national development plans through inter-sectoral strategies;
4. affordable technologies ensuring self-sufficiency and effective basic health care with the support of secondary and tertiary care; and
5. collective, not individual, efforts.

PHC has its origins in a stream of seventeenth to twentieth-century classical epidemiological studies that observed the links between human health and the total environment—social, economic, political, physical, and biological. This emerging holistic view of disease however, was overshadowed, first by the sanitary approach of the Chadwickian model and later by the germ theory, both undermining the "predisposing" host factors and promoting "external" causality (Hamlin 1992). The germ theory promoted linear therapeutic disease control programs and individualistic and institutional care to the detriment of focus on the host and the social environmental factors. The debate was revived only after the second half of the twentieth century when despite all available technology, Third World countries remained riddled with disease.

Two kinds of country experiences revived the debate. One, where health declined following transformation of agricultural economies into markets for raw material, as in Africa. The other, where basic health services were a part of a broader socio-economic change leading to improved health, as in China. A combination of repeated failures of technocentric approaches, researches that emphasized the links between socio-economic and demographic factors and health transitions, and available country experiences led to the 1978 Alma-Ata Declaration. It stated that mere formal government support would not be sufficient to achieve the desired level of health and that PHC would require a reorientation of national strategies for health planning. It would imply a transfer of health resources to the under-served. The health budget might have to be increased until the total population received essential care and institutions supporting PHC were made effective.

Soon after this conference where PHC was hailed as a step forward, the World Health Organization—the very organization that had helped it to evolve—was forced to question and criticize the concept. It was argued that handling complex systems would be impractical and too costly as compared to specific medical technological interventions (Kenneth 1988). While the issue of costs was pushed center-stage, questions regarding nature of development and costs to whom were sidelined. The so-called soft states of South Asia, signatories to the declaration, conceded to the demands of their funding agencies and made no case for comprehensive as against selective PHC.

This is amply reflected across the subcontinent where only Sri Lanka built a strong basic infrastructure and succeeded in bringing down its infant and maternal mortality rates and general diseases over 1980–90. Nepal and Bangladesh are still struggling with these elementary challenges and trying to build a village-level infrastructure to be linked to district and medical college hospitals (WHO 1993). India, on the other hand, despite its advantage of having started earlier, has chosen to put on paper a number of independent programs and call them its PHC strategy. In brief then, the political nature of PHC defined its limits. Whatever the limitations, a commitment, however, was made and a bargaining instrument conceded to the people.

International institutions concerned with monetary controls acknowledged the importance of PHC but attempted to further transform its nature. By the eighties, the International Monetary Fund and World Bank were freely using the debt trap of Third World countries to compel them to accept a set of new economic deals, of which health sector reform was a part. By the early nineties, South Asian countries were made to agree to plans which were conceived for them, but not necessarily by them (World Bank 1993). They adopted bank-driven, narrow, techno-centric interventive strategies in the area of population control, reproductive and child health, and treatment of communicable diseases. They opened up medical care to the private sector and introduced a slow dismantling of the public sector, first by depriving it of funds and second by taking advantage of people's dissatisfaction with it. The cuts in subsidies for food and basic services further marginalized the role of the public sector in health care. Contrary to the very essence of PHC, in India, health was officially declared a "non-essential" service (Ghosh 1997). Inevitable for the sake of stability of reforms, a theoretical rationalization had to be found for this restructuring.

A moratorium was placed on any debate on the nature and direction of development in the UN Conferences at Cairo, Copenhagen, and Beijing. Issues of health and population had to be debated within the overall framework of structural adjustment. A number of ideas were pulled out from old debates in health economics and revived. Public good versus individual consumption, withdrawal of state investment on goods without externalities, importance of informed choice, uncertainty factor of illness, and the value of insurance began to be re-emphasized. Most of these notions have been debated extensively in the past and the limitations of the market in dealing with health needs of deprived populations is well-recognized. Yet, a massive onslaught was launched against public sector participation in health care through colorfully illustrated "data-based" packages of *World Development Report–1993*, whose quality was as unreliable as the cause they advocated.

The packaged PHC that has emerged as an alternative to comprehensive PHC is obviously rooted in a very different notion of public health. If its theoretical moorings are extracted out of the mesh of policy recommendations, it seems to have the following basic characteristics:

1. There is a shift in emphasis from programs rooted in the needs and priorities of different sections to age and sex-based clusters, arising out of the prerogatives of the donor–provider nexus.
2. The alternative to the state medical-care service is the market-driven model where quality, costs, and efficiency will be ensured by the competition between providers and by informed consumers.
3. It recognizes neither the importance of planning for regional priorities nor the necessity of a central coordinating (not controlling) agency. It advocates "decentralization", which is nothing but the diversification of health financing and services.
4. The brunt of this fragmentation falls on the national programs for disease control, whose curative components are now offered in the market as lucrative goods for sale.
5. Clearly, it takes public health back to the bio-medical model where technology dominates and there is no feel for the social, political, cultural, and economic realities of a people.

Thus, for this variant of public health, financial considerations are the prime concern. Costs are seen in purely monetary terms and their societal dimensions become irrelevant. Cost reduction is then sought, not for the optimization of social welfare, but for savings and debt repayment by the national governments.

Within this altered frame, the notion of efficiency also shrinks conceptually. The cost-efficiency link devoid of social concerns no longer examines the contribution of social initiatives to health improvement but becomes the domain of technology alone. Even at the technological level, once the essence of efficiency as conceived in public health—maximum good of the largest number—is lost, an inevitable tension is introduced between quality and coverage. Quality is de-linked from numbers covered, yet it requires very high inputs. There is no impetus for distinguishing between social and individual gains or for accommodating various levels of health. The concept of costs logically leads to choices wherein short-term individual gains get priority over long-term societal gains. The concept of "discounting" is then used to rationalize this, totally disregarding the fact that the future cannot be mortgaged to the present. That loss of lives, cultures, and human plurality is something that cannot be reduced to monetary discounts.

Shifting the burden of growth on to the shoulders of the already marginalized poor under SAP is thus accommodated by this variant of public health. This public health diminishes local autonomy as well as the social responsibility of the state that was at the very core of classical public health. These reforms need to be evaluated on the basis of evidence as much as the successes and failures of the public sector. Despite all the talk of "evidence-based medicine," it is important to reiterate that there is no linear relation between research and utilization of its results. Selective use of research is a historical reality as much as distortion of methodologies to suit unslated objectives. Therefore, without exploring the ideology behind collecting the "evidence," it will not be possible to explain why, for instance, public health that was theoretically acceptable in the seventies is rejected so vehemently in the nineties, particularly when the evidence of the links of poverty with disease have been universally accepted.

To understand the ideological moorings of the South Asian governments and their perspectives on public health, we examine the shared past of their health service systems till the forties. We argue that the reasons why public sector planning failed in the past are a part of the same mind-set that has now led us to accept a new round of "reforms."

II

In the early period of the British rule, apart from providing health care to the army of the East India Company, its medical officers extended their services to British civilians through dispensaries, district, and jail hospitals. This rudimentary Indian Medical Service (IMS) was consolidated after the Mutiny of 1857. Though sanitary commissioners were appointed in 1869, the work of sanitation remained confined to the cantonments. No investments were made for the general population on the pretext of not imposing reforms on people. It was only the threat of loss of revenue and trade caused by epidemics such as malaria, cholera, and plague that finally changed the colonial policy in favor of interventionist strategies.

Contact with "natives," which was earlier seen as a "sanitary problem" confronting Europeans (Harrison 1994: 76), became a necessity when it was realized that the British could not rule by isolated grandeur alone. The 1909 Morley–Minto reforms consolidated provincial governments and helped shift costs on to the local elite. The district and provincial boards of health added to their cadre (Ramasubban 1988). A sanitary policy enunciated in 1914 acknowledged the importance of proper survey and studies. Yet, the bacteriological research wing was moved out of the sanitary commissioner's charge and given to the IMS wing on the basis that it interfered with their touring and that separation of research and clinical work deterred men from entering the clinical departments (GOI 1927). While the IMS administration alone was formally under military administration, the latter also used the provincial services. For example:

1. It helped retain large army reserves over peace time.
2. Provincial services kept the army doctors trim and trained them in handling large populations.
3. Civil posting was a carrot offered to the European doctors, who found it remunerative as they could do private practice.

4. These IMS officers ensured for the white civilian population care from physicians of their own color and creed.

Meeting international criticism of its policies and protecting international trade and local revenue was also linked to building provincial infrastructure for safety of ports and trade centers. The indifference of the British government to the plague epidemic until it threatened Bombay's trade (Catanach 1989), and its neglect of famines till its own revenues were affected (Zurbrigg 1992) are examples of the nature of British concern about the problem of health in India.

Apart from the political control of the health department, there were also internal adjustments within the health services structure. After the mutiny, the amalgamation of the IMS and the Army Medical Division of Her Majesty's Service (AMD) was considered over 1860–64. It was proposed that a royal medical service be constituted with complete authority vested with the Government of India. A subordinate civil medical service was also proposed. This was not acceptable to the military department as it neither wished to give up control over AMD nor lose the provincial control through the IMS (Crawford 1914). On the one hand, the army held the IMS captive, and on the other, the newly awakened political forces pressed for expansion of services, Indianization, and rural health services. The demand for a civil medical service was raised in the Legislative Assembly by professional associations and Indians (Government of India 1921, 1991). The representatives objected to the large number of posts reserved for IMS officers (62 percent of the entire strength of service) and to subordinating people's needs to those of the army. In 1936, at the Council of States, it was again pointed out that the prescribed ratio of one Indian to two British officers had to change (Government of India 1936a). Under these pressures the defense department had to consider a reduction in its military reserves, reorganization of the Military Medical Services, and the position of the IMS under the new constitution.

The importance of rural services too was accepted because of the constant threat of epidemics and the inability of provincial services to reach out to the villages. The 1914 public health policy talked of travelling dispensaries, local organizations, voluntary agencies, disinfection of wells, and sanitary activities, but the paucity of funds in the provincial governments restricted the building of an effective service infrastructure. The services were not only inadequate but also totally unrelated to social conditions. By 1926, only 13 percent of the population had access to the civil hospitals (Government of India 1949). The medical and sanitary activities for the public were in fact a part of the "noble task" of civilizing the "native" and controlling the "untamed tropical environment." Disease was a reflection of social and moral inferiority and biological determinism inspired by Darwin's ideas justified that the weak and the vulnerable perished (Arnold 1989). In other words, the British rationalized both their action and inaction in the medical field.

The adjustments then were for political advantages and not necessarily for the benefit of the public. It was for the same reason that the British moved from a strategy of legislative control and limited medical services toward mass interventive strategies of an order never attempted before. Vaccination of large populations against smallpox in the early eighteenth century, cholera during 1893–96, plague over 1901–20, and efforts to control malaria are examples. Official records of the period reveal the inadequacy of, both the coverage by vaccination and the availability and supply of quinine (Government of India 1936b). Yet, the official perceptions were heavily biased against the people. For example, the British officials were aware that irrigation canals in Punjab and roads and railway tract construction in Bengal added to the menace of malaria. Yet they insisted that the deciding factor was "the aggregation of labour and the expansion of trade caused by the opening of the railway line" (Clemisha 1917). Thus, the blame for being diseased was shifted on to the people.

The army showed a decline in death rate from 25 per 1000 in 1869–70 to less than 5 per 1000 in 1909–10 (Harrison 1994), while the mortality rates among the general population declined from 44 to 30 per 1000 over the nineteenth century and early decades of the twentieth century (Government of India 1975). In spite of this stark contrast in mortality of two sets of the same population, the reasons for the difference were never explored. Instead, the tropical climate and the unwillingness of the natives to make use of a "superior" science were considered sufficient explanations. The differences in their living conditions, and access to and availability of food, apart from the age differences, were completely ignored. The link between famine and disease, which was repeatedly recorded, was not taken seriously and hunger was taken for granted among the general population. It was seen as an outcome of their "lifestyles" and backwardness rather than an outcome of the British agricultural and economic policies.

The discipline of public health in early nineteenth century Britain was dominated by the sanitarians. In the subcontinent, however, only the cantonments were the focus of sanitary activity; the rest of the population received very little attention. Even after the establishment of a sanitary commission, provincial and district sanitary activities remained lukewarm. The "hopeless climate" of the tropics was initially considered the reason for high mortality. Later, mortality was seen as preventable and it was argued that India could be helped. This shift in thinking, however, was not universal. Resistance of the medical bureaucracy to this shift was reflected in their conflicts with scientific circles of the imperial metropolis and those who attempted to evolve methods of disease control applicable to general populations. Opposition to Haffkine's efforts to evolve the plague vaccine is a good example. In 1899, when his work held promise, several Indian princes offered to fully finance the cost of a research institute under his directorship. Though the institute was established, neither the Indian offer nor its conditions were ever mentioned (Ramasubban 1988).

When the germ theory replaced the sanitarian's popularity, it enabled the medical bureaucracy in India to avoid expansion of sanitary activities beyond the cantonment. The causal theory of indigenous local conditions that gave rise to disease was thus never given up. Similarly, while the science of nutrition influenced British welfare policies to introduce feeding programs for the vulnerable, in the subcontinent the idea was entertained only after the vast devastation caused by the Bengal famine of 1942.

We see then that in British India the policy for health services was not necessarily guided by the trends and principles of public health as they evolved in Britain. The military and political interests shaped the services till the forties. This points towards the overreaching power of economic, political, and social factors on the use of science. As a result, health services that evolved were fragmented and imbalanced. Political compromises were made through Indianization and expansion but with an eye to retaining subtle political control and reducing costs. Research was highly centralized, focused on bacteriology and clinical medicine, and controlled by the medical department. For all this, a series of structural adjustments were made. Establishment of voluntary and charitable health care institutions by the elite was encouraged to cut down state costs and enhance the philanthropic image of the government. These trends had a deep impact on the growth of public health structures and ideas after independence.

III

The Indian national movement not only compelled the British government to set up the Health Planning and Development Committee in 1944 (Government of India 1946), it also set up its own subcommittee on health under the National Planning Committee in 1944 (National Planning Committee 1948). Three additional exercises of this kind through the forties were the Gandhian Plan of Economic Development (Agarwal 1944), the People's Plan of Economic Development of the Indian Federation of Labor (Banerjee, Parikh and Tarkunde 1944), and the Bombay Plan of Economic Development (Thakurdas et al. 1944). All these constitute studies in contrast. Striving to achieve a broadly common objective, each differs in its thrust and strategies. The Gandhian and People's Plans along with Sokhey Committee emphasized the role of agriculture and health of the people in rural areas. The Bombay Plan focused on urban services for industrial growth and proposed to deal with rural problems "through proper instructions and education" and well-organized propaganda. People's Plan held the state solely responsible for health. The Bombay Plan held it responsible for infrastructure but not for controlling the private sector in health. Both the Sokhey and Bhore committees proposed banning private practice by public sector doctors while leaving the private sector to wither away with the growth of the public sector.

The notion of technological excellence remained common to the two ideological opponents—the Bombay Plan and the People's Plan. Both visualized the best hospitals and technologies for disease control—the former through initial dependence on foreign countries for "machines and technical skills", the latter through equity as an incentive to generate and acquire technology. Both saw doctors and nurses as the key personnel in health care. Only the Bhore and Sokhey committees talked of short-term training to health assistants, while the Gandhian Plan emphasized people's role in self care. It is not difficult to see then that within their economic policies and ideological positions, these groups were groping to achieve different levels of the same objective with differing priorities and perspectives.

The independent democracies of the subcontinent started charting their own trajectories based on these liberal ideas, each country building its infrastructure with a system for providing basic health services to the common people. Despite shortcomings, the effort to reach out to the largest numbers in a short period as compared to the past cannot be overlooked. In India, the First and Second Five Year Plans gave priority to building infrastructure, water supply and sanitation, and maternity and child health (MCH). In both, health sector planning was visualized as a technical and managerial exercise. The central problem of poverty was left for the economic planners after recognizing the link between poverty and disease. This separation led to a disjunction between nutritional planning, agricultural policies, sanitation, control of communicable and occupational diseases, and welfare sector planning.

Though independence was won by an alliance of different classes, planning, as it unfolded itself, revealed that some were more equal than others. The ruling party's domination by the bourgeois-landlord combine ensued half-hearted land reforms and freedom from taxes on agricultural earnings. Except for setting up heavy industry the public sector remained low key, while the small market was captured by private industry. The latter produced luxury goods and consumption items while basic goods production was scarce. In the absence of adequate agricultural growth, both sectors tended to stagnate and pushed the state into more and more dependence on foreign aid at unfavorable terms (Bagchi 1982). These failures and delays were explained by trickle-down theories, failure of rains, and high rates of population growth. While the disparities increased, the working class was asked to have patience and "work for nation building" (Government of India 1969).

The tensions within the national fabric were evident by the early seventies when the first nationwide strike of railway workers was declared.

The health sector could not remain isolated over the Third and Fourth Five Year Plans. Not only did the rate of expansion of infrastructure slow down, there was also a shift from building peripheral health centers and training paramedical professionals to hospitals and specializations. Vertical technocentric programs were accepted for disease control and maternal and child health services were kept separate from the vertical Family Planning Program (FPP) with the fear that they may suck all the funds given their very poor status. Force and coercion became the hallmarks of FPP and the height of arrogance was reached during the emergency when officially inflicted atrocities became the main reason for the downfall of the Congress government in 1977.

After this experience, some adjustments were made in terms of expanding the primary health center network in rural areas under the Minimum Needs Program, Community Health Guide Scheme at the village level, and a move toward integrating services for nutrition, MCH, FPP, and malaria into general health services (GHS) (Government of India 1974). As population control remained the priority at the national level, this integration converted the FPP into the "black hole" of health services which sucked into it the resources of all other programs. The last in the series of these comprehensive strategies was the acceptance of the Alma-Ata Declaration in 1978. The crunch came in the eighties. The national debt by then was of an order that the Indian ruling class could no longer keep the common man hopeful while taking care of itself. It made its choice, no doubt at the cost of the poor. The Five Year Plans were undermined to give space to market forces, welfare sectors were drastically pruned and handed over to the private sector, and dependence replaced the goal of self-sufficiency in the name of globalization and one world!

In the British period, services such as railways, roads, and postal systems became popular because common people could appreciate their value for their own welfare. In the area of public health, people's experience with health campaigns was very limited and often negative because of the use of force and coercion as in the plague epidemic and early variolation and vaccination campaigns. Medical services were restricted and people's experience of public health was barely sufficient to generate confidence in it. After independence, programs against malaria, smallpox, and tuberculosis did reach out to people, though in a limited way. However, given their curative nature, they only strengthened the hold of clinical medicine on popular imagination. The only exception was vaccination against smallpox.

This devolution of PHC strategy and the ease with which it happened cannot be understood without understanding popular perceptions which were not independent of the professional view of public health. Molded by British education, public health continued to operate within the bio-medical paradigm and strengthened the hold of allopathic cures. The Indian planners thus contributed to the glamorization of technology by separating health, economic, and social sector planning. This led to dissociation of technological from possible social strategies of disease control and to de-linking poverty and hunger from disease. Over time, the notion of prevention got restricted to only immunization and health education, and even modern epidemiology dubbed socio-economic determinants of disease as "co founding factors." In spite of most disease prevention programs being therapeutic in nature, the preventive significance of mass therapeutics never became a popular perception.

These trends in professional and popular perceptions determined peoples' expectations and actions. For example, while the urban middle class took civic amenities for granted and pressed for better and more hospitals, the poor despite realizing the value of shelter, water, and food for health never could perceive these as part of public health facilities. Hence, both classes shared a mind-set where health service system is synonymous with curative services. Similarly, while the planners and politicians, in a hurry to show results, depended heavily upon technology at the cost of improving environment and living conditions of people, the poor too saved time by seeking cures when actually sick, instead of losing wages to take preventive action. Both classes had short-term visions, one by choice and the other by compulsion.

Interestingly, the effort of the poor to access hi-tech medical care is used to justify the pruning of the public sector in health care rather than to improve PHC. In other words, adequate experience of comprehensive public health service remains beyond the pale of people's experience.

So, when "comprehensive PHC" was accepted as a goal by the government, it was hardly on popular demand. It was, in fact, a political move by the Government of India to regain its democratic image that had been sullied by the emergency and its excesses. The implementation of comprehensive PHC continued to be weak and ineffective. Though PHC was officially accepted by the health ministry and inter-sectoral planning was debated, it could not break the conceptual barriers created by bio-medical models of intervention.

IV

A certain contradiction between public-health practice and ideas through the years reflects a continuity, which is important to grasp. The interests of the Indian ruling classes replaced the British military interests and are today being dissociated from the interests of the other classes as well and linked to those of the international elite. Thus, IMF and World Bank proposals of absorbing South Asian economies into the global market are seen by them as an advantage. As we have seen, at different points in time, shifting interests of the ruling classes have resulted in adjustments and restructuring of the health services. These adjustments are not necessarily a response to either people's needs or the growing body of public health knowledge.

In the nineteenth and early twentieth century, it suited the Government of England to let the colonial Government of India neglect public health till the early forties, when they were forced to set up the Bhore Committee to propose a blueprint for health care. Today the World Bank and other international bodies are pressing for undoing whatever was built by the national government. State responsibility for health care is no more considered desirable as it hinders unleashing market forces in the health sector. The contradiction is not restricted to the British who, in their time, preached the value of modern service to Indians but practiced a public health that did not match their own tenets. The independent Government of India too accepted PHC but chose to implement only the selective PHC as it could not bring about the required policy changes necessary for the comprehensive PHC.

The health care system is rooted in the political economy of each country and its links with the global processes of economic and political change. Ideas about public health influence the pattern of shifts by generating awareness and therefore public support or resistance. There has been little resistance to selective PHC as the idea of comprehensive PHC had never taken root in the social consciousness of the classes in India. Neither the majority of professionals nor the articulate middle-class users saw the limitations of rising technocentricism, the undermining of the public sector, and market and technology-based notion of efficiency inherent in health sector reforms. As a consequence, more often than not, borrowed technology became central to disease-control programs and more aid and increasing dependence became a part of health sector reforms.

The declining official interest in PHC in the eighties is a reflection of the reassertion of the powerful with a difference, yet the element of continuity is not insignificant. In the history of public health—as it unfolds in South Asia—the glimmer of hope and relief for the majority has been brief and is dwindling fast. Images similar to the colonial past are becoming difficult to ignore. For example, the burden of costs has again been shifted on to the shoulders of the poor; epidemics are again being treated, not as issues of right to life, but as problems of national prestige and trade interests; charity and paid voluntarism are being resurrected through foreign funds which ultimately leads to controlling the spheres of investment.

These parallels are not accidental. They represent a growing inclination of the ruling classes for short-term returns on investments at the cost of social and economic environment. The present health sector reforms favor this as long-term policies cannot be pursued on short-term loans. Its demands, therefore, are contrary to the demands of comprehensive PHC which seeks social reforms and economic growth with equity. In other words, this too needs structural adjustments but of another order.

It is this contradiction between SAP and PHC that explains why, after complete rejection at the practical level, the very idea of PHC had to be attacked. Even selective PHC was not spared and is now being replaced by WHO's new public health (NPH). This is perhaps due to the fact that selective PHC carries within it both the burden of state responsibility and the shadow of people's needs. WHO's new public health (WHO 1996) gives up both these pretensions and is in harmony with the World Bank's essential package of services.

1. It does away with the notion of planning for population as a national agenda and talks of healthy "cities" and "communities," thereby shifting responsibility to the local organizations (a strategy that the colonial government used to push costs on to local governments!). What it does not do, however, is decentralize control over resources and their use. That is left for the moneyed and the market forces.
2. Within NPH, the role of the state becomes so insignificant that it is forced to seek partners in the private, corporate, and NGO sectors.
3. The PHC approach emphasizes adequately and equitably distributed health resources and social measures, whereas the NPH only concerns itself with "health status."
4. From essential health care for the main health problems it moves on to "prevention of the preventable."
5. Despite these shifts it claims, "socio-economic growth is its anchor, wherein priorities have to be set between treatment of disease and affecting its determinants." However, since it accepts "the finiteness" of resources and the logic of cutbacks in the social sector and also hazardous and iniquitous growth of the economy, its only recourse is in encouraging individuals to take action and make "practical work plan" to save themselves from increasing risks. It does not question the risks themselves.
6. It claims "operational freedom from the subordination of medicine." At the same time it states that, "the greatest insights into determinants of health are held by the staff of health facilities and hospitals." Thus, while it reduces disease control activities in health sector, it retains the emphasis on therapeutics.
7. It focuses on the special needs of individuals through their "*life cycles*." Interestingly, the emphasis of the life cycle approach is on the reproductive phase of the life of women. While the market is allowed to occupy the empty spaces created by a receding public sector in health, the latter influenced by the truncated vision of life cycle depends entirely on reproductive health strategy to control fertility.

8. Technology-based disease control programs replace social strategy-based programs of public distribution systems or food and drinking water.

WHO's NPH has the same roots as described in section I. It swings the pendulum in a way that though it apparently moves away from technological approaches of disease control to socio-economic growth models, it actually leaves out of its domain specific intervention at that level. It unquestioningly accepts the creation and continuation of risk-ridden environments and calls upon individuals to live "life and physical styles" conducive to ecologically sustainable environments. The latter is equated to "psychological, social surroundings" in which participation is reflected by conscious preventive action of individuals (and not the state) against risks (Peterson and Lupton 1996). NPH, therefore, carves even the selective PHC to fit smoothly into the slot provided to a reformed health sector within the overall frame of SAP.

We need to ask then what individual action and self-protective strategies can be expected of a population where 40–50 percent of the people live below the poverty line and another 30–40 percent just manage to scrape through. Where people are fast losing their control over their livelihood and natural resources, essential need-based technologies are inaccessible to the poor and inter-sectoral development is being undermined by SAP. While seeking answers, it is also important to be cautious of tools that come with the conceptual biases—be they cost-efficiency measurements, participatory rapid assessments, or disability adjusted life years (DALYs) that have stormed the field of public health research. These are simplistic short cuts to complex challenges, which are meant to impress, not to improve us.

Take DALYs for example, a tool that has been acclaimed as a sophisticated instrument for planning. It converts death and disability into a common denominator—the time lost. In public health, decline in total mortality is the first step towards success which in poor countries may often be associated with increase in morbidity. DALYs tend to overshadow these early successes by compensating declines in "time lost" through death by time lost through increased morbidity. They may not show any marked shifts over periods of transition and thus undermine achievements in public health in poor countries with high morbidity.

The formulators of DALYs proclaim that it includes in it any health outcome that reflects a loss of welfare (Murray 1994). Such comprehensiveness, irrespective of the relevance and value of the loss or the quality of data, is at the cost of reliability and specificity. Thus, DALYs create a myth of scientific measurement and distract public health planning in the Third World from making social choices, using simple though reliable epidemiological tools, making projections, and monitoring health outcomes.

This NPH and its tools are in stark contrast to another vision of new public health whose conceptual base is the political economy of health, wherein epidemiology, health behavior of populations, and health service systems are rooted (Banerji 1988). The two new public health visions are studies in contrast. Since choices are being made between them, we can at least lay bare the underlying myth of "science and rationality."

References

Agarwal, B.N. (1944): *The Gandhian Plan of Economic Development for India.* Bombay: Padma Publications.

Arnold, D. (1989): Introduction: Disease, Medicine and Empire. In D. Arnold (ed.). *Imperial Medicine and Indigenous Societies.* Delhi: Oxford University Press.

Bagchi, A. (1982): *The Political Economy of Under Development.* Cambridge: Cambridge University Press.

Banerjee, B.H., Parikh, S.D., and **Tarkunde, V.M.** (1944): *People's Plan for Economic Development of India.* Delhi: Indian Federation of Labor.

Banerji, D. (1988): New Public Health. *Journal of Sociological Studies,* 7: 161–73.

Catanach, I.J. (1989): Plague and the Tensions of Empire: India, 1896–1918. In D. Arnold (ed.). *Imperial Medicine and Indigenous Societies.* Delhi: Oxford University Press.

Clemisha, H.H. (1917): *Note on the Influence of Railway Construction on Public Health. Record of the Malaria Survey of India: Collected Memorandum on the Subject of Malaria.* Reprinted from Government of India Reports (1847–1924), March 1930, 1(2): 171–73.

Crawford, D.G. (1914): *A History of the Indian Medical Service, 1600–1913.* Vol. 2. London: Thacker & Co. pp. 268, 298, 301.

Ghosh, J. (1997): *Frontline,* 30 May.

Government of India (1921): Resolution in Legislative Assembly by B.S. Kamath regarding Reorganization of Medical Services in India. Department of Education (Medical), File No. 23–26. New Delhi: National Archives of India.

——— (1927): *India Sanitary Policy, 1914.* Calcutta: Central Publication Branch.

Government of India (1936a): Department of Education, Health and Land. File No. 53–63/36. New Delhi: National Archives of India.

——— (1936b): *Annual Report of the Public Health Commissioner*. Vol. 1: 54.

——— (1946): *Report of the Health Survey and Development Committee (Chairman Sir Joseph Bhore)*. Delhi: Manager of Publications.

——— (1949): *Indian Statistical Abstract*.

——— (1969): *Report of the National Commission on Labour, Employment and Rehabilitation*. New Delhi.

——— (1974): *Minimum Needs Programme*. Draft Fifth Five Year Plan, 1974–79. New Delhi: Planning Commission.

——— (1975): *Pocket Book of Health Statistics*. Central Bureau of Health Intelligence. New Delhi: Ministry of Health and Family Welfare.

——— (1991): Resolution of the Delhi Medical Association. Department of Home (Medical). File No. F.48/49, September. New Delhi: National Archives of India.

Hamlin, C. (1992): Predisposing Causes and Public Health in Early Nineteenth Century Medical Thought. *The Social History of Medicine*, 5(1): 43.

Harrison, M. (1994): *Public Health in British India: Anglo-Indian Preventive Medicine 1859–1914*. Cambridge: Cambridge University Press.

Kenneth, W. (1988): The Evolution of Selective Primary Health Care. *Social Science and Medicine*, 26(9): 891–98.

McKeown, T. (1971): Sociological Approach to the History of Medicine. In T. McKeown (ed.). *Medical History and Medical Care: A Symposium of Perspective*. London: Nullfield Provincial Hospitals Trust, 1–21.

Murray, C.S.L. (1994): Qualifying the Burden of Disease: The Technical Bases of Disability Adjusted Life Years. *Bulletin of WHO*, 72(3): 429–45.

National Planning Committee (1948): *Sub-committee on National Health, Report of Sokhey Committee*. Bombay: Vera Publishers.

Petersen, A., and **Lupton, D.** (1996): *The New Public Health: Health and Self in the Age of Risk*. London: Sage Publications.

Ramasubban, R. (1988): Imperial Health in British India, 1857–1900. In R.M. Macleod, and M. Lewis (eds.). *Disease, Medicine and Empire*. London: Routledge.

Thakur Das, P., Tata, J.R.D., Birla, J.D., Dalal, A., Ram, S., Shroff, A.D., and **Mathai, J.** (1944): A Brief Memorandum Outlining a Plan of Economic Development for India. Calcutta: Central Publications Branch, Pt I.

WHO (1993): *Implementation of the Global Strategy for Health for All by the Year 2000. Second Evaluation – Eighth Report on the World Health Situation*. Delhi, Nepal, Bangladesh: Regional office for South-east Asia.

——— (1996): *New Challenges for Public Health*. Report of Inter-regional Meetings, Nos. 27–30, 1995, Geneva: WHO HRP 96.4.

World Bank (1993): *World Development Report 1993—Investing in Health*. Washington: World Bank.

Zurbrigg, S. (1992): Hunger and Epidemic: Malaria in Punjab 1868–1940. *Economic and Political Weekly*, 27(4): 2–25.

8

Health Reforms and Developing Countries—A Critique

Kasturi Sen

Background

In the eagerness among donors to introduce changes to the financing and organization of health care in developing countries, a number of critical issues pertaining to the provision of public services have been overlooked:

- The relatively recent history of public health provision in the majority of these countries, where few services had been available to the general populace until independence from colonial rule.
- The linkages between macro-economic policies such as structural adjustment and its overall effects upon the provision of health care.
- The meaning of the term "reform" and the relevance of the term "efficiency," as utilized under reforms have escaped clear thinking and evaluation.

Historically, reform of health services in developing countries has entailed altering pre-existing inequalities in the organization and distribution of health services established during the colonial era. However, during the past decade, the meaning of the term "reform" has been restricted to an exclusive focus on the cost and economic value of health services.

Of late, arguments have been raised, both from developing and developed nations, challenging the application of a competitive market model to the provision of social goods such as health care (Banerji 1997; Qadeer 1994). Critics suggest that there is little evidence that a model premised upon introduction of competitive charges and cost containment would ever operate effectively in distribution of social goods such as health and social care.

In light of the evidence of recent structural changes in the health sector, this chapter examines critically some of the assumptions behind these reforms and assesses their potential health and social consequences.

Why Reforms?

There has been an abundance of literature over the past decade on the financing and reorganization of health care. The thematic content of much of this literature is rooted in market economics, with an unquestioning acceptance of its guiding principles as the most rational means to reorganize health care throughout the world. There is common use of terminology such as "demand" and "supply" led services, and the need for the provision of consumer "choice," reinforced by the key and often repeated phrases, "efficiency," "effectiveness," and "cost containment" (Akin and Birdsall 1987; World Bank 1987, 1993). Health planning had clearly been transformed during the eighties.

The reform of public services is premised on the view that the public sector is unable to act as sole provider of services within a context of economic recession. Advocates of this view claim that owing to the "poor" economic performance of the public sector, greater competition in the provision of services is the only means of providing better quality care and improving the efficiency of public services (World Bank 1987, 1993). During the eighties and nineties, the utilization of public health care provision, such as primary health care services, has varied in much of the developing world owing to specific economic and political factors (Qadeer 1994). The decline in usage in some regions has been held by the advocates of the reform as evidence of poor quality of services and as the main indicator of growing consumer dissatisfaction with public services. This continues to be referred to as crucial in the argument for the privatization of health services (Mills 1993).

The relevance of creating an analogy between public services and the operations of a market is simply accepted as given in a world overshadowed by notions of cost containment (Health Policy and Planning 1995; World Bank 1993). However, there is growing concern that evidence to reduce public provision is not only historically inaccurate, but is also yet to be justified on the grounds of current evidence. Also, the private sector in most developing countries is an amorphous group, comprising modern allopathic as well as traditional medical practitioners, who are usually excluded from contemporary evaluation of the private sector.

The strength of the pro-reform lobby suggests that there has been a major ideological shift in outlook towards public service provision during the past decade. A number of authors argue that there has been a shift from the neo-Keynesian outlook of the post-war years, that recognized state responsibility for basic services, to an outlook based upon free market theory and "consumer choice" as prerequisites for the organization of services (Green 1995). The argument which follows is that health systems need to be overhauled through a redefinition of the functions of government in order to ensure effective functioning of the welfare sector as a whole and to satisfy consumer choice and demand. Reform advocates also hold that the state should undertake only minimal intervention in economy and society and, by definition, should run only essential services. The incompatibility between public welfare and private provision continues to remain largely unquestioned among the advocates of reform.

Development in this new paradigm is reform through competition and privatization, whereas public services or public welfare is viewed as anachronistic and antagonistic to quality services and consumer choice. The problem of such a linear approach to development is that it equates economic growth with a process of modernization whose prerequisite is de-regulation. This approach excludes the impact of material factors such as poverty, inequality, social class, gender, and age divisions in society upon the process of development, and in particular the disproportionate dependence among the poor upon public provision. This reveals that the value and relevance of current arguments for the retrenchment of public provision is largely motivated by ideological factors.

It is ironic that while major changes to the organization and delivery of services based on market-formulae are proposed for the developing world, few such changes are being contemplated for the developed world. The state continues to play a major role in the organization and delivery of health care in developed countries, especially in western Europe and North America (Green 1995). In these countries any proposed changes to the existing division of responsibilities between public and private sectors would receive little popular support. In the past two to three years, many countries of western Europe have reversed some of their reforms which attempted to introduce internal markets and competition in the financing of health services provision (see Koivusalo in this collection).

There is clear historical evidence to show that public provision ensures some element of redistributive justice and that in its absence, a growth-oriented and market-led economy is "development" conceived of in a highly restrictive way and by solely economistic criteria. Many of the gains in public health over the past 100 years have been premised upon measures of public welfare and public service provision in both the developed and developing countries. The period before such gains were made was marked by the blight of hunger, starvation, and high levels of infant and child mortality. It was the desire to avoid the perpetuation of precisely such effects that many postcolonial states attempted to provide the safety net of public services following decades if not centuries of ingrained inequality through the colonial experience (Banerji 1997). But for some exceptions (Green 1995; Koivusalo and Ollila 1997; Qadeer 1994; Werner et al. 1996), this historical perspective is absent in much of the literature advocating reforms. It fails to acknowledge global evidence on and widespread acceptance of the socio-economic origins of ill health by a majority of policy-makers throughout the world. The historic declaration of Alma-Ata (1978) in support of comprehensive primary health care is testimony to this.

The Origins of the Structural Adjustment Policy

Few studies acknowledge that the changes are being made more for the benefit of the overall economic policy rather than for the improvements in performance of public health services. The relationship between macro-economic policies, such as structural adjustment and population health, continues to be largely neglected. However, it is essential to understand some of the events leading to the implementation of Structural Adjustment Policies in developing countries. This will serve as an essential backdrop to understanding some of the possible consequences for health services and for the public sector as a whole.

Structural Adjustment Policies are rooted in the economic crises experienced by many countries during the latter half of the seventies. The preceding decade is now re-known as a period of excessive lending by international banks at a time characterized by inequitable international trade agreements between developed and developing countries. The excess funds had been obtained by banks from oil revenues accrued during the seventies. These were lent out with exceptionally lax credit rules to governments, institutions, and businesses and most often spent on white elephant or wasteful projects such as those among large hospitals, dams, airports, and luxury hotels. Such patterns of conspicuous consumption generated a process of unsustainable development. According to some "...the rich got the loans and the poor got the debts" (Kent 1991).

The repayment crisis which followed led to a dramatic deterioration in the economies of the developing world owing to the fact that the interest to be repaid accumulated and often exceeded the total incomes of these countries from their export earnings. Brazil, for example, had one of the highest debts. Its interest repayments were $30 million per day. In Mexico, one of the earliest debtors, with a similar repayment schedule as Brazil's, minimum urban salaries fell by 50 percent through devaluation between 1980 and 1990. Prices rocketed as wages continued to fall. In 1987, the Mexican National Institute of Nutrition reported that 80–90 percent of Mexican children were experiencing early malnutrition with irreversible losses in mental and physical capacity. In other countries as far apart as Brazil and Ghana, infant mortality rates began to increase significantly in comparison to the slowing down of the rate in several countries (Kent 1991; Watson 1994).

The donor-led debt crisis of the early eighties, together with the prospect of instability to the banking system in the North, sets the backdrop for Structural Adjustment Policies. The IMF together with the World Bank stepped in to help developing countries pay off loans, on the condition that the countries adopt economic policies which would generate "economic growth" and in their terms, create the climate for repayment and the requisite economic and social stability. It is clear from the literature, however, that part of this strategy was to replace the state sector in public services or to reduce its role to a minimum (Kanji et al. 1991; Loewenson 1993; Werner et al. 1996).

Structural Adjustment Policies have involved (Werner et al. 1996):

- Sharp cuts in public spending on health education and other social services.
- The removal of subsidies and lifting of price controls on staple foods and other basic commodities.
- Freezing of wages.
- A shift from production of food and goods for domestic consumption to production for export.
- Liberalization of trade policies (through tariff elimination and restrictions on imports).
- Efforts to attract foreign investors by providing them incentives, such as lax regulation and tax breaks.
- Privatization of public services and state enterprises.
- Devaluation of the local currency.

These economic measures were adopted by countries at different times, but the general conditions applied to all, with a concerted move to implement SAPs from mid-late eighties through to the nineties. In the latter period, and owing to growing concern voiced by those working in the health sector, which included pressure from multilateral agencies such as UNICEF, adjustment with a "human face" was advocated. Some refinements were made to the original objectives, particularly those targeted at the social sector (health and education). However, the basic economic changes advocated for the reorganization of public services did not alter.

Evidence of Effect upon Economy

Economic reforms have been introduced at different times in different countries. Yet the reported effects for the health and social sectors appear to share remarkable similarity (Kanji et al. 1991; Loewenson 1993).

Some of the evidence of the impact of SAPs that has begun to emerge during the past five years reveals that they have led to an overall chaos in the public sector, in addition to the impact on employment, food, and transport. Judged even by conventional economic standards, they have generated impoverishment and reduced considerably the capacity for the reconstruction of economies—a stated aim of the policy itself (Emeagwali 1995;

UNRISD 1995). For example, the economic policies of lifting price controls, freezing wages, devaluing local currencies, and reducing subsidies on basic essentials such as food and transport have had the effect of reducing purchasing power. Several studies highlight reductions in the consumption of nutritional staple foods as a result of these changes, especially among vulnerable groups such as children and elderly people. This has occurred most notably in the early adjusting countries of Africa and Latin America, such as Mexico and Brazil (Watson 1994; Werner et al. 1996).

Overall, the ability of poor people to buy food, transport, education, and health care has been reduced. A number of studies also highlight the serious effects of SAPs on women—both as producers and consumers. The cumulative evidence from countries as far apart as Zimbabwe and India shows that women have to work for longer hours, with lower wages and also have less access to food (Costello, Watson, and Woodward 1994; Emeagwali 1995; Kanji and Jazdowska 1993; Patel 1992).

As early as 1994, Oxfam challenged the World Bank report on the success of adjustment in Africa and its position that SAPs had brought recovery to the continent in terms of poverty reduction. The report argued that it was difficult to support the evidence on many of the so-called success stories of growth. For example, in Ghana, a country often held up as a success story, economic growth was artificially sustained through substantial injections of foreign aid. In Gambia, growth was linked to tourism alone and that too, only on a seasonal basis. In Zimbabwe, the figures provided for sustained economic growth appeared to be highly selective (Watkins 1994). On the contrary, by the early nineties a clear correlation had been established between the introduction of user fees for health care and a marked fall in women's attendance at antenatal clinics in Zimbabwe, one of the first African countries to experience reforms. Adverse health trends were beginning to emerge in infant mortality and maternal mortality levels at Harare General Hospital; here, mortality rate among children booked to mothers who did not attend antenatal clinics was almost five times that of their registered counterparts (Bijlmakers, Bassett, and Sanders 1994).

The core adjustment policy of reorienting agriculture for export promotion, without a balance with domestic consumption and production, also appeared to have created a scarcity for locally produced and often the only nutritious foods available for people in many countries of Africa. Cash cropping generated internecine conflict and problems for the peasantry and small holders, with land being lost to transnational corporations (TNCs) and large landowners for the production of luxury crops for export. The impact on nutrition at the level of the household and on the intra-household allocation of food is gradually emerging, mainly from Africa, but also from Latin America. These show that the prospects for the already vulnerable groups are negative as reflected by higher levels of malnutrition and related conditions of morbidity. Many of the studies show that some of the gains in health status, in terms of improved nutritional and improved mortality of the eighties, are being reversed owing to the gross inequalities introduced in the distribution of income and resources (Sen 1996; Watson 1994; Werner et al. 1996).

The literature on the overall impact of the economic policies is substantial. There is a growing body of evidence to reinforce the long held view that Structural Adjustment Policies can only intensify economic inequalities within and in between regions, and reinforce those which already existed at the international level. This is linked to the liberalization of trade and lifting of import restrictions, which act to the advantage of TNCs. At the national level, SAPs have created new inequalities by advocating drastic cuts in the real earnings of the majority of the population while encouraging unsustainable consumption patterns among the wealthiest for imported goods.

Health Services—Overall Evidence on Reorganization and Transformation

From prescribing changes to the overall economies of developing countries, there was growing interest in the reform of health services. In its first report on *Financing Health Services in Developing Countries*, the World Bank set out some of the basic strategies proposed in terms of introducing market reforms (World Bank 1987). These were elaborated and reinforced in the *World Development Report* of 1993, where the predominant role of markets becomes evident from the subtitle—Investing in Health. In brief, this report advocates that the state or the public sector should provide only essential services such as "clinical packages" for the needy whilst the tertiary sector opens up to full global competition (Qadeer 1994; World Bank 1993). In the ideological thrust to introduce changes in the economy, the relationship between macro-economic policy and health services among other social measures has not been sufficiently considered. Hence, the effects of macro-economic policy upon social sectors such as health and education only became visible when direct changes such as the introduction of charges were made.

Among changes brought about to varying degrees in the health sector of developing countries were:

- The introduction of health insurance (with compulsory purchasing) in some cases deducted from salary payments as in Thailand.
- The introduction of user charges for specific services.
- The introduction of community-based financing.
- The advocacy of de-centralized services.
- The location of NGOs as a key reference point in service provision.

While the *World Development Report—Investing in Health* (World Bank 1993) advocates reforms in the health sector, there has been little attempt to define what the "health sector" might mean for most developing countries. Health systems of developing countries include a plurality of services, where often the public sector provides much of basic health care for the majority of rural populations. This complexity and inter-dependency is excluded from the common definition and the ensuing analysis of health service provision. Some critics have argued against oversimplification and the application of a universal reform prescription for economic reforms to the diverse settings that exist in the different countries as well as regions within them.

For example, in some of the literature, the notion of "a health market" is discussed coterminously for developed and developing countries, whereas, in reality health services have historically evolved very differently in the regions in question (Newbrander 1997). There is little understanding also of the historical location of public service provision or of the political and economic factors that may have contributed to the serious underfunding of the public health services and the donor pressures for vertical rather than comprehensive programs. It is through an understanding of precisely the chequered history of public health that led organizations such as the WHO to advocate extreme caution in the implementation of reforms. But this word of caution appears to have largely been ignored (WHO 1995).

The analogy of "performance" between public and private sectors in terms of efficiency is also questionable owing to the intrinsic differences of outlook and motivation in each of these sectors (Creese 1991; Evans 1997; Reinhardt 1998). Reinhardt, for example, suggests that economists who have advocated reform in its current mode (in the US), singularly fail to acknowledge the ideological content of the word "efficiency." "Efficiency" is not and cannot be an objective term since it is enmeshed in a subjective context or order (Evans 1997; Reinhardt 1998).

Falling rates of utilization in public sector provision have often served as the rationale for its reform and reorganization. The latter has been associated with (*i*) the inability of the public sector to fund services in the future; and (*ii*) its inability, in particular, to deliver the quality of service demanded by patients. These two factors, associated with a market analysis (demand and supply), have been the cornerstone for relegating this sector to essential clinical services (World Bank 1993). However, there are few critical studies of the performance of the private sector by a breakdown of several necessary variables in order to explain the differential rates in utilization.

The few studies which exist point to escalating costs of private sector provision owing to: the use of inappropriate and unsustainable technologies (Bennett 1991), overprescription (VCAN 1996; Yang 1997), and a captive market (Bennett 1991), where there is little choice for people seeking health care in a private supplier led health service. In India, for example, there is particular concern about quality and standards of hygiene in the private sector in one state as well as considerable overprescribing in several major states (VCAN 1996; Yesudian 1994).

Dilemmas of Public Provision

It would be inaccurate to claim that prior to the reforms, public provision of health services was flourishing in much of the developing world. The substitution of comprehensive services by selective and vertical programs in countries across the world systematically undermined the ability of the public sector to provide low cost and accessible services to the majority of the population. The ability of doctors to charge for services also paved the way for public sector subsidizing for private sector activity. This was to become a major drain on public sector activity.

Increasing rates of utilization following introduction of user charges are often used as the rationale to beat the public sector. But these can be interpreted very differently when micro-level studies on the process of care are undertaken. In many cases, utilization rates actually rise owing to the increase in the number of visits as requested by the physician for the same condition, usually for greater profit. This is the case in countries as far apart as Burkina Faso (Sauerborn, Nougtara, and Latimer 1994) and Korea (Yang 1997). The reality emphasizes a rise in the profit margin rather than expressing patient preference for a particular type of health service provided, as the advocates of reform suggest. Such in-depth micro-level studies which focus on the operational process of reforms are few and far between and are not actively encouraged by funding agencies. Often, their findings are ignored.

There is also much evidence to suggest that even on grounds of efficiency and effectiveness as defined by economists, the reforms in the majority of cases are of poor value. A number of micro-level studies show that cost recovery, for example, may be feasible, but it is rare to have this translated into better quality services, thereby sacrificing the goals of efficiency and equity. Efficient cost-recovery, by definition, needs to act as revenue for re-funding services in accordance with the terms of the reforms. However, the evidence for this according to conservative estimates is virtually non-existent in the African region where the earliest experiments with cost recovery took place (Creese and Kutzin 1995). At the macro level, de-regulation has clearly strengthened the hand of multinationals in the pharmaceutical and health-insurance fields. It is likely to escalate health care costs further as technology and pharmacology intensive care continues to grow in this sector (Koivusalo and Ollila 1997; Smith 1996; Werner et al. 1996; Yang 1997).

The evidence from the OECD countries on the impact of reforms upon efficiency is thin on the ground. There is little evidence to show that competition has improved efficiency in health care markets even in the crude economic terms that efficiency is described. Studies from different regions of the world carry indications of the impact on distribution of changes in the structure of health services in the developed market economies of eastern and central Europe (Mastilica 1996). In terms of the organization of health care, many of the services previously funded by the state no longer exist, or have moved to a competitive mode, where payment for staff is made on the basis of performance. Specific services have introduced user charges to prevent their overuse and obtain revenue. However, there are no procedures to evaluate changes in utilization or levels of cost recovery. Some studies clearly show evidence of the myth of cost recovery (Bijlmakers, Bassett, and Sanders 1994; Chabot, Harnmeijer, and Streefland 1995; Sauerborn, Nougtara, and Latimer 1994). In some countries, the changes in the terms of trade have meant an expansion of private tertiary care, with import of expensive drugs and technology, with few controls over their usage, and a guarantee of rising per capita expenditure in health services (Yang 1997).

The reforms as outlined in *Investing in Health* (World Bank 1993) openly advocate segmented care. This entails one system of underfunded care for the poor (essential clinical services), and another, consisting of high technology for those who can afford to pay. There is ample evidence to show that where a so-called public–private mix is advocated as a policy measure and the private sector is armed with most of the resources, there is little possibility for the former to survive. Consequently "consumer choice" remains restricted only to those who can afford to pay for services in the private sector. Despite the interest in reforms, the social and health consequences of segmentation of health care are not being sufficiently evaluated. We need to know, for example, whether vulnerable groups continue to try and pay for health services they can ill afford or do they resort to alternative systems.

Several studies over the past five years are beginning to acknowledge that elasticity of demand for health care only applies to the better off (Creese 1991; Ensor and Bich San 1996; Sauerborn, Nougtara, and Latimer 1994; WHO 1995). When expensive health care is unavoidable for vulnerable groups, a heavy price is usually paid, either by incurring debts or families foregoing some basic essentials, such as a minimum adequate diet and schooling for girl children in particular.

For vulnerable groups, such as elderly people, who often suffer from multiple chronic conditions, this is likely to be a major calamity in both economic and social terms. As it is not in the interest of the private and for-profit sector to support programs of primary care or of prevention, the cost of health care falls upon families. Among the effects of the high cost of treating emerging chronic diseases is a breakdown in intra-household and in particular inter-generational relations, owing to conflicts in duties, obligations, and economic survival (Sen 1996).

The overall evidence on the other aspects of reforms, such as decentralization, community financing, and the introduction of user charges, does not reveal positive outcomes (Bijlmakers, Bassett, and Sanders 1994; Green 1995; Kanji et al. 1991; Sen 1996; Smith 1996; Watkins 1994). Instead, they reinforce the already known view that under conditions of gross structural inequality, the application of market formulae can only act to the advantage of the more wealthy and powerful and strengthen the gradients of poverty and inequality (Evans 1997). As mentioned earlier, mechanisms such as user charges are very specific to developing countries. Reforms in countries of Europe and in North America consist of introduction of competition between and within providers and contracting out of specific services; there has been no introduction of user charges for public sector services.

The issue in the OECD countries has been that of equity—that a population's capacity to benefit from health care is likely to be distributed very differently from its purchasing power. In Canada, the policy debates have been against user fees. Some describe them as a "tax on those unfortunate enough to become ill" (Barer, Evans, and Stodard 1979). It has been argued that high fees are likely to deter precisely those people who most need access to care as the ability to pay is a very different notion from "willingness to pay," that has been the premise of advocating user charges. This is also echoed in a number of studies that have been undertaken in developing countries since the late eighties (Bijlmakers, Bassett, and Sanders 1994; Kanji et al. 1991).

Conclusion

Despite the above-delineated problems of definition and validity of comparison, there appears to be a concerted effort to highlight weaknesses in public provision and an ideologically motivated onslaught for dismantling state involvement in public services. It appears that policies over the past two decades have been formulated to ensure the predominance of multinational drug companies in the health and social sectors of debt-ridden and vulnerable nations. Health services, which are a social asset, are being treated as any other economic service. The appropriateness of this correlation is increasingly being questioned (Nittayaramphong 1997). Quality of health care means technology intensive and expensive health care. The appropriateness of such a model in countries where the majority lives at subsistence level remains unquestioned.

It has for long been established that health care is a basic need, and poor health is not determined by the whims of the marketplace nor by supply and demand (Rice 1997). The evidence on the incidence of morbidity and mortality in most regions of the world clearly shows that it is a consequence of structured conditions of poverty and inequality. Introducing competition and costs in the health sector will discriminate against those who are poor and sick.

It would be inaccurate to claim that prior to reforms, public provision of health services was flourishing in much of the developing world (Green 1995; Koivasulo and Ollila 1997; Werner et al. 1996). Resource constraints have been awesome and have starved public facilities of basic health resources, such as medicines and personnel. This has affected the quality of services and made the onslaught of medical-pharmaceutical lobby only too easy (Qadeer 1994). There is a need, therefore, to provide a historical dimension to the limitations as well as relevance of public services in developed and developing countries. There is also a need to explore the economic and political means to generate progress in this sector since much of the health gains of the past several decades were made to a large degree by the availability and accessibility of public provision. If such consideration is taken on board in a scientific manner, devoid of ideological underpinnings, it is likely to provide the true criteria for improving service provision.

Given some of the challenges and growing doubts facing current reforms, there is need to accumulate detailed evidence on the implementation of the reform process in order to question its efficacy and relevance. There is need to continue to support studies of process rather than place undue emphasis on single measures of outcome, such as attendance, drug availability, and waiting times to judge the overall impact of changes. We need to know the cumulative impact and over a period in time.

The visible absence of such a scientific evaluation of the quality and impact of the reforms has led some to conclude that there has been a process of engineering. Experimental projects have sprung up in different parts of the world, it would appear, not to test but rather vindicate the dominant paradigm in terms of market reforms as a valid and relevant alternative to public sector provision (Health Policy and Planning 1995). The growing voices of concern from different regions of the world for evaluations and micro-level studies of the health effects of SAPs are either ignored or are simply not funded. Not only is evaluation of policy measures lacking, there is also no evaluation of the services provided under the aegis of the private sector. This is so despite the fact that the private sector has had a long history and a good share of the health sector in most of the developing sector.

This vacuum serves to reinforce the view that the debate on public versus private has been largely motivated by the ideology of monopoly capital for profit, as the collection of empirical data is avoided or disregarded (Sen and Roy 1996). In brief, the far-reaching reforms of the past decade are yet to be justified on the grounds of efficiency.

The overall evidence from both developed and developing countries suggests that these reforms have simply aggravated existing disparities and created a situation which will generate lasting damage to the health and well-being of populations worldwide.

References

Akin, J.N., and **Birdsall, D. de Ferranti** (1987): Financing Health Services in Developing Countries: An Agenda for Reform. A World Bank Policy Study, Washington.

Banerji, D. (1997): Structural Adjustment and Health in India—A Critique. Discussion paper at the International Meeting on Health Impact of Structural Adjustment in South Asia, September, New Delhi.

Barer, M.L., **Evans, R.G.**, and **Stodard, G.L.** (1979): Controlling Health Care Costs by Direct Charges to Patients: Snare or Delusion? Occasional Paper, No. 10. Ontario: Ontario Economic Council.

Bennett, S. (1991): *The Mystique of Markets: Public and Private Health Care in Developing Countries*. PHP Departmental Publication, No. 4. London: London School of Hygiene and Tropical Medicine.

Bijlmakers, L., Bassett, M., and **Sanders, D.** (1994): Health and Structural Adjustment in Rural and Urban Settings in Zimbabwe. Interim Research Report, mimeo. Community Medicine Department, University of Zimbabwe, Harare.

Chabot, J., Harnmeijer, J.W., and **Streefland, P.H.** (1995): *African Primary Health Care: The Times of Economic Turbulence*. Amsterdam: Royal Tropical Institute.

Costello, A., Watson, F., and **Woodward, D.** (1994): *Adjustment and the Health of Mothers and Children*. London: Centre for International Child Health.

Creese, A.L. (1991): User Charges for Health Care: A Review of Recent Experience. SHS Paper No. 1. Geneva: WHO.

Creese, A.L., and **Kutzin, J.** (1995): Lessons from Cost Recovery in Health. Discussion Paper No. 2, Forum on Health Sector Reform. Geneva: WHO.

Emeagwali, G.T. (1995): *Women Pay the Price*. New Jersey: Africa World Press.

Ensor, T., and **Bich San, P.** (1996): Access and Payment for Health Care: The Poor of Northern Vietnam. *International Journal of Health Planning and Management*, 11(1): 69–83.

Evans, R.G. (1997): Health Care Reform: Who's Selling the Market and Why? *Journal of Public Health Medicine*, 19(1): 45–49.

Green, A. (1995): The State of Health Planning in the 90s. *Health Policy and Planning*, 10: 22–29.

Kanji, N., and **Jazdowska, N.** (1993): Structural Adjustment and Women in Zimbabwe. *Review of African Political Economy*, 56: 11–26.

Kanji, N., Kanji, N., and **Manji, F.** (1991): From Development to Sustained Crisis: Structural Adjustment, Equity and Health. *Social Science and Medicine*, 33: 985–93.

Kent, G. (1991): *The Politics of Children's Survival*. New York: Praeger.

Koivusalo, M., and **Ollila, E.** (1997): *Making a Healthy World. Agencies, Actors and Policies in International Health*. London and New York: Zed Books Limited.

Leighton, C., and **Terrell, N.** (eds.) (1995): Special Issue on Improving Quality, Equity and Access to Health Services through Health Financing Reforms in Africa. *Health, Policy and Planning*, 10(3).

Loewenson, R. (1993): Structural Adjustment and Health Policy in Africa. *International Journal of Health Services*, 23: 17–30.

Mastilica, M. (1996): Health Care Reform in Croatia. In *Health Care Reforms in Central and Eastern European Countries*. European Public Health Association, Department of Social Medicine, University Medical School. Debrecen: Soros Foundation.

Mills, A. (1993): *Improving the Efficiency of Public Sector Health Services in Developing Countries: Bureaucratic versus Market Approaches*. PHP Departmental Publication No. 17. London: London School of Tropical Medicine and Hygiene.

Newbrander, W. (1997): *Private Health Sector Growth: Issues and Implications*. Chichester, UK: John Wiley and Sons.

Nittayaramphong, S. (ed.) (1997): *Health Care Reform: At the Frontier of Research and Policy Decisions*. Bangkok, Thailand: Ministry of Public Health.

Patel, V. (1992): Women and Structural Adjustment in India. Cited in: F. Watson (1994): *Human Face or Human Façade. Adjustment and the Health of Mothers and Children*. London: Centre for International Child Health.

Qadeer, I. (1994): The World Development Report 1993: The Brave New World of Primary Health Care. *Social Scientist,* 22(9–12): 27–40.

Reinhardt, U.E. (1998): *Accountable Health Care: Is it Compatible with Social Solidarity*. Office of Health Economics Annual Lecture 1997. London: Mimeo Office of Health Economics.

Rice, T. (1997): Can Markets Give us the Health System that We Want? *Journal of Health Politics, Policy Law,* 22(2): 382–424.

Sauerborn, R., Nougtara, A., and **Latimer, E.** (1994): The Elasticity of Demand for Health Care in Burkina Faso: Differences Across Age and Income Groups. *Health Policy and Planning,* 9(2): 185–92.

Sen, K. (1996): Health Sector Reforms and the Implications for Later Life from a Comparative Perspective. *Health Care in Later Life,* 1(2): 73–83.

Sen, K., and **Roy, S.G.** (1996): *Demographic and Epidemiologic Transition in India and Impact upon Utilization of Health Services*. Report submitted to the European Commission in the Fourth Framework for Health Systems Research. Unpublished.

Smith, R. (1996): Global Competition in Health Care. *British Medical Journal,* 313: 764–65.

United Nations Research Institute for Social Development (UNRISD) (1995): *Adjustment, Globalization and Social Development*. Geneva: UNRISD.

Voluntary Consumer Association of India (VCAN) (1996): Prescription Audit Analysis in Metropolitan Cities: A Study of Drug Utilisation in Urban Community. R. Krishnangshu et al. Unpublished. Calcutta.

Watkins, K. (1994): *The Oxfam Poverty Report*. Oxford: Oxfam.

Watson, F. (1994) *Human Face or Human Facade? Adjustment and the Health of Mothers and Children: Annotated Bibliography Pt 1 and Pt 2*. London: Centre for International Child Health.

Werner, D., Sanders, D., Weston, J., Babb, S., and **Rodriguez, B.** (1996): *Questioning the Solution: The Politics of Primary Health Care and Child Survival*. Palo Alto: Health Wrights.

World Bank (1987): *Financing Health Services in Developing Countries: An Agenda for Reform*. Washington D.C.: World Bank.

——— (1993): *World Development Report*. New York: Oxford University Press.

World Health Organisation (1995): *Lessons from Cost Recovery in Health*. Discussion Paper No. 2. Forum on Health Sector Reform. Geneva: WHO.

Yang, Bong-min (1997): The Role of Health Insurance in the Growth of the Private Health Sector in Korea. In New Brander (ed.). *Private Health Sector Growth Issues and Implications*. Chichester, UK: John Wiley and Sons.

Yesudian, C.A.K. (1994): Behaviour of the Private Sector in the Health Market in Bombay. *Health Policy and Planning,* 9(1): 72–80.

9

Disability Adjusted Life Years as a Tool for Public Health Policy: A Critical Assessment

Ritu Priya

It was well-recognized by the seventies that a major reason for the poor health status in the Third World was the physical, social, and cultural gap between planned public health care and the people. People's health in people's hands was the official response (Newell 1975). In India, several strategies including the Community Health Volunteer Scheme, meant to act as a channel of communication between the "people" and the health care services, were adopted. The Health Policy document of 1982 acknowledged the shortcomings of the health policies followed since independence (Government of India 1982). People's participation and decentralization became rhetoric. Control over local health services through the panchayati raj (local government) institutions was advocated through the eighties and nineties as a possible corrective to basic ills (Antia and Bhatia 1993). In response to the failure of the health programs that they had initiated or helped plan earlier, international experts took to re-prioritization of problems and shifts in strategies of intervention. One line of enquiry to aid this valid exercise was the development of DALYs during the eighties and nineties. DALYs is being widely promoted as an epidemiological tool for assessing "burden of disease," for identifying priority problems, and for evaluation of optional interventions (World Bank 1993). It is being hailed as a significant advance in providing a comparable database for enunciating public health policy, and planning and program evaluation.

This chapter attempts to analyze the technical bases of DALYs, and its potential and limitations. Given the very nature of the discipline, the "technical" basis for public health has to be a mix of quantified statistical data dealing with measurable phenomena such as quantum and distribution of health problems, and qualitative data dealing with social processes and perceptions (Susser 1994). In fact, all quantitative data have underlying qualitative assumptions and conceptual bases. The choices between various methodological options and value positions, and the assumptions used in constructing it represent this qualitative dimension of DALYs (Murray 1994).

This analysis of DALYs explicitly incorporates qualitative and quantitative aspects into its framework. The questions addressed are:

- Does DALYs help in a better epidemiological understanding of the burden of ill health?
- Does it improve prioritization of public health problems and evaluation of optional public health interventions?
- Can it be used for bridging the gap between people's perceptions/aspirations and health policy? If so, how?

Conceptual Issues

DALYs is a composite index quantitatively representing "burden of disease," incorporating into one figure morbidity, disability, and mortality, expressed in terms of estimated years of human life affected. Each disease is quantified in terms of number of deaths caused and the age at death converted into standard number of years of human life lost "prematurely" and weighted for value of human life at different ages. To this is added the incidence of the disease multiplied by a weight for degree of disability caused and the average duration diseased persons are estimated to suffer with the disability (i.e., for severity of disease). Then a 3 percent discounting (reduction from previous calculations) is done per year on the assumption that, as the calculation includes potential loss of healthy years in the future, the value placed on them as compared to healthy years in the present is less. By, at least theoretically, including all "disability" caused by disease, even of least severity or shortest duration, DALYs is claimed to quantitatively represent "any health outcome that affects social welfare," and to be the most comprehensive measure of "loss of welfare" due to a "health outcome" (Jamison and Jardel 1994).

DALYs evolved primarily out of the World Bank's efforts to intervene in public health policy to limit public sector spending. The experts felt the need to estimate and compare global and regional burden of disease, as well as to undertake a cost-effectiveness analysis for major diseases. It was felt that a rational evaluation of policies for health improvement requires "a detailed, reliable assessment of demographic conditions and the burden of disease, with comparative data across country or across a broad range of interventions" (Murray, Lopez, and Jamison 1994). The epidemiologists catered to the accounting needs of economists by reducing all disease experience to a single numerical figure, DALYs.

However, given the complexity of the problem and the lack of good data from most countries, this is a very difficult task. There are genuine problems of data and of social values faced in any epidemiological analysis. These are handled differently by epidemiologists, depending upon their primary objectives, perspective and value positions, resulting in significant variations in analyses of "burden of disease" (Murray 1994), and thereby in policy. In this section, we will set out the methodological choices made by the proponents of DALYs, and their underlying assumptions. In the next, we examine empirically the outcome of a DALYs-based analysis of Indian data. Finally, we compare the DALYs perspective with other epidemiological approaches that incorporate people's perceptions to develop a reliable assessment of health problems.

The first problem faced in such an exercise is that of obtaining reliable data sets. With incomplete and unreliable reporting from most countries, the WHO–World Bank team undertook an extensive exercise for bringing reasonable accuracy to the data sets. This was a valid exercise, which needed to be done irrespective of DALYs, but an appropriate methodology was crucial. The methodology adopted was to get groups of experts to prepare estimates of disease for each country based on available data. They were cross-checked by other international experts, and modified through several rounds of revision, ensuring "internal consistency." For instance, often the number of deaths obtained by summing up estimates for all diseases exceeded the actual total deaths in the population during the period. Therefore, the specific disease experts were asked to lower the estimates to make the two consistent. The underlying assumption was "one death, one disease."

The second problem, of deciding weights for different types and degrees of disability, was overcome by getting groups of experts to rank the disability caused on a six-point scale. Weights were assigned between zero (as no disability) and one (representing death) (Murray 1994), based on their own rough assessment of impact of the disease on the functional capacities of affected persons.

The third issue was of setting a discount rate for disability expected to occur in the future. Weights for disability at different ages also needed to be decided upon. Both these explicitly reflect social values. Discounting was considered important because of "the economic concept that individuals prefer benefits now rather than in the future." With no comparative data from different societies on such valuation in health, an arbitrary figure of 3 percent was set (Murray 1994). Similarly, based on the notion of "human capital" for productivity, greatest weight was assigned to morbidity and mortality in young adults than in childhood or old age. Having evolved out of these value choices, DALYs exhibits the following qualities.

Internally Consistent, Inconsistent with Reality

Multi-causality, linking of multiple factors, and linking health problems to their context is well accepted in epidemiology. Similarly, coexisting pathologies and their inter-linkages are well recognized. The understanding is that multiple pathologies have a multiplier effect on each other, and the total "burden of disease" is not additive (MacMohan and Pugh 1970). However, this has been obscured by the quantification involved in computing DALYs, which conceptually takes us back to a simplistic primitive mode of bio-medical representation and analysis. DALYs is calculated separately for each disease in isolation from all others. The figures so obtained are then aggregated to compute the total burden of disease. The method adopted to enhance accuracy of data begins by ignoring multiple causes of death, thus generating data sets that are far from reality. All further statistical computations on the "internally consistent" but inconsistent-with-reality data sets compound the inaccuracies. Later, in response to criticism, the proponents of DALYs attempted isolated exercises to use DALYs to compute the multiple burden of disease caused by one factor (such as diabetes, malnutrition, and water supply) (Murray and Lopez 1997). Once again the burden of multiple diseases is added, not taking into account the complex non-linear relationships between them.

Another means of representing epidemiological linkages is by grouping of diseases, such as by causal mechanism or mode of transmission. While computing DALYs three major categories—communicable diseases, non-communicable diseases, and injuries (Murray, Lopez, and Jamison 1994)—have been used with epidemiological correctness. However, the basis of smaller groupings within these is diverse, and not always in keeping with epidemiological logic. For example, the group called "childhood cluster" consists of diseases targeted by the Universal Immunization Program, i.e., the technological intervention package has decided the grouping. "Tropical cluster" is based on geographical distribution. Similarly, including pelvic inflammatory diseases (PID) in sexually transmitted diseases (STDs) is against the existing understanding that a majority of PID cases in India result from chronic manifestation of puerperal sepsis, and not from sexual intercourse per se. Staphylococcal and other non-specific infections are prime suspects. Studies show that about 20 percent of the cases of infertility are due to tubercular infection and in only a very small percentage is gonococal infection found (Tripathi 1998). Categorizing it under STD excludes the role of nutritional status, obstetric services, and curative care, and reduces it to simply a problem of "risky individual behaviour."

Comparability and Equality in the Abstract

The value choices made by the proponents of DALYs include consideration of only those social variables "that are general to all communities and households, namely age and sex" (Murray 1994). Other variables such as occupation, income, educational attainment, religion, and ethnicity, have been excluded, with the plea that this would mean "total relativism" (Murray 1994). This label completely sidetracks the issue of stratification of social groups. This may have little impact in a socio-political milieu where these issues are squarely tackled. But, where it is not so, technical tools such as DALYs become political instruments for obscuring inequalities/realities.

Equality as a value is catered to by "treating like health outcomes as like," by making no difference in quantifying death or disability of individuals (except by age and sex). For example, the premature death of the 40-year-old woman should contribute equally to estimates of the global burden of disease irrespective of whether she lives in the slums of Bogota or a wealthy suburb of Boston (Murray 1994). This is consistent with the needs of effective global comparability based on equality. However, comparison of health problems in two widely differing, and hence absolutely non-comparable, contexts requires going beyond simple quantification, into causal differences. Viewing them 'as like' obscures these differences in the determinants of ill health and death in the two contexts. To believe that "community-specific characteristics such as local levels of mortality should not change the assumptions incorporated into the indicator design" is to say that local realities must not "contaminate" the "comprehensive" indicator!

Other value choices involved in developing DALYs are no less debatable. For instance, the question as to how to quantify death due to different causes. Does death averted due to a condition such as diabetes or malnutrition leave the person with an expected disability free lifespan equal to others, or is it to be estimated at less than, say, death averted by accident? Different assumptions for the weights significantly influence the calculated DALYs. A sensitivity analysis shows that corresponding to different values of discount rate, the proportion of communicable or non-communicable diseases gets modified (Murray, Lopez, and Jamison 1994). A higher discount rate favors old-age problems, while a lower one will shift the DALYs computation towards childhood diseases. Also, discounting is a culturally-loaded choice. Large parts of the debate on discounting come from theoretical economics and are likely to be irrelevant for health outcomes. But then DALYs is a theoretical exercise. The abstract value placed on "equity" may be good in theory, but is poor in depiction of reality as it ignores diversity of context.

"Scientific Advance" with Loss of Reliability

As already discussed, the raw data sets used for computing DALYs are largely estimates based on uncertain information, and therefore inaccurate or at best broad approximations. The computations involved in calculating DALYs add to the uncertainty. For instance, disability estimates when added to mortality data decrease the reliability of the latter. Further, the universal assumptions and homogenizing arbitrary weights that incorporate all the biases of experts, compound the inaccuracies inherent in the estimates. That the theoretical statistical exercise is no protection against the compounding of inaccuracies is evident in computer simulations on weights. One such shows that a deviation of just 1 percent in age data due to error in the raw data for a disability suffered at 60 years scales up the variability to 6.7 percent (Sayers and Fieldner 1997).

Thus, in the development of a seemingly comprehensive, statistically sophisticated single indicator such as DALYs, there is an inherent compounding of inaccuracies, and a simplistic representation of "burden of disease" that is far removed from the reality of people's life and experience of health.

The Utility of DALYs

Until now multiple indicators were commonly used to obtain a multi-faceted picture of health status and disease patterns and trends. Data sets were available in India on morbidity, mortality, disability, and nutritional status but with varying degrees of reliability (GOI 1968–95; 1973–94; NIN 1996). Special surveys and a multitude of community-level studies provided further information. In this context, the multiple sources of information provided counterchecks or corroboration of data that were otherwise inadequate. To some extent, the prevalence data incorporated measurement of duration, and mortality indicated the severity. Based on experience, the severity and duration were also derived from the local pattern of the disease by experts familiar with the local context of each data set. These experts could make epidemiologically sound analyses, especially of trends in magnitude and severity (Gopalan 1992; Nagpaul 1978; Panikar and Soman 1984; Qadeer 1998). This required a certain analytical skill for interpreting each set of data with due consideration to: (*i*) the quality of data; (*ii*) the implications for other data sets; (*iii*) linkages between diseases; and (*iv*) the social and epidemiological context from which the data were drawn. DALYs is based on the same data sets and uses all the multiple indicators. However, DALYs not just limits, but excludes the analytical exercise itself.

Table 9.1
Prioritization of Disease Conditions for India by DALYs and in National Plan Documents

	*Ranking of Problems in National Plan Documents**	*Ranking by DALYs-lost Estimated by the WHO–WB***
1.	Acute respiratory infections (ARI)	ARI
2.	Diarrheal disease	Cardio-vascular diseases
3.	Fevers (non-specific infectious diseases, malaria, typhoid, viral fevers, including influenza)	Diarrheal disease
4.	Tuberculosis	Injuries
5.	Leprosy	Peri-natal causes
6.	STDs	Childhood cluster
7.	Blindness	Nutritional/endocrine
8.	Maternal conditions	Neuro-psychiatric
9.	Peri-natal causes	Malignancy
10.	Cancer	Non-communicable digestive disorders
11.	Cardio-vascular diseases	Tuberculosis
12.	Diabetes	Congenital
13.	Accidents	Chronic respiratory conditions
14.	Mental health	Maternal causes
15.	Oral health	HIV

Source: *Government of India 1980, 1985 and 1989.
** Murray, Lopez, and Jamison 1994.

The arbitrary, predetermined parameters of DALYs incorporate all the biases of international experts. The attempt is to have a decontextualized, universalizing framework favoring international comparability over detailed and reliable depiction of complex epidemiological linkages, which is indispensable for meaningful national and subnational planning.

Ranking of Health Problems: Shifts in Priorities

Comparison of the World Bank–WHO analyses for India with the national data and the priorities, as reflected in national planning documents, shows how the process of construction of DALYs tilts priorities. The priorities indicated by the two methods are apparently similar, with both according greater importance to communicable diseases, and 11 of the top 15 diseases being common (see Table 9.1). However, it is the differences that are significant. The

Table 9.2
Ranking of Disease Categories by Different Indices during Computation of DALYs for India, 1990

By DALYs[*]	*By Estimated Deaths Caused*[**]	*By Morbidity/Disability (Computed as YLDs-lost)*[***]
1. ARI	2	12
2. Cardio-vascular diseases	1	4
3. Diarrheal diseases	3	21
4. Injuries	6	3
5. Perinatal diseases	5	5
6. Childhood cluster	7	18
7. Nutritional/endocrine	11	2
8. Neuro-psychiatric	13	1
9. Malignancy	4	10
10. Non-communicable digestive disorders	9	6
11. Tuberculosis	8	14
12. Congenital	12	9
13. Chronic respiratory conditions	10	8
14. Maternal causes	16	7
15. HIV	-	24

Source: [*]Murray, Lopez, and Jamison 1994.
[**]Murray and Lopez 1994a.
[***]Murray and Lopez 1994b.

eminence given to communicable diseases in national planning till the late eighties is narrowed by computing their contribution to DALYs to be only 54 percent of the burden of disease, as against 46 percent by non-communicable diseases (excluding "injury" and considering only "disease") (Murray, Lopez, and Jamison 1994). Among the communicable diseases only the "childhood cluster" (Universal Immunization Program target diseases) and several non-communicable conditions move up in the DALYs ranking. Tuberculosis, fevers, leprosy, STDs, and maternal conditions move down.

Given the same database, how do the two methodologies lead to such differences? Examination of the two components for the computation of burden of each disease—its mortality and morbidity/disability—suggests that there are methodological reasons. Table 9.2 ranks the DALYs ranking by estimated contribution to mortality and to morbidity and disability in Years of Life Disabled (YLDs), while Table 9.3 ranks national priorities

Table 9.3
Ranking of Disease Categories in National Planning and in Different National Data Sets (1985–89)

	*National Planning Priority**	*Ranking by Cause of Death Data***	*Ranking by Morbidity (as No. of Reported Cases)****
1.	ARI	7	2
2.	Diarrheal disease	10	1
3.	Fevers	6	3
4.	Tuberculosis	8	7
5.	Leprosy	20	4
6.	STDs	-	5
7.	Blindness		-
8.	Maternal conditions	13	12
9.	Perinatal	3	18
10.	Cancer	9	11
11.	Cardio-vascular diseases	2	9
12.	Diabetes	15	15
13.	Accidents	4	6
14.	Mental health	17	16
15.	Oral health	-	-

Source: *Government of India 1980, 1985, 1989.
**Government of India 1990.
***Government of India 1991.

by reported cause of death and cases coming to medical institutions. Even though the major advantage of DALYs in measuring "burden of disease" is perceived to be its incorporation of morbidity and disability along with mortality, the consolidated DALYs is actually less influenced by the former and reflects mortality much more. The national planning documents, however, reflect much more the morbidity burden! The first six diseases in each column of Tables 9.2 and 9.3 make this point evident.

Second, the statistical computations reflect neglect of epidemiological specificities. For instance, the computation of morbidity due to diarrheal disease as YLDs brings it down to the 21st place. All Indian data sets on the other hand place diarrheal disease at the first or second position. Given that it is endemic in populations with high levels of under-nutrition, as in India (Government of India 1989), its low ranking in YLDs could only be due to the assumption that the condition is of short duration, self-limiting, and mild in nature! These assumptions run contrary to available evidence.

Third, the different categories used for ill health lead to variations in analysis. In the Indian data sets, local classification based on reporting by laypersons was used, and that captured social perceptions. For computing DALYs, the same data were converted into bio-medical categories. For example, in the original data, a single category of fevers covering specific and non-specific infections is recognized. The latter contributes 50 percent of deaths due to "fevers," which is equal to the magnitude of diarrheal deaths and is three times the maternity deaths. The DALYs classification on the other hand is unable to reflect this reality, as it has no space for "non-specific infections." It may appear to be more scientifically sound to divide "fevers" into specific diseases, moving from symptom to pathology, but this has led to arbitrary selection of specific diagnosis and distortion of data, as reflected in the use of "childhood cluster," malaria, tuberculosis, etc., as categories. These distortions then become handles to promote specific disease control programs. Only those fevers have been chosen against which preventive technological intervention is possible and improvements in nutritional status, drinking water, and sanitation can be avoided.

Similarly, "senility" is a cause for 25 percent of deaths, as reported by laypersons in the systematic survey. This represents what is socially perceived as "mature" death within the existing Indian context. When converted into bio-medical causes such as "cardio-vascular diseases" and "dementia" to compute DALYs, it enhances priority to be given to them and also to geriatric services. Data based on social perception in India, on the other hand, suggest a greater priority to other problems.

Thus, those disease conditions that have been declared major global public health problems, for which there are universal technocentric programs, have been taken higher on the list. The homogenizing quality of DALYs also pushed to the fore the priorities and experiences of the industrialized North and small elite sections of the Third World.

Prioritizing Interventions: The Technocentric Bias

DALYs is claimed to be of great value for evaluating interventions. Two epidemiological exercises are necessary for choosing between diverse intervention options: (*i*) identifying the determinants of disease pattern and the processes by which they influence disease and (*ii*) empirical evaluation of the various intervention options. In both instances the researcher would need to know separately the change in incidence, prevalence, duration, severity, and nature of morbidity, and the outcome in terms of recovery, disability, or death, as different interventions could act on the disease process in different ways. For this, one would have to disaggregate all the data so painstakingly put together as DALYs! Use of DALYs per se would tell us next to nothing about the nature of the interventions and therefore lead to a very superficial comparison. For instance, the possible public health interventions for diarrheal disease control would be promotion of oral rehydration solution (ORS), safe water supply, improving nutritional intake, or a curative care service. ORS will not alter incidence or prevalence but will decrease case fatality. Provision of safe potable water will decrease incidence and thereby mortality, though case fatality rates could remain unaltered. Improved nutritional status would decrease duration and severity of illness, decrease prevalence, and case fatality. Knowledge of these diverse processes is essential for informed decision-making. Given the mortality bias in DALYs any cost-effectiveness analyses using it will tend to favor life-saving interventions over primary prevention. The WHO–World Bank analysis does exactly that (World Bank 1993). Further, assessing cost-effectiveness for each disease for separate interventions bypasses the likely multiplier effects, e.g., interventions for provision of safe water and nutritional improvement will lead to the decline in morbidity and mortality more than the addition of each intervention separately. Also, burden of disease would decrease not only for diarrhea, but for several other water-borne and nutritional-deficiency diseases as well. Finally, water supply and nutrition are important not just as "preventive and promotive health measures" for decreasing "burden of disease," but are crucial for human well-being beyond survival. A DALYs based cost-effectiveness analysis does not even begin to acknowledge such "benefits."

The complexity of epidemiological processes and impact of interventions discussed above is evidenced in most cases of communicable and non-communicable diseases. However, DALYs cannot depict this complexity. Hence, its use only ends up as an abstract simplistic exercise. It is true that in the old methodology intuition plays a significant role. But until DALYs or some other single measure can quantify underlying epidemiological relationships, we must content ourselves with the more intuitive process of interpretation of morbidity and mortality, quantitative and qualitative data, by public health workers who are intimately familiar with the real life situation.

The Undemocratic Technocratic Agenda

Clearly, the ease of use of one figure is attractive. However, such a sanitized tool promotes technocentric and isolated disease control programs, alienates public health from the local context, and has no regard for people's experience and perceptions. Even a democratic political process responding to different demands of its constituencies is not considered desirable, as evident from this statement: "If the process of choosing relative weights of different types of health outcomes is left entirely to the political or bureaucratic process, there is a high probability that similar health outcomes may be weighted inconsistently, perhaps reflecting the political voices of different constituencies" (Murray 1994). Instead, the proponents of DALYs claim: "*We* [the international technocrats] can explicitly choose a set of relative values for different health outcomes and construct a single indicator of health. The black box of the decision maker's relative values is then opened for public scrutiny and influence" (emphasis and parenthesis added).

By explicitly stating in specialized professional journals the relative values implicit in the construction of the indicator, its proponents hope to fulfill their obligation towards scientific debate and public scrutiny. Whereas, the "explicit" value choices lead to denial of people's life context as well as their experience of ill health!

One needs to draw distinctions between the "black box" of the international technocratic epidemiologist and that of the national bureaucratic, public health planner–administrator. It is true that the elite bureaucratic and political systems of governance in our region often act as bottlenecks to public health provisions reaching large sections of the deprived. Yet, whatever gains the latter have achieved is largely through these systemic processes (Banerji 1984). They at least allow some space for people's democratic pressure and incorporation of people's perspectives. The international technocratic black box forecloses any such possibility. Pandering to it can only widen the gap between people's "felt need" and public health policies and programs.

DALYs versus People's Perceptions of Public Health

Today there are three visible streams within epidemiology. The most dominant one, which informs the majority of studies, deals with statistical association between "risk factor" and extent of disease in a linear manner; conclusions of causality are drawn from this in a universalized manner, without: (*i*) relating to social context or (*ii*) establishing processes behind the association. This is what has been called "black box" epidemiology (Susser 1996). Clearly, DALYs is located in this stream. It ignores all the advances made over the century in modern epidemiological understanding of disease and health in human societies. A second set of studies uses statistical methods, but also takes into account biological, environmental, and social contexts at macro and micro levels. This is what has been called eco-epidemiology (Susser 1996). A third stream, still minuscule in proportion of studies, adds to the "eco-epidemiology" by integrating people's perceptions and behaviors into the epidemiological conceptual framework (Banerji and Andersen 1963; Bose 1988; Sathyamala 1997; and Sukhatme 1972).

If linkages and the context of public health policy are viewed as essential, then people's perceptions become highly relevant for policy. They contribute a perspective that is rooted in their socio-historical context, that is responsive to changes in context, and that highlights those linkages that they perceive as critical to health. They provide the "target population" a means of coping with health problems within their context, and can therefore point to public health planners the most feasible interventions. This advantage, of incorporating people's perceptions, as illustrated by the use of "senility" as a cause of morality, is over and above its value in being able to provide comprehensive measures of illness, as shown in the national data on fevers.

Most studies on people's perceptions of health and health-behavior have focused on treatment-seeking behavior and perception of illness, not of "health." Some have brought forth the "people's perspective" more comprehensively and with greater depth by placing their behavior within their morbidity profile, social conditions, and health service conditions. They indicate the role of laypeople's wider concerns in determining their health and priorities and "felt needs." For instance: the issue of health of different family members in a situation of economic scarcity, where fulfilling basic needs of all members has to be weighed against treatment of one, reflects the perception of basic needs for survival of the household and not the neglect of some members. Similarly, a hierarchical health care system generates the perception of loss of dignity in availing of treatment from government personnel, and thereby discourages use of such a system. When slum dwellers in Indian cities demand services like water and sewage connections, it is a demand for well-being and for "health" (Priya 1995a). These are "health perceptions" which indicate the linking of illness-related perceptions with factors contributing to physical and social well-being. The conceptual and methodological limitations, the blinkers and blind-spots of those studying health perceptions do not allow such recognition or interpretation.

A study by the author attempted to understand the perceptions of health and illness of a group of construction workers (Priya 1995b). These workers were poor peasants, formerly untouchables, and had migrated from villages of Rajasthan to Delhi. They lived in makeshift hutments at construction sites and moved from site to site depending upon availability of work. Their non-technocentric, holistic approach is evident in several ways, which contrasts sharply with the conceptual basis of DALYs.

Two major findings are relevant here. The workers viewed illness or "burden of disease" as one component of health, and health as one component of well-being. Illness is thus encompassed within the larger frame of health, and both in the still larger frame of well-being. This is reflected in their health perceptions and behavior, which exhibited the following characteristics:

- A basic needs approach, which included physical amenities, social dignity and emotional support. "Well-being" was the central concern of the workers, while it is "disease" in the conceptual framework of DALYs. For the workers, while illness necessitated action, the nature of action was determined by the impact of different options on well-being. The issue of how the basic needs are fulfilled was the essence of "dignity." Therefore, they evaluated health care interventions on this criterion, along with that of efficacy, cost, and access.

- A historical perspective, their own historical experience, and future aspiration acting as reference points to assessing the present, and not just a comparison with others at the present point in time.
- A collectivist, and not individualist, outlook. The workers considered the fortunes and status of family and caste group for evaluating their own well-being and health, the most common reference point being their collective past. The principles of DALYs consciously use the individuals as unit, stating that the value of a person's health status is his or her own and does not depend on his or her neighbor's health status (Murray 1994). Read together with the earlier quote against use of any social group categories, this makes explicit the anti-collective thrust of the DALYs approach. This is not only counter to the workers' perception, it is also counter-productive for their health and well-being, as the family and community are important for emotional well-being, and are the workers' only social support system. Further, it is also counter-productive for public health interventions based on "community initiative" and collective action. This issue is of significance as it points to the clear difference in world-view of the international professional and the poor of our region. All healthy collectivities are under pressure today from the ethos of individualism and competition, and are tending to break down as supportive structures (Dube 1988).
- An integrated view: The dynamic interaction between different health problems was well recognized by the construction workers, and preventive or therapeutic choices were accordingly made. For instance, they associated physical labor and nutritional status, poor nutritional status and proneness to disease, measles and post-measles pneumonia, etc. We have seen that DALYs does not incorporate such linkages.

The second significant finding was the high value that the construction workers placed on the role of the state and a democratic polity for their well-being, and thereby, health. These are perceived as the structures which have led to improvements in their condition in the past decades and which, they presume, will continue to do so in future. The proponents of DALYs consciously attempt to suppress the influence of this democratic political process on public health policy. They believe in the technocratic, managerial process.

The workers' perspective on health and illness can form a conceptual basis different from that of DALYs for developing measures of ill health and evaluating optional interventions. This would influence the categories of ill health and thereby all subsequent analysis. Second, any health intervention must be evaluated not only for its preventive/curative efficacy, but also for its impact on well-being which has to be defined more broadly than by the individual disability/death it averts. Third, if at all one health indicator is to be constructed, it should incorporate parameters that represent a wide range of dimensions related to health and well-being, and not just the bio-medical factors. For instance, it could incorporate life expectancy and nutritional status as positive correlates and morbidity plus violence/crime/suicide rate as negative correlates.

Why is it that there are such diverse perspectives on health priorities and "burden of disease?" Is it a question of differing kinds of rationality? The rational mental processes appear to be very similar as both are inductive and deductive, analytical and synthetic. Even with the same motivation, that of improving human life, what differs are (*i*) the exposure to diverse contexts and so differing perceptions of "realities"; and (*ii*) differing primary objectives and priorities. These lead to diverse perspectives of the technocentric expert, the socially-oriented expert, and the laypeople. The objective of the technocentric experts to improve human health through technology and expertise leads them to represent reality in "manageable" ways. Bureaucratic management becomes essential as the system becomes bigger and more centralized. The distanced technocrat bureaucrat then needs single qualitative indicators, being unable to analyze "multiple qualitative indicators in the light of qualitative contextual knowledge," and DALYs is the answer.

Implications of the Use of DALYs

In the past two decades, there has been, on the one hand, an increasing recognition of the developmental and social dimensions of health and health care. Attempts had been made to develop measures for "well-being" and to incorporate social choices within medical and public health decision-making. On the other hand, there has also been increasing medicalization. On the one hand there has been democratization within the medical system (patient's voice and choice given importance in deciding between management options, recognition of the worth of other "complementary healing systems," etc.). On the other, there has been an increasing strangehold of specialities and super-specialities, hi-tech clinical care, and expensive private sector expansion.

DALYs is a step forward in terms of incorporation of all levels of suffering from ill health. But it has resulted in a narrowing of the definition of health and health care. It moves back from "well-being as health" to a greater disease-orientation. It also takes a step back to "experts" making social choices related to health care, and consciously attempts to pre-empt social and political processes. It gives a decontextualized, universalistic meaning to health problems, and creates a hegemony of the international technocrat. It shifts the focus from diseases that continue to be the major problems among deprived majorities of the Third World, to problems which are priorities for the industrialized North and the elite sections of the Third World. Its use, so far, has been to rationalize further the selective primary health care package of medical technologies as against the primary health care approach, that had a far-sighted vision, respect for social and political process and local context, and involved intersectoral coordination (Chen 1988). The technocentric and biomedical bias severely restricts the potential for analytical use. The minor bureaucratic benefit of DALYs is certainly not adequate as a trade-off against the technical drawbacks and its cultural and political implications. There is a danger of such tools being given greater value than they deserve, as they create illusions of an "objective description of disease and suffering." Such a depiction will further stall deeper analysis and understanding of the gap between health policy and people's needs and perceptions.

History shows us that if we accept this now, it may take decades to correct this conceptual narrowing of health and its medicalization. It also shows that the "recovery" is never complete.

References

Antia, N.H., and **Bhatia, D.** (eds.) (1993): *People's Health in People's Hands—Indian Experiences in Decentralised Health Care: A Model for Health in Panchayati Raj*. Bombay: Foundation for Research in Community Health.

Banerji, D. (1984): The Political Economy of Western Medicine in Third World Countries. In J.B. Mckinlay (ed.). *Issues in the Political Economy of Health Care*. New York and London: Tavistock Publishers.

Banerji, D., and **Andersen, S.** (1963): A Sociological Study of the Awareness of Symptoms Suggestive of Pulmonary Tuberculosis. *Bulletin of WHO*, 29(5): 665–83.

Bose, A. (1988): *From Population to People*. Delhi: B.R. Publishing Corporation.

Chen, L.C. (1988): Ten Years After Alma Ata—Balancing Different Primary Health Care Strategies. In A. de Geus (ed.). State of the Art Lectures—12th International Congress for Tropical Medicine and Malaria, Supplement to *Tropical and Geographical Medicine*, 40(3).

Dube, S.C. (1988): *Modernization and Development—The Search for Alternative Paradigms*. New Delhi: Vistaar Publications, Tokyo: UNU.

Gopalan, C. (1992): *Nutrition in Developmental Transition in South East Asia*. Regional Health Paper, No. 21. New Delhi: WHO–SEARO.

Government of India (1968–95): *Survey of Causes of Death (Rural)*. Annual Reports, Registrar-General of India. New Delhi: Ministry of Home Affairs.

——— (1973–94): *Health Information of India*. Annual Reports. New Delhi: Central Bureau of Health Intelligence, Ministry of Health and Family Welfare.

——— (1980): *Sixth Five Year Plan*. New Delhi: Planning Commission.

——— (1982): *Statement on National Health Policy*. New Delhi: Ministry of Health and Family Welfare.

——— (1985): *Seventh Five Year Plan*. Vol. 2. New Delhi: Planning Commission.

——— (1989): Proceedings of the Second Conference of Central Council of Health and Family Welfare, 1–3 February. New Delhi: Ministry of Health and Family Welfare.

——— (1990): Survey of Causes of Death (Rural). Annual Report. Registriar General of India. New Delhi: Ministry of Home Affairs.

——— (1991): Health Information of India. Annual Report, Central Bureau of Health Intelligence. New Delhi: Ministry of Health and Family Welfare.

Jamison, D.T., and **Jardel, J.P.** (1994): Foreword to C.J.L. Murray and A.D. Lopez (eds.). *Comparative Health Data and Analyses: Global Comparative Assessments in the Health Sector*. Geneva: WHO.

MacMohan, B., and **Pugh, T.F.** (1970): *Epidemiology—Principles and Methods*. Boston: Little Brown.

Murray, C.J.L. (1994): Quantifying the Burden of Disease : The Technical Basis for Disability Adjusted Life Years. *Bulletin of WHO*, 72(3): 429–45.

Murray, C.J.L., and **Lopez, A.D.** (1994a): Global and Regional Cause of Death Patterns in 1990 (annexed table on estimated deaths by age, sex and cause, 1990, India). *Bulletin of WHO*, 72(3): 447–80.

——— (1994b): Quantifying Disability: Data, Methods and Results (annexed table on years lived with a disability, India). *Bulletin of WHO*, 72(3): 481–94.

——— (1997): The Utility of DALYs for Public Health Policy and Research—A Reply. *Bulletin of WHO*, 75(4): 377–81.

Murray, C.J.L., Lopez, A.D., and **Jamison, D.T.** (1994): The Global Burden of Disease in 1990—Summary Result, Sensitivity Analysis and Future Directions. *Bulletin of WHO*, 72(3): 495–509.

Nagpaul, D.R. (1978): Tuberculosis in India—A Perspective. *Journal of Indian Medical Association*, 71(2): 44–48.

National Institute of Nutrition (NIN) (1996): *Nutritional Status of Rural Population*. Report of Surveys. Hyderabad: National Nutrition Monitoring Bureau.

Newell, K.W. (1975): *Health by the People*. Geneva: WHO.

Panikar, P.G.K., and **Soman, C.R.** (1984): *Health Status of Kerala*. Trivandrum: Center for Development Studies.

Priya, Ritu (1995a): Dalit Perceptions of Health. *Seminar*, 428: 15–19.

——— (1995b): The Meaning of Health for a Group of Migrant Construction Workers—Implications for Health Planning. *IASSI Quarterly*, 14(1&2): 81–102.

Qadeer, I. (1998): Reproductive Health—A Public Health Perspective. *Economic and Political Weekly*, 33(41): 2675–84.

Sathyamala, C. (1997): Reproductive Health Consequences of Bhopal Gas Leak. *Economic and Political Weekly*, 31(1): 43–57.

Sayers, B. McA and **Fieldner, T.M.** (1997): The Critique of DALYs: A Counter-reply. *Bulletin of WHO*, 75(4): 383–84.

Sukhatme, P.V. (1972): India and the Protein Problem. *Ecology of Food and Nutrition*, 1: 268.

Susser, M. (1994): The Logic in Ecological: The Logic of Analysis. *American Journal of Public Health*, 84(5): 825–29.

——— (1996): Choosing a Future for Epidemology: From Black Box to Chinese Boxes and Eco-Epidemiology. *American Journal of Public Health*, 86(5): 674–82.

Tripathi, R. (1998): Reproductive Tract Infections—Analysis of Data from Studies Conducted at Maulana Azad Medical College, New Delhi. Reproductive Health in India's Primary Health Care. New Delhi: Center for Social Medicine and Community Health, Jawaharlal Nehru University.

World Bank (1993): *World Development Report: Investing in Health*. New York: Oxford University Press.

10

Re-thinking Public Health: Food, Hunger, and Mortality Decline in South Asian History

Sheila Zurbrigg

History of Public Health

Ever since the sanitarian movements of the mid- and late nineteenth century in Europe—personified in England by the activities of Edwin Chadwick—the concept of public health has increasingly been restricted to the microbiological realm, in particular, to the task of controlling transmission of microscopic disease agents (microorganisms) based upon public sanitation services and promotion of individual hygiene. This Chadwickian view of public health came to replace an earlier understanding, which encompassed the full range of social and economic factors affecting human survival: living and working conditions, unemployment, poverty, and hunger in addition to filth and miasma (Hamlin 1992).

Public health in this larger sense is reflected in overall mortality levels in a society. Throughout most of human history, life expectancy fluctuated in the low and mid-twenties in virtually all regions of the world. By contrast, many people in much of the world today can expect to live well beyond their seventies. This vast extension in average human lifespan is primarily the result of the dramatic decline in the risk of death from an infectious disease.[1] The history of this "public health" thus confronts the basic "epidemic equation," bringing together

[1] This low life expectancy reflected recurring subsistence crises and political instability/internecine conflict/war, a potent trigger of famine and compromised resistance to disease. Even during times of war, however, epidemic mortality far outweighed deaths directly due to violence.

secular trends in levels of human exposure to disease on the one hand, and changes in human (host) resistance to infectious disease on the other.

Strangely enough, the history of rising life expectancy (mortality decline) is to a very large extent unwritten. This is in sharp contrast to medical history, i.e., the history of medical discoveries, techniques, innovators, and institutions. Indeed, the very question of health history is rarely posed either in modern medical or public health texts and is one that has slipped between the cracks of the major historical subdisciplines as well. An explanation for this omission probably lies in the assumption that we already had the answer, that it lay in modern scientific medicine.

The subject of mortality decline has been taken up in historiography as a question only in recent times. McKeown and coworkers looked at yearly death rates in England and Wales from 1841 to the present for each of the major infectious diseases and the time at which effective modern medical prevention and treatment techniques became available. It was observed that most of the decline in death rates for almost all the major infectious diseases occurred well before the discovery and general availability of modern medical techniques such as antibiotics, immunization, intravenous rehydration, and vitamin supplements (see Figures 10.1–10.3). Modern medicine as we know it today could account for only a very small part of the increase in English life expectancy to 70 years by the mid-twentieth century (McKeown 1976). After detailed examinations, he concluded that increased general resistance to infectious disease through improvements in nutrition was probably the main factor underlying this transformation in health. He acknowledged that clean water supplies and sewage systems in the final decades of the nineteenth century played an important role in reducing exposure to water- and food-borne diseases, such as diarrhea, dysentery, and typhoid fever. But these public health measures could explain at most one-quarter to one-third of the total mortality decline. Even here, he suggested, the same factor that had reduced lethality of air-borne diseases, viz. increased human resistance, may well have contributed to the fall in death rate of water-borne infections. More recent historical anthropometric analysis for a number of European populations has shown strong correlation between improved nutrition and decline in mortality (Fogel 1992).

Figure 10.1
Respiratory Tuberculosis: Mean Annual Death Rate (standardized to 1901 population): England and Wales

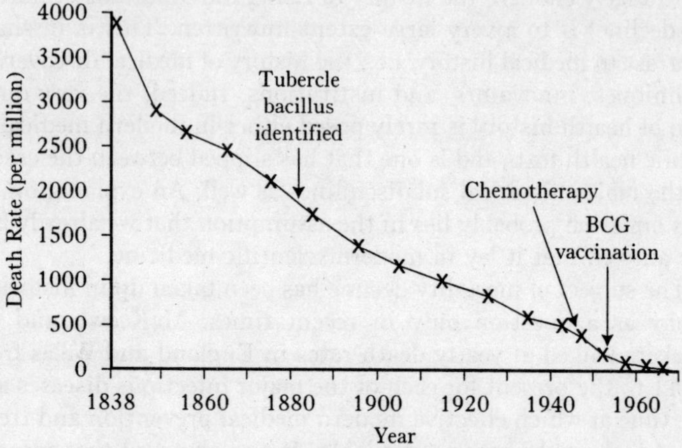

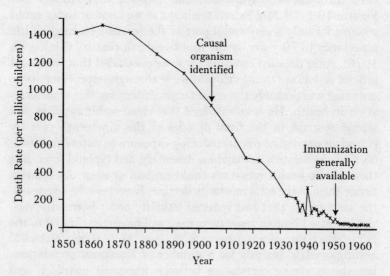

Figure 10.2
Whooping Cough: Death Rate of Children under 15: England and Wales

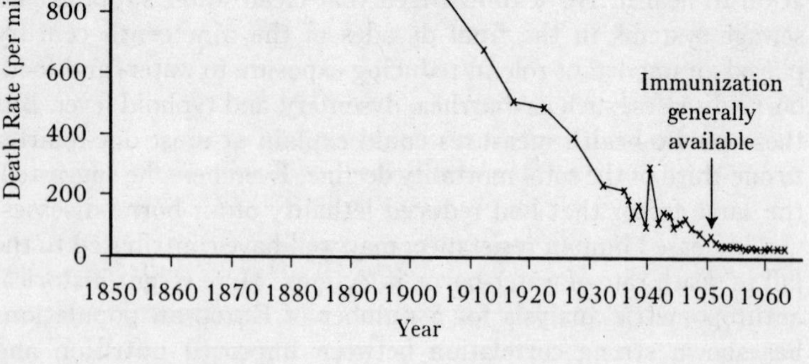

Source: McKeown 1979.

Figure 10.3
Measles: Death Rate of Children under 15: England and Wales

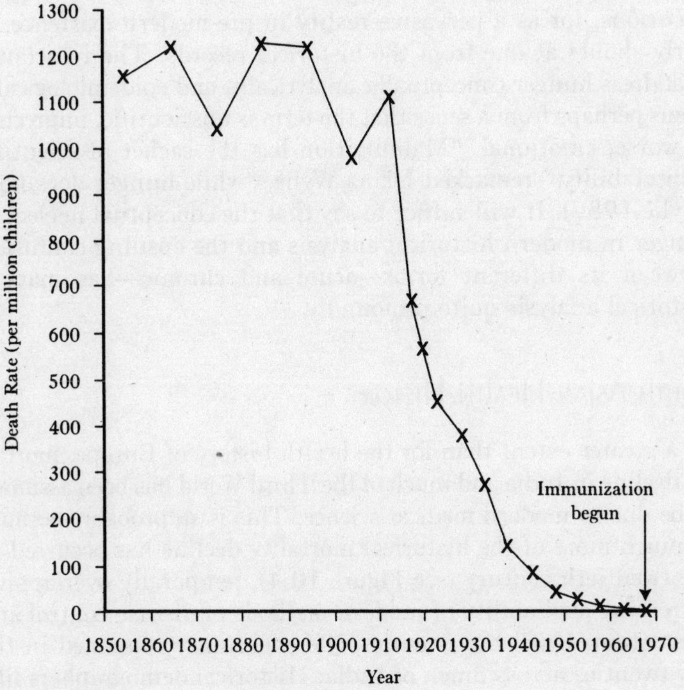

Source: McKeown 1979.

Through the eighties, there has been some questioning (contesting) of McKeown's nutrition thesis, particularly by demographic historians. Some have even gone so far as to suggest that the link between famine and epidemic mortality may be related primarily to increased exposure to disease through famine migration and lack of hygiene (dysfunctional social behavior) rather than reduced immunity and resistance to disease (Livi-Bacci 1991; Post 1985).[2] A great deal of the "ambiguity" which critics of the nutrition thesis find with respect to the nutrition-infection link may stem from an inadequate conceptual understanding and

[2] For an important rebuttal to specific criticism of the McKeown thesis, see Guha 1994.

methodological approach to the issue of hunger in history. We discuss this in the later sections.

The relative neglect of hunger in modern historical inquiry is curious, for as a pervasive reality in pre-modern existence, it fairly shouts at one from the historical records. The reluctance to address hunger conceptually, analytically, and epidemiologically stems perhaps from a sense that the term is unscientific, imprecise, or worse, emotional. "Malnutrition has the cachet of scientific respectability," remarked Diana Wylie, "while hunger does not" (Wylie 1989). It will suffice to say that the conceptual neglect of hunger in modern historical analysis and the ensuing confusion between its different forms—acute and chronic—has marked historical analysis quite profoundly.

South Asian Health History

To a greater extent than for the health history of Europe, mortality decline in India and much of the Third World has been assumed to be due to modern medical science. This is so probably because so much more of the historical mortality decline has occurred in the twentieth century (see Figure 10.4), temporally overlapping increasing availability of modern methods of disease control and prevention. Until the twenties, life expectancy remained in the low twenties across much of India. Historical demographers like Kingsley Davis have most explicitly and tenaciously argued the case for modern medical science (Davis and Bernstam 1991). We can see the medical technology assumption repeatedly occurring also in textbooks of Indian demography, public health, and indeed economic history, such as the 1983 *Cambridge Economic History of India*. The Visarias too are of the opinion that, "After 1921 a progressive control of cholera and plague epidemics began to lower mortality.... Among the factors contributing to the mortality decline is the introduction of universal immunization in the mid-1970s" (Visaria and Visaria 1994). While one form of hunger, epidemic starvation, or famine is referred to briefly, the role of famine control in mortality decline is generally assumed modest at best. Among those techniques credited with bringing down death rates, the use of DDT in malaria control programs has been considered the paramount example.

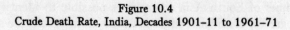

Figure 10.4
Crude Death Rate, India, Decades 1901–11 to 1961–71

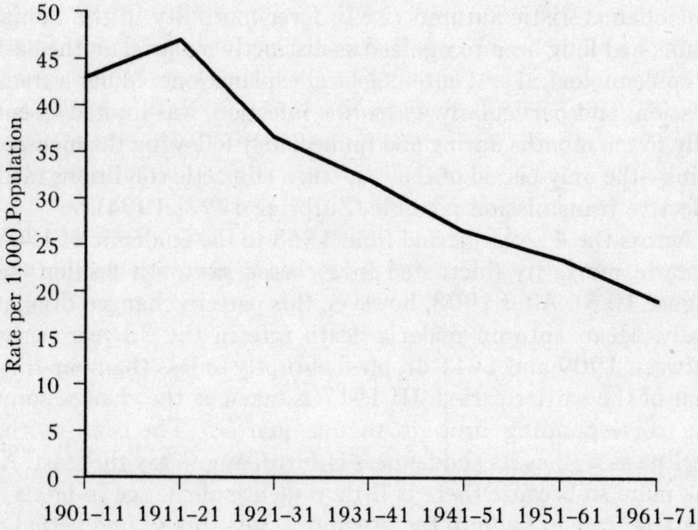

Source: Census of India 1901–71.

It is only in the last few years that the subject of mortality decline in the Indian subcontinent has begun to be addressed as a question meriting empirical analysis (Guha 1991; Guilmoto 1992).

Re-examining the History of Malaria Mortality Decline: The Case of Punjab

My observations in rural Tamil Nadu in the late seventies of the difficulties faced by communities in obtaining basic health care services made me skeptical of the medical technology thesis of mortality decline in India. This along with the fact that the DDT explanation for malaria mortality decline in India had never been subjected to empirical analysis, made me pursue research on South Asian health and epidemic history.

Malaria was considered a leading cause of death in the pre-1920 period. Punjab province became the regional focus for re-examining malaria mortality decline for pragmatic reasons. It is one of the few regions of South Asia where it is possible to identify with some degree of confidence malaria deaths from within the general category of fever deaths recorded in the colonial sanitary reports. The characteristic autumn rise in fever mortality in the Punjab plains had long been recognized as distinctly malarial on the basis of epidemiological and entomological explanations. Malaria transmission, and particularly *falciparum* infection, was limited essentially to the months during and immediately following the monsoon rains—the only period of the year when climactic conditions made effective transmission possible (Zurbrigg 1992, 1994).[3]

Across the 41-year period from 1868 to the epidemic of 1908, malaria mortality fluctuated in a classic sawtooth fashion (see Figure 10.5). After 1908, however, this pattern changed dramatically. Mean autumn malaria death rate in the 33-year period between 1909 and 1941 dropped abruptly to less than one-third that of the earlier period. (If 1917 is taken as the change point, the corresponding drop is to one-quarter.) The size of this decline as well as its suddenness is surprising to say the least. All the more so because there is little evidence of change in levels of malaria transmission in the province across this second period as reflected in spleen and parasite rates. There was no significant change in rainfall in the province nor substantial change in incidence of flooding across the 1868–1941 period. Indeed, post-monsoon prevalence of *falciparum* infection continued to rise to high levels in years of above-normal rains well into the thirties also (Zurbrigg, 1992, 1994, in preparation).

What appears to have changed after 1908 then was not the incidence of malaria infection in the province so much as its lethality, that is, the proportion of infected people dying from the infection—in epidemiological terms, a shift in case fatality rate. One explanation for declining lethality of malaria could be medical treatment. Yet per capita availability of quinine in the province was so low even by the late thirties, in particular for the rural areas, as to make this explanation extremely unlikely. By the late thirties, the amount of quinine distributed free or at

[3] I have used two different measures of annual malaria mortality. The first was simply the (autumn) October–December fever death rate per 1000 population. The second measure is simply the numerical difference between the autumn fever death rate and the spring–summer (April–July) fever death rate. This helps control non-malarial fever death rates included within the autumn data.

Figure 10.5
Malaria Mortality, Punjab, 1875–1940

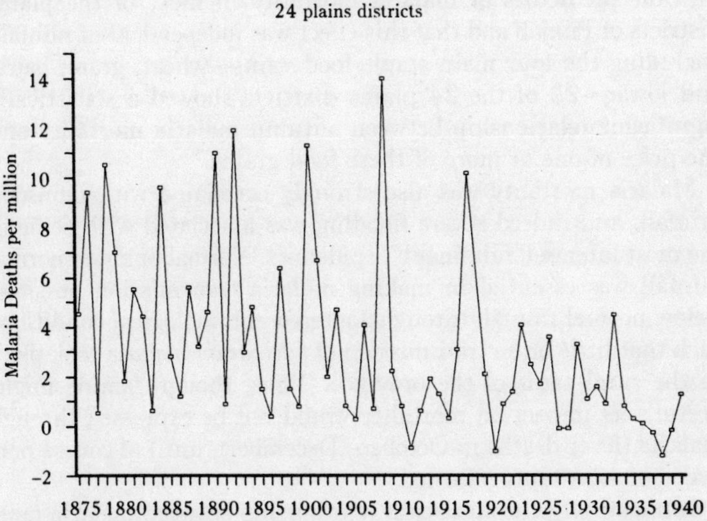

Source: *Ann. Sanitary Rpts.*, Punjab.
1918 omitted.
Malaria mortality calculated as Oct–Dec fever deaths minus Apr–July fever deaths × .75 per million. See Zurbrigg 1992.

subsidized rates through the public dispensaries and rural "depots" by the Punjab government amounted to only 1.1 grains per capita, annually. By comparison, the amount of chloroquine—roughly equivalent by weight to quinine—required to treat malaria today is 46 grains.[4] The one factor that did clearly change after 1908, on the other hand, was the incidence of famine.

Going back to the pre-1909 period of notorious malaria epidemics, all but one of the peaks in the 1868–1908 period were periods of either frank (officially-declared) famine or severe economic crisis, secondary to sudden massive grain exports. The one exception, the epidemic of 1876, was preceded by catastrophic floods in 1875, which had destroyed standing crops and prevented agricultural activities well into the subsequent year.

[4] Private sales of quinine amounted to a further 1.5 grains per capita, but because of the cost, it was beyond the reach of the large majority of the population. See Zurbrigg 1992, note 120.

Multiple regression analysis confirmed that for the 41-year period between 1868 and 1908, food grain price levels were significant predictors of malaria mortality in most of the plains districts of Punjab and that this effect was independent of rainfall. Including the four main staple foodgrains—wheat, gram, bajra, and jowar—22 of the 24 plains districts showed a statistically significant relationship between autumn malaria mortality and the price of one or more of these food grains.[5]

Malaria mortality was also strongly correlated with monsoon rainfall, and indeed severe flooding was associated with some of the most intense ("fulminant") epidemics. Normal or above normal rainfall was essential in making malaria transmission possible. Below normal rainfall (drought) altered entomological conditions such that little or no transmission of *falciparum* malaria took place in the rural areas of the province. Thus, though famine might prevail, its impact on mortality would not be expressed through malaria (fever deaths in October– December), until of course normal monsoon rains returned.

Interestingly, the statistical relationship between malaria mortality and rainfall remains equally strong after 1908 even as levels of mortality from these epidemics declined dramatically. Together these findings suggest that adequate rainfall was a necessary (entomologically) but not sufficient factor in explaining the severe (highly lethal) epidemics of the pre-1909 period. Indeed, highly destructive floods continued to occur after 1908 in years of exceptionally heavy rains. Yet they did not trigger epidemic mortality anywhere near the scale characteristic of the earlier period.

To what can we attribute this change in malaria mortality in Punjab? Malaria control activities of this period were extremely localized efforts, limited essentially to a few urban areas. Insofar as control efforts also included quinine distribution, the amounts

[5]Interesting regional differences in the impact of food grain prices and rainfall were apparent. In the south-eastern districts, where agriculture was primarily rain-dependent, wheat price was more consistently a predictor of autumn mortality than rainfall. The opposite pattern was the case in the north-central and western districts, where a much larger proportion of crops were protected by irrigation, either natural inundation from the Himalayas or well-irrigation. Here crop losses, unemployment, and starvation were triggered more by severe flooding in years of heavy rainfall than by drought.

involved were too inadequate to account for the decrease in mortality observed.[6] There were, on the other hand, major changes in famine relief policy, changes which have been documented in detail elsewhere (Zurbrigg 1996).

From palliative relief of established famine as set out in the initial 1883 famine code, relief policy after the turn of the century increasingly shifted to early, pre-emptive support of the agricultural economy before frank famine "had declared itself." The 1880 Famine Commission had restricted relief to only those years of exceptional (catastrophic) harvest failure. After 1908 however, drought relief became increasingly a policy of routine application at times of local harvest shortfall. From 1920 onward, relief also began to be sanctioned for crop losses due to flooding. Floods along the Jumna river in 1924–25, for example, occasioned Rs 2.9 million in agricultural loans and Rs 150,000 distributed as gratuitous relief. In 1928–29, the first account appears of the army being called in to distribute food and agricultural supplies in flooded districts (Punjab Administration 1929). Subsequent revisions to the Punjab famine code in 1930 made provision for relief simply on the basis of scarcity—by definition, whenever staple foodgrain prices rose 40 percent above normal levels.

The effect of these policy changes was to make relief available earlier and far more frequently, in effect, catching starvation with a finer, or to be more accurate, less coarse net. In other words, after 1908, there appears to have been a marked decrease in the frequency with which drought and/or floods proceeded on to economic collapse and epidemic starvation (famine).

Not too surprisingly in this context, the statistical relationship between food grain price levels and malaria mortality disappears after 1908. Relief however continued to be limited to periods of acute crisis, and thus prevalence of chronic hunger (undernourishment) and endemic acute hunger in the province probably

[6] As late as the thirties, there were numerous reports regarding the reluctance to give quinine to young children. To some extent this must also have included directing quinine supplies. Yet the total amount of quinine made available for free or subsidized distribution remained so low that it is difficult to conclude that access was anywhere near effective. Further, it seems quite unlikely that those most vulnerable—the poor and the young—would have had priority to those supplies at the village level.

Table 10.1
Mortality Trends in Ludhiana District, Punjab, 1930–60

	Crude Death Rate	*Infant Mortality Rate*	*Life Expectancy at Birth*
1930	40.9	237	25.5
1931	27.8	249	35.1
1932	25.0	170	38.3
1933	24.8	181	38.3
1934	28.8	191	34.5
1935	23.4	165	39.8
1936	22.3	185	41.5
1937	24.0	159	39.8
1938	23.3	142	40.8
1939	23.7	157	40.0
1940	27.4	175	36.2
1941	23.8	152	39.9
1942	30.3	192	33.3
1943	25.5	168	36.8
1944	23.3	143	39.5
1945	19.5	129	44.1
1946	19.3	172	44.0
1947	19.0	193	43.2
1948	12.5	129	52.8
1949	12.3	121	53.6
1950	15.2	125	49.1
1951	13.1	115	52.7
1952	13.1	126	52.8
1953	14.2	124	51.3
1954	11.7	109	56.2
1955	12.1	105	56.3
1956	13.6	116	54.0
1957	12.8	107	55.5
1958	13.6	116	54.2
1959	12.1	109	56.7
1960	12.6	115	55.6

Source: Dyson and M. Das Gupta (1996).

changed little during this period. Nevertheless, the impact of famine control—removing the tip of the hunger iceberg, so to speak—appears to have been profound with respect to lethality of malaria infection.

The impact on mortality—both crude death rates and malarial—of residual insecticide (DDT) spraying in India has never been

Figure 10.6
Crude Death Rate, Ludhiana District 1930–60

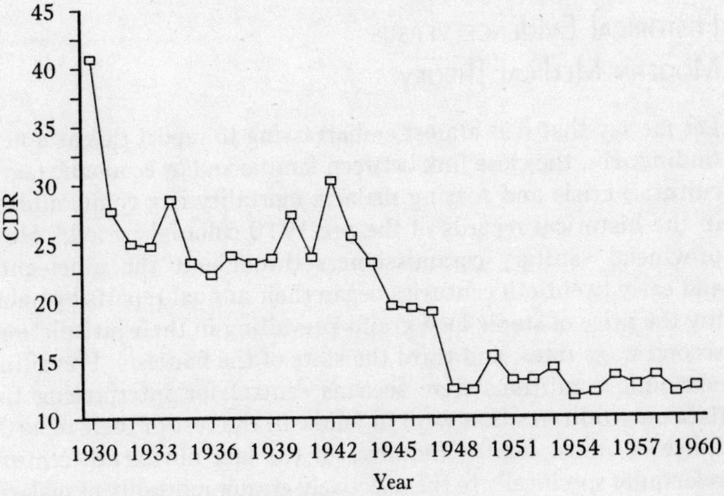

directly assessed. It has been difficult tracking down monthly vital registration data for Punjab districts during the forties and fifties, so I have been unable as yet to estimate actual malaria mortality trends across the period of the dramatic reduction in malaria transmission brought about in the early mid-fifties by mass application of residual insecticides (DDT). On the other hand, data on annual crude death rates are available from Census reports for individual districts. For Ludhiana district, Dyson and Das Gupta have traced crude death rates between 1881 and 1981 (Dyson and Das Gupta 1996) (see Table 10.1 and Figure 10.6). The major initial period of DDT spraying in the district took place across late 1953 and 1954. By 1955, malaria infection rates had come down markedly in the district (Mehta 1955). The impact of this near eradication of malarial infection in the district on crude death rate trends was modest to say the least, barely discernible in terms of overall crude death decline. Infant mortality for the district did show slight decline between 1952 and 1954–55, yet relative to the amount of decline already evident by 1950, this improvement was quite limited. What is also apparent from this series is that by 1948, well before residual insecticide malaria control efforts, average life expectancy in the district had already reached a level of over 50 years.[7]

Historical Evidence versus Modern Medical Theory

Let me say that it is almost embarrassing to report this as a new finding. For, the close link between famine and/or economic (agricultural) crisis and soaring malaria mortality is a commonplace in the historical records of the pre-1910 colonial period.[8] Most provincial sanitary commissioners throughout the nineteenth and early twentieth centuries began their annual reports by quoting the price of staple food grains prevailing in their jurisdiction; second wage rates, and third the state of the harvests. Prevailing economic conditions were seen as central for interpreting the data on vital rates that were to follow in the rest of their reports. Likewise, most famine inquiries of the late nineteenth century refer quite specifically to the selectively greater mortality of malaria among the starving. In effect, they were making the important distinction between infection on the one hand and mortality from that infection (lethality) on the other. This does not necessarily mean that most sanitary officials were unusually socially-conscious; they simply could not help noticing. One can find this relationship expressed in folkloric terms even more clearly, as Braudel has in the Tuscan proverb "The best cure for malaria is a full cooking pot."

Yet such a conclusion flies in the face of current medical and historical understanding of the relationship between nutritional

[7] Much research needs to be done in exploring the factors underlying the remarkable rise in physical survival in the immediate post-World War II years. It mirrors not only the celebrated pattern in Sri Lanka (also assumed incorrectly to be due to DDT), but that of many other developing countries. It may possibly be related to the transient economic boom and the related increase in employment among the primary producing (developing) countries, that was triggered by favorable terms of trade, in other words, economic factors. See Dyson and Murphy (1991).

[8] S.R. Christophers, one of the leading malariologists in colonial India, concluded his 120-page investigation of the 1908 epidemic in Punjab with the words "malaria only reaped the harvest prepared for it by famine" (Government of India 1911). His attempt to measure statistically the relationship between epidemic malaria mortality and scarcity (high food-grain prices) is what stimulated my own efforts in this direction.

status and malaria. For example, a recent major textbook on malaria suggests little, if any, role for malnutrition in enhancing malaria mortality, a view which is echoed in recent historical writing (Rotberg and Rabb 1985; Wernsdorfer and MacGregor 1988).

Much of the confusion, I believe, stems from conceptual confusion with respect to the term nutrition. The emergence of nutritional science in the earlier decades of the twentieth century replaced very specific and practical understandings of hunger in human experience with the unfortunate—and I might suggest euphemistic—term nutrition (and malnutrition). In the process, key distinctions between acute hunger (starvation) and chronic hunger (undernourishment) were effectively lost,[9] a distinction that any village laboring woman, if asked, could most precisely delineate.

To the extent that modern medical literature addresses the malaria–nutrition relationship, the focus, overwhelmingly, is on micro-nutrient deficiencies (qualitative issues of diet) and chronic hunger (malnutrition). Acute hunger (starvation) on the other hand is virtually absent, both conceptually and investigationally. In the absence of adequate terminology, these differences have been obscured with major interpretative problems arising.

During the course of the Sahelian famine, the Murrays observed that some children at the relief centers showed rising malaria parasite levels and fever once in receipt of relief feeding. They interpreted this as suggesting that the earlier period of starvation (acute hunger) protected the children from malaria and that starvation in general may protect from malaria and coined the term "refeeding malaria" to describe this observation. This thesis has been highly influential within both the medical and historical disciplines (Dyson 1991).

The protection thesis put forward by the Murrays is problematic in that it conflates severity of malaria infection as measured by malaria parasite levels, with lethality of malaria in terms of host survival rates. Their interpretation of protection was a microbiological one; no information was offered with respect to mortality rates or survival rates. It was assumed that lower parasite rates meant lower mortality. While this may be so in particular instances, such a relationship cannot be taken for granted necessarily nor

[9] For a discussion of the conceptual, biological, and epidemiological distinction between acute and chronic hunger see Zurbrigg 1997.

extended automatically to seriously altered host states such as starvation, where the suppressive effect on the human host of that star- vation may well exceed the suppressive effect on the micro-organisms. This "refeeding malaria" thesis confuses microbiological observations with epidemiological outcome. Second, the malaria observed during the Sahelian famine was not new infection, rather it was recrudescence of existing infection and hence unrepresentative of malaria epidemics of South Asian and most other historical famines.[10]

The Murrays as well as prominent malariologists cite also the 1943 Bengal famine as further evidence of the protective effect of starvation in malaria, in spite of the 1945 Famine Commission's observation that the starving succumbed far more readily to the disease in spite of the lower parasite levels and also were particularly unresponsive to medical treatment. It appears that the "re-feeding" malaria thesis has also influenced Elizabeth Whitcombe's recent study of late nineteenth-century Indian famines (Whitcombe 1993). She concludes that malaria mortality was primarily entomologically driven—a function of prodigious proliferation of anopheline mosquito vectors, and secondarily increased human exposure to these vectors because of famine-induced cattle mortality (deviation of mosquito feeding from cattle to humans). A role for starvation was dismissed with a single (unreferenced) comment that the relation of (malaria) infectivity to the nutritional status of the host is even today obscure.

All these speak volumes for the extraordinary power of the germ theory in shaping interpretation of human health/mortality experience. In the name of scientific explanations, what is offered is a highly selective application of scientific theory, one restricted to the microbiological domain—the germ/vector side of the epidemic equation. One could argue that it is equally scientific to be addressing the condition of the human host, assessing prevalence of acute hunger and its relationship to lethality of infection and soaring (epidemic) malaria mortality. A number of leading malariologists (such as Christophers, Bentley, and Ramakrishnan) attempted to do this in the early decades of this century.[11] There is another conflation here, namely, scientific is microbiological. In

[10] The potential significance of this distinction was highlighted in the research by S.P. Ramakrishna 1953, 1954.

[11] See notes 8 and 10.

the nineties, germ explanations are somehow much more credible than socio-economic ones. This is so even though Whitcombe's theses of prodigious vectors or cattle deviation remain entirely in the theoretical realm. Remarkably, no attempt whatsoever is made to provide supportive evidence with, say, some kind of cattle mortality data. Nor does the theory explain the malaria mortality decline post-1920 or for that matter other severe famine-related malaria epidemics, such as that in the Bengal famine, where climactic or cattle mortality-vector deviation explanations are not possible even theoretically. Any microbiological hypothesis, no matter how unsubstantiated empirically, is better (more credible) it seems, than a social explanation. Such is the power of the microbiological explanation (Zurbrigg 1997). All the extremely rich, credible, and consistent historical evidence is dismissed, consigned to the dustbin of history, in the thesis that starvation offered relative protection from malaria. Not only historians, but even leading economists have been bamboozled by this reductionist germ theory. For instance, Bagchi has observed, "fall in (South Asian) mortality...was caused not by a rise in private living standards nor even by an improvement in public health facilities and sanitation. It seems rather to have been caused by spectacular advances in the medical technology for controlling such bacterial diseases as malaria, smallpox and cholera" (Bagchi 1982).

Whitcombe is correct that modern medical research suggests little evidence of a synergistic relationship between malnutrition and malaria. The question remains: how representative is this research of the historical experience of famine and malaria? As we have seen, malaria-nutrition research has focused on micronutrient deficiencies and to a limited extent undernourishment (chronic hunger); acute hunger on the other hand is largely missing. Thus, conceptual limitations of modern epidemiological theory make interpretation of historical health and mortality experience problematic. The error lies not in referring to modern medical theory, but rather in deferring to such theory to the exclusion of historical experience and inquiry.

While much more empirical analysis is needed, still, these preliminary observations suggest that the medical technology view of South Asian health history needs a great deal of rethinking. It appears that the main decline in malaria mortality, at least in Punjab, predates DDT.

Is this to suggest that malaria parasites are irrelevant to public health as long as one has access to two square meals a day? Or that there was no more hunger (chronic or acute) in Punjab by the fifties? Clearly not. Malaria infection, particularly *falciparum* malaria, has an inherent lethality which is by no means inconsequential (even with a full stomach). Many, perhaps thousands of young children in Ludhiana district and elsewhere in the country were spared malarial deaths in the fifties through the control program based on residual insecticides. It simply means that the number of deaths prevented was very small relative to the toll exacted historically by the disease when combined with recurrent epidemic starvation. Similarly, it is not that public health in the narrow nineteenth-century Chadwickian sense of germ control is unimportant.

The issue here is that of framing of health history debate in oppositional terms, between nutrition (hunger) and public health (disease exposure), and creating a false dichotomy where none exists.

Re-thinking Public Health

We can get glimpses in twentieth-century health experience of the continuing importance of access to food. For, the issue of hunger is by no means limited only to epidemic starvation (famine). Child mortality in Sri Lanka increased in 1974, a result of soaring international food grain prices in 1973–74 and consequent disruptions in the national program of food subsidies. Infant mortality rose 44 percent (from about 97 to 144 per 1000 live births) with post-neonatal death rate rising by 250 percent (from 30 to 76 deaths per 1000 live births). There was little if any change in health care or sanitation, making it difficult to explain the mortality increase except in nutritional (hunger) terms (Isenman 1980; Meegama 1980). Another study on British civilian life expectancy trends across the decades of the two World Wars showed an unprecedented rise of seven years (see Table 10.2). This was so in spite of: (*i*) a tremendous increase in urban crowding (and presumably greater exposure to air-borne infection) during the war years; (*ii*) a reduction in medical services (half of all doctors and nurses in Britain

Table 10.2
Longevity Expansion in England and Wales

Decade	*Increase in Life Expectancy per Decade (years)*	
	Male	*Female*
1901–11	4.1	4.0
1911–21	6.6	6.5
1921–31	2.3	2.4
1931–40	1.2	1.5
1940–51	6.5	7.0
1951–60	2.4	3.2

Source: Dreze and Sen 1989.

during World War I being recruited into military service); and (*iii*) the 1918 influenza epidemic. Death rates fell most among the working class across World War I (Winter 1986). These were periods marked by dramatic increases in many forms of government support, including public employment, food price control, and food rationing, which ens ured access to basic foods.

Endemic starvation was, and still is, also extremely important. Households slip into destitution through sudden loss of work, illness, or death of individual "breadwinners." Then there is the enormous prevalence of chronic hunger (undernourishment) which takes such a toll on young children and is intimately linked with conditions of women's work, conditions which preclude adequate feeding and care of themselves and their children, including those *in utero*.

Health analysis in the nineties is by no means immune to the reductionist germ theory. The fact that the above examples are only "glimpses" reflects the fact that modern health analysis has abjectly failed to pursue, measure, or assess the impact of shifts in hunger, both acute and chronic, on mortality trends.[12]

[12] One important exception to this has been the modest on-going survey by the National Institute of Nutrition, tracing undernourishment (weight-for-age) among children under five. IIowever, there has been little analysis of the relationship between the dramatic decline in prevalence of "severe malnutrition" in states like Kerala and plummeting child mortality. (Regrettably, recent cutbacks appear to be putting current survey reliability at jeopardy.)

"Nutrition" is considered at most secondary to modern medical techniques of disease control as a factor in falling mortality and is simply ignored as an issue. This is parallel to mid-nineteenth century Europe, where the pre-Chadwickian understanding of the importance of factors such as unemployment, destitution, and hunger in explaining epidemic mortality "was not something that could be disproved. It could be ignored, as the questions preoccupying medical inquirers shifted from a focus on the lives and well-being of individuals to general questions about the presence of particular diseases in particular populations, and as questions arose of what were the most easily taken public actions that could make a significant difference in the incidence of disease" (Hamlin 1992).

Does this mean that medical care is not a priority for the poor? That they can only be interested in economic concerns, in filling their stomachs and those of their children? Once again, this sets up an entirely false dichotomy. This "preventive" and "curative services" dichotomy is as false as that between economic (food) security and medical care. Public health care technology becomes problematic only when offered to the exclusion of broader socio-economic policies and reforms, when offered as a technical fix, that is, as a substitute for economic (food) security.

There can be little doubt that access to basic curative medical care saves lives, and thus is of extraordinary importance to the concerned individuals and households. All citizens have an absolute right to basic health and medical care. Under existing levels of poverty and economic inequality, this right of access is of even greater importance for those living near or below the poverty line (viz. bare subsistence). It is because of:

1. the far greater morbidity and risk of death from ordinary diseases that they and their children face, a risk which is a direct and immediate function of high rates of undernourishment. It is well-documented that Indian children in severe undernourishment have a ten- to twelve-fold greater risk of dying than those of standard weight and growth like our own (Kielman and McCord 1978). This far greater sickness and mortality risk means of course a correspondingly greater need for curative care and food than for the elite in society; and

2. the catastrophic economic impact of even non-lethal illness among those living at or below bare subsistence levels. Inability to work even for a few days throws households into economic crisis. I have come across the not infrequent phenomenon of suicide in rural Tamil Nadu among men suffering from tuberculosis. Such decisions can be explained by the insupportable economic burden of incapacity (a non-contributing mouth to feed) for the household.

This argument applies equally to preventive public health services—clean water, sewage disposal, etc. The morbidity and mortality costs of inadequate services are so much higher for the poor, again, because of hunger-compromised resistance to disease in general and because they cannot hope to buy their way out of the failure of basic public services through bottled mineral water and the like. These observations are self-evident, yet perhaps important to stress in the context of historical research, which suggests an overwhelming role for hunger and shifts in food security in explaining mortality decline in India. Just because acute hunger appears to have been of such import for malaria lethality does not mean malaria treatment and prevention are not important public health issues today. They most certainly are important for the poor, for apart from saving individual lives, malaria morbidity and incapacity represent a serious economic (i.e., hunger and ultimately, health) cost for the poor.

We can see the centrality of larger socio-economic issues to health even in the so-called affluent West. Among industrialized countries, it is increasingly clear that mortality levels and life expectancy are predicted not by per capita levels of wealth (GNP) and per capita health expenditures. By far the strongest predictor is distribution of income, that is, economic inequality. Those countries where wealth is distributed most equitably (or least inequitably) are those with the highest life expectancy levels (namely, lowest premature mortality rates) (Wilkinson 1994). It has recently been estimated that if economic inequality in Britain were to be reduced to levels prevailing in Sweden, life expectancy could be expected to increase by two full years—representing a fall in premature deaths annually in the range of tens of thousands throughout society. This would be cost-effective health economics and make the World Bank's head spin.

Figure 10.7
Mean Heights of 7-year-old Boys of High (•) and Low (○) Socio-economic Status in Various Developing Countries

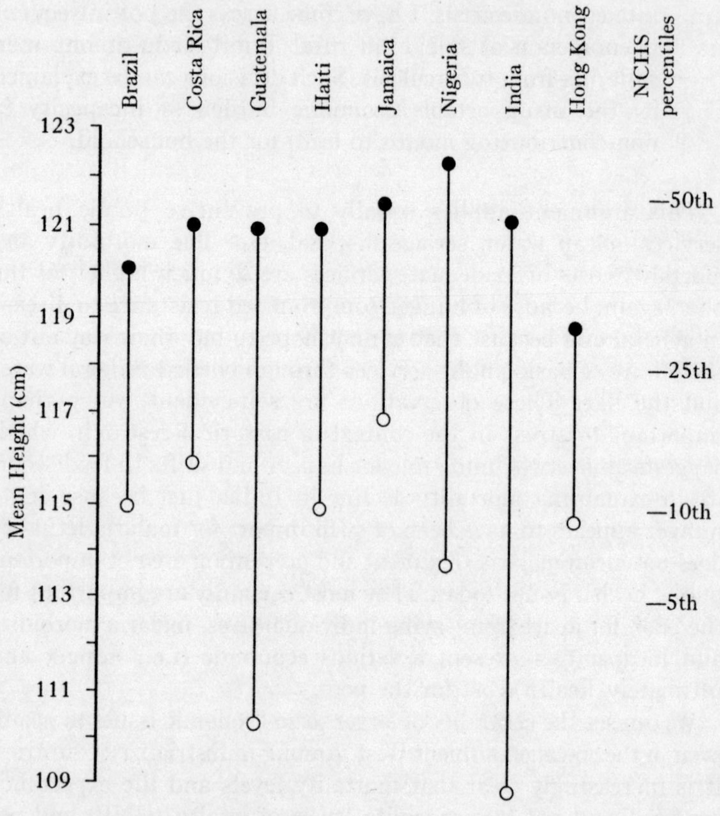

Source: Martorell and Habicht 1986.

Investing in Health

The World Bank's health report (World Bank 1993) is perhaps the most prominent example of current reductionist health analysis. Within the extraordinary maze of DALYs calculations, the subject of food merits only several sentences in the entire report, with reference to food security programs. Here again, it is qualified—rather tainted—with the suggestion that food subsidies are often not "cost-effective." Except for frank famine, a role for government intervention in food security policies as central health policy is largely overlooked. Similarly, a recent UNICEF analysis of the causes of child undernourishment in India focuses primarily on the cultural issues, the social devaluation of women (UNICEF 1996). As important as this issue is, one might never know from the study that there is a single female domestic servant, construction worker, or agricultural laborer in India. Women's work, waged and unwaged, is invisible, and thus also the conditions of that work—conditions which so utterly preclude adequate feeding and care of their children and themselves. Alongside pulse polio targets, where are, for example, targets for minimum wage implementation, village creches, rural fair price shops, labor legislation for female domestic servants, etc.? Likewise, nowhere are data presented on the extraordinary class differentials in birth weight, "nutritional"/hunger stunting (see Figure 10.7). Like hunger, it seems, conditions of laboring women's work is something not talked about in polite company. It is only the end result—the clinical state, "malnutrition" with the societal dimensions removed so to speak—that qualifies for discussion.

The point is that addressing these questions, of food, work, and other broader socio-economic parameters is public health, but of a kind not generally found in modern textbooks. It would be "public health" in the earlier and broader pre-Chadwickian understanding.

References

Bagchi, A.K. (1982): *The Political Economy of Underdevelopment*. Cambridge: Cambridge University Press.

Davis, K., and **Bernstam, S.** (eds.) (1991): *Resources, Environment and Population*. New York: Oxford University Press. p. 16.

Dreze, J., and **Sen, A.** (1989): *Hunger and Public Action*. Oxford: Oxford University Press.

Dyson, T. (1991): On the Demography of South Asian Famines. *Population Studies*, 4: 5–25, 279–97.

Dyson, T., and **Das Gupta, M.** (1996): Mortality Trends in Ludhiana District, Punjab 1881–1981. Paper read at the IUSSP Conference on Asian Demographic History, January, Taipei.

Dyson, T., and **Murphy, M.** (1991): Macro-level Study of Socio-economic Development and Mortality: Adequacy of Indicators and Methods of Statistical Analysis. In J. Cleland and A. Hill (eds.). *The Health Transition: Methods and Measures*. Health Transition Series, No. 3. Canberra: Australian National University.

Fogel, R. (1992): *Second Thoughts on European Escape from Hunger: Famines, Chronic Malnutrition and Mortality Rates*. In S.R. Osmani: *Nutrition and Poverty*. Oxford: Oxford University Press.

Government of India (1911): *Malaria in the Punjab. Scientific Memoirs by Officers of the Medical and Sanitary Departments of the Government of India*. New Series, No. 46. Calcutta: Superintendent, Government Printing.

——— (1901–71): *Census of India*.

Guha, S. (1991): Mortality Decline in Early Twentieth Century in India. *Indian Economic and Social History Review*, 28: 371–87.

——— (1994): The Importance of Social Intervention in England's Mortality Decline: The Evidence Reviewed. *Social History of Medicine*, 7(1)(April): 89–113.

Guilmoto, C.Z. (1992): Towards a New Demographic Equilibrium: The Inception of Demographic Transition in South India. *Indian Economic and Social History Review*, 29: 247–89.

Hamlin, C. (1992): Predisposing Causes and Public Health in Early Nineteenth-Century Medical Thought. *Society for the Social History of Medicine*, 5(1) (April): 43–70.

Isenman, I. (1980): Basic Needs: The Case of Sri Lanka. *World Development, 10*: 237–58.

Kielman, A., and **McCord, C.** (1978): Weight-for-Age as an Index of Death in Children. *Lancet*, 1: 1247–50.

Livi-Bacci, M. (1991): *Population and Nutrition: An Essay on European Demographic History*. Cambridge: Cambridge University Press.

Martorell, R., and **Habicht, J.P.** (1986): Growth in Early Childhood in Developing Countries. In F. Falkner and J.M. Tanner (eds.): *Human Growth*. New York: Plenum Press.

McKeown, T. (1976): *The Modern Rise of Population*. London: E. Arnold.

——— (1979): *The Role of Medicine: Dream, Mirage or Nemesis*? New Jersey: Princeton University Press.

Meegama, S. (1980): Infant and Child Mortality in the (Sri Lankan) Estates. Scientific Reports, No. 8, World Fertility Survey, International Statistical Institute. pp. 38–55.

Mehta, D.R. (1955): Malaria Control in the Punjab (India) with Special Reference to the National Malaria Control Programme. *Indian Journal of Malariology*, 9(4): 327–42.

Post, J.D. (1985): *Food Shortage, Climactic Variability and Epidemic Disease in Pre-industrial Europe*. Ithaca: Cornell University Press.

Punjab Administration (1929): *Punjab Land Revenue Administration Report*. Punjab: Government Printing.

Ramakrishna, S.P. (1953, 1954): *Indian Journal of Malariology*, 7: 53–59, 8: 89–96, 8: 327–32.

Rotberg, R.I., and **Rabb, T.K.** (eds.) (1985): *Hunger and History*. Cambridge: Cambridge University Press.

UNICEF (1996): *Progress of Nations*. New York: UNICEF.

Visaria, P., and **Visaria, L.** (1994): Demographic Transition. *Economic and Political Weekly*, 29(51): 3281.

Wernsdorfer, W.H., and **MacGregor, I.** (eds.) (1988): *Malaria: Principles and Practice of Malariology*. Vol. 1. Edinburgh: Churchill Livingstone, 763.

Whitcombe, E. (1993): Famine Mortality. *Economic and Political Weekly*, 28(23): 1169–79.

Wilkinson, R. (1994): Health, Re-distribution and Growth. In A. Glyn and D. Miliband (eds.). *Paying for Inequality: The Economic Cost of Social Injustice*. London: IPPR/Rivers Oram Press.

Winter, J.M. (1986): *The Great War and the British People*. Harvard: Harvard University Press.

World Bank (1993): *World Development Report: Investing in Health.* New York: Oxford University Press.

Wylie, D. (1989): The Changing Face of Hunger in Southern African History. *Past and Present*, (122)(February): 160.

Zurbrigg, S. (1992): Hunger and Epidemic Malaria in Punjab, 1868–1920. *Economic and Political Weekly*, 27(4): PE2–PE26.

——— (1994): Re-thinking the "Human Factor" in Malaria Mortality: The Case of Punjab, 1868–1940. *Parassitologia*, 36: 121–35.

——— (1996): Evolution of Colonial Famine Policy in South Asia, 1880–1940. Paper presented at the IUSSP Conference on Asian Historical Demography, January, Taipei.

——— (1997): Did Starvation Protect from Malaria? Distinguishing Between Severity and Lethality of Infectious Disease in Colonial India. *Social Science History*, 21(1)(Spring): 45–79.

——— *Hunger in India's Epidemic History*. In press.

11

Biological Stress and History from Below: The Millet Zone of India 1970–92

Lalita Chakravarty

Study of biological stress signals helps to construct history from below. In this chapter, an attempt has been made to interpret biological stress signals and their evolution over three decades in a country like India, where mass poverty has been, and still is, written large.

The millet zone of India (Gujarat, Karnataka, Maharashtra, and Rajasthan) was studied over the period from 1970 to 1992. This zone suffered from repeated famines, big as well as small, throughout the last decade of the nineteenth century (Maharatna 1996a). Biological stress signals of heightened mortality rates in the populace of a particular administrative area would be accompanied by a fall in conception rates. Birth rate would also fall as crop failure due to droughts hit the area. Famines would be declared, generally later than the appearance of early warnings of "slump" in agricultural activity and employment; death-toll would rise from month to month; there would be relief camps for dislocated communities which, in turn, would be victims of epidemics. The catastrophe would take its toll, both in terms of the dead as well as in terms of those who failed to be born. Agricultural dislocation due to "slump" would, however, abate and disappear when monsoon rains reappeared. The present story of biological stress signals begins in the early seventies in the millet zone, with exactly such a scenario of "slump" famines,[1] as marked by the two signals,

[1] There are two types of entitlement failure in the literature, i.e., a failure of entitlement caused by lack of employment and a failure of entitlement due to fall in real purchasing power. "Slump famines" refer to the first whereas "boom famines" refer to the second. This chapter discusses situations of short-term entitlement failure though trend factors are working in favor of "food security" (Dreze et al. 1995).

namely, heightened mortality rates and a dip in the birth rate, adjusted for a nine-month lead. As the story proceeded to the early nineties, "slump" famine was replaced by "boom famine" of much smaller magnitude. Evolution of many institutions in the intervening period has also taken place.

I

To build the story around biological stress signals we need the following six presuppositions:

1. Heightened mortality and depressed fertility of a short duration are easily discernible from random fluctuations if appropriate statistical tests are applied. These statistical tests are stated under sign tests and simultaneity criteria as far as mortality indicators are concerned; sign tests for fertility indicators (FI) are briefly stated in section II.
2. There is inequality in death between the poor and the nonpoor and between the two sexes. The former was commented upon by Pressant while discussing mortality patterns in different countries of Western Europe during industrial revolution in the respective countries. We shall not dwell upon it here. It is one of the basic assumptions and is related to assumptions regarding micro units that are listed as fifth and sixth assumptions.
3. Men are responsible for the material reproduction scheme of an agrarian society and women for the biological reproduction scheme.[2] As we shall connect heightened mortality rates to "entitlement failure," either through employment failure or through depression of real wages or of real earnings in

[2] It can be shown with the help of N.S.S. data that, to date, men and women of this subcontinent are differentially "responsible" for two different reproduction schemes. Men are entitled to rewards for being responsible for "work" and thus keeping the material reproduction scheme going. Women are responsible for keeping the biological reproduction scheme going and thus are not "primary workers." If we analyze a set of three dualities, namely, the duality of primary versus secondary worker, the duality of labor market exchange versus household (reciprocity mode) exchange, and the duality of ownership rights to the material means of production versus usufruct rights only, then we can see that the first claim of higher entitlement as a primary worker, busy in the labor market and free to own, are men and men only. This note summarizes earlier work by the present author (Chakravarty 1991; Agarwal 1994).

kind, our main focus will be on mortality pattern of men. Mortality signals of the two genders (M for men and F for females) rather than on fertility signal (FI) will be discussed in section II. Infant mortality (I) and heightened mortality of children (C) will be brought in as corroborative evidence only but will not be the central focus.[3]

4. The event of entitlement failure precedes epidemiological outbreaks in the post-independence India, when old killers like cholera or smallpox have been brought under control and new killers like endemic tuberculosis, AIDS, or hepatitis B have not given rise to new outbreaks of epidemics. In the period of stagnant health transition in a poor country, the main culprit need not be any particular disease and need not even be declared "starvation death." A host of endemic diseases flare up when there are "gaps" or even prolonged periods of "reduced caloric intakes," and the attrition rate rises (Fogel 1989, 1994; McKeown 1976; Zurbrigg 1992, 1994).
5. This presupposition is regarding micro units that suffer attrition. Consumption loan or consumption grant (CLG) is essential in many agronomic tracts where dry spells, if prolonged beyond the usual three months of pre-monsoon inactive period, mean starvation for the casual agricultural laborers. Dreze (1995) has shown that other occupational groups that are in poverty or even those which are relatively better off also suffered a precipitous drop in calorie intake in 1972–73, when large tracts of Maharashtra were in the grip of severe drought and crop failure. It is assumed here that the lower strata of these groups of "poor" do need consumption loan and/or grant when entitlement fails due to "slump" in activity. It is further implied that if

[3] Women in the reciprocity mode, working as "helpers" or secondary workers only, are worse sufferers under conditions of biological stress in the sense that they are hit first by intensified hunger and prolonged "gaps" in calorie intake as and when the "shock" begins. If the shock is inflationary price rise, they suffer longer than men. Indices of "fertility failure" are thus important for the study of gender-differentiated biological stress. We have not brought in either the data or relevant analysis in this chapter. As far as infant and child mortality are concerned, these indices have been thoroughly discussed and used by Maharatna (1996a, 1996b).

inflationary price rise of food grains reduces the real value of money wages, then also consumption grant/loan is required to prevent rise in attrition rates. This second scenario, however, may be different from the first "slump" scenario. The second scenario means "boom" for members of the upper strata of rural and agricultural occupations who can sell some marketable surplus. Two necessary conditions for entitlement failure are: (*i*) geographical boundary of both labor circulation and commodity circulation is narrow and the same; and (*ii*) there is no institutional support to the base of real agriculture wages.

6. This assumption is regarding adjustment between price rise, wage rise and the length of the CLG period. Though the exante length of the period of CLG is essentially dependent on the rate of inflation (or duration of "slump" in case of droughts), the ex post length of the duration of CLG is equal to the wage-price adjustment lag for local casual agricultural laborer. These assumptions regarding "entitlement failure" in the context of "boom" in agriculture, as well as in the context of slump induced by natural calamity are essential for "mortality" signals. These assumptions go well with the long-term trends in India where real wages have not deteriorated in spite of steady inflationary pressure on food prices, and in spite of the fact that agriculture and rural territory sector have emerged as labor-sinks. Entitlement failure in any geographical area and drying up of CLG due to institutional failures are two necessary conditions for linking deep poverty and biological stress signals.

II

Basic data used here are age-specific mortality rates (ASMRs) published by Vital Statistics Department (Office of the Registrar General of India) in their periodic bulletins, Sample Registration Survey (SRS) Data. These data can be arranged in a matrix, where the rows give annual mortality rates for ages 10 to 70+, given in five-year age brackets. Infant and children mortality as separate age-cohorts are ignored. These last two, however, enter the last reading of the row, where "all age" mortality is given. Thus there are 14 readings of "mortality rates" in any row pertaining to any calendar year. Any column of this matrix, however, gives a time series covering 1970 to 1992. Marking peaks between two lower readings and reading along any one column will give the nature of random fluctuations in any one of these 14 columns, as peaks defined in this way are also "turning points" (Nagar and Das 1990). Tests for random fluctuation do indicate that each one of these 14 time series is full of random elements, much more so than standard mortality data of advanced countries would show.

There is, however, a qualitative test, "sign test" in short, which can be performed on the rows of this matrix to test whether some calendar years are full of random peaks and thus qualitatively different, i.e., qualitatively worse than the adjacent years. Moreover, by fixing a carefully-chosen base year and sliding it down the period 1970–92, any current year (t) may be compared to the "base value" and tested for "mortality signal," as contrasted to random elements in both the years. This is basically "indexing by shifting base" to take care of the trend factor.

Ten or more "peaks" out of 14 readings in a row pass the sign test at 10 percent and 5 percent significance level. This is a "strong result" according to our method of detecting any one year of biological crisis. However, we do take into account nine peaks as "weak result." But they do demand attention because of some specificity of the grouped data that could be discussed under "cohort effect."[4]

We could do this test on adult male mortality only to isolate years of "biological stress" and then look for causative factors. In

[4] An age cohort (x+4) in period (t) may suffer and lose some members due to stress in this period and carry forward some who are morbid and also near the upper end of the age limit (x+4). Thus, a heightened mortality at t in age group (25–29) may get carried forward to (t+1) in age-group (30–34). Therefore, there is often high degree of co-relation between two adjacent columns in the vicinity of crisis periods in age-groups 30 to 40 years. Adjacent rows, however, go through a process of adjustment immediately after a crisis period which may be explained in terms of new entrants of better health status entering a particular age-group. New entrants may also have different relative weightage between "poor" and "non-poor." The two attributes, "health" and "poverty" are of course highly correlated by one basic presupposition of this chapter. Net result is that after a peak in period (t) in age group (x+4), there is a relative dip in period (t+1) for the same age-group. This very often goes a long way in giving a "weak" sign test for a calendar year that follows a crisis period.

order to give more substance to the idea of biological stress at a particular point of time, we supplement male mortality signal (M) by female mortality signal (F) and female infant mortality (I) as well as female child (0–4 years) mortality (C). Thus if simultaneously four groups of data, male, female, infants, and children show higher than contemporaneous mortality rates, then we get a "complete stress signal." However, some of the groups, such as children, infants, or young mothers may not show stress as they are target groups for policy measures. We then get incomplete stress signals. It is obvious that various combinations of "strength"and "completeness," or their absence, are possible and may be found to be interesting as "leads" to causal factors.

A third aspect of this "stress mortality signal" is to do with the downward time trend in Indian mortality data, though the present data-set would rather not be subjected to parametric time-trend analysis. If we choose a fixed base, any normal year, for comparing a crisis year mortality then we get an idea regarding the comparative severity of the crisis. If we shift the "base" from 1970 to 1980 and then to 1990, we get some idea of de-trended short-term fluctuations. This is like a fixed-base index, whereas the other method is like a chain-base index. A crisis year can be isolated by any one of these two methods, but due to strong trend factors in mortality, stress signals of the eighties and the nineties come into sharp focus when "fixed-base year" is recent or when chain-base method is used. Although no difference has been made between the two methods in the tables given here, it will be relevant to keep the above factors in mind. The distress signals of the 1991–92 period are far below the attrition rates of the early seventies. This is "trend effect."

We have described the tests for "mortality stress signal." A crisis year that is noted for biological stress must also indicate a fall in birth rate, adjusted for a nine-month lead in conception index. All the SRS bulletins give crude birth rate, total fertility rate for rural areas and total fertility rate for urban and rural areas combined {CBR, TFR(R), and TFR}. If all the three indices show a temporary dip then fertility indices are moving in the same direction and FI is clear. If, however, CBR gets disjunct from TFR, say, due to rising net reproduction rate and/or due to quick replacement births, then the fertility indicator is giving an enigmatic response and we take due note of it.

Table 11.1
Gujarat: Stress Signals, Mortality Behavior, and Causal Variables

(1)	*(2)*	*(3)*	
Years of "Stress"	*Drought*	*AGCLPI (3A)*	*Increase (3B)*
1970**			
1971	D/P		
1972	D/T		
1973**W			
1974	D/T	24	–9
1975**WA		dx	–dx
1976		–17	dx
1977		dx	dx
1978		dx	12
1979		7	10
1980		10	12
1981(*) W		16	dx
1982	D/T	dx	11
1983* AW		12	dx
1984	D/P	dx	11
1985	D/P	dx	dx
1986	D/T	dx	13
1987	D/T	10	dx
1988**A		dx	dx
1989		16	12
1990		12	24
1991		17	dx
1992*W		20	dx
1993			dx

Source: Government of India 1970–93.

We may now turn to the adjoining tables. When mortality stress signal is complemented by fertility drop, we put two stars against that year to show that full biological stress is indicated. If fertility signal is enigmatic, then we put only one star, i.e., only the mortality signal indicates some kind of biological stress. However, the mortality signal itself can be weak (W) when either M or F (male or female mortality) does not cross 10 peaks, and is short by one reading. If the mortality signal is incomplete, either due to absence of any one or two of its four components, which happens very often with I and/or C, then that absence is indicated by the letter A next to the stars. Although emphasis has been given to mortality stress signal, it has been considered important to complete the picture of stress as borne by women by marking out those years when both

Table 11.2
Karnataka: Stress Signals, Mortality Behavior, and Causal Variables

(1)	*(2)*	*(3)*	
Years of "Stress"	*Drought*	*AGCLP (3A)*	*Increase (3B)*
1970			
1971			
1972**W	D/P		
1973			
1974		24	–dx
1975*A		dx	–dx
1976*WA	D/P	–12	0
1977**W		dx	–dx
1978		–dx	dx
1979		11	19
1980		15	17
1981		24	–dx
1982	D/P	–dx	15
1983		14	dx
1984*WA		0	0
1985	D/P	0	0
1986	D/P	–dx	11
1987		10	20
1988		20	dx
1989		12	dx
1990	D/P	dx	25
1991**A		19	–13
1992*A		23	–dx

Source: Government of India 1970–93.

M and F are "weak," but fertility crisis is very strongly indicated. This is indicated by one star within brackets.

Turning to the causal factors we come to examine two of these, namely, drought that may be total or partial (D/T and D/P) [5] and inflation rate as reflected in consumer price index for agricultural laborers—CPIAL, annual rise in two complementary calculations (as in Chandak's series, who uses financial year—April to March—averages, or alternatively, agricultural year averages—July to June—lagged forward one period), as given in columns

[5] Data were supplied by S.R. Sikka, Director of the Meteorological Division, at the request of Prof R. Ramaswami of the Centre of Physical Sciences, Jawaharlal Nehru University, New Delhi. Mean rainfall is calculated for twenty years and negative standard deviation is "drought." If all agro-climactic regions are affected, then it is total drought (D/T); otherwise it is D/P.

Table 11.3
Maharashtra: Stress Signals, Mortality Behavior, and Causal Variables

(1)	*(2)*	*(3)*	
Years of "Stress"	*Drought*	*AGCLP (3A)*	*Increase (3B)*
1970			
1971	D/P		
1972**A	D/P		
1973(*)AW			
1974	D/P		
1975			
1976			
1977**A	D/P		
1978			
1979			
1980			
1981	D/P	20	–
1982		–	13
1983		+	dx
1984*AW	D/P	+	dx
1985	D/P	+	dx
1986	D/P	–	–
1987	D/P	dx	dx
1988		dx	dx
1989		20	dx
1990		dx	33
1991**		27	dx
1992*AW		17	–dx

Source: Government of India 1970–93.

3A and 3B.[6] When annual point to point rise is between 5 and 9 points only, dx has been put in the columns.

It is clear from the above tables that till 1977 natural disaster like drought produced mortality signal in all the four states of the millet zone. This was the period of "slump little famines." A new phase begins from 1980–81, when mortality signals start becoming weak and incomplete.[7] Definitely, they do not appear

[6] H.L. Chandak's series can be obtained from CMIE 1994. The agricultural year averages have been provided by Abhijit Sen of School for Social Sciences, Jawaharlal Nehru University, New Delhi.

[7] There is an exhaustive official literature on various "public works" programmes. For unofficial but exhaustive research work one may consult Dev (1996) and Dev, Parikh, and Suryanarayanan 1994.

Table 11.4
Rajasthan: Stress Signals, Mortality Behavior, and Causal Variables

(1)	*(2)*	*(3)*	
Years of "Stress"	*Drought*	*AGCLP (3A)*	*Increase (3B)*
1970			
1971			
1972*A	D/T		
1973**			
1974	D/P	33	–21
1975		–10	–dx
1976**AW		–17	+37
1977		21	–dx
1978		–dx	+14
1979	D/T	dx	+18
1980		19	dx
1981**AW		12	–dx
1982	D/T	–dx	+dx
1983	D/T	+dx	11
1984**W		+dx	11
1985		16	–dx
1986	D/T	–dx	17
1987	D/T	–dx	14
1988**		25	+dx
1989		13	14
1990		13	16
1991**AW		dx	dx
1992*AW		dx	17

Source: Government of India 1970–93.

as and when droughts are declared. If at all mortality rises, as it does in the state of Rajasthan, then it is with a lag when "relief" to drought is dismantled (as in 1981 and 1988). Double stars do appear, indicating a full biological crisis in 1991 in the states of Karnataka, Maharashtra, and Rajasthan; Gujarat followed suit in a weaker way in 1992 when poverty index rose in all states and also for all-India level.

What are the factors that may account for this sudden reappearance of mortality signal? It was not price rise alone. The floor value of wages collapsed as all "public works" were stopped under SAP and no other institutional support for consumption loan or grant (CLG) replaced the older institutional support. In short, the evolutionary process of better crisis management was reversed by SAP in 1991–92.

References

Agarwal, B. (1994): *A Field of One's Own: Gender and Land Rights in South Asia.* Cambridge South Asian Studies. New Delhi: Oxford University Press.

Center for Monitoring Indian Economy (CMIE) (1994): India: The Economy. Mumbai: Economic Intelligence Service.

Chakravarty, L. (1991): Agrarian Economies and Demographic Regimes in India 1951–81. In J. Breman and S. Mundle (eds.). *Rural Transformation in Asia*. New Delhi: Oxford University Press.

Dev, M. (1996): Food Security: PDS versus EGS—A Tale of States. *Economic and Political Weekly*, 31(27): 1752–64.

Dev, M., Parikh, K., and **Suryanarayanan, M.H.** (1994): India. In M.G. Quibria (ed.). *Rural Poverty in Developing Asia*. Vol. I. Manila: Asian Development Bank.

Dreze, J. (1995): Famine Prevention in India. In J. Dreze, A. Sen, and A. Hussain (eds.). *Political Economy of Hunger*. New Delhi: Oxford University Press.

Dreze, J., Sen, A., and **Hussain, A.** (eds.) (1995): *The Political Economy of Hunger*. New Delhi: Oxford University Press.

Fogel, R.W. (1989): Second Thoughts on the European Escape from Hunger Famines, Chronic Malnutrition, and Mortality Rates. In J. Walter and R. Schofield (eds.). *Famine, Disease and Social Order in Early Modern Society*. Cambridge: Cambridge University Press.

——— (1994): The Relevance of Malthus for the Study of Mortality Today: Long-Run Influences on Health, Mortality, Labour Force Participation and Population Growth. In K. Lindah-Kiessling and H. Landberg (eds.). *Population, Economic Development and the Environment*. Oxford: Oxford University Press.

Government of India (1970–93): *Sample Registration Survey*. New Delhi: Vital Statistics Division, Office of the Registrar-General, Ministry of Home Affairs.

Maharatna, A. (1996a): *The Demography of Famines: An Indian Historical Perspective*. New Delhi: Oxford University Press.

——— (1996b): Infant and Child Mortality during Famines in the Late Nineteenth and Early Twentieth Century. *Economic and Political Weekly*, 31(27): 1774–83.

McKeown, T. (1976): *The Modern Rise of Population*. London: Edward Arnold.

Nagar, A.L., and **Das, R.K.** (1990): *Basic Statistics*. New Delhi: Oxford University Press.

Zurbrigg, S. (1992): Hunger and Epidemic Malaria in Punjab (1968–1940). *Economic and Political Weekly*, 27(4): PE2–26.

——— (1994): Recent Insights into the Role of Hunger in the History of Health. Presented at the Centre for Health Studies. 29 March, York University. Mimeo.

Part III

Shifts in Health Services and Health Financing

The importance of the public sector in health needs no belaboring, given the proportion of South Asians living under poverty. The World Bank has played an increasingly significant role in changing the patterns of investment and production in health and associated sectors, depending upon the country's pre-reform status. The weakening of existing structures is tragic, given the investments made by previous governments to create the essential infrastructure. This section explores the neo-liberal thrust of the current adjustment programs which, in chasing corporate profits, transform and weaken public sector health services by segmenting and universalizing it, irrespective of regional diversities. The first three chapters take up state-level analysis for India. The rest present national perspectives from the region on overall or specific services.

Raman Kutty provides a succinct account of HSR being followed in Kerala. Acknowledging the need to change the financing and organization of current services, he queries the options being offered. Baru provides a cogent overview of the funding of health services at the state level in India and its relationship to SAP. She argues that SAPs are transferring the profitable elements of health care into the market, leaving only underfunded and poor quality essential packages for the poor. Prabhu compares and contrasts how the investments in health services and the health indicators of two states, Maharashtra and Tamil Nadu, are being affected by the current reforms. She meticulously explores the nature and trends of these effects and offers some interesting insights into the complexity of inter-sectoral linkages.

Akbar Zaidi argues that the major factors contributing to the improvement of Pakistan's HDI over time have been high economic growth rate and declining poverty levels over the decades. SAPs, by slowing the growth rate and undermining the welfare sector, contribute to the recent reversal of some development indicators. Dulitha Fernando, examining two decades of reforms in Sri Lanka, reveals that though the basic structure of the public health sector remains unchanged, yet the nutritional status has declined over the past 18 years. She discusses why the data available may not be reflecting this impact. A.K. Chakraborty reviews the structure and functioning of one of the most significant disease control programs in India—the Revised National Tuberculosis Control Program. With impeccable rigor he demonstrates how distorted monitoring methodologies provide false evidence to support a costly, inappropriate, technocentric approach. B.R. Chatterjee's incisive analysis yet again brings out the weaknesses of the present vertical strategy to eliminate leprosy in India. He highlights the dangers of ignoring the basics of epidemiological requirements in program formulation and of a growing dependency, both technical and administrative, on international sources. A.Q. Khan provides a historical background of health services in Bangladesh. Placing mortality and morbidity loads in the context of poverty, he forcefully argues that service failures were responsible for creating a market in health, which the proponents of SAP took advantage of.

12

Health Sector Reforms and Structural Adjustment: A State-level Analysis

Rama V. Baru

Introduction

Private provisioning of medical care has been a significant feature of the Indian health sector. Private interests were present in medical care, the pharmaceutical, and medical equipment industries even at the time of independence. During the last five decades, these interests have become well-entrenched and grown in size and outreach. Thus, the private penetration of capital in the health sector predates Structural Adjustment Programs (SAPs). Commercialization of public services began in the late sixties and early seventies with the introduction of paying wards, graded user charges, and the like. Under SAP, there has been an acceleration of these trends; also certain new directions are being given to privatization. This chapter analyzes the content and directions of privatization and health sector reform in India under SAP, with a focus on the states of Karnataka, Punjab, West Bengal, and Andhra Pradesh, where these structural changes have been initiated.

The chapter is divided into four sections. The first examines the basis for the emergence of the World Bank (WB) as the single largest financier of the health sector in developing countries and the shifts that have taken place in the bank's understanding regarding the relative role of public and private sectors in health. It also examines certain ideas like efficiency, quality, and effectiveness, which are central to the bank's approach. The second section examines the effect of SAP on the health sector, both in terms of cutback on public expenditure and growth of the private sector. The third section analyzes the package of public health care reforms in the four Indian states. The last section examines the implications of the reform package for health care and public health in India.

I

The WB is playing an increasingly dominant role in the health sector in developing countries. As mentioned earlier, it has emerged as the single largest external source of financing during the nineties, although the volume of funding may not be large. This is a shift from the eighties, when bilateral funding played a substantial role in the health sector (Michaud and Murray 1994). The reasons for this development lie in:

1. the fact that investment in social sectors is seen as necessary for cushioning the vulnerable sections from the adverse impact of SAP; and
2. WB's desire to be seen as addressing the problem of inadequate investment in the social sectors and human development.

This trend is clearly visible in India too. The WB does not limit its role to only financing of health programs, but is also setting priorities regarding where and how this money is to be spent. The bilateral agencies are merely playing a supportive role for specific disease control programs in the country (Baru, Nayar, and Gopal 1996).

Between the eighties and nineties, there has been a shift in the bank's understanding of its role in the health sector. The reasons for this shift arise out of the negative experiences of market-oriented polices in the health sector during the eighties, when the libertarian philosophical approach of the bank emphasized blanket privatization policies for the health sector by scaling down the public sector and promoting pro-market policy reforms. This approach was prescribed for the early adjusting countries in Africa and Latin America. As a result of the adverse impact of these policies, many of these countries had to step up public investments in the health sector. As Creese observes:

> Chile's commitment to privatization proved difficult to implement, at least initially, as the country was in deep recession, so resources for additional private spending were simply

not available as real incomes were falling. Chile's subsequent restructuring changed patterns of access to care, making it harder for the poor to get care, and mortality and morbidity trends in most age groups rose reflecting inequities of access. Since 1990 Chile has been increasing the government contribution to health financing, in an attempt to prevent further decline in equity (Creese 1994: 322).

These negative experiences of the Latin American countries opened up a major international debate regarding the health and nutritional consequences of SAP. The United Nations Children's Fund (UNICEF) along with several bilateral donors from the Nordic countries called for protection of the poor and vulnerable sections and coined the slogan "Adjustment with a Human Face." This debate led to "some sections backing off from strong libertarian positions, and promoted efforts to strengthen the State's capacity to protect social welfare, a more utilitarian view" (Reich 1995). The dominant philosophical approach for health sector reform in the nineties is the utilitarian perspective, which "employs a consequentialist calculation and comparison of policies to determine which reform will achieve the most results for the least inputs" (Reich 1995). Tools such as Disability Adjusted Life Years (DALYs) were essentially devised as a measure to determine cost-effectiveness of interventions. DALYs largely focuses on medical interventions for preventing illnesses, rather than address the determinants of health.

The utilitarian perspective carries certain in-built assumptions regarding issues of efficiency, quality, and effectiveness of public and private provisioning. Private and voluntary sectors are viewed as being more efficient, as providing better quality services, and as being more effective than the public sector. However the former two sectors, specially the private sector, do not invest in a host of preventive services since it is not profitable to do so. Preventive services are indispensable for disease control programs and therefore the state should assume responsibility for delivery of "public goods." Hence, the *World Development Report 1993* emphasizes the need for selective state intervention at the primary level and reforms at the secondary and tertiary to become self-financing in the long run. This document has spelt out in fair detail the guidelines for health sector reform in developing countries. Some of the recommendations are:

1. Cutback on tertiary medical care in the public sector.
2. Private sector to play a more prominent role in providing care.
3. Introducing cost recovery mechanisms in the public sector.
4. Implementing an "essential clinical package for primary level care" (World Bank 1993).

II

Impact of SAP on Health Services in India

One of the most significant impact of SAP on the health sector was a sharp cutback in public expenditures during the early nineties. This resulted in a steep fall in central grants to the disease control programs during this period. Tulasidhar's work shows that central grants for disease control programs fell from 41 percent in 1984–85 to 29 percent in 1988–89 and to 18.5 percent in 1992–93 (Tulasidhar 1994). The poorer states, which were much more dependent on central outlays, suffered as a result. During 1992–93 some of the cutbacks were restored through World Bank loans for specific diseases programs. Much of this restoration could be attributable to a 34 percent increase for AIDS control and a marginal increase for tuberculosis and blindness control programs.

During 1993–94, there was a marginal increase for malaria but other communicable diseases registered a decline. In this entire period, the outlays for curative services had stagnated and in some states even registered a decline. The restoration of the cutbacks for communicable disease programs was necessitated by outbreaks of several epidemics resulting in a large number of deaths. The deaths due to the plague epidemic in Surat and malaria in western Rajasthan in 1994 were attributed to two important reasons: (*i*) the slashing of budgets for communicable diseases in the early nineties; and (*ii*) declining standards of public health in general (Qadeer et al. 1994). The breakdown of the public health services became apparent from the Surat plague epidemic. As Shah observes: "The public health system revealed glaring weaknesses. First, there was no co-ordination among various department[s], needed for efficient management of crisis"

(Shah 1997). There was lack of coordination at various levels. Information regarding diagnosis and treatment was inadequate and there were conflicts between hospital staff and public health officials. Government hospitals, which do not have the infrastructural facilities to function properly even during normal times, were burdened during the crisis. Private hospitals refused to treat patients. In fact, during the epidemic a large number of private practitioners either fled from Surat or refused to treat patients. The plague epidemic thus brought out the indispensability of public hospitals despite all their limitations.

Growth of the Private Sector

Notwithstanding its limitations, the public sector continues to be the single largest provider of inpatient services. The cutbacks in financing have affected the quality of service provided by these institutions. Individual private practitioners play an important role in providing outpatient care in both rural and urban areas. Several studies have commented on the role of private practitioners in rural areas and their high levels of utilization for outpatient care (Baru 1994).

The growth of private nursing homes and hospitals took place essentially during the late seventies, mainly in urban areas and in agriculturally prosperous states (Baru 1993). The eighties saw the rise of the corporate sector in medical care with active support from the government. The promoters of these enterprises were only regional business groups and non-resident Indian doctors. Interestingly, the rise of corporate sector in medical care was largely confined to the southern cities of Hyderabad and Madras.

Through the nineties, there has been an expansion of secondary-level private hospitals in several states. Increasingly, the private sector is no longer a mere urban phenomenon, but due to intense competition within this sector, they are being forced to move into peri-urban and rural areas. The real significant changes have taken place at the tertiary level. One of these is that corporate and trust hospitals at this level have started collaborating with state governments and very recently with multinational corporations (MNCs) (see Table 12.1). This is a new trend as against the presence so far of indigenous business groups. Given the growth of the middle class, there is a market for speciality services for the middle and upper middle classes in both urban and rural areas.

Table 12.1
Collaborations in the Tertiary Private Hospital Sector, 1997

S.No.	*Indian Company*	*Collaborators*	*Type of Hospital*	*Location*
1.	C.K. Birla Group	Kleveland Klinik of the U.S.	Super Speciality 350-bedded Hospital	Jaipur
2.	Escorts Heart Institute	Gleneagles Singapore	Duncan's Gleneagles Super Speciality—900 Beds	Calcutta
3.	Wockhardt	-	Health Care Center	Mumbai
4.	Sterling Gujarat	-	Corporate Hospital	Baroda
5.	Ranbaxy Laboratories	-	Corporate Hospital	Mohali, Chandigarh
6.	Apollo Hospital	Jardine, Insurance U.K.	Health Maintenance Organization	Delhi
7.	Apollo Hospital	Delhi Admn.	Apollo Indraprastha Multi Speciality Hospital	Delhi
8.	-do-	-do-	800 Beds Hospital	Delhi
9.	Royalton Health Care (India) Pvt Ltd	Montreal based Royalton Medical Management	Tertiary	Gandhinagar, Gujarat

Source: Compiled from newspaper and magazine clippings 1997.

This demand has also fueled the import of high technology equipment.

Medical Technology and Private Sector Growth

Investments in tertiary care have become profitable also because of relaxation in import policies for high technology medical equipment. In the 1996–97 budget, there has been a drastic cut on import duties on equipment from 120 percent to 30 percent. Further, foreign manufacturers are making inroads into the Indian market (see Table 12.2).

Table 12.2
Foreign Investors in Medical Equipment

No.	*Company*	*Investment Type*	*Equipment*	*Location*
1.	Becaton, Dickinson & Co., USA	$100 million (Rs 360 crore) over next five years	Syringes, catheters, blood tubes	Rajasthan
2.	Siemens, Germany	Rs 30 crore	CT Scanners, models, ultra-sound devices, X-ray machines	Goa
3.	Philips	NA	Flat screen ultrasounds	Pondicherry

Source: Newspaper clippings 1997.

With the growth of the tertiary private sector, the demand for medical equipment is on the rise. According to the managing director of Philips Medical Systems India: "The health care business is a $3,000 billion industry worldwide. If we attract even 1 percent of that here, the potential for the medical equipment industry is tremendous" (*Business World* 1997).

Apart from high technology medical equipment, there is a tremendous demand for items like syringes and surgical instruments. Indigenous production of these items is low; there has been no public or private investment in the manufacture of medical equipment. The rate of growth of the disposable syringes market, which is about 750 million units a year at present, is 20 percent per annum (*Business World* 1997).

Heterogeneity of the Private Sector and Debates over Quality of Care

The private sector is heterogeneous and largely unregulated. The assumption that they offer better quality and more efficient services than the public sector needs to be reviewed. Studies on private practitioners and secondary-level institutions clearly show that even minimum physical standards do not exist for quality assessment.

Studies in Hyderabad and two talukas of Satara district in Maharashtra show that there are differences between small and large nursing homes in terms of physical infrastructure, staffing, and services provided. A survey of private nursing homes in Hyderabad showed that 63 percent of the larger nursing homes were housed in separate buildings while the remaining 27 percent were extensions to residences. In the small nursing home category, nearly 70 percent of the owners were using their residences to house the nursing home (Baru 1998). In Satara district, 82 percent of the hospitals were located near a marketplace and 66 percent were functioning from an independent building (Nandraj and Duggal 1995). A study in Bombay found that 62.50 percent of the hospitals were located in residential premises and 12.50 percent were run from sheds that had roofs of asbestos, etc. (Nandraj and Duggal 1995). The uneven physical standards, coupled with variance in other inputs like staffing and equipment, are bound to affect quality and efficiency in the private sector.

There are very few studies on quality and efficiency of private practitioners and institutions in India. Studies on private providers in India reveal that a fairly large percentage of them are untrained. Vishwanathan and Rhode's study on rural private practitioner in UP found that a substantial percentage of them did not have any formal training in allopathic or indigenous systems but they were dispensing allopathic medicines (Rhode and Vishwanathan 1994). Many private practitioners get access to medicines from chemists and some micro studies have found that they administer medicines ranging from analgesics, vitamins to even steroids. Even trained practitioners use irrational combinations. Phadke's analysis of prescriptions from private clinics found that 28.9 percent were irrational drug combinations, 9.6 percent were hazardous drugs, 45.7 percent were unnecessary drugs, and 26.5 percent were unnecessary injections (Phadke et al. 1995). Most practitioners, both trained and untrained, receive information of drugs from drug representatives and chemists. There have been some efforts at training private practitioners in rural areas of West Bengal by a Calcutta-based NGO. However, their efforts are limited and given the large numbers of practitioners, it does not seem like a feasible alternative. Uplekar's study shows that there is a gross lack of knowledge and awareness regarding major communicable diseases like leprosy and tuberculosis (Uplekar and Shephard 1991). Lack of training in a large percentage is an important factor for the differential quality of care among private providers.

The myth that the private sector provides better quality care was shattered when cases of medical negligence in private hospitals were brought to light through the consumer courts under the Consumer Protection Act, 1986.

There are some serious methodological problems in evaluation and in drawing comparisons of efficiency and quality of public and private medical institutions.

1. There are certain fundamental differences in the nature of outputs and the type of consumers that each of these institutional forms serve. The private sector largely focuses on a narrow range of curative services and because of its pricing structure selects out certain social groups based on the ability to pay. The public hospital, on the other hand, offers a mix of preventive and curative services and is technically accessible to all social groups, whether or not they can pay. The patterns of financing and investments in these two institutional forms are fundamentally different making comparisons in costing of care difficult.

   Given these differences, the units have to be matched for parameters like bed strength, type of services, number of medical and paramedical personnel, location of hospitals, investments, and availability of technology. This really means that studies on efficiency and quality become highly specific to the units being studied. Therefore, it is not possible to make generalizations about relative efficiency or quality at a macro level.
2. A systematic search for studies on efficiency has drawn a blank. With respect to quality, there are few studies on institutions delivering family planning services.
3. Studies on quality in the private sector are problematic because of the heterogeneity. Hence, the difficulty in generalizing.

A recent study from Trivandrum examines the experiences of patients from public and private sector hospitals and evaluates the performance of hospitals from both sectors (Homan and Thankappan 1997). This is the only study that has tried to compare efficiency of the two institutional forms. The sets of parameters used to measure hospital performance were:

1. occupancy rates, performance of outpatient area, performance of surgery programs, laboratory, and X-ray services.

2. staffing, both medical and paramedical.
3. cost of care delivered.

The authors admit that there were limitations. The case mix could not be matched for the hospitals and there was paucity of data for other variables. What comes out fairly clearly is that the public sector is providing services beyond its intended capacity, which clearly has an impact on the quality of care. The private sector hospitals had low levels of occupancy, partly related to the pricing structure, which also has a negative effect on efficiency. They find that price remains a significant barrier to using the private sector. This study does not in any way provide empirical evidence that the private sector is more efficient than the public.

This study also assessed patient preferences, patient satisfaction with the care received, and perceptions of hospital quality. Interestingly, it revealed that two-fifths of those interviewed preferred private hospitals. The proportion of patients reporting complete satisfaction with the public sector was lower than that for private hospitals. However, the proportion of patients reporting dissatisfaction with public hospital was also quite low. The important reasons for preferring private hospitals were: distant location of government hospital, lack of attention, bad behavior of staff, and lack of hygiene. These can be explained by the fact that public hospitals are providing services beyond their capacity. Significantly, only 11.7 percent of patients preferred private hospitals because they offered better care.

The above study is one of the first to systematically try and open up a debate on the methodological problems of measuring efficiency and quality of health care and to raise the need for developing parameters to measure these. It is important to highlight these aspects because the rationale for limiting and restructuring the public sector is largely based on these assumptions of better quality and efficiency of private sector. More empirical evidence is needed to effectively question and counter these assumptions.

III

Reform of public sector was initiated in 1995 in Punjab, West Bengal, Karnataka, and Andhra Pradesh, which opted for a state sector adjustment loan. Both the *India Country Document 1991* and the *World Development Report 1993* had clearly articulated the need to limit the role of the public sector and encourage private provisioning of medical care. They opined that public investments could be cut back from secondary and tertiary levels of care and channeled into the primary level. The *WDR 1993* clearly articulates this as follows:

> Although both the public and private sectors have important roles in the delivery of clinical services, government run health systems in many developing countries are over extended and need to be scaled back. This can be done through legal and administrative changes designed to facilitate private (NGO and for profit) involvement in the provision of health services, by public subsidies to NGOs for supplying the essential package, and by curtailment of new investments in public tertiary hospitals. At the same time, the efficiency of public health services can be greatly enhanced through decentralization and improved management of government hospitals and programs (World Bank 1993: 108).

The State Health Systems Project formulated by the World Bank is based on this understanding. Loans have been provided to the selected states of Karnataka, Punjab, and West Bengal in 1995. Recently Andhra Pradesh was also included in this project.

Ten state governments had submitted project proposals, of which these three states were chosen on the grounds that they capture the heterogeneity of this country in terms of epidemiological profiles, levels of economic development, health services development, and political structures. For the bank, the experiences of health sector reform in these states will be invaluable for evolving strategies for the entire country. In a sense, the health systems project in these states is a "test run" for the bank since "together, they represent sufficient diversity applicable at the state level generally" (World Bank 1997).

The WB has loaned a total of $350 million repayable at 12 percent per annum over 35 years. The bank describes this as "an investment loan with policy reform in areas of resource allocation for the health sector, capacity development for sector analysis and management strengthening, enhance participation of the private and voluntary sectors in the delivery of health services, and implementation of user charges for those who can afford to pay" (World Bank 1996: 18).

These reforms are geared towards restructuring, both financially and administratively, secondary and tertiary levels of care. Public expenditures earmarked for secondary and tertiary care will gradually be shifted to primary-level care and will be directed towards an essential clinical package consisting of specific interventions which are considered to be "cost-effective," based on DALYs.

Break-up of Investment Costs from 1996 to 2001

The pattern of investment is almost uniform across the states. A substantial part of the investments are earmarked for civil works, ranging from 39 percent of the total investments in Karnataka to 43.7 percent in West Bengal to 48.8 percent in Punjab. Civil works cover renovation and new construction or extensions to existing hospitals. In Karnataka, the next major item for investment is medicines (13.6 percent of the total investment) followed by purchase of equipment (10.7 percent) and major medical equipment (10.6 percent). In West Bengal, 14.7 percent of the total investment is earmarked for purchase of major medical equipment and 10 percent for other equipment. In Punjab, 14.8 percent of the total investment for major medical equipment is followed by 7.6 percent for vehicles (see Table 12.3).

Across all three states, the items that have a high foreign exchange percentage are major medical equipment (60 percent), vehicles (15 percent), medicines (50 percent), and studies (90 percent). The high foreign exchange component is indicative of high import potential for these items. The WB's document explicitly states that up to certain levels of purchases of the above-mentioned items will be done through national tendering and above that level through global tendering. Most of civil works contracts are being given to private firms in all the three states.

The issue of sustainability of these reforms once the loan period is over should be of concern to all state governments. The understanding is that state governments must recover these costs through user fees, shifting the burden once again on households to pay for care.

Restructuring of State-level Health Care

The primary-level care is essentially to provide a safety net for the poor and vulnerable sections of the population by reducing the burden of disease. In addition, the project proposes to strengthen the performance of state health systems to deal with the evolving

Table 12.3
Break-up of Total Investment Costs for Selected States 1996–2001 (in Million Rs)

Sl. No.	Items	Karnataka	Percent of Foreign Exchange	West Bengal	Percent of Foreign Exchange	Punjab	Percent of Foreign Exchange
1.	Civil works (renovation)	251.6(8.0)	15	922.8(19.8)	15	156.4(5.8)	15
2.	Civil works (new construction or extension)	954.4(31)	15	1,110.0(23.9)	15	1,560.0(43.0)	15
3.	Professional services	110.6(3.4)	20	203.3(4.4)	20	131.2(4.9)	20
4.	Furniture	104.1(3.4)	10	169.2(3.6)	10	65.2(2.4)	10
5.	Major medical equipment	326.5(10.6)	60	482.8(14.7)	60	397.5(14.8)	60
6.	Minor medical equipment	-	-	36.7(0.8)	20	17.5(0.65)	20
7.	Medical equipment surgical packs	-	-	78.1(1.7)	20	23.2(0.86)	20
8.	Equipment (other)	327.7(10.7)	20	468.7(10.0)	20	157.5(5.8)	20
9.	Vehicles	151.4(4.8)	75	203.4(4.5)	75	84.9(3.2)	75
10.	Medical lab supplies	124.8(2.5)	20	24.1(0.5)	20	11.0(0.4)	20
11.	Medicines	418.2(13.6)	50	180.8(3.9)	50	204.0(7.6)	50
12.	Other supplies	116.1(3.7)	-	384.3(8.3)	-	50.0(1.9)	-
13.	MIS/IEC materials	32.3(1.0)	25	64.6(1.4)	25	111.4(4.1)	25
14.	Local training	100.1(3.2)	-	61.2(1.3)	-	59.2(2.2)	-
15.	Studies	19.5(0.6)	90	16.0(0.3)	-	31.2(1.2)	-
16.	Fellowships	28.0(0.9)	-	12.8(0.8)	90	21.0(0.8)	90
17.	Workshops	21.5(0.7)	-	20.9(0.4)	-	9.1(0.33)	-
18.	Consultants	8.4(0.3)	-	3.4(0.05)	-	1.6(0.06)	-
19.	NGOs	12.7(0.4)	-	3.6(8.0)	-	2.4(0.09)	-
	Total	3,107.6(100)		4,645.5(100)		2,690.3(100)	

Source: The World Bank 1996, Report No. 15106-IN.

burden of disease by providing more efficient and effective health care (World Bank 1997).

In order to improve efficiency, quality, and effectiveness of public hospitals it is proposed to:

- cutback on secondary and tertiary spending and channel it into selective interventions at the primary level;
- contract out ancillary services in public hospitals to private contractors;
- involve private providers in national communicable disease programs;
- institute user charges in all public hospitals;
- encourage private sector growth at secondary and tertiary levels by instituting regulations; and
- initiate decentralization measures (Qadeer 1997).

In this kind of restructuring, the role of the public sector is gradually limited to only primary-level provisioning. Secondary and tertiary care is commercialized through user charges for outpatient and inpatient services, diagnostic, and other facilities. This kind of delinking of the primary and higher levels of care will clearly affect the effectiveness of any public health. As Qadeer observes: "If the middle level hospital system does not provide the support to basic institutions and is not supported in turn by tertiary care institutions, the delivery of primary health care is bound to be differential and mutilated in its preventive endeavours" (Qadeer 1997). The viability of each of these recommendations need to be assessed based on data available from India and other countries, where they have been tried as a part of their adjustment programs.

Contracting out of Ancillary Services to the Private Sector

Much of the debate regarding contracting out of ancillary services took place in Britain when Thatcher was trying to restructure the National Health Services. It was considered more cost-efficient to cut back on salaries of workers who provided ancillary services in hospitals. The WB too feels that contracting out to the private sector is "more efficient and effective than directly hired labor. In view of the difficulties of employing government staff, such as slow recruitment procedures and poor attendance, contracting out certain services, especially support services, is an attractive alternative.

The State governments should, wherever economically attractive, contract out support services such as laundry, kitchen, landscaping, dietary services, sanitation, security and mainstream diagnostic and clinical services" (World Bank 1997: 26–27).

Limited experiences of contracting out—mainly non-clinical services in public hospitals—in developing countries suggests that the belief that competition leads to efficiency may not always be realized.

McPake and Banda (1994) argue that while contracting out may theoretically appear to have advantages, there are questions regarding its viability. The basic conditions required for contracting out are competition and regulation. The four main questions that they raise are:

1. Will real competition take place?
2. Will competition promote efficiency?
3. Are the necessary skills for management of markets available?
4. Is public financing viable?

There are problems associated with the issue of efficiency because it is difficult to specify the output in contract, particularly with respect to quality. Very often contractors will choose only those services where they are assured returns. Some of the problems concerning contracting out identified by managers in the National Health Services (NHS) are:

- A very rigid service is provided, restricted to a literal interpretation of the contract.
- Selection of contractors could be hit and miss and it is difficult to get rid of an unsatisfactory contractor quickly.
- There are constant disagreements on standards of service with contractors reluctant to erode profit margins by eliminating any low standard brought to their attention (McPake and Banda 1994).

These problems will have far-reaching impact on quality, efficiency, and even continuity of services. In Zimbabwe, the failure to define performance expectations clearly and to link them to penalties for non-performance has undermined the contracting of laundry. Another important issue that comes to the fore is that certain kinds of management and administrative skills are required in order to implement and monitor services that are contracted out. Very often public systems do not have these in place and this adds to the existing burden of human resource development requirements within the health systems of developing countries.

Involvement of Private Providers in National Health Programs

The *WDR 1993* and subsequent documents call for greater involvement of private providers and NGOs in disease control programs. Given the situation vis-à-vis the performance of private practitioners (see earlier section on this), involving private practitioners without a proper system for registration and monitoring would prove to be detrimental to people's health and public health in the country.

User Fees

In the health care reforms package, specially in secondary public hospitals, institution of user fees assumes a very important role. The introduction of user fees is seen as a way of "substituting public funds with private funds in secondary and tertiary hospitals by instituting means tested user-charges" (World Bank 1995: 103). User charges are seen as fundamental to generating the necessary revenue to cover the running costs for secondary and tertiary hospitals. The experiences of cost recovery through user fees are not very encouraging; it often does not ensure returns high enough to cover recurrent expenditures, and in many countries it has excluded the poor from access to services. This is a feature of developing as well as developed countries. Canada's experience of user fees is illustrative in this regard. A recent study on revenue-contribution from user fees, as a percentage of recurrent government expenditures on health in some African countries, shows an average of 5.2 percent. Few countries have recovered more than 10 percent (see Table 12.4).

In India, user charges in public hospitals predates SAP and varies from state to state. Under SAP, there is a strong push towards charging for outpatient, inpatient, and diagnostic services in government hospitals, while developing means to exempt the poor. Experiences of states like Andhra Pradesh and Maharashtra indicate that recovery has been very low. In fact, across states the average is 3.8 percent and this is hardly adequate to make public hospitals self-sufficient (see Table 12.5). The State Health Systems

Table 12.4
Revenue from User Charges as a Percentage of Recurrent Government Expenditures on Health in Selected African Countries

Country	*Percent*
Botswana	
1979	1.3
1983	2.8
Burkina Faso	
1981	0.5
Burundi	
1982	4.0
Cote d'Ivoire	
1986	3.1
1993	7.2
Ethiopia	
1982	12.0
mid-1980s	15.0–20.0
Ghana	
1984	5.2
1987	12.1
Kenya	
1984	2.0
Lesotho	
1984	5.7
1991/92	9.0
Malawi	
1983	3.3
Mali	
1986	2.7
Mauritania	
1986	2.7
Mozambique	
1985	8.0
Rwanda	
1984	7.0
Senegal	
1986	4.7
Swaziland	
1984	2.1
Zimbabwe	
1986	2.2
1991/92	3.5

Source: Nolan and Turbat 1993; Vogel 1988; World Bank 1994. Cited in Shaw and Griffin 1995.

Table 12.5
Cost Recovery in Medical and Public Health Services (Non-ESIS)
(in percent)

	1975–76	*1980–81*	*1984–85*	*1988–89*	*Average*
15 Major States	6.4	4.1	3.04	1.6	3.8
Andhra Pradesh	2.9	3.4	3.8	0.8	2.7
Assam	3.9	3.5	-	1.6	2.2
Bihar	17.0	8.5	3.3	-	7.2
Gujarat	3.7	5.0	1.9	2.6	3.3
Haryana	6.4	3.9	7.7	1.5	4.9
Karnataka	11.0	3.2	2.7	6.6	5.9
Kerala	3.8	4.1	3.7	1.6	3.3
Madhya Pradesh	4.9	2.4	6.4	2.4	4.0
Maharashtra	12.9	3.5	1.7	1.7	5.0
Orissa	2.6	3.0	4.3	1.1	2.8
Punjab	15.6	5.6	4.3	5.4	7.7
Rajasthan	4.0	3.9	2.5	0.8	2.8
Tamil Nadu	4.0	3.9	2.5	0.8	2.8
Uttar Pradesh	5.3	1.9	1.3	0.5	2.3
West Bengal	2.2	2.1	2.1	0.8	1.4

Source: Tulsidhar 1992, p. 85. Cited in World Bank 1997.

Project proposes to implement existing user charges more rigorously. As the report outlines: "The system of user charges proposed by each state would be a combination of voluntary payments and targeting the poor for exemptions. In order to generate revenue and provide services for those willing to pay, district and subdivisional hospitals will provide private paying bed facilities and begin to charge for services in a phased manner after improvements in the quality of basic services and infrastructure development have been completed" (World Bank 1995). The revenue from user charges will be used for meeting non-salary recurrent costs in public hospitals.

The poor will be exempted from paying user fees; the three states have evolved certain guidelines for protecting them. It is the high and middle-income groups that will be tapped for user fees. However, an analysis of utilization of health services across income groups for states shows variations between those which have a significant presence of the private sector and those which do not. In those states where the private sector is substantial, viz., Kerala, Andhra Pradesh, Gujarat, a significant percentage of middle and upper-income categories in rural areas are utilizing the

Table 12.6
Distribution of Rural Hospitalized Cases across Fractile Groups in Private and Voluntary Institutions (in percent)

S.No.	*States*	*Total Hospital Cases in Public*	*Share of Bottom 20%*	*Share of Top 20%*
1.	Andhra Pradesh	69	55	73
2.	Bihar	29	32	31
3.	Gujarat	51	32	69
4.	Haryana	47	40	38
5.	Himachal Pradesh	10	08	00
6.	Karnataka	41	36	44
7.	Kerala	56	55	68
8.	Madhya Pradesh	20	13	30
9.	Maharashtra	56	43	75
10.	Orissa	10	03	12
11.	Punjab	51	39	70
12.	Rajasthan	17	15	16
13.	Tamil Nadu	43	37	44
14.	Uttar Pradesh	41	24	44
15.	West Bengal	08	02	20

Source: Government of India 1989.

private sector. Among the top 20 percent, 73 percent in Andhra Pradesh, 69 percent in Gujarat, 75 percent in Maharashtra, 70 percent in Punjab, and 68 percent in Kerala are utilizing private hospitals. Among the bottom 20 percent of the population, a fairly substantial percentage are resorting to the private sector in Andhra Pradesh (55 percent), Kerala 55 (percent), Maharashtra (43 percent), Gujarat (32 percent), and Punjab (39 percent) (see Tables 12.6 and 12.7).

In states where the public sector is in a dominant position, the percentage of total hospital cases is high—in Karnataka 82 percent, Madhya Pradesh 79 percent, Orissa 88 percent, and West Bengal 92 percent. In these states the differential in utilization of public hospital between the top 20 percent and bottom 20 percent is not as sharp when compared to those states where the private sector is significant.

Given these varied patterns of provisioning and utilization, there is bound to be an impact on how much user fees will contribute to revenues of public hospitals. In Karnataka and West Bengal, where of the top 20 percent, 62 percent and 80 percent respectively utilize public hospitals from rural areas, there is

Table 12.7
Percentage Distribution of Rural Hospitalized Cases across Fractile Groups in Public Institutions

S.No.	*States*	*Total Hospital Cases in Public*	*Share of Bottom 20%*	*Share of Top 20%*
1.	Andhra Pradesh	29	40	24
2.	Bihar	51	46	51
3.	Gujarat	49	67	29
4.	Haryana	51	58	61
5.	Himachal Pradesh	16	26	83
6.	Karnataka	82	80	62
7.	Kerala	43	44	30
8.	Madhya Pradesh	79	87	72
9.	Maharashtra	44	58	28
10.	Orissa	88	24	92
11.	Punjab	48	60	33
12.	Rajasthan	80	88	78
13.	Tamil Nadu	56	64	36
14.	Uttar Pradesh	55	74	52
15.	West Bengal	92	98	80
16.	All India	60	67	50

Source: Government of India 1989.

some possibility of cost recovery through user charges. However, in Punjab and Andhra Pradesh, only 33 percent and 24 percent respectively, of the top 20 percent use public hospitals. With such low levels of utilization by sections that are "capable of paying," the revenues generated through user fees would be very low. Thus, even in those states where the health systems projects are being implemented there is bound to be difference in revenue generated through user fees. This has very serious implications for the financial sustainability of the secondary and tertiary sectors.

Exempting the poor from paying user fees is important and must be implemented in all states. Several states have devised administrative mechanisms towards this end. However, targeting of services for the poor coupled with declining levels of utilization by the middle and upper middle classes has far-reaching effects on quality of care. As Burgess and Stern observe: "Targeting of public services for the poor is beset with many problems, namely, mechanisms of identification and delivery of services to the non-needy, who have the political power to force the effective and sustained implementation of any given scheme" (Burgess and Stern 1991).

The administrative problems involved are well-documented in India. In Maharashtra, a number of social groups were exempt from being charged. These included: those with monthly income less than Rs 180 (urban areas) and Rs 150 (rural areas); civil servants and their families, medical and nursing staff, and medical students. Despite detailed administrative guidelines, hospitals collected less than 1 percent of the costs in 1984–85 (Griffin 1992). What is important is that effective administrative guidelines do not automatically ensure better recovery; very often the influential sections use political or social clout to get free treatment even when they can afford to pay.

Experiences of Regulating the Private Sector

An area of emphasis in the *WDR 1993* was regulation of the private sector. There has been little effort to regulate the growth and quality of services provided by the private sector both at the national and state levels.

As far as the central government is concerned, the only conditions laid down relate to the import of high-technology equipment, namely, that all private hospitals importing medical equipment have to treat a certain percentage of in- and outpatients free of cost. However, there are no mechanisms to check whether they are being fulfilled.

Efforts by state governments to regulate the private sector, such as in Andhra Pradesh, Kerala, and Tamil Nadu have met with tremendous resistance from the doctor-owners of these enterprises. The professional community perceives this as an autocratic act and feels that they should not be regulated. Neither the Indian Medical Association nor the Medical Council of India has shown any interest in this important issue.

Efforts at banning private practice by government doctors have also met with a similar fate. The fact that doctors belong to the elite sections has meant that they have the social and political clout to safeguard their interests. In Madhya Pradesh and Delhi, recent experiences of banning private practice have resulted in an exodus of doctors from public to private hospitals, leading to a genuine fear that the quality of services in government hospitals will be affected.

Implications of Health Reforms

The push for privatization of medical care is based largely on inadequate empirical evidence regarding the quality and efficency of medical care provided by both private and public sectors.

The commercialization of secondary and tertiary-level services, when viewed in conjunction with the nature of commercialization (entry of multinationals in the medical equipment and pharmaceutical industry, and opening of speciality hospitals), seems to have more to do with creating markets for the medical industry.

The restructuring opens up spaces for penetration of the market also in specific areas of medical care. The introduction of user fees shifts the burden on to individuals. The recommendation for decentralization is essentially for tapping additional resources from the community.

Clearly, the reforms lack a systemic view as well as the welfare perspective. The linkages between various levels of providers, rational use of technology that permits maximum coverage with optimum results, and inter-sectoral approach to health which is extremely crucial for handling public health problems, have been consciously sidelined. The focus is only on health financing, which, as Banerji observes, "is a part of the wider academic field of health economics, which in turn forms only one component of health systems research for developing effective public health policies under given conditions" (Banerji 1993). The reforms are obsessed with cutting costs and reducing state involvement in health-care. This undermines the principles of equity and universal access, which are essential for public health.

References

Banerji, D. (1993): Simplistic Approach to Health Policy Analysis: World Bank Team on Indian Health Sector. *Economic and Political Weekly*, 28(24): 1207.

Baru, R. (1993): Inter-regional Variations in Health Services in Andhra Pradesh. *Economic and Political Weekly*, 28(20): 963.

——— (1994): Structure and Utilization of Health Services: An Inter-state Analysis. *Social Scientist*, 22(9–12): 105.

——— (1998): *Private Health Care in India: Social Characteristics and Trends*. New Delhi: Sage Publications.

Baru, R., Nayar, K.R., and **Gopal, M.** (1996): Patterns of Funding by Bilateral and Multilateral Agencies in Health. Paper submitted to the Independent Health Commission. New Delhi: Voluntary Health Association of India.

Burgess, R., and **Stern, N.** (1991): Social Security in Developing Countries: What, When, Who and How? In E. Ahmad, J. Dreze, J. Mills, and A. Sen (eds.). *Social Security in Developing Countries*. New Delhi: Oxford University Press.

Business World, 22 May 1997.

Chiutsu, S.H., Hongoro, C., Chandiwana, S.K., Kodzwa, G.M., and **Katsumbe, T.** (1993): A Study of the Public/Private Sector Mix for Health Care in Zimbabwe. Background Paper for Workshop of the Collaborative Research Network on the Public/Private Mix for Health Care, 11–15 January, London School of Hygiene and Tropical Medicine, London.

Creese, A. (1994): Global Trends in Health Care Reform. *World Health Forum*, 15: 322.

Griffin, C. (1992): *Health Care in Asia: Comparative Study of Cost and Financing*. Washington, D.C.: The World Bank.

Government of India (1989): Morbidity and Utilization of Medical Services 42nd Round. National Sample Survey No. 364. New Delhi: Central Statistical Organization.

Homan, R.K., and **Thankappan, K.R.** (1997): An Examination of Public and Private Providers in Thiruvananthapuram District, Kerala. Discussion Paper Series, No. 20. Trivandrum: Center for Development Studies.

McPake, B., and **Banda, E.** (1994): Contracting Out of Health Services in Developing Countries. *Health Policy and Planning*, 9(1): 27.

Michaud, C., and **Murray, C.** (1994): Aid Flows to the Health Sector in Developing Countries: A Detailed Analysis, 1972–1990. Background Paper No. 11. *World Development Report, 1993: Investing in Health*. Washington D.C.: The World Bank.

Nandraj, S., and **Duggal, R.** (1995): *Physical Standards in the Private Health Sector: A Case-study of Rural Maharashtra*. Bombay: CEHAT.

Phadke, A., Fernandes, A., Sharada, L., and **Mane, P.** (1995): *A Study of Supply and Use of Pharmaceuticals in Satara District: A Summary Report*. Bombay: Foundation for Research in Community Health.

Qadeer, I. (1997): Health. In *Alternative Economic Survey*. Delhi: Delhi Science Forum.

Qadeer, I., Nayar, K.R., and **Baru, R.** (1994): Contextualising Plague: A Reconstruction and an Analysis. *Economic and Political Weekly*, 29(47): 2981.

Reich, M.R. (1995): The Politics of Health Sector Reform in Developing Countries: Three Cases of Pharmaceutical Policy. In P. Berman (ed.). *Health Sector Reform in Developing Countries: Making Health Development Sustainable*. Harvard series on Population and International Health, Boston. Boston: Harvard School of Public Health.

Rhode, J., and **Vishwanathan, H.** (1994): The Rural Private Practitioner. *Health for the Millions*, 2(1) (February): 13–16.

Shah, G. (1997): *Public Health and Urban Development: The Plague in Surat*. New Delhi: Sage Publications.

Shaw, P., and **Griffin, C.** (1995): *Financing Health-care in Sub-Saharan Africa through User Fees and Insurance*. Washington: The World Bank.

Tulasidhar, V.B. (1994): Expenditure Compression and Health Sector Outlays. *Economic and Political Weekly*, 28(45): 2473.

Uplekar, M.W., and **Shephard, D.H.** (1991): *The Private GP and Treatment of Tuberculosis. A Study*. Bombay: Foundation for Research in Community Health.

World Bank (1993): *World Development Report: Investing in Health*. New York: Oxford University Press.

——— (1995): *India: Policy and Finance Strategies for Strengthening Primary Health Care Service*. Report No. 1304-IN. Washington D.C.: World Bank.

——— (1996): *India Health Systems Project II*. Report No. 15106-IN. Washington D.C.: World Bank.

——— (1997): *India—New Directions in Health Sector Development at the State Level: An Operational Perspective*. Report No. 15753-IN. Washington D.C.: World Bank.

13

Reforms and Their Relevance: The Kerala Experience

V. Raman Kutty

Introduction

Study of health sector expenditure by government and its trends over time constitute an important tool in health policy analysis. Analysis of sources of finance and the bodies controlling the spending is an essential element in the planning and implementation of health policy (WHO 1978). It helps to focus attention on resource flows in the health sector and often unmasks hidden inequities. It can also bring to light the response of the health system to external influences which curtail the availability of funds.

Although Kerala is one of the smaller states in India, it has rightly been in the limelight in the matter of health, because of the better health status of its people in comparison to other Third World countries and other states in India. Table 13.1 reviews the major health status indicators in the state in comparison to all-India figures. It is generally agreed that the health services of the state government have had an important role to play in this achievement (Panikar and Soman 1984). But of late, the importance of the government sector in health care in the state has waned greatly. A very relevant question is whether inadequate financing of the health sector by the government has been at least partly responsible for this trend.

Acknowledgments: The author wishes to record his appreciation of the fruitful collaboration he had with Professor P.G.K. Panikar which made the analysis more complete. He is also grateful to Abraham Babu for help in compilation and computer entry of the data. The work would not have been possible without the active support of the Directorate of Health Services, Kerala; Secretary for Health, Kerala; and UNICEF, Madras, which funded the study. Thanks are due to all of them. The author also appreciates the extremely useful comments of the reviewers.

Table 13.1
Crude Birth Rate (CBR), Crude Death Rate (CDR), and Infant Mortality Rate (IMR), India and Kerala, 1993

Indicator	*India*	*Kerala*
CBR (per 1,000 population)	28.5	17.3
CDR (per 1,000 population)	9.2	6.0
IMR (per 1,000 live births)	74	13

Source: Government of India 1993.

Kerala's lead in social development through public investment in education and health has been acknowledged as a uniquely successful model. Recently, the question has been raised whether the state can sustain such levels of public spending in the social sector (George 1993), thus challenging the relevance of its development experience. The eighties have been difficult times economically for most developing countries and India has been no exception. During this time the Government of India accepted the position that government spending needs to be reduced if budgetary deficits are to be contained. According to one analyst, "expenditure compression," or cutbacks in spending by the central Indian government and, as part of it, contraction in money transfers to states started some years before the Government of India officially proclaimed a policy of curtailment of government spending (Tulasidhar 1993). Since part of the health programs of the states are financed by central government funding, this has affected their expenditure on health. Kerala too has been subject to this tightening of expenditure controls by the central government. It is important to see what effect this "fiscal crisis" has had on the social sector spending including health.

The last two decades have been a time of increasing fiscal difficulty for the state in other ways also. These fiscal problems have not arisen completely independent of the national and international economic climate. This period coincided with the global economic recession of the eighties, which affected Third World economies very badly. International agencies dominated by the Western industrialized nations have been actively advocating "Structural Adjustment Programs" as a remedial measure. In essence, these consist of a drastic reduction of government expenditure in all sectors including social sectors and allowing the market forces a free reign in many of these areas. In health this would mean introduction of user charges for services. Kerala is not directly subject to pressures by international bodies in policy formulation. Nevertheless, their very strong indirect influence in the form of control of funding for specific health projects and lobbying of administrators has resulted in a strong policy environment favoring "structural adjustment." This chapter attempts to look at the government allocations for the health sector during this crucial period. It is to be emphasized here that only the state expenditures in health have been examined; this does not give us a true picture of the overall health expenditure trends, which would include the household and private spending on health during the period. Nevertheless, since the government is a leading player in deciding the direction of health policy, this becomes important.

This chapter attempts to answer the following questions:

1. To what extent and how have the fiscal difficulties of the Kerala state government involved the health sector during the period 1977–78 to 1992–93?
2. What are the adjustments in expenditure in the government health sector as a reaction to this situation?
3. What are the policy implications of these?

To answer the first two questions we review published material on budget trends and secondary data culled from the budget documents. Every year the government publishes the detailed break-up of the government budget. This gives: (*i*) the estimated expenditure under different heads in the coming fiscal year; (*ii*) revised estimates of expenditure under various heads in the current year; and (*iii*) final statement about expenditure under various heads in the immediate past fiscal year. The analysis is based on final statements of government expenditures.

The period from 1977–78 to 1992–93 saw an initial growth in the health sector expenditure followed by a trend towards cutbacks. To smoothen out the trends over time, the three-year moving averages were calculated. The fiscal year in India runs from 1 April to 31 March. Wherever appropriate, the figures in current rupees were deflated using the wholesale price index (WPI) to retain the comparability over time. The WPI was based on the year 1981–82, which meant that all figures were converted into 1981–82 rupee value.

Budget statements in Kerala, like in other Indian states, divide the expenditure into revenue accounts and capital accounts. Capital accounts list mainly the expenditure on buildings and structures, which are one-time investments. Expenditure on machinery, though conventionally considered capital, is not included under the capital accounts. Revenue accounts include all recurrent expenditures such as salaries, wages, expenditure on consumable items, maintenance, as well as on machinery and equipment. Revenue expenditure on health was examined (*i*) category-wise, i.e., the proportions spent on salaries/wages, and supplies, the two most important categories of spending; and (*ii*) sector-wise, i.e., divided into primary, secondary, and tertiary sectors. Primary health centers, family welfare, preventive and promotive programs, and the national disease control programs were considered as constituting the primary care sector, the teaching institutions and the hospitals affiliated to them as the tertiary sector, and by default, all institutions of intermediate size not falling into these two categories as the secondary sector. Thus, the secondary sector consisted of the community health centers, taluk (subunit of district) hospitals, and district hospitals.

Patterns in Government Spending

Figure 13.1 shows the trend of expenditure on health by the government in the period under discussion, as a proportion of total government expenditure. Spending on health varies between 4 and 7 percent. Table 13.2 shows total expenditure by government under the revenue (recurrent) account, total revenue receipts, state domestic product, and surplus or deficit of receipts over expenditure under the revenue account for various years covering the period under review. From Table 13.2 we see that money received by the government failed to keep pace with the spending, leaving an ever increasing deficit in the revenue account. The growing revenue expenditure is constituted by two main components: development expenditure and non-development expenditure. Development expenditure traditionally comprises the total of government spending on such items as health, education, animal husbandry, agriculture development, and housing. Non-development expenditure comprises money spent on repayment of debts, interest payments,

Figure 13.1
Percentage Share of Health Sector in (a) Total Government Expenditure, and (b) Revenue Expenditure by Government, in Kerala State, 1977–78 to 1992–93

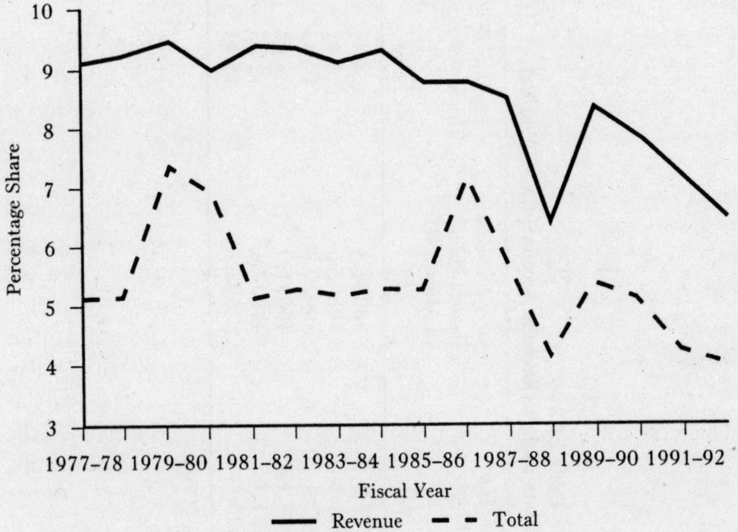

and such. Table 13.3 shows the figures under these various heads from 1985–86 to 1992–93.

Figure 13.2 shows three-year moving averages of capital and revenue expenditure on health by the government after adjustment to 1981–82 rupees. The steady growth of revenue expenditure in health throughout the eighties is evident, whereas capital expenditure shows a tendency to drop after the mid-eighties.

Figure 13.3 shows that salaries display a sharp and upward trend from the mid-eighties onward, which has been somewhat curbed starting the beginning of the nineties. But it does not show any tendency to drop down as yet, whereas the curve for supplies shows that it has followed a much slower rate of increase in the eighties, followed by cutbacks beginning the late eighties.

Figure 13.4 shows the break-up of the expenditure on supplies in the primary, secondary, and tertiary sectors. Primary sector shows an almost flat curve, registering not much growth nor contraction. Secondary sector, which is by far the largest of the three

Table 13.2
Trends in Overall Position of the State Budget (Revenue Account) (in Million Rs)

Year	*Revenue Receipts*	*Revenue Expenditure*	*Surplus/ Deficit (S/D) (–)*	*State Domestic Product (SDP) in Million Rs*	*S/D as % of Revenue Received*	*S/D as % of SDP*
(1)	*(2)*	*(3)*	*(4)*	*(5)*	*(6)*	*(7)*
1980–81	6403.8	6676.1	–272.3	38227.3	4.25	0.71
1985–86	13714.7	14443.4	–741.7	40863.6	5.41	1.81
1986–87	15025.3	16547.7	–1522.4	39929.7	10.43	3.81
1988–89	18970.6	20610.0	–1639.4	45841.0	8.64	3.58
1989–90	20476.4	22680.9	–2504.5	48923.6	12.23	5.12
1990–91	24929.8	28249.5	–4220.2	52693.7	16.93	8.01

Source: Government of Kerala 1993b; Government of Kerala (1993c).

Table 13.3
Total Revenue Expenditure, Expenditure under Medical and Public Health Accounts, and Proportions, from 1985/86 to 1992/93

I *Year*	*II* *Total Revenue Expenditure (in Million Rs)*	*III* *Medical and Public Health (in Million Rs)*	*III as % of II*	*III as % of Development Expenditure by the State*
1985–86	14453.4	1205.5	8.34	11.63
1986–87	16547.7	1437.5	8.69	12.89
1987–88	17806.5	1665.3	9.35	14.32
1988–89	20610.0	2142.0	10.39	15.76
1989–90	22930.9	2395.6	10.45	16.40
1990–91	28249.5	2785.0	9.86	15.45
1991–92	32164.6	2920.0	9.08	14.83
1992–93	38512.5	3379.8	8.78	13.76

Source: Government of Kerala 1993b.

Figure 13.2
Total Government Expenditure on Health, Kerala State, under Capital and Revenue in Million Rupees, 1977–78 to 1992–93—3-year Moving Averages

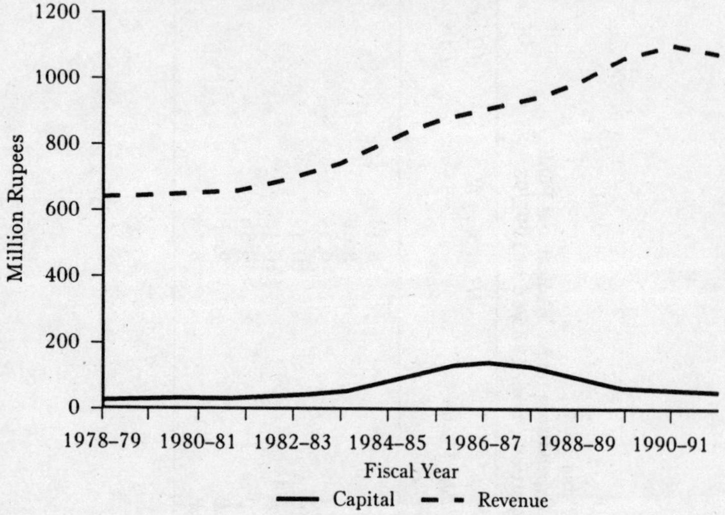

and consists of district and taluk-level hospitals, shows a steady upward trend during the eighties followed by a sharp fall from the start of the nineties. Tertiary sector shows a milder increase all through the eighties, with a tendency to flatten in the recent years.

The question of the existence and nature of fiscal crisis in this state is put to detailed analysis in an in-depth study brought out recently (George 1993). The main points highlighted in this study are: (*i*) though budgetary deficit has become a common feature for all states in India, the magnitude of the deficit in Kerala has been steadily growing and is substantively higher than the all-states average; and (*ii*) unlike in other states, the deficit here has its genesis in the revenue account. This means that the recurrent expenditure by the state has been growing at a greater rate than the total spending. The gap between government receipts of money or revenue and expenditure has been steadily widening. This mounting and recurring revenue deficit has been financed by drawing on capital receipts, or funds meant for capital expansion.

Figure 13.3
Expenditure by Government on Salaries and Wages ("Salaries") and Supplies in the Health Sector, Kerala State, in Million Rupees, 1977–78 to 1992–93—3-year Moving Averages

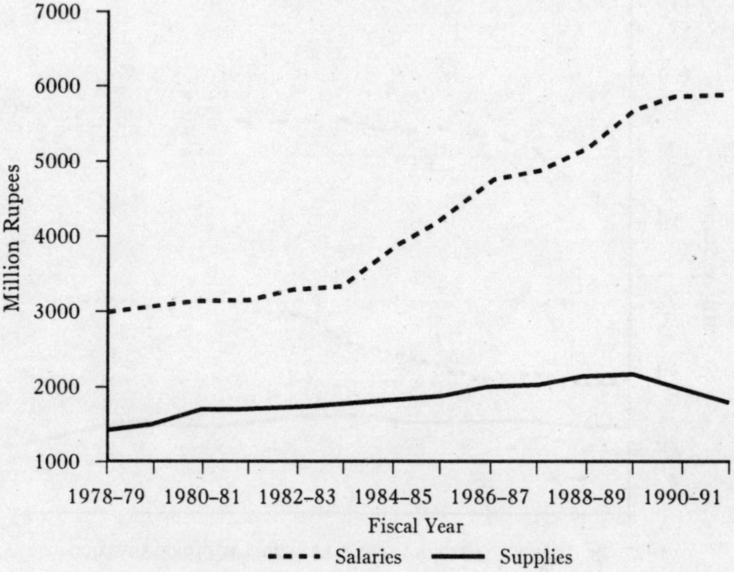

Spending on health as a proportion of total revenue expenditure remained steady all through this period of expansion, whereas as a proportion of total development expenditure, it actually showed an increase (see Table 13.3). In fact, after education, health forms the second most important head of revenue expenditure for the state government. As such, the health sector expense has been a major component of the mounting revenue spending. Capital expenditure on health has been cut back, probably as an attempt to contain the growing fiscal deficit, even by the mid-eighties (see Figure 13.2). It is reasonable to conclude that the adjustment in health expenditure first affected capital and only later, after 1990, was the revenue expenditure affected. Total revenue spending on health has continued growing, at least till the beginning of the nineties. This is because of two reasons: (*i*) Having built up the health infrastructure, the government found it difficult to close down facilities for fear of public reprisal. Thus,

Figure 13.4
Expenditure by Government on Supplies in the Primary, Secondary, and Tertiary Sectors in Kerala State, in Million Rupees, 1977–78 to 1992–93—3-year Moving Averages

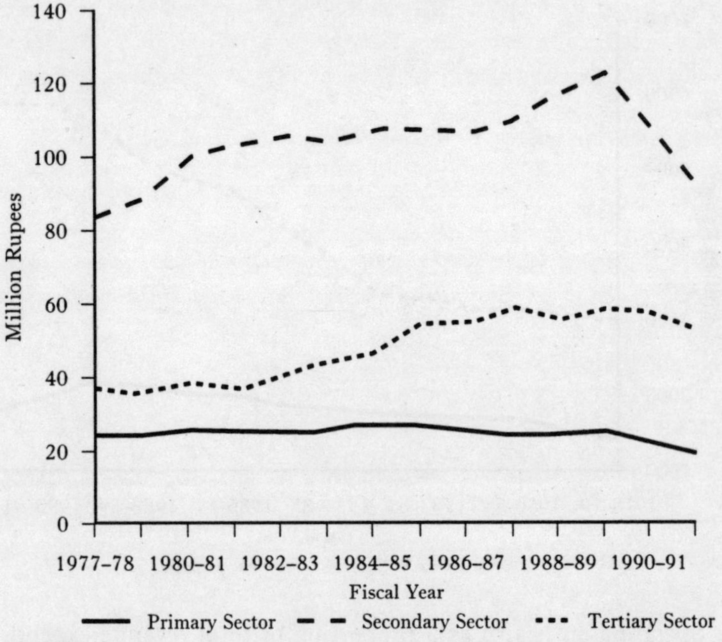

the momentum of spending could not be contained. (*ii*) There was an increasing demand for more services, which the government tried to provide within the existing physical infrastructure by recruiting more personnel.

The curve showing the growth of expenditure on salaries is remarkably parallel to the curve for total revenue expenditure on health, thus confirming that rising salary expense has been a main contributor to growth in revenue spending in health (see Figure 13.3). Increase in salaries comprises two elements: (*i*) increase in value of salaries and wages over the years and (*ii*) increase in number of employees. Both these have probably contributed to the observed trend. The high level of political consciousness in the state, strong unions, and precariously balanced governments, together create a political environment in which curtailment of salary expense is not easy. On the other hand, the curve for supplies shows a much gentler upward slope all throughout the eighties, indicating a moderate degree of increase. By the beginning of the nineties, this curve already shows a tendency to drop down, whereas the curve for salaries continues to go up and only shows a mild tendency to flatten towards the end of the period under review. Successive governments, faced with the necessity of controlling revenue expenditure but denied the choice of even trying to check the growth of salaries, were left with no option but to reduce spending on supplies. Figure 13.4 shows that supplies in the primary sector were largely unaffected because a good proportion of these is constituted by vaccines, oral rehydration salts, and such, whose supply is supported by international agencies and the central government. A good number of programs for disease prevention and the Family Welfare Program, which are all supported by the central government, also come under the primary sector. Possibly because of this, supplies in the primary sector have been unaffected by the crisis in the state government's finances. A similar picture, where the primary sector was unaffected and in fact continued to grow at a greater rate than the overall growth of the health sector in the eighties, has been reported from Andhra Pradesh (Mahapatra and Berman 1991).

The medical colleges and other large hospitals which form the tertiary sector have also been comparatively spared from the worst effects of the adjustment. Possible reasons are the greater amount of public attention they receive, their urban location, and their perceived strategic importance in the medical care setup in the state. The brunt of the adjustment, therefore, has been borne by the secondary sector. This sector comprises the large number of smaller hospitals which cater mostly to the vast rural population in the state.

Reviewing the whole picture, we see that fiscal adjustment, in the form of expenditure compression, has affected capital earlier and to a greater degree than revenue expenditure. Moreover, in revenue expenditure, supplies have been affected much more than salaries; supplies to the secondary sector have been affected more acutely than those to the primary or tertiary sectors. What this means in real terms is that expansion of facilities and provision of good quality care have suffered and this has affected selectively the secondary sector to the greatest extent. Since the secondary sector caters to the curative care needs of a large section of the population, this has in effect meant erosion of the standards of health care in the public sector.

Fiscal problems of the government affecting health sector has been a recurring theme in developing countries. Loewenson comments on the adverse health consequences of "Structural Adjustment Policies" (SAP) which have been introduced in sub-Saharan Africa (Loewenson 1993). In the case of Kerala, though SAP may not be directly responsible for the crisis situation, the state's finances have not been unaffected by the national and international economic trends.

Policy Implications

Improving the standards of care in the government sector envisages, as a necessary condition, improvement in the financial situation also. A priori, there are several possible ways of improving the health care financing situation in the public hospitals and health centers:

1. Increasing the share of health in the budget;
2. finding ways of augmenting the state's revenues, so that total expenditure, and the share of health sector, can be enhanced;
3. cost containment and deployment of available resources more effectively; and
4. raising resources within the health sector.

As we have seen, one has to seriously look at option 1, namely, enhancing health sector's share in the total government spending. Government spending on health, as a share of total government revenue expenditure in Kerala, is around 8 percent and cannot be said to be too high. In industrialized countries, it is often a higher percentage of the total government expenditure: in 1991, in the United States, reportedly around 20 percent of the government expenditure was used by the states on health (Calkins, Fernandopulle, and Marino 1995). There is a definite case for increasing the public spending on health in the state, contrary to the popular notion that the state already spends too much on health.

At present, the lion's share of spending on health comes from the state's own revenues. There is a case for further flow of funds from the central government to the state in the health sector. Performance indicators for most of the centrally sponsored health schemes in Kerala, such as the family welfare program and universal immunization are much better compared to other states. These achievements can be attributed to developments outside the health sector in the state, such as high levels of literacy, especially female literacy, and political awareness. It is often argued that since the state is already a high performer in health, it does not need more central funds. In reality, there is a case for an even greater share of central resources being allocated to the state for its health programs, especially in the area of control of infectious diseases. The recent outbreak of malaria in the state after being free from endemic cases for a long time and epidemics of viral encephalitis and dengue underscore this need.

Option 2. viz., enhancing revenue collection in general is the one which, however justifiable, is socially and politically unpalatable and will meet with wide resistance; nevertheless, its feasibility should be explored.

Option 3. i.e., cost containment is another important policy option geared towards better performance of the health sector. It is important to see if costs can be contained without affecting the level of services. The savings thus generated could obviously contribute to expanding services in quality and/or quantity. Currently, most of the energy of the administrative machinery in the health services is taken up by transfers, postings, and such non-productive activity, which are all done centrally. By delegating this authority to the local administrative bodies, a lot of efficiency could be introduced into the functioning of the health services. The state has to evolve a long-term manpower policy in health to make sure that available skilled personnel are put to the greatest use.

Option 4. i.e., raising finances within the health sector should be examined in the context of the proposed decentralization, which envisages conferring more administrative power and financial resources to the local bodies.

The interim report of the Resources Commission in the state, a body appointed by government to look into ways of improving the financial position of the government, recommended levying user charges for outpatient services and introducing differential charges depending upon the income of the patient (Government of Kerala 1993a). One can see here the influence of the policy environment created by the Structural Adjustment Programs. Many developing countries have experimented with the introduction of user charges in the health facilities, even in primary health centers. Not only has this met with great opposition from the public, this has also proved to be disastrous in areas like sub-Saharan Africa (Moses et al. 1992). User charges, though perhaps simple to operate, have some built-in problems in a developing community:

1. Sick people are already at a disadvantage economically because of their sickness. To be obliged to pay for hospital services to get well puts an additional burden on them, which is contrary to the principles of equity.
2. Charging uniformly for similar services puts differential burden on different classes of people. What may be an insignificant amount to the richer households, may be a considerable encumbrance for a poor household. This introduces an additional element of inequity: the poor are asked to pay a relatively greater price for getting well. If to tide over this problem we introduce differential charges, then the additional administrative cost of categorizing people may make the whole exercise counter-productive.

But user charges are not the sole means of improving the financial status of the health sector. Other policy options need to be examined with a view to their suitability in the Kerala context:

1. *Community financing*: In a well-defined community, such as a panchayat, a specific amount per household can be collected as decided by the panchayat, the poorer households being exempted; this amount can be set apart specifically for running of the local-level health institutions such as the primary health center. There are two preconditions which have to be met for the success of this policy: (*i*) The local level health institution should be under the control of the local administration such as the panchayat. The first step towards this has already been taken with the promulgation of the panchayati raj law, devolving responsibility

of local-level health institutions to the gram, block, and district panchayats. (*ii*) Basic health services which will be available at the local level have to be decided on sound epidemiological principles, with a system of referral to higher institutions run by the state. The amount collected locally as health tax can be specifically used for augmenting the facilities of the health center including its drug supply since the state government already pays the salaries of the staff. A considerable amount of improvement in the conditions of care can be brought about this way without collecting charges from the users at the facility. Here the emphasis should be on local control of the facility and not merely on the collection of taxes. The Resources Commission of the state also favors entrusting management of the health facilities in the rural sector to local-level bodies such as panchayats (Government of Kerala 1993a). Recently, the state government and the state planning board took initiatives to set apart 40 percent of the funds for schemes in the Ninth Five Year Plan in the state for allocation by the panchayats themselves.

2. *Health insurance*: Health insurance is another potential resource base which is much favored in the international health policy circles currently. However, for health insurance to be successful, total coverage is a must. The problems of copying the Western model of private insurance for health in developing countries have been documented: it leads to inadequate coverage, inappropriate use, and exclusion of the most needy sections from the health network (Mills 1983). If insurance is to be effective and equitable, coverage must be total and risks pooled.

There are certain realities which may make the conventional type of health insurance not the ideal option for a country like India:

1. Only a small proportion of the working age population is employed formally; the others who make up the large informal sector have a very unpredictable income and as such cannot be expected to contribute insurance premiums regularly. Moreover, in the informal sector, the logistics of collecting the premium is itself formidable.

2. There is also a large section of the people, unemployed or under-employed, who are too poor to pay even the insurance premiums, however low. A just and equitable policy should take care of their health needs also.

One way out of this situation is to make the village councils, panchayats, responsible for payment of premiums for the whole village. The panchayats can decide which are the households that are too poor to pay and find some mechanism for payment on their behalf. The local body can decide how they are going to raise this collective premium: probably this would include a certain amount of subsidizing for the poor families. Thus, each panchayat can pay the insurance agency an annual sum depending on the population in the village it represents. This would amount to a kind of community rating. Each government health institution can make claims to the company for reimbursement of charges on the number of people they have treated. It is also desirable to create a single insurance agency which will cover the whole population of the state, which will provide adequate pooling of risks and total coverage. A single agency in health financing offers certain advantages such as low cost of procurement of drugs on account of large volumes.

In the matter of raising additional revenue for the health facilities, pre-payment is more equitable because those who have the misfortune to fall ill are not penalized by the system. Since nobody can discount the small risk of falling sick and since every family knows that all families in the village are paying, there would be very little resentment against this. As it is a designated tax and it is administered by the panchayat, there can be greater accountability and public participation. In fact, the panchayat can be required to publish the annual revenues and expenditures for the local health center, which can be scrutinized by the public. We do not as yet have models in the state where such experiments have been undertaken.

Both pre-payment at the panchayat level and group health insurance, as outlined above, have certain features in common. They envisage (*i*) a more active role for the local governments such as panchayats and (*ii*) greater resource mobilization at the local level. The difference is that local-level financing of health institutions leads to more direct control for the local governments on the health centers. The state could adopt one of the choices:

either local level-health tax or insurance through a single agency. It is also possible to think of a system where after the panchayat collects the health tax, part of it is given over to the health center and part paid to a central agency with a clear-cut division of responsibilities between the two.

Conclusion

Kerala presents a unique experience among developing countries where a commitment to investment in social sectors such as health and education has reaped great benefits in the improvement of the health status of its people. Growing fiscal problems of the state administration pose a serious threat to the health services in the state. Policy prescriptions now in vogue all propose a conscious orientation towards less of public spending and more privatization in health. Our analysis shows that: (*i*) the proposition that there cannot be expansion in public spending in health is not necessarily correct; (*ii*) some remedies that are planned, such as user charges, will undermine the very foundation of the health care network in Kerala, which is based on a premise of universal access; and (*iii*) there are alternative policy instruments which can lead to greater resource mobilization as well as efficiency in resource use in health. All these presuppose a more decentralized administration of health care. Decentralization of overall government is a national commitment ever since India's independence and is reiterated periodically. With more powers for administration of the local health institutions vested with the three-tier panchayats, the opportunity has arisen for reorganizing health care to provide greater services to the people.

Policy-making in health demonstrates the need for an in-depth understanding of the health situation. Improving health finances is not a simple question of collecting more money. Each option carries its own implications for equity and efficiency. Unless there is a deep understanding of the local health system, we are likely to end up with more problems than we started with.

Referencess

Calkins, D., Fernandopulle, R.J., and **Marino, B.S.** (1995): *Health Care Policy*. Cambridge: Blackwell Science.

George, K.K. (1993): *Limits to the Kerala Model of Development*. Trivandrum: Centre for Development Studies.

Government of India (1993): Sample Registration System—Selected Demographic Indicators. New Delhi: Office of the Registrar-General, Vital Statistics Division, Ministry of Home Affairs. Mimeo.

Government of Kerala (1993a): Report of the Resources Commission. Trivandrum.

——— (1993b): Kerala Budget in Brief 1993–94. Trivandrum.

——— (1993c): Economic Review. Trivandrum.

Loewenson, R. (1993): Structural Adjustment and Health Policy in Africa. *International Journal of Health Services*, 4: 717–30.

Mahapatra, P., and **Berman, P.** (1991): Allocation of Government Health Services Expenditure in Andhra Pradesh, India, during the Eighties. *Demography India*, 20: 297–310.

Mills, A. (1983): Economic Aspects of Health Insurance. In K. Lee and A. Mills (eds.). *The Economics of Health in Developing Countries*. Oxford: Oxford University Press.

Moses, S., Manji, F., Bradley, J.E., Nagelkerke, N.J.D., Malisa, M.A., and **Plummer, F.A.** (1992): Impact of User Fees on Attendance at a Referral Centre for Sexually Transmitted Diseases in Kenya. *Lancet*, 340: 463–66.

Panikar, P.G.K., and **Soman, C.R.** (1984): *Health Status of Kerala: Paradox of Economic Backwardness and Health Development*. Trivandrum: Centre for Development Studies.

Tulasidhar, V.B. (1993): Expenditure Compression and Health Sector Outlays. *Economic and Political Weekly*, 28(45): 2473–77.

World Health Organization (1978): *Financing of Health Services*. Report of WHO Study Group. Geneva: WHO.

14

Health Sector and Economic Reform: A Study of Maharashtra and Tamil Nadu

K. Seeta Prabhu

Introduction

The impact of economic reform on the social sector is a keenly debated issue. Critics argue that the post-economic reform government policy for restructuring Third World countries would contribute to the worsening health status of the people, particularly the poor. This would be an outcome of (*i*) reduced government expenditure on health, particularly primary health care; (*ii*) first and second order/direct and indirect effects of the withdrawal of subsidies from various welfare programs and social sector services (including health, education, nutrition, Minimum Needs Program, etc.); and (*iii*) increasing inequalities. The available evidence from countries of sub-Saharan Africa and Latin America indicates that the process of economic reforms has had adverse repercussions on the health sector in countries of these regions (Jayarajah, Branson, and Sen 1996).[1] A study of the impact of economic reform on the health sector is of particular importance in a low income country like India, where poverty and inequality are major contributors to hunger, disease, and

[1] Jayarajah, Branson, and Sen (1996) report that the index of real per capita health spending (1981=100) in sub-Saharan Africa declined from 117.7 to 97.7 after structural adjustment, though in Latin America the index increased from 94.6 before adjustment to 103.6 during adjustment (p. 85). The rate of decline in infant mortality slowed down in both sub-Saharan Africa and Latin America, from –1.8 percent per annum to –1.6 percent in Africa. In Latin America, the slowdown was sharper, from –5.0 percent to –2.9 percent.

debility.[2] With the initiation of economic reforms in India in July 1991, fears have been voiced of further deterioration in the health status of the population. The trends in government health expenditure in the initial two years of reform lent support to such apprehensions (Tulasidhar 1993).

At the outset, it needs to be mentioned that although government expenditure on health constitutes only around one-fifth of the total expenditure on the sector (World Bank 1995), this is more important for health attainment than immediately apparent for the following reasons: (*i*) public sector health facilities are utilized to a greater extent by the poor (NCAER 1992);[3] and (*ii*) higher per capita government expenditure improves utilization of primary health centers as well as public hospitals, particularly free wards (Purohit and Siddiqui 1994).[4]

A significant feature of government health expenditure in India is that the bulk of such expenditure (75 percent) is incurred by the state governments. In view of this, the chapter attempts

[2] India has a high burden of diseases of poverty and in fact has the dubious distinction of having half of the world's 20 million tuberculosis patients and one-third of the 12 million leprosy patients (Uplekar and George 1993). The Disability Adjusted Life Years (DALYs)—a controversial measure used by the World Bank—lost due to diseases in India in 1990 was 292 million which is over 21 percent of the global burden of disease (World Bank 1993).

[3] Income group-wise data indicate a greater reliance on public facilities by the poor. NCAER 1992 indicates that 40 percent of illness episodes in poorer households and 25 percent in richer households were attended to by government doctors. NSSO 1992 data on hospitalization indicate that the intensity of use of government hospitals (defined as the percentage of hospitalized cases in a quintile using government facilities) was 61 percent and 70 percent for the households belonging to the lowest 20 percent of the consumer expenditure class in rural and urban areas respectively. The corresponding percentages for the top 20 percent of households were 49 and 45 percent.

[4] Purohit and Siddiqui (1994) report that the highest utilization of public hospitals has been observed to be in states where per capita government expenditure on health is high (above Rs 200 in 1986–87). The rate of utilization of hospitals in these states in 1986–87 was 81.38 percent and 87.36 percent for rural and urban areas respectively (p. 1074). Corresponding inversely to the low average per capita expenditure levels of state governments, the private rural hospitals were used more by respondents (27.10 percent) belonging to the low expenditure group states. Furthermore, utilization of free wards was also higher in the high expenditure states. The utilization of PHCs, both in rural and urban areas, was observed to be the highest among the high expenditure states.

to examine the main trends in health sector expenditures of the governments of two Indian states, viz., Maharashtra and Tamil Nadu, during the period of economic reforms, to assess whether there have been any changes since the introduction of SAPs in 1991. Maharashtra represents a high-income state which ranked third among 15 major states in terms of per capita income in 1988–91, whereas Tamil Nadu is a middle-income state ranked eighth during the same period (Prabhu and Chatterjee 1993). What is of special interest is the fact that, with respect to health and other human development indicators, the performance of the two states is similar. In terms of priorities, Maharashtra spends the highest proportion of health expenditure on public health though its spending on welfare measures such as nutrition is minimal. Tamil Nadu, on the other hand, is known for a wide range of nutrition programs, though the direct emphasis on public health seems to be lower. Thus, the two states provide an interesting contrast in terms of their emphasis on different components of human development and their responses during a period of economic reform could provide valuable insights for the future.

In this chapter, the next section sets out the main features of health attainment as well as health infrastructure in the two states during the period prior to the initiation of economic reforms. Section three provides an analysis of the level of state government expenditures on the health sector during the period 1988–89 to 1994–95. Section four briefly discusses the intra-sectoral allocation of these health sector expenditures. While expenditures are reported at the state level, they are in fact incurred at the district level. Section five presents an analysis of district level expenditures on health during two time periods, 1988–89 to 1990–91 (1988–91) which represents the pre-adjustment period and 1991–92 to 1993–94 (1991–94) which is the post-adjustment period. Section six presents a brief analysis of the perceptions of users of primary health centers regarding both quality of services as well as change in such quality during the adjustment years in five selected villages in Maharashtra and Tamil Nadu. This is very important because the utilization of available public health services would depend a lot on the quality and efficacy of these as perceived by the people. The last section highlights the main conclusions of the study.

Pre-adjustment Period

Table 14.1 sets out the attainment of the two states in terms of key indicators of health during the period 1985–87 and 1990–92. It may be stated that though data on two time points are presented, this in no way is to be construed as comparing the pre- and post-adjustment periods. The attainment data till 1992 have been reported as they are the latest available estimates. The prevalence rate of illness is higher in Tamil Nadu. This is confirmed by the National Council of Applied Economic Research (NCAER) data for 1990 (NCAER 1992).

Maharashtra's provision of health infrastructure was better for tertiary care whereas Tamil Nadu recorded a higher number of primary health centers (PHCs) per 100 sq km. The same tendency was observed in PHCs as well as medical personnel per lakh population (CMIE 1992). Data pertaining to distance traveled per illness episode indicate that two-thirds of the illness episodes in urban Maharashtra were treated within a range of one kilometer whereas the figure for rural Maharashtra was less than 50 percent. In Tamil Nadu, only 45 percent of illness episodes in urban areas and 10 percent in rural areas were treated within a range of one kilometer. In fact, in rural Tamil Nadu, 36 percent of the population traveled 3–5 kilometers and 30 percent traveled 6–10 kilometers for medical treatment (NCAER 1992).

A perusal of infrastructure for nutrition indicates higher per capita production in Maharashtra though in terms of indicators of distribution, Tamil Nadu's performance was better. Both states implement nutrition programs apart from operating the public distribution system, though the effectiveness of these programs is noteworthy in Tamil Nadu (Prabhu 1997a).

Data on utilization of health facilities available from the NCAER (1992) indicate higher reliance on private facilities in Tamil Nadu in 1990, with over half the cases in both rural and urban areas being referred to private doctors. In Maharashtra, less than half the illness episodes were referred to private doctors. The PHCs in Maharashtra accounted for 16 and 21 percent of illness episodes in rural and urban Maharashtra respectively, whereas the corresponding percentages for Tamil Nadu were extremely low at 4 and 3 percent despite physical access to

Table 14.1
Main Indicators of Human Development

S.No. (1)	*Indicator* (2)	*Year* (3)	*Maharashtra* (4)	*Tamil Nadu* (5)	*India* (6)
1.	IMR	1985–87—C*	66	79	96
		Rural (R)	75	91	105
		Urban (U)	47	54	60
		1990–92—C	59	58	80
		R	67	67	86
		U	41	40	52
2.	Birth rate	1985–87—C	29.3	24.1	32.6
		R	30.6	24.5	34.1
		U	27.1	23.5	27.5
		1990–92—C	26.3	21.0	29.5
		R	28.2	21.2	31.1
		U	22.7	20.6	24.0
3.	Death rate	1985–87—C	8.4	9.6	11.3
		R	9.6	10.6	12.4
		U	6.3	7.2	7.6
		1990–92—C	7.8	8.6	9.8
		R	8.9	9.4	10.7
		U	5.7	6.9	7.0

Source: EPW Research Foundation 1994: 21 May, p. 1302. Mumbai.
C*—Combined
IMR—Infant mortality rate represents number of infant deaths per 1,000 live births.
Birth rate and Death rate represent number of live births and deaths respectively per 1,000 of mid-year population.

such facilities being better. NSSO data for 1986–87 indicate similar trends (NSSO 1992). The lower average cost of treatment given by private doctors, Rs 106 per illness episode in Tamil Nadu as against Rs 208 in Maharashtra according to NCAER data explains the differences in utilization of government services to some extent. NSSO data for 1986–87 report an average cost of Rs 901 in private hospitals in rural Maharashtra, and Rs 681 in rural Tamil Nadu (NSSO 1992). The relative burden of treatment, defined by Krishnan (1995) as the ratio of treatment cost to annual per capita expenditure of the corresponding decile of population, indicated that the burden of treatment per illness episode in private hospitals was 75 percent in rural Tamil Nadu as compared to 110 percent in rural Maharashtra, indicating that households had to incur debt in order to seek medical treatment.

Regarding social sector expenditure, the bias in both the states was towards higher level facilities. Maharashtra spent 28 percent of medical and health expenditures on public health in 1990–91 as compared to 11 percent in Tamil Nadu. There has been a deceleration in the growth of real per capita social sector expenditure and real per capita health expenditure since the mid-eighties in both the states, from 6.97 to 2.34 percent in Maharashtra between 1974–75 and 1984–85, and 1985–86 and 1991–92, and from 7.49 to 4.43 percent for Tamil Nadu during the same time period. In sum, deceleration in social sector expenditure is evident in both states. More significant is the dramatic reduction in growth rate in the health sector in terms of both quantum and pace in Maharashtra, from 7.46 to –3.54 percent, which is better sustained in Tamil Nadu (Prabhu and Chatterjee 1993).

In the case of Maharashtra, despite higher per capita incomes and provision of rural employment on a sustained basis since 1982, the levels of poverty are high. In 1993–94, the proportion of population below the poverty line (estimated by the Expert Group of the Planning Commission) was 38 percent in rural Maharashtra, which had declined only marginally from the 41 percent recorded in 1987–88. This is in contrast to Tamil Nadu where rural poverty had declined from 46 percent in 1987–88 to 32 percent in 1993–94 (Malhotra 1997). One of the main reasons for this differential performance of the two states is that Maharashtra pays very little attention to the nutrition sector though the attention paid to public health is noteworthy. The state has, in fact, recorded several deaths of children due to malnourishment in recent years in tribal pockets such as Melghat in Amravati district.

Trends in State Government Expenditure on Health

Before proceeding to an analysis of trends in health sector expenditure by the state governments, it is necessary to recognize the differences in the fiscal situation of the two states. Maharashtra is generally considered to be well-managed in terms of state finances, whereas Tamil Nadu's fiscal situation would be considered none too prudent by conventional norms. Tamil Nadu has a higher component of non-plan expenditure as well as revenue expenditure though the bulk of revenue expenditure is for developmental purposes. The higher non-plan expenditure is due to the continuation of various social sector schemes initiated during the plan period. Both states reported a deceleration in revenue receipts as well as gross transfers from the center during the years of economic reform. However, Tamil Nadu embarked on a fiscal policy, wherein the ratio of consumption expenditure to current expenditure as well as subsidies to current expenditure increased, further widening the gap between the two states on this account. The fiscal stress experienced by Tamil Nadu was also higher as indicated by its higher revenue deficit to gross fiscal deficit ratio (Prabhu 1997b). While conventional fiscal wisdom would tend to characterize this as alarming, Tamil Nadu's better performance in nutritional attainment, despite being a middle-income state, could be attributed to such expansionary fiscal policies.

Tables 14.2–14.4 provide data on trends in revenue expenditure on social services, health, and nutrition in Maharashtra and Tamil Nadu between 1988–89 and 1994–95. It may be noted that revenue expenditure constitutes the bulk of expenditure on these sectors, accounting for 81 and 86 percent of total expenditure in Maharashtra and Tamil Nadu respectively during 1988–91. The share of education and health in total revenue expenditure was between 96 and 98 percent, whereas in the nutrition sector the entire expenditure was on revenue account in both states. The expenditure on health includes expenditure on medical, public health, family welfare, and water supply and sanitation. Nutrition expenditures have been included in the analysis in view of the importance of nutrition for health attainment. All data have been compiled from various issues of the *Reserve Bank of India Bulletin*.

A perusal of Table 14.2 indicates that the expenditure on social services and health sectors in Maharashtra in general kept pace with total expenditure, though the same cannot be said of the nutrition sector where the expenditure declined in three of the post-1991 years. Consequently, in 1994–95, the total expenditure on this sector was 22 percent lower than that in 1990–91. In Tamil Nadu, revenue expenditure increased in 1991–92 by 54 percent due mainly to book adjustments, such as writing off State Electricity Board dues, and remained at that level in subsequent years. The expenditure on social services recorded increases of 7 to 16 percent during the post-1991 years. The expenditure on health increased sharply by 30 percent in 1993–94, though the next year the expenditure declined marginally by 4 percent. The nutrition sector recorded modest increases ranging between 4 and 9 percent in the post-1991 years except in 1994–95 when it increased by over 26 percent.

In terms of share in total revenue expenditure (see Table 14.3), Maharashtra's expenditure on social services and health remained more or less constant between the years 1988–89 and 1994–95 at 35 percent and 7 percent respectively. The low emphasis on nutrition expenditures is evident in the negligible proportion of total revenue expenditure allocated to this sector. The data thus indicate no major change in the levels of expenditure during the period under consideration. In the case of Tamil Nadu, the share of MPH in total revenue expenditure was around 9 percent in the pre-adjustment years, declined to 7 to 8 percent in the next two years and recovered to over 9 percent subsequently. Expenditure on nutrition followed similar trends with the share being restored to the pre-adjustment level of 4 percent in 1994–95. The experience of the state is marked by an effort to maintain sectoral priorities.

A more meaningful picture may be available by examining the real per capita expenditure, which is calculated using state specific SDP deflators. It is important to note that the price level is higher in Maharashtra and the state also experienced a sharper rise in prices, particularly in the Consumer Price Index for

Table 14.2

Trends in Revenue Expenditure on Human Development (in Million Rs)

S. No. (1)	Expenditure on (2)	1988–89 (Acc.) (3)	1989–90 (Acc.) (4)	1990–91 (Acc.) (5)	1991–92 (Acc.) (6)	1992–93 (Acc.) (7)	1993–94 (Acc.) (8)	1994–95 (R.E.) (9)
					Maharashtra			
1.	Total	65406.50	79025.50 (20.02)	87536.70 (10.77)	100487.0 (14.79)	115467.0 (14.91)	131006.9 (13.53)	146683.5 (11.9)
2.	Social services	23436.00	28665.9 (22.32)	30966.8 (8.03)	36022.5 (16.33)	41178.5 (14.31)	46313.1 (12.47)	52834.4 (16.24)
3.	Medical & public health*	5571.0	6108.1 (9.63)	6843.0 (12.03)	7313.5 (6.88)	8522.9 (16.54)	9539.3 (11.93)	10594.5 (11.06)
4.	Nutrition	331.00	414.90 (25.05)	555.20 (32.82)	500.20 (4.5)	744.90 (28.39)	672.20 (–9.76)	431.50 (–35.81)
					Tamil Nadu			
1.	Total	37630.4	47307.9 (25.72)	56412.9 (19.25)	86795.3 (–1.58)	85425.3 (–1.58)	87580.0 (2.52)	91871.6 (4.9)
2.	Social services	15660.4	20517.0 (31.01)	24919.1 (21.46)	28805.5 (15.60)	31609.5 (9.73)	35860.7 (13.45)	38408.5 (7.10)
3.	Medical & public health*	3527.1	4738.30 (34.34)	5183.40 (9.39)	6066.00 (17.03)	6740.10 (11.11)	8768.00 (30.09)	8392.30 (–4.28)
4.	Nutrition	905.77	1396.86 (54.22)	2353.30 (68.47)	2555.60 (8.60)	2723.10 (6.55)	2825.10 (3.75)	3565.00 (26.19)

Source: *Reserve Bank of India Bulletin*, various issues.

*including family welfare, water supply, and sanitation.

Acc.: Accounts; R.E.: Recurring expenditure.

Figures in parentheses indicate percentage change over previous year.

Table 14.3
Human Development Expenditure Ratios (in percent)

S.No. (1)	*Item* (2)	*1988–89* (*Acc.*) (3)	*1989–90* (*Acc.*) (4)	*1990–91* (*Acc.*) (5)	*1991–92* (*Acc.*) (6)	*1992–93* (*Acc.*) (7)	*1993–94* (*Acc.*) (8)	*1994–95* (*R.E.*) (9)
					Maharashtra			
1.	Social services/ Total revenue expenditure	35.83	36.27	35.30	35.85	35.66	35.33	36.70
2.	MPH/Total revenue expenditure	8.52	7.73	7.82	7.28	7.30	7.14	7.22
3.	Nutrition/Total revenue expenditure	0.51	0.53	0.63	0.58	0.65	0.51	0.29
					Tamil Nadu			
1.	Social services/ Total revenue expenditure	41.62	45.37	44.17	33.19	37.00	41.95	41.81
2.	MPH/Total revenue expenditure	9.37	10.02	9.19	6.99	7.89	10.01	9.13
3.	Nutrition/Total revenue expenditure	2.41	2.95	4.17	2.94	3.19	3.23	3.00

Source: Computed from *Reserve Bank of India Bulletin*, various issues.
MPH: Medical and public health; Acc.: Accounts; R.E.: Recurring expenditure.

Table 14.4
Trends in Real Per Capita* Revenue Expenditure on Select Items of Human Development (in Rs)

S.No. (1)	*Expenditure on* (2)	*1988–89* (*Acc.*) (3)	*1989–90* (*Acc.*) (4)	*1990–91* (*Acc.*) (5)	*1991–92* (*Acc.*) (6)	*1992–93* (*Acc.*) (7)	*1993–94* (*Acc.*) (8)
				Maharashtra			
1.	Total	488.07	547.59 (12.20)	529.60 (–3.29)	529.05 (–0.10)	546.97 (3.39)	563.40 (3.00)
2.	Social services	174.00	198.63 (13.58)	187.35 (–5.68)	189.65 (1.23)	195.06 (2.85)	199.05 (2.04)
3.	MPH**	41.58	42.32 (1.00)	41.40 (–2.18)	38.50 (–7.00)	40.37 (4.85)	40.23 (2.89)
4.	Nutrition	1.11	2.87 (157.54)	3.36 (17.07)	3.05 (–9.23)	3.53 (15.74)	2.09 (–18.13)
				Tamil Nadu			
1.	Total	367.45	415.30 (13.02)	456.96 (10.03)	608.34 (33.13)	533.24 (–12.35)	502.00 (–5.86)
2.	Social services	152.92	180.11 (17.78)	201.85 (12.07)	201.90 (0.01)	197.30 (–2.27)	205.55 (4.17)
3.	MPH**	34.44	41.60 (20.79)	41.99 (0.94)	42.52 (1.26)	42.07 (–1.06)	50.26 (19.47)
4.	Nutrition	8.84	12.26 (38.69)	19.06 (55.46)	17.91 (–6.03)	17.00 (–5.00)	16.19 (–4.76)

Source: Expenditure Budgets of Government of Maharashtra and Government of Tamil Nadu for 1988–89 to 1993–94.
*Using state specific SDP deflators and mid-year population.
**Medical & public health including family welfare, water supply, and sanitation.
Figures in parentheses indicate percentage change over previous year/period.

Agricultural Laborers (CPIAL) during the economic reform period. The situation on the price front is partly influenced by the differing policies of the two states with respect to PDS prices. The Central Issue Price (CIP) for rice and wheat has been revised upward substantially since 1991 and the states are at liberty to fix the prices at which food grains are issued from the PDS outlets. In February 1994, in Maharashtra the price was 23 percent higher than the CIP for rice and 24 percent higher for wheat. In Tamil Nadu, the policy was just the reverse. The price that was charged for rice, the main cereal consumed, was 35 percent lower, though for wheat the state charged a price that was 12 percent higher than its CIP. The completely different policy approach to the relationship between CIP and PDS prices in the two states underlines and explains their attitude toward and performance in health. It is obvious that the subsidy on rice, the principal cereal consumed in Tamil Nadu, would contribute to greater food accessibility and therefore better nutritional status of the poor. Whereas, Maharashtra, in its pursuit of the so-called fiscal discipline, chose not to subsidize. On the contrary, it levied a surcharge on the CIP. Health was approached more through professional medical delivery systems. This is a direct outcome of SAPs, whereby subsidies are sought to be cut drastically everywhere and food subsidies reduced by raising the CIP and PDS prices.

The data in Table 14.4 clearly show that the difference between the two states in real per capita expenditure on social services (RSE) narrowed down, though it continued to be higher in Tamil Nadu.

Intra-sectoral Allocations

Some clarification is essential while considering intra-sectoral allocations in the health sector, particularly the expenditures included under the categories, medical, and public health. Generally, medical expenditures are associated with the medical department's spending on hospital-based care in urban areas, whereas public health expenditure is the spending of the public health department of the state on preventive measures. Centrally sponsored disease control programs and the shared schemes get included under this head.

State budgetary documents and the reported expenditure on minor heads therein indicate that Maharashtra has been incurring a higher share of medical and public health expenditures on public health. In fact, it recorded the highest share of 27 percent on public health among 15 major states during the years 1988–91 and managed to retain this during the adjustment years. In Tamil Nadu, the share of public health during 1988–91 was 7 percent and this increased to 13 percent in 1991–94 indicating a welcome retargeting of expenditures towards this sector. In case of family welfare, Maharashtra's spending constituted 9 percent of the total health budget, whereas in Tamil Nadu, the share was higher at 13 percent. No discernible change was noticed in the allocations to this item during the adjustment period in both the states.

In Maharashtra, the Minimum Needs Program claimed a substantial share of about 20–23 percent of total expenditures on public health. Another important item with a share of 32 to 35 percent was prevention and control of diseases. Direction and administration had a share of 38 percent in 1988–91 and 46 percent in 1991–94.

In Tamil Nadu, the Minimum Needs Program was conspicuous by its absence. The bulk of the expenditure (over 70 percent) was on disease control programs. Direction and administration accounted for about 10 percent of public health expenditures, which is around one-fourth of that in Maharashtra. In Maharashtra, the contribution of the center towards disease control programs declined sharply from 1990–91 and ranged between 16 and 60 percent. In Tamil Nadu, the center's contribution to these programs was over 70 percent during 1988–89 to 1993–94. Interestingly, the share of materials and supplies in Maharashtra's disease control programs ranged between 11 and 25 percent in the years 1990–91 and 1993–94, whereas in Tamil Nadu, the proportion was much smaller, around 5 percent or even less during the post-1991 period.

Perusal of real per capita expenditures on public health, maternal and child health, and nutrition points to the differing priorities of the two states (see Table 14.5). Maharashtra's expenditure on public health was maintained around Rs 10 in most years after 1991, though in 1993–94 it fell to less than Rs 7. Despite this decline, the level of spending far exceeds that in Tamil Nadu which was lower than Rs 3 per capita in most years.

Table 14.5
Trends in Real Per Capita Expenditure* on Select Items of Health and Nutrition

S.No. *(1)*	*Item* *(2)*	*1988–89* *(3)*	*1989–90* *(4)*	*1990–91* *(5)*	*1991–92* *(6)*	*1992–93* *(7)*	*1993–94* *(8)*
				Maharashtra			
1.	Public health	10.96	11.55 (5.33)	10.69 (–7.40)	10.18 (–4.79)	10.77 (5.83)	6.77 (–37.21)
2.	MCH	0.32	0.72 (126.91)	0.73 (1.05)	0.72 (–0.21)	0.62 (–14.6)	0.55 (–11.37)
3.	Water supply & sanitation	13.37	11.92 (–10.02)	12.52 (4.96)	10.74 (–14.2)	11.20 (4.31)	10.22 (–0.77)
4.	Nutrition	1.11	1.24 (10.05)	1.37 (11.14)	1.14 (–17.17)	2.18 (91.64)	2.09 (32.68)
				Tamil Nadu			
1.	Public health	2.32	2.54 (9.00)	2.86 (12.36)	2.67 (–6.67)	2.81 (5.48)	1.18 (–58.04)
2.	MCH	0.32	0.48 (47.88)	0.31 (–35.54)	0.63 (104.5)	0.5 (–19.95)	-
3.	Water supply & sanitation	0.99	13.60 (52.27)	1.13 (–91.72)	12.85 (1034.07)	11.52 (–10.35)	18.78 (63.00)
4.	Nutrition	8.84	12.26 (38.64)	19.06 (55.46)	17.91 (–6.03)	17.00 (–5.11)	16.19 (–4.73)

Source: Expenditure Budgets of Government of Maharashtra and Government of Tamil Nadu for 1988–89 to 1993–94.
Figures in parentheses indicate percentage change over previous years.

In the case of nutrition, the situation is exactly the reverse. Tamil Nadu recorded higher levels of expenditure, which was around Rs 17 per capita in the post-1991 period, whereas in Maharashtra it was less than Rs 3 per capita.

The analysis indicates the excessively sectoral biases of the two state governments. Despite the strong linkages between the provision of nutrition and health, both the state governments have chosen to concentrate on one sector to the utter neglect of the other, thereby limiting the success of their interventions. In Tamil Nadu, this is reflected in the fact that while infant mortality rates have declined, the extent of female morbidity continues to be high. In Maharashtra, despite relatively good public health facilities, the mortality of children in tribal areas such as Melghat is high owing to starvation. The ICDS program in the district has not been able to make any substantial dent in view of the poverty and subsequent low nutrition status of the families in this region (Chinai 1996).

District-level Expenditures

District-level analysis assumes particular importance as (*i*) there exist considerable intra-state differences in human development attainment and (*ii*) new initiatives have been taken in recent years to revive panchayati raj institutions. In view of the importance of this issue, an attempt has been made to examine the district-level expenditures on health and nutrition in the two states during the period 1988–89 to 1993–94. In Maharashtra, the district-level expenditure data are available only for plan outlays. In 1990–91, the share of plan component in medical and public health was 26 percent, whereas in water supply and sanitation it was 93 percent and in nutrition 52 percent. Thus, the extent to which trends in plan outlays reflect trends in non-plan spending could differ depending on the sector on which attention is focused. In Maharashtra, data on total plan outlay were available so that comparisons were possible between the extent of increase in sectoral outlays and total outlays.

A word of caution regarding this analysis is in order. The data pertain at best to the allocable part of sectoral expenditure at the state level and do not constitute the total expenditure incurred on the sector. In view of this, only the extent of change in district-level

Table 14.6
Percentage Change in District Level Plan Outlay on Select Items during Adjustment: Maharashtra Percentage Change between 1988–91 and 1991–94

S.No. (1)	*Districts* (2)	*Total Outlay* (3)	*Health Services* (4)
1.	Bombay City	105.74	914.69
2.	Bombay Sub.	-	-
3.	Thane	256.78	479.57
4.	Raigad	242.36	234.15
5.	Ratnagiri	242.92	121.51
6.	Sindhudurg	–2.37	145.81
7.	Nashik	268.52	539.32
8.	Dhule	282.46	782.03
9.	Jalgaon	281.98	332.51
10.	Ahmadnagar	231.82	365.87
11.	Pune	287.91	99.95
12.	Satara	282.81	574.24
13.	Sangli	296.56	845.12
14.	Solapur	216.79	454.43
15.	Kolhapur	272.27	519.79
16.	Buldana	299.14	308.59
17.	Akola	259.58	261.80
18.	Amaravati	277.54	740.50
19.	Yavatmal	269.10	474.71
20.	Nagpur	255.64	321.26
21.	Wardha	266.78	176.20
22.	Bhandara	274.21	307.92
23.	Chandrapur	309.49	184.67
24.	Gadchiroli	410.94	744.60
25.	Aurangabad	319.95	659.67
26.	Jalna	299.69	553.30
27.	Beed	291.35	802.26
28.	Parbhani	267.29	359.72
29.	Nanded	250.85	106.89
30.	Osmanabad	314.22	339.65
31.	Latur	279.73	171.14
32.	Undistrib.	141.28	-
33.	Total	274.75	380.50

Source: Compiled from Government of Maharashtra, Planning Department data.

spending is reported and no attempt is made to analyze the level of per capita expenditure on the relevant sectors. The changes in levels of expenditure between 1988 and 1991, the period prior to

Table 14.7
Percentage Change in District Level Government Expenditure on Select Items during Adjustment: Tamil Nadu Percentage Change between 1988–91 and 1991–94

S.No. (1)	*Districts* (2)	*MPH* (3)	*Nutrition* (4)
1.	Kanyakumari	48.42	149.75
2.	Pasumpon M. Thevar	46.43	108.74
3.	Kamarajar	48.93	175.10
4.	Madurai	6.62	134.24
5.	Ramanathapuram	44.97	141.49
6.	Dindigul–Anna	46.01	164.83
7.	Tiruchirapalli	50.92	159.72
8.	Pudukottai	48.47	195.75
9.	Thanjavur	25.51	51.35
10.	Nagapattinam Q. Milleth	70.82	626.60
11.	Coimbatore	42.62	180.81
12.	The Nilgiris	48.98	160.25
13.	Periyar	44.28	166.24
14.	Salem	53.20	170.13
15.	Dharmapuri	51.99	189.87
16.	North Arcot–Ambedkar	11.84	87.90
17.	Chengalpattu–MGR	41.15	159.38
18.	Tirunelveli–Kattabomman	41.80	148.04
19.	South Arcot	45.47	161.94
20.	Total	55.79	89.93

Source: Computed from data provided by Government Data Center, Chennai, Tamil Nadu.

economic reform, and the reform period 1991–94, are reported for total outlay and health in Maharashtra and for health and nutrition sectors in Tamil Nadu. The data are presented in Tables 14.6 and 14.7 for Maharashtra and Tamil Nadu respectively.

It may be observed that in Maharashtra almost all the districts recorded considerable increase in total plan outlays of 200 percent or more. The only exceptions were Bombay city (106 percent) and Sindhudurg district where there was a marginal decline. Significantly, backward districts such as Chandrapur, Gadchiroli, and Osmanabad along with the relatively developed district of

Aurangabad experienced an increase in plan outlay in nominal terms of over 300 percent. In the health sector, a large number of 16 districts reported an increase in outlays that was higher than the increase recorded in total plan outlay. Of these Amravati, Aurangabad, Beed, Bombay city, Dhule, Gadchiroli, Jalna, Nashik, Satara, and Sangli recorded particularly high increases.

A question that arises in this context is whether the increase in outlays was recorded in those districts with low levels of health attainment. A perusal of the data indicates that of the districts which experienced substantial increases in medical and public health expenditures in 1991–94, Sangli had a relatively better record in terms of life expectancy ranking fourth among Maharashtra's districts in 1981.[5] Satara ranked seventh while Beed, Aurangabad (including Jalna into which it was bifurcated subsequently), and Dhule represent medium-level districts with ranks in life expectancy ranging between 10 and 16. Amravati was a relatively less developed district with a rank of 19 in life expectancy in 1981. Thus, a sharp increase in outlays occurred in districts with relatively better health attainment as well.

The data for Tamil Nadu are in terms of total expenditure incurred on the sector. It is clear that only four districts, viz., Dharmapuri, Nagapattinam, Thiruchirapalli, and Salem, recorded increases above 50 percent. Whereas Thanjavur, in 1981, ranked fourth in life expectancy among the districts of Tamil Nadu; the ranks of Thiruchirapalli and Dharmapuri were 12 and 8 respectively. In sharp contrast, expenditure on the nutrition sector recorded over 100 percent increase in nominal expenditure between 1988–91 and 1991–94. Only two districts, North Arcot and Thanjavur recorded lower growth rates of 88 and 51 percent respectively. Dharmapuri, Coimbatore, and Kamarajar recorded increase between 175 and 190 percent, whereas Nagapattinam district recorded a phenomenal increase of over 627 percent.

The analysis in this section reiterates the observations made in the earlier section regarding the different priorities of the two states. The importance given to nutrition in Tamil Nadu and to public health in Maharashtra is clearly reflected in the changes in district-level expenditures during the period of economic reforms.

[5] The latest data available on district-level life expectancy are for 1981.

There was no evidence of conscious targeting of expenditures towards districts with lower attainment levels. On the contrary, health outlay increased more in districts with moderate to high attainment levels.

Health Delivery Systems

The translation of state and district-level expenditures into improved health outcomes depends, among other factors, on the efficacy of health delivery systems. A survey of 286 households in five selected villages, Rise, Pise, and Mandhar in Maharashtra and Eguvaripalayam and Verkadu in Tamil Nadu was conducted for the reference year 1993–94 to gain insights into the pattern of utilization of social sector services, the household expenditure incurred on such services, as well as perceptions of households regarding the quality of services rendered in government facilities (Prabhu 1997b). A study of three PHCs, two in Purandhar taluka of Pune district of Maharashtra and one in Gummadipoondi taluka of Chengalpattu-MGR district in Tamil Nadu, indicated that the functioning of the health delivery systems at the village level was unsatisfactory. One indication of the commitment of the governments to reforming the health delivery systems may be obtained from the speed with which they have adopted the policy initiative to create block community health centers containing 32 beds. This conversion was formally sanctioned in Gummadipoondi in 1993, but the rural hospital had not started functioning even in March 1995 at the time of the field survey. In Saswad taluka of Maharashtra, the conversion was effective and led to the provision of additional facilities such as availability of 32 beds, appointment of a child specialist, improvements in the operation theatre, and appointment of requisite staff.

The selected PHCs in both states were used only for treatment of minor ailments. Eighty percent of the patients interviewed at the PHCs on a particular day reported that they sought treatment for minor ailments like fever, headache, and dysentery. The Eguvaripalayam PHC in Tamil Nadu reported a high incidence of tuberculosis cases. Less than half the patients interviewed in the PHCs in both states were satisfied with the services provided.

An examination of the expenditure pattern of the PHCs indicated that less than 2 percent of the expenditure was incurred on the non-salary component. A large part of the non-salary expenditure in both states was on fuel for vehicles. All medicines in both states were procured at the state level and distributed to the PHCs. No major change in the expenditure pattern of the PHCs could be discerned. Thus, a major issue in service delivery was related to the availability of qualified practitioners. Their conspicuous absence contributed to negative perceptions about the quality of care in these centers.

The utilization of government health services varied considerably across villages and income groups. Utilization of private facilities even by households belonging to the lower-income groups was common, particularly in the two Tamil Nadu villages and in Pise in Maharashtra. Expenditure on medicines constituted a very high proportion of household expenditure on health, especially for major ailments.

Analysis of perceptions of households regarding quality of health services in the PHCs indicated that higher-income groups in both the Tamil Nadu villages and Rise in Maharashtra perceived the doctor to be irregular. Significantly, a higher proportion of households in these villages reported the use of private facilities. In Mandhar, where the Parinche PHC was located in close proximity to the selected village, 60 to 80 percent of selected households in all categories except the lowest-income group perceived the doctor to be regular. One factor that may explain the perceived irregularity of doctors is the fact that they are frequently required to attend meetings at the taluka and district headquarters. Invariably, other PHC personnel were considered to be regular whereas the supply of medicines was considered irregular. In Verkadu in Tamil Nadu, all income groups reported irregular supply of medicines, whereas in Enathimelpakkam also in Tamil Nadu, this perception increased steadily as one proceeded from low to high-income groups. Twenty-five to 50 percent of households in all income groups in Mandhar, 40 to 95 percent in Rise, and 40 to 70 percent in Pise reported irregular supply of medicines.

When questioned about change in the quality of services in the past three years, coinciding with the economic reform period, a large proportion of households in all categories in each of the five selected villages did not perceive any change in the quality of services rendered in PHCs. It was only in the case of the PDS outlets that a substantial proportion of households, particularly in the very low income category, reported a deterioration during the adjustment years. This issue is likely to be of increasing and critical significance in the coming years, as the reforms are institutionalized.

Summary and Implications

The objective of this chapter was to examine the changes in government policy in the health sector during the period of economic reforms in two Indian states, viz., Maharashtra and Tamil Nadu. While the two states differ substantially in terms of levels of per capita income and patterns of government expenditure on health and nutrition, they record similar levels of attainment in crucial human development indicators. Despite better physical access to primary health centers, resorting to private medical practitioners is high in Tamil Nadu. In Maharashtra, while utilization of primary health facilities is better, the prevalence of high levels of rural poverty and occurrence of starvation deaths of infants in certain pockets such as Melghat taluka point to the inadequacy of government interventions in the nutrition sector. Furthermore, the policy of the two state governments toward food grain prices is diametrically opposite. Since 1994, Maharashtra has been charging prices that are 23–24 percent higher than the Central Issue Price, while the Tamil Nadu government has been charging 35 percent lower price for rice, the main consumption item.

The analysis indicates that the relative share of medical and public health in total revenue expenditure was maintained during the adjustment years in Maharashtra, whereas in Tamil Nadu there was a decline in the first two years and a recovery to pre-reform levels subsequently. A perusal of real per capita expenditure on public health and nutrition sectors highlights not only the sharp difference between the two states in their approach towards human development, but also points to the utter lack of recognition on the part of two state governments of the synergies accruing from the implementation of an integrated package comprising both health and nutrition interventions.

The priorities at the state level get reflected in the changes in spending at the district as well as village levels. Thus, in Maharashtra, the plan outlays on medical and public health recorded substantial increases in a large number of districts between 1988–89 and 1991–94 even as nutrition expenditures more than doubled in most districts of Tamil Nadu. There was however no evidence of targeting of expenditures towards districts with low attainment levels.

The services provided in the government primary health delivery systems were considered to be unsatisfactory by a majority of the respondents in the five selected villages in the two states. There was evidence of restructuring of health services at the taluka level only in Saswad in Maharashtra. There was no observable change in either the level or pattern of expenditure incurred by the primary health centers in both the states. The perceptions of respondents in the selected villages indicated that there was no change in the quality of services of the primary health care services during the economic reform period, though a distinct deterioration of services of the public distribution system was perceived, particularly by respondents belonging to the lower-income groups.

The inadequacy of government interventions in ensuring a reasonable level of health attainment even in economically better-off states such as Maharashtra and Tamil Nadu is clearly evident. The less than satisfactory outcomes in this sphere may be traced to the unduly sectoral, segmented, and short-sighted approach to health adopted by state governments, which focuses on select interventions without recognizing the other factors affecting the health status of the population. The neglect of primary health care in Tamil Nadu and the high importance given to family welfare have resulted in the peculiar situation, where despite improvement in key indicators of health, morbidity rate is high among females. The Maharashtra experience suggests that better attention to public health is wasted in the absence of adequate nutrition. For sustained benefits, there is no alternative to a more integrated package of measures that is built around the synergistic relationship between several well-balanced sectoral initiatives, so that even the modest amounts spent on each component yields results far in excess of those that can be expected from sectoral expenditures.

It is clear how SAPs and economic liberalization affect the actual and potential health status of the people by attempting to identify changes in government policy and expenditure which impinge on health. Health attainment is a function of several, often interrelated factors, which includes income, income distribution, poverty, government expenditure, access to, and quality of health care facilities, etc. Economic reform has undermined both the states following different routes to health.

References

Centre for Monitoring Indian Economy (CMIE) (1992): *Basic Statistics Relating to Indian Economy*. Vol. 2, States. Bombay: CMIE.

Chinai, R. (1996): Heaven and Hell Co-exist in the Villages of Melghat. *The Times of India*, 26 August, p. 13.

Jayarajah, C., Branson, W., and **Sen, B.** (1996): Social Dimensions of Adjustment: World Bank Experience, 1980–83. World Bank Operations Evaluation Study. Washington D.C.: World Bank.

Krishnan, T.N. (1995): *Access to Health and Burden of Treatment in India: An Inter-State Comparison*. Discussion Paper Series, No. 2. UNDP Research Project on Strategies and Financing for Human Development. Thiruvananthapuram: Centre for Development Studies.

Malhotra, R. (1997): Incidence of Poverty in India: Towards a Consensus on Estimating the Poor. *Indian Journal of Labour Economics*, 40(1): 67–102.

National Council of Applied Economic Research (NCAER) (1992): *Household Survey of Medical Care*. New Delhi: NCAER.

National Sample Survey Organisation (NSSO) (1992): Morbidity and Utilisation of Medical Services. NSSO 42nd Round (1986–87). *Sarvekshana*, 15(4) (April–June.)

Prabhu, K.S. (1997a): Promotional and Protective Social Security during Economic Reforms: A Study of Maharashtra and Tamil Nadu. *Review of Development and Change*, II(1): 24–51.

——— (1997b): Structural Adjustment and Human Development: A Study of Two Indian States. Report prepared for the UNDP Research Project on Strategies and Financing for Human Development. Thiruvananthapuram: Centre for Development Studies.

Prabhu, K.S., and **Chatterjee, S.** (1993): Social Sector Expenditures and Human Development: A Study of Indian States. DRG Study No. 6. Bombay: Reserve Bank of India.

Purohit, B.C., and **Siddiqui, T.A.** (1994): Utilization of Health Services in India. *Economic and Political Weekly*, 29(18): 1071–80.

Reserve Bank of India Bulletin (various years). New Delhi: RBI.

Tulasidhar, V.B. (1993): Expenditure Compression and Health Sector Outlays. *Economic and Political Weekly*, 27(45): 2473–77.

Uplekar, M., and **George, A.** (1993): Access to Health Care in India: Present Situation and Innovative Approaches. Discussion Paper prepared for the UNDP Research Project on Strategies and Financing for Human Development. Thiruvananthapuram: Centre for Development Studies.

World Bank (1993): *World Development Report: Investing in Health*. New York: Oxford University Press.

——— (1995): *India: Policy and Finance Strategies for Strenghthening Primary Health Care Services*. Report No. 13042-IN. Washington D.C.: World Bank.

15

Structural Adjustment and Economic Slowdown: Likely Impact on Health Outcomes in Pakistan

S. Akbar Zaidi

Evidence accumulated from numerous countries over the last five decades suggests that as economic growth takes place, the overall health status of the populations tends to improve. Life expectancy is seen to rise, infant mortality rate falls, as does the maternal mortality rate; the crude death rate and child mortality rate also show a decreasing trend. There is also some degree of increase in the literacy rate and in other human development indicators. For a very large number of countries, there seems to be a secular relationship between economic growth/development and improvement in human development indicators. This is also evidenced spatially where, at any given time, countries with higher GDP per capita tend to have better health and other social sector indicators.

However, numerous exceptions show that this is not necessarily an immutable law. Perhaps, public policy interventions determine the extent of the difference. This is most marked in the case of present and former socialist states. Vietnam, Cuba, and China have human development indicators far better than what a strict relationship with economic growth would suggest. This was so also in every single one of the former Soviet states, although there has been a decline in the health indicators in recent times. Costa Rica, Sri Lanka, and the Indian state of Kerala also form a group of countries/regions which detract from the norm, as do the oil-rich high-income countries.

This is a considerably abridged and edited version of the paper read at the conference. I gratefully acknowledge the numerous comments made by the participants at the conference, particularly those by Professors Imrana Qadeer, Kasturi Sen, and Mozzaffer Ahmad.

If it is likely that a secular increase in growth rates will result in an improvement in health outcomes, an inverse relationship should also hold. This chapter tries to understand and document the nature of the Structural Adjustment Programs pursued in Pakistan since 1988 and tries to evaluate their impact upon the economy and the health sector and the welfare of the people. It examines the outcome of lower government expenditure, cuts in subsidies, and the promotion of the private sector at the expense of the state sector. In Pakistan, the overall growth rate prior to reforms has been relatively high; public policy has been particularly absent in providing health facilities, with the private sector expenditure dominating spending in the health sector by a ratio of 3:1. In this case, economic growth and its distribution become important pointers for health outcomes. The argument in this chapter rests on the premise that since most spending in the health sector is in the private sector, changes in economic growth affecting population below poverty line, and per capita income will have an impact on health expenditure, and hence on health outcomes. The underlying assumption is that despite a cure-oriented, urban-based health system, which is the outcome of a skewed social policy, the increasing growth rates did succeed in lowering poverty levels. Hence, people could spend on basic requirements of food, drinking water, housing, clothing, medicine, and education through private expenditure. Expenditure on health, therefore, has to be assessed within a broader definition of the determinants of health, which goes beyond the bio-medical perspective.

Nature of Pakistan's Structural Adjustment Program

Pakistan has had a close relationship with the IMF and the World Bank since the fifties. However, the real involvement with both institutions began with great gusto in 1988 with the implementation of the SAP following an Extended Structural Adjustment Facility (ESAF) worth $1.2 billion. Since then, Pakistan has had recourse to three standby arrangements, and two more ESAFs worth $1.1 billion in 1993–94 and $1.6 billion in October 1997.

The three ESAFs contain all the regular components which are part of such programs. The IMF and the World Bank have repeatedly asked (told?) Pakistan to cut its tariffs, which have subsequently been cut from a maximum tariff rate of 225 percent in 1992 to 45 percent in 1997; in addition, the tariff structure has been "rationalized", with fewer slabs operative. A cut in public expenditure has been insisted on in order to make the fiscal deficit sustainable at (at first) 4 percent of GDP in the earlier agreements, to 5 percent according to the agreement signed in 1997. Privatization continues to be an important condition for the release of funds with 62 of the 109 industries and units privatized over the last nine years. Government subsidy on wheat and fertilizer has been either dramatically reduced or totally eliminated and the prices of utilities, such as gas, electricity, and kerosene, have been raised repeatedly and substantially in order to "get prices right." The control over the interest rate by the State Bank of Pakistan has diminished as market-determined operations have determined the rate doubling it over the reform period. Two of the nationalized commercial banks have been privatized, with the largest two of the remaining three likely to be privatized in the near future; simultaneously, multinational banks, probably the single biggest beneficiary of the Structural Adjustment Process, have been given increasing room in deference to promoting competition. Numerous smaller government institutions and departments have been closed down over the last few years. The "downsizing" of the government sector has been underway for a few years, with a freeze on the hiring of new public sector employees and voluntary redundancy. Even public sector utilities, such as water, sewerage, and electricity are scheduled for privatization as part of the agreement with the IMF and the World Bank (Khan 1997; Zaidi 1994, 1999; Zaman 1995).

The devaluation of the Pakistani rupee in order to make Pakistani exports more competitive has taken place at a consistent pace. In order to curtail the fiscal deficit, taxation reforms have taken place and a consumption-based general sales tax has been imposed. Government expenditure has also been cut over the last few years, although the fiscal deficit has fluctuated between a high of 8.7 percent of GDP in 1990–91 and a low of 5.5 percent in 1994–95.

The overall budgetary allocation for the social sector for the fiscal year 1997–98 was cut by 9 percent (20 percent inflation adjusted). Education was the worst hit, with a reduction of

19 percent (30 percent inflation adjusted). Federal development expenditure on the health sector was cut by 17.5 percent (27 percent inflation adjusted). The health sector budget for the four provinces fell by 25 percent between 1995–96 and 1996–97. Moreover, the amount allocated for the health sector in 1997–98 for the four provinces and for the federal government fell in real terms over that utilized in 1996–97 by 13 percent.

Health Care System

Pakistan's health care system is typical of that of many post-colonial Third World countries, although it has its particularities. For the most part, the health care model has changed little from the time of the British. It is essentially doctor-oriented, has a curative rather than a preventive emphasis, and is urban-biased in terms of resources and personnel. Given the now dominant role of the private sector over the public sector health facilities, it is highly inequitable, where ability to pay rather than need determines access to health care (Zaidi 1988, 1999).

A doctor-oriented curative care model implies that there is an inverted pyramid of health personnel, with more than three doctors for each nurse and 17 doctors for each lady health visitor. The little money that is available for training health personnel gets utilized disproportionately for training doctors. These doctors usually belong to urban areas and to the relatively prosperous economic and social class. This restricts their mobility as they are less likely to opt for hardship postings, which for them is any place outside the environs of a district headquarter or teaching hospital. The perennial problem of doctor absenteeism at smaller, more remote government health facilities, such as rural health centers and basic health units is due to this overdependence on doctors to deliver health (read, medical) care and their reluctance to go to so-called remote regions. A health care system with doctors as the main focus also results in the dominance of curative care over preventive care, with medical students specializing in disciplines which affect or can be purchased by the more affluent urban residents. Urban, hospital-oriented, curative care is a natural outcome of the training and rewards system, which creates the medical care model in Pakistan. For the government health care availability is a numbers game, where targets are set each year for increasing the number of facilities or doctors, but the important aspect of quality of care is usually not considered. As of January 1992, there were 613 hospitals, with a total of 50,323 beds; only 18 percent were in rural areas. Of these, 309 were state and federal public hospitals with 32,617 beds (or 65 percent of the total beds). There were 304 rural health centers and 1,679 basic health facilities (Haq 1997; UNDP 1997).

A significant development in the health care system has been the shift toward the private sector from the government health sector, with the private sector now being the main provider of medical care. Seventy-five percent of expenditure by patients takes place in the private health sector. Private doctors are to be found even in the remote regions, where government doctors refuse to go. Often, it is the very same government doctor who, while being posted in a rural area, will set up a private clinic near the rural health center in the closest town. The government facility is left to be handled by a medical auxiliary or technician, who dons the role of the doctor. Even in urban slums, private doctors are usually available. The only criterion for the availability of doctors is the prospect of making profits. If consumers are willing to pay, doctors will be available.

Given this private doctor dominated medical care system, the public health care system has been severely undermined. The lack of an effective public health program for disease control, other than some immunization interventions, highlights this aspect. Also, a doctor-oriented model of health care causes distortions in the allocation of resources for training public health personnel and in proportion to doctors, other health staff are almost non-existent. For instance, in 1984–89, while there was one doctor for a population of 2,940, there was one nurse for a population of 5,040 (World Bank 1991). A consequence of this has been that the health status of the Pakistani population has been much worse than what it should have been for the development level, as measured by per capita income.

Some Special Features of Pakistan's Economy

Although the official GNP per capita of Pakistan makes it the 35th poorest country out of 133 placing it in the low-income

Table 15.1
Incidence of Poverty in Pakistan

Year	*Population (in million)*	*No. of Poor (in million)*	*Percent of Poor*
1960	50	19	38
1965	58	23	40
1975	80	28	35
1980	90	34	38
1985	105	26	25
1990	120	24	20
1995	140	42	30

Source: Haq 1997, p. 18.

category, Pakistan's economy has many of the characteristics associated with that of a middle-income country (Burki 1986). One reason for this could be that the large underground or illegal economy, estimated to be between 30 and 40 percent of the official GDP, results in a real increase in the overall per capita income of the inhabitants. Another reason for low levels of poverty has been the consistent, near 6 percent growth rates in the economy, with employment and incomes also growing. The population below the poverty line decreased from 46 percent in 1984–85, to 34 percent by 1990–91 (World Bank 1995a). As a consequence, income inequality has also decreased over the seventies and eighties. A single digit inflation rate for most of the decades prior to the nineties has also not affected the real income and purchasing power of the people (see Table 15.1).

Possibly, the most important factor which has stopped the health and welfare statistics from being far worse has been the large amount of money remitted from the Middle East by Pakistani workers. Around $30 billion were remitted between 1977 and 1988 (on average, 6.5 percent of GDP throughout the eighties), through official channels alone, rising to a far higher figure if we include unofficial remittances as well. These remittances have got dispersed to numerous villages and hamlets all across Pakistan and have not been concentrated in one large city or area. This dispersion has resulted in a fall in income inequality. Much of this money has been spent in either creating small-scale employment, house improvements resulting in better living conditions with a more hygienic and healthier environment and in better consumption patterns, especially in food intake. All these factors have helped improve the condition of a very large number of Pakistani families, majority of whom are rural-based (Addleton 1992).

Trends in Health Indicators

Not surprisingly, there has been some improvement in terms of key health indicators over the last few decades (see Table 15.2). The IMR shows a clear downward trend up till 1993. MMR has come down to 340 in 1990, from 600 in 1980. Life expectancy too has increased over the years from 45 in the sixties to 55 in 1989. Moreover, daily calorie supply (per capita) shows an upward trend till 1995. Though this does not reveal the access of those below poverty line (who may still suffer from under-nutrition), it indicates at least gross availability of food, which if distributed adequately will suffice. The percentage of births attended by trained health personnel went up from 24 (1985) to 70 in 1988–90.

Given the specific nature of the health delivery system and the consumption pattern by users, household income and overall growth may perhaps have played a critical role in this pattern. In fact, while Pakistan's health indicators are still very poor as compared to other low-income countries, it is quite possible that this consistent high growth rate has saved them from being far worse. It seems to have compensated for the poorly managed, inefficient public health and medical care system by allowing most inhabitants to have private access to some health and basic minimum facilities care.

However, since the initiation of the SAPs in 1988, much of the nature and status of the economy has changed and so has the implicit impact on health care, health status, and overall welfare. The reversal in proportion of population living below the poverty line, reduction in public expenditure on health, reversal in IMR and child mortality rates, and access to health sources may be early indicators of things to come (see Table 15.2).

Probable Impact of SAPs on Health

Although it is difficult to prove causality, some interesting observations on the economy after 1988 help show how the economy has performed after the initiation of the SAPs. First, the overall

Table 15.2
Trends in Some Health Indicators

Year	*IMR*	*Child Death Rate (per 1,000 live births; under 5)*	*Daily Calorie Supply (per capita)*	*Population with Access to Health Services %*	*MMR*	*Births Attended by Trained Personnel %*	*Life Expectancy*
1980	124	-	-	65	600		51
1984	116	-	-	-	-		
1985	115	-	2,159	-	-	24	
1986	-	-	2,315	-	-		
1987	109	-	-	-	-		
1988	-	-	2,200	-	-		
1989	106	136	2,280	-	-		55
1990				85*	340	70	
1991	101	138	-	-	-		
1992	92	130	-		-		
1993	88	-	-		-		
1995	90	-	2,471	-	-		
1996	95	136	-	55**	19		

Source: World Bank 1987, 1989, 1990, 1991, 1994, and 1995b; UNDP 1993, 1994, and 1998.
*Figure is for the period 1987–90.
**Figure is for the period 1990–96.

Table 15.3
Pakistan's Economic Performance

	Annual Average 1980–88	*Annual Average 1988–97*
GDP (growth rate)	6.51	4.7
CPI (growth rate)	7.12	10.69
Manufacturing (growth rate)	9.06	4.9
Development Expenditure (as % of GDP)	7.5	5.5
Current Account Deficit (as % of GDP)	3.6	4.9

Source: Government of Pakistan 1997.

growth rate of GDP has fallen well below trend levels and appreciably below the average of the eighties (see Table 15.3). In the nine years since the implementation of the program, in only one of those nine years was growth in GDP more than the average 6 percent observed since 1977; in two of those nine years, in 1992–93 and in 1996–97, the growth in GDP was 2.27 percent and 3.1 percent respectively, the lowest in more than three decades. In the nine years since 1988, inflation was in double digits in seven of those nine years, while previously in the 40 years between 1947 and 1987, inflation was in double digits on only seven occasions.

The current account deficit, reduction of which is one of the goals of the Structural Adjustment Program, was more than 4 percent of GDP in seven of the nine years. It was 3.6 percent between 1980 and 1988, rising thereafter due to the trade liberalization reforms. Manufacturing growth rates, which averaged 9.1 percent between 1980 and 1988, fell to 4.9 percent in the period 1988–97, dropping to a mere 1.78 percent growth rate in 1996–97, the lowest in the last 30 years. It is important to emphasize that while these numbers show a very obvious downward trend since 1988 when the Structural Adjustment Program was introduced, we cannot prove that this is on account of the program, since there are numerous other factors which have also affected the economy since 1988. Nevertheless, given the dramatic changes that have taken place as a consequence of the program, common sense suggests that it is more than likely that the adjustment program had a significant contribution in this downtrend. The result of these dramatic trends is likely to be deleterious.

In countries like Chile, where the SAP has been in operation for more than a decade and a half, there is evidence to show that the health status of the people has deteriorated sharply and that human and social conditions have worsened markedly (Veltmayer 1993). In Pakistan, however, it is important to emphasize that not enough research has been conducted and there is lack of hard, indisputable evidence to prove that the health status of Pakistanis has deteriorated on account of the program. We have as yet not been able to capture statistically the second and third round effects due to the adjustment process, as there are problems in measuring the impact (Lundy 1996; Peabody 1996). Nevertheless, available research seems to endorse the results from Chile as well as from many other countries. In fact, IMF and World Bank publications also acknowledge these significant human and social costs, but consider them transitory and propose "safety nets" as mitigative measures.

Research shows that after 1988, poverty has returned to Pakistan in a big way, increasing the number and percentage of people below the poverty line (see Table 15.1). Public sector employment, historically an important anti-poverty measure, is estimated to have fallen by 10 percent during 1990–93, and 43.2 percent of workers previously employed in public enterprises were laid off by their new employees. Real wages, which increased by 0.7 percent between 1980 and 1991, fell by 2 percent between 1991 and 1995 (Sayeed and Aisha 1996). Moreover, it has been seen that "overall unemployment in occupations with a high incidence of the poor has increased dramatically and real wages of skilled and unskilled labor have declined sharply. Not surprisingly, there has been an increase in poverty and equality, particularly in the rural areas" (Khan 1997). Kemal (1994) has shown that the share of wages in national income fell from 32.3 percent in 1987–88 to 30 percent in 1990–91. Personal income distribution, which improved between 1979 and 1988, worsened considerably between 1987 and 1991, with the overall Gini coefficient increasing from 0.35 in 1987 to 0.41 in 1991. In rural areas, the Gini coefficient increased from 0.307 to 0.41 in the same period (Kemal 1994). Not only was there a cut of 22.4 percent in food subsidies between

Table 15.4
Central Government Expenditure on Various Sectors
(as percentage of total expenditure)

Year	*Defense*	*Education*	*Health*	*Housing, Social Security, Welfare*
1980	30.6	2.7	1.5	4.1
1983	34.8	3.1	1.0	9.3
1988–1990	-	3.4	4.5	-
1991	27.9	1.6	1.0	3.4
1993	26.9	1.1	0.4	2.8

Source: World Bank 1987, 1989, 1990, 1991, 1994.

1991 and 1995 (Sayeed and Aisha 1996), but the "rationalized" tax structure resulted in more indirect taxes, with a decline of 4.3 percent of the tax burden on the rich and an increase of the tax burden on the poor by 10.3 percent (Kemal 1994). Just as the high growth period prior to 1988 had highly beneficial indirect effects on health and welfare, we can concur that the downward trend since 1988 has had (or is going to have) equally negative consequences on health and welfare. This is not all.

In the obsession to reduce the fiscal deficit, public expenditure has been cut and development expenditure in particular has borne this brunt. From a high of 9.3 percent of GDP in 1980–81, development expenditure has been falling since and in 1997–98, only a little over 3 percent of GDP has been allocated for this sector. With increasing domestic and foreign debt together accounting for 88 percent of GDP, interest payments dominate all forms of public expenditure. In the 1997–98 budget, as much as 45 percent of the expenditure was set aside for interest payments, with the ubiquitous defense expenditure exceeding 27 percent of the total expenditure (see Table 15.4). With increasing domestic policing and administrative requirements to address the ever-increasing law and order problem across the country, very little is left for development purposes.

With reduction of the fiscal deficit, the most important target in the Structural Adjustment Program under the ESAF, it is very probable that development rather than defense will bear the brunt of further cuts as has been the scenario in the past. This has also been the pattern in other countries (Reed 1992).

Some issues specific to the health sector are also likely to have negative impacts on the health and welfare of the people. Cuts in government recurring expenditure will curtail more recruitment in the public sector including the health sector and cuts in capital expenditure will either stop or slow down the process of the expansion in health facilities (Zaidi 1999). Private medical colleges are a booming business as is all private sector education. They charge market tuition rates unlike governmental colleges; this will probably result in the production of even more doctors in a doctor-dominated health care model and will probably encourage doctors to charge higher consultation fees so that they can make a reasonable return on their rather large investment. Moreover, it is very likely that the government will be forced to stop subsidizing government medical colleges, which currently charge fees which are one-thirtieth of those charged by private sector medical colleges. The consequences of the cut in education subsidies should be quite clear. The privatization of health and medical education also has consequences on the availability of health auxiliaries. At present, the government does pay lip service to the need for nurses and lady health visitors and has state-run schools for training them; if much of the health sector is privatized, it is possible that even more emphasis will be placed on doctors at the expense of essential auxiliary staff.

As the government is finding it increasingly difficult to meet even its running costs in the medical sector, it has floated the idea of privatizing existing government hospitals, rural health centers, and even basic health units by selling them off or renting them out to one or more doctors. These doctors can then use these facilities as their private clinics. Given the general lack of political opposition, activism, and collective action, it will not be surprising that this process gets going in a big and organized way in the near future. Not only will the government cut its recurring costs, but it will also raise revenue to pay for the interest payments on the loans that it took earlier, all in the name of fiscal balance.

The getting-prices-right preoccupation and the desire to cut "wasteful" public expenditure is also likely to be reflected in the health sector. Health and medical services are currently heavily subsidized in Pakistan. It is likely that not only will user fees and other charges for health care be introduced where they are lacking at the moment, but the opening up of certain hospital services, such as food, laundry, and construction, to private contractors will push medical costs much above the true costs of these services (Rachlis and Kushner 1994). Need and demand for health services will be replaced by considerations of cost-effectiveness, covering full costs, eliminating subsidies, and making the public sector indistinguishable from the private sector, where the market will determine price and allocation. In the smaller cities and rural areas, where the government sector does still provide a service, albeit of poor quality, it is possible that that service will be taken away from those who need health care. In the urban areas where the private sector dominates, it is usually the poor and under-privileged who make greater use of state-owned health services; it seems that sooner rather than later, this group will lose this benefit and will also be forced to go to the private sector. Given these possibilities, and the broader macro-economic discipline and conditions of the SAP, there is a real possibility that the public sector will cease to exist as a provider of health care, especially primary and secondary-level care. All that it will be required to do would be to regulate the private sector and provide an "enabling" environment in which the private sector can function more smoothly.

The burden of adjustment and of the changed health system is likely to fall unevenly on different groups. Not surprisingly, the poor will suffer the most as the economic situation worsens and low growth results in fewer employment possibilities. Higher inflation and lower food subsidies will make life even more difficult for this section of the population and private health care will be beyond their reach. Hence, not only will they be more vulnerable to disease, but also less able to acquire health care. In addition, if utilities like water and sewerage are privatized, they may not be available for those who cannot afford the higher prices. Women usually bear the brunt of austerity before men; this suggests that while the whole population will be affected, women and especially those from lower-income groups, will be affected more adversely. Because, in terms of food intake and access to health care, women and girls come last; now, with greater austerity, it is probable that their already dismal health status will worsen further (Zaidi 1996).

Conclusions

The health status of Pakistanis is poor by any comparison, but would have been far worse had it not been for ameliorative factors in the economy. A prosperous and growing economy for most of the latter half of the seventies and the eighties has acted as a palliative for a very large section of the population. An unrecorded economy possibly equivalent to 40 percent of the official economy; comparatively higher growth rates; growing employment opportunities in the public and private sector; and large amounts of remittances from the Middle East had all helped in improving the situation. The benefits of this had filtered down reaching poor economic and regional populations. This may have resulted in a little more equality in terms of income and wealth and certainly in lowering the poverty level in the country. All these factors did have a real wealth and welfare enhancing effect. This has been reflected in the trends in health indices of the people by allowing them access to food, education, housing, drinking water, sanitation, medical care, etc. However, after the implementation of the SAP in 1988, all positive trends and economic gains made in the previous decade have been lost. The 1988–97 period is likely to be the worst in Pakistan's 50 year history affecting more than just health care and the health status of the population (see Table 15.1).

With economic growth not just slowing down but screeching to a halt, matters have been made worse by key conditions imposed in the SAP. Privatization, cuts in government spending, getting prices right, and more market-dominated incentives are likely to affect health and the health sector adversely. The central argument in this chapter is that SAP has further distorted the welfare policy of Pakistan and marginalized public health. Second, economic prosperity that allowed the health status of the population to improve, both as a consequence of better inputs at the family and individual level and also in terms of affordability of medical services, can no more do so. A large section of the population will now be marginalized due to the changed economic conditions in terms of lower economic prosperity. This, in all likelihood, may also worsen their health status.

References

Addleton, J. (1992): *Undermining the Centre: Gulf Migration and Pakistan.* Karachi: Oxford University Press.

Burki, S.J. (1986): *Pakistan: A Nation in the Making.* Boulder: Westview Press.

Government of Pakistan (1997): *Pakistan Economic Survey 1996–97*, Islamabad: Finance Division.

Haq, M. (1997): *Human Development in South Asia.* Karachi: Oxford University Press.

Kemal, A.R. (1994): Structural Adjustment, Employment, Income Distribution and Poverty. *Pakistan Development Review*: 33(4).

Khan, S.R. (1997): *Do IMF and World Bank Policies Work?* SDPI Monograph Series No. 6, Islamabad.

Lundy, P. (1996): Limitations of Quantitative Research in the Study of Structural Adjustment. *Social Science and Medicine*, 42(3): 313–24.

Peabody, J. (1996): Economic Reforms and Health Sector Policy: Lessons from Structural Adjustment Programs. *Social Science and Medicine*, 43(5): 823–35.

Rachlis, M., and **Kushner, C.** (1994): *Strong Medicine: How to Save Canada's Health Care Systems.* Toronto: Harper-Collins Publishers Ltd.

Reed, D. (1992): *Structural Adjustment and the Environment.* Boulder: Westview Press.

Sayeed, A., and **Aisha, G.** (1996): Has Poverty Returned to Pakistan? Karachi: Social Policy and Development Centre. Mimeo.

United Nations Development Program (UNDP) (1993): *Human Development Report.* New York: Oxford University Press.

——— (1994): *Human Development Report.* New York: Oxford University Press.

——— (1997): *Human Development Report.* New York: Oxford University Press.

——— (1998): *Human Development Report.* New York: Oxford University Press.

Veltmayer, V. (1993): Liberalisation and Structural Adjustment in Latin America: In Search of an Alternative. *Economic and Political Weekly*, 28(39): 2080–86.

World Bank (1987): *World Development Report.* New York: Oxford University Press.

——— (1989): *World Development Report.* New York: Oxford University Press.

——— (1990): *Poverty: World Development Report.* New York: Oxford University Press.

——— (1991): The Challenge of Development: *World Development Report.* New York: Oxford University Press.

——— (1994): *Infrastructure for Development: World Development Report.* New York: Oxford University Press.

——— (1995a): *Pakistan: Poverty Assessment.* Report No. 14397-PAK. Islamabad: Sustainable Development Policy Institute.

——— (1995b): *Workers in an Integrating World: World Development Report.* New York: Oxford University Press.

Zaidi, S.A. (1988): *The Political Economy of Health Care in Pakistan.* Lahore: Vanguard.

——— (1994): The Structural Adjustment Programme and Pakistan: External Influence or Internal Acquiescence. *Pakistan Journal of Applied Economics*, 10(1&2).

Zaidi, S.A. (1996): Gender Perspectives and the Quality of Care in Underdeveloped Countries: Disease, Gender and Contextuality. *Social Science and Medicine,* 43(5).

——— (1999): *Issues in Pakistan's Economy.* Karachi: Oxford University Press.

Zaman, A. (1995): The Government's Present Agreement with the IMF: Misgovernment or Folly? *Pakistan Journal of Applied Economics,* 11(1&2).

16

Health Services in Bangladesh: Development and Structural Reforms

A.Q. Khan

Country Profile

Bangladesh lies in the delta of three large rivers. Its geographical location and climactic conditions make it prone to natural catastrophes such as cyclones and floods. As much as one-third of the land gets flooded in the monsoon. Its population is 128 million (1998 estimates) (HDC 1999) and about 65 percent of the labor force is employed in agriculture (1994 estimates) (HDC 1999). Bangladesh is primarily an agricultural country, with GNP per capita of US $360 (1997 estimates) (HDC 1999). The country is managed through a network of administrative units, such as wards, unions, and districts, as shown in Table 16.1.

Table 16.1
Administrative Divisions in Bangladesh

Name of the Division	*Number*	*Average Population Per Division (in million)*
Divisions	6	20
Districts	64	18,75,000
Thana (of 9–10 unions)	460 urban–63 rural–397	2,61,000
Unions (of 9 wards)	4,500	27,000
Wards (of 2 or more villages)	40,500	3,000
Villages	85,650	1,400

Some Socio-economic Indicators

Bangladesh's early success in reducing poverty has reversed since the mid-eighties as evident from Table 16.2.

Table 16.2
Rural and Urban Poverty in Bangladesh

Year	*Head Count Measure of Poverty*		
	National	*Rural*	*Urban*
1973–74	70.5	71.3	63.2
1981–82	63.5	65.3	48.4
1985–86	43.9	45.9	30.8
1988–89	47.8	49.7	35.9
1991–92	49.7	52.9	33.6
1995–96	47.0	51.1	26.3

Source: HDC 1999.

Table 16.3
Some Basic Indicators for Bangladesh

Life expectancy at birth	1970	44 years
	1997	58 years
Adult literacy rate percent	1970	24
	1995	38
Female literacy rate percent	1970	9
	1995	26
IMR per 1000 live births	1970	148
	1996	83
	1997	81
MMR per lakh live births	1990–96	850
Under 5 mortality per 1000 live births*	1970	239
	1997	109

Source: HDC 1998, 1999.
*UNDP 1999.

Table 16.4
Per Capita Calorie Supply in Bangladesh

1970:2177*	1992:2019**	1964:2301***
1996:2105*	1995:2001**	1976:2094***

Source: *UNDP 1999.
**HDC 1999.
***Government of Bangladesh 1980.

This overall reversal is primarily due to increasing poverty in rural areas. The decline in urban poverty is consistent, though relatively slow as compared to the previous decade. The depth and severity of poverty also increased, demonstrating the worsening conditions of the poor (HDC 1999). Some human development indicators are as shown in Table 16.3.

There has been a progressive decline in daily per capita calorie supply. While different sources have arrived at different figures, all show a consistent fall, as shown in Table 16.4.

Development of Health Services

The health care system inherited from British times has been traditionally cure-oriented, urban-based, directed to the alleviation of suffering due to sickness and catering to the needs of a privileged group concentrated in urban areas. With the passage of time, the grace was, however, extended to the sub-divisional towns in the form of small hospitals with 20 beds.

After attaining independence from British rule in 1947, it was planned that every year 100 rural dispensaries would be set up containing four beds. This plan was not pursued beyond the first year as the country lacked any broad and persistent policy in the field of public health. Thereafter, an ambitious scheme envisaging one rural health center (RHC) with three subcenters covering a population of 50,000 (block-wise) was undertaken. But the malaria eradication program and its continuation, led to the disproportionate allocation of funds to the detriment of development of RHC and the vital rural network of basic health infrastructure. In 1958, an integrated post of director of health services was created at the directorate level and was redesignated as director general of health services in 1980. Integration of service at various other levels also took place.

After the formation of Bangladesh in 1971, development of rural health complexes in place of RHCs was taken up (Government of Bangladesh 1980). It was proposed to have one RHC with 31-bedded hospital for each thana police station. Various vertical projects were integrated over 1976–77. The existing staff of vertical programs was converted to multipurpose health workers, permitting rational utilization of manpower. Family planning however managed to remain outside the domain of integration on the plea of a so-called "top priority" program. A three-year medical assistants' training program was launched in 1976.

The findings of a survey conducted in 1977 to assess access to health care revealed that:

- 10.82 percent of villagers had access to government practitioners, namely, graduate and other trained health workers;
- 26.02 percent had access to private practitioners (rarely qualified as doctors, mostly compounders and quacks);
- 27.21 percent sought the help of traditional healers;
- 7.32 percent did not seek any medical care at all; and
- there was no information regarding the remaining 2.07 percent (Khan 1989; WHO 1977).

Basic health service need not be highly technocentric and market-oriented. The bulk of interventions, hitherto regarded as the sole responsibility of qualified doctors, can be undertaken by suitably trained health personnel working under the supervision of more qualified persons.

In 1978, in order to bridge the increasing gap between rural and urban health services, a new cadre of field-level health workers, named *palli chikitsak* (village doctors), was introduced. This scheme was rooted in the notion that much of the rural population suffered from common diseases, majority of which could either be prevented or cured by the use of a limited number of drugs. It was proposed to have one such *chikitsak* for each of the 65,000 villages. Unfortunately, this scheme of delegating responsibilities to less-qualified personnel met with resistance and criticism by qualified doctors on the pretext that it would undermine the "quality" of services provided. They looked down upon it as a "second-grade" and "dangerous health service." These doctors conveniently overlooked the reality that a large section of the population including the marginalized is deprived of any medical care whatsoever. And that doctors also cannot really "care" for all the needy people, given especially their aversion to serve in rural areas. Further, the medical specialists and super specialists are mainly engaged in highly technocentric and market-oriented practice. Hyper specialization has led to escalation in cost of medical care and increasingly pushed these services beyond the reach of the average citizen. This resistance seemingly stems from the fear of possible shrinkage of private practice in a society where medicine has become more a trade and less a social service and has also given birth to uncontrolled and vested interests.

The *palli chikitsak* proposal was eventually shelved and the program of training medical assistants was reduced in size. Admittedly, the root of the problem lies in the conflicting interests of different classes of the society that is predominantly based on the exploitation of the poor.

Present-day Health Services

The structure of the health services, like that of the general administrative set-up, is highly centralized. The Ministry of Health and Family Welfare is officially responsible for policy and planning. There are two separate directorates within this ministry, one of health and the other of population control. The former is responsible for the management and implementation of health programs, while the latter is responsible for implementing the maternal and child health-based family planning program, throughout the country.

Some figures relating to the availability of health facility and health functionaries are shown in Table 16.5.

By and large, the total number of fieldworkers for family planning (36,952) far exceeds the number for general health services (27,091).

Disease Profile

Some of the health indicators and trends over the years 1977 to 1996 are shown in Table 16.6. (Source for all figures: Government of Bangladesh, various years.)

We see that in this period there has been a reduction in infant as well as maternal mortality and an increase in life expectancy from 47 to 59.5 years. Reduction in mortality from diarrhea has been effected by prompt rehydration therapy. However, morbidity due to diarrhea has not changed much in this period. This is so in spite of increased coverage by tube-wells. This is a reflection of inadequate sanitation measures. Only about 20 percent of diarrhea cases belonged to households having access to both safe drinking water (tap and tube-well) and hygienic latrines. Whereas, about 72 percent belonged to households having access to only safe drinking water and not to hygienic latrines. The remaining 8 percent had neither such facilities (Government of Bangladesh 1995a). The prevalence of worm infestation follows a similar pattern. There is no change in prevalence over the

Table 16.5
Health Facilities and Functionaries at Various Levels

Administrative Division	*Health Facility Available*	*Field-level IIealth Functionaries*	
		Name/Post	*Number*
National and divisional level	Various institutions and specialized hospitals that provide investigation services and act as tertiary-level referral centers.	-	-
District level	About 59 hospitals, with 50–100 beds; provide general, specialized, and investigation services; act as secondary referral centers.	-	-
Thana level	About 379 thana health complexes with facilities for 31 beds; provide health family planning services; act as first referral centers.	Doctors (including specialists in medicine, surgery, gynecology, dental surgery, and MCH)	9 5
		Nurses	-
		Paramedical and non-medical staff	-
Union level	Union Health and Family Welfare Center (UHFWS) provides static services; holds eight satellite clinics a month in the villages.	Medical officer/Medical assistant	1 1
		Family welfare • visitor	
		Pharmacist	1
Village/Ward level	Primary health care at the domiciliary level, covering a fixed number of house-visits per day on a fortnightly round; by one male health assistant (IIA) and one female family planning worker·	Family planning workers (FWW)	23,500
		Family planning assistants•	4,500
		IIealth assistants (HA)	21,000
		IIealth inspectors (HI)	1,400
		Assistant HI	4,200
		Sanitary inspectors	491

Source: Bangladesh Bureau of Statistics (various years), DGMS 1989.
•(FPA) There are other categories of fieldworkers for FP services such as family welfare visitor.

Table 16.6
Selected Health Indices: Disease Profile—Trends and Shifts
(Morbidity in percent if not otherwise stated)

	1977	*1980*	*1985*	*1990*	*1991*	*1992*	*1993*	*1994*	*1995*	*1996*
Crude birth rate/1000 live births/year	48.0	43.3	39	33				31		24.9
Crude death rate/1000 deaths/year	20.9	16.8	15	11.4				11		7.9
Annual growth rate/ 1000 pop./year	27.1	26.5	24	21.6				20		17
Infant mortality rate/1000 live births/year (39 percent of all deaths were due to infant mortality in 1980)	150	140	125	94.4	92	88	85	77		76.8
Child (1–4 years) mortality rate/1000 children/year		23	22	13 (1989)	11.2					7
Maternal mortality rate/ 1000 live births/year (accounting 27% of all deaths of females aged 15–45 years)		7	6	5.1 (1988)	4.7		4.9			3.9
Life expectancy (at birth)		47	50	56			57			59.5
Diarrheal disease	17.5	17.1	16.9	15.9	15.1	17.3	14.5	12.5	13.4	14.3
D.D. (Mortality)	0.28	0.16	0.10	0.09						
Worm infestation 80% (Prev. 15 years)	12.2	12.4	13.0	15.2	9.4	11.9	8.9	10.1	11.5	12.3

(Contd.)

(Contd.)

	1977	*1980*	*1985*	*1990*	*1991*	*1992*	*1993*	*1994*	*1995*	*1996*
Malaria (clinical malaria)	1.09	0.95	0.87	0.26	0.55	0.77	0.63	0.62	0.33	0.88
Kala-azar	0.03	0.01	0.02	0.01	0.01	0.01	0.01	0.01	0.02	0.02
Tetanus	0.06	0.04	0.02	0.01	0.01	0.01	0.002	0.01	0.02	0.01
Diphtheria (1,714 cases in 1995, 1,096 in 1996)	0.04	0.02	0.04	0.001	0.03	0.003	0.003	0.001	0.000	0.000
Pertussis	1.37	1.11	0.65	0.11	0.26	0.24	0.07	0.02	0.03	0.09
Measles	0.58	0.53	0.25	0.04	0.05	0.02	0.02	0.02	0.02	0.02
Skin disease (mostly – scabies)	10.6	10.1	9.30	4.94	8.75	11.4	9.60	8.90	12.9	9.30
Hepatitis B	0.62	0.50	0.37	0.07	0.18	0.17	0.26	0.08	0.08	0.09
Night-blindness	1.67	1.52	1.15	0.25	0.44	0.25	2.31	0.21	0.25	0.24
Anemia	8.36	8.50	8.50	3.99	6.78	8.01	6.74	7.98	6.7	9.85
Deficiency goiter	5.84	6.25	6.38	10.1	8.42	6.44	6.39	2.97	-	-
Diabetes	0.18	0.20	0.47	0.04	0.11	0.17	0.13	0.08	0.17	0.14
Maternal mort./1,000 live births	5.96	5.72	5.08	4.78	4.72	4.68	4.52	4.50	-	-
Infant mort./1,000 live births.	113	110	98.0	94.0	92.0	88.0	84.0	77.0	-	-
Safe water supply (pop. coverage per tube-well—250 rural pop. within 50m of a tube-well)		40%			80%			85%		
Coverage of households by sanitary/water sealed latrine/rural sanitation		0.4%		0.6%			33%			

Source: Government of Bangladesh (various years).

years. Further, in about 292 cases, about 14 percent were from households with both safe drinking water and hygienic latrines, whereas about 80 percent were from households with access to safe drinking water but no hygienic latrine facilities.

There has also been a consistent reduction in morbidity from diseases like diphtheria, pertussis, tetanus, and measles. However, among the diseases, proportion of measles prevalence is still the highest; among morbid infants (less than 1 year), morbidity due to measles is high (4.9 percent). The estimated annual mortality from measles, in 1994, was 45,000. Majority of the victims were either severely or moderately malnourished.

Malnutrition is both a cause and effect of ill health. Severe malnutrition exists among families of landless agricultural laborers and farmers with small holdings, affecting women the most. "A significantly higher proportion of the members of women-headed households live in extreme poverty as compared to the members of men-headed households. The bottom 20–30 percent of women-headed households are amongst the poorest in Bangladesh" (Hossain and Begum 1995). Children under five, and pregnant and lactating women are the worst sufferers. Non-pregnant mothers in slums also suffer from severe malnutrition. Other problems like nutritional anemia, endemic goiter, and cretinism are also common.

Some specific causes of maternal mortality are: post-partum hemorrhage (26 percent), post-partum sepsis (11 percent), obstructed labor (8 percent), eclampsia (16 percent), abortion (21 percent), and other obstetric problems (18 percent). About 94 percent of deliveries take place at home (Das 1992). Only 2 and 3.2 percent of births in rural areas are attended to by doctors and nurses respectively, about 35.2 percent are taken care of by relatives, and 59.4 percent by trained birth attendants (TBAs). About 70 percent mothers suffer from iron-deficiency anemia, and 45 percent have low body mass index. The average weight gain in pregnancy is 4.5 kg. The estimated current maternal mortality rate of 4.5 per 1,000 live births is among the highest in the world (*Bangladesh Observer* 1998). There seems to be a wide discrepancy in the figures. Another source places maternal mortality at 8.5 per 1,000 live births (HDC 1999), which is even higher.

Infant mortality has dropped from 150/1,000 live births in 1977 to 76.8/1,000 live births in 1996. Other related mortality rates for 1994 were: neonatal – 51.1/1,000 and post-natal – 3.1/1,000 (1994 estimates) (Government of Bangladesh 1995b). The main causes of under-five mortality are: diarrhea, diarrheal diseases, acute respiratory infections (ARIs), low-birth weight, tetanus, measles and its complications, pertussis, and malnutrition (Das 1992). The mortality and morbidity patterns and other health indicators when viewed against the socio-economic parameters of land-ownership, etc., illustrate yet again the close association between health and the extent of poverty and deprivation of basic needs.

Paradigm of Disease Control

Malaria Control

Clinical malaria cases ranged from 1.09 to 0.62 percent of the total reported diseases during 1986 to 1994, with occasional fluctuations. About 582 malaria deaths were reported in 1994 by the Malaria and Parasitic Disease Control Division.

In 1997, Malaria Control Program was initiated in many countries including Bangladesh with commendable results and the World Health Organization had no real reason to be remorseful of its fine record in the field of malaria control. Despite encouraging results, "control" became a dirty word in international malariological circles. Nothing less than world eradication could suffice (WHO 1972).

In 1961, the control program was converted to a program for eradication in complete disregard of the prevailing socio-economic milieu that required a holistic approach and a comprehensive plan. Hundreds and thousands of tonnes of DDT were dumped in Bangladesh, promoting market economy and causing environmental degradation. The achievement in the reduction of malaria, though at a huge cost, almost beyond the limited resources of many developing countries, has been great. However, the fanfare with which the doctrine of eradication was announced was nullified when malaria reappeared in the form of huge epidemics in Sri Lanka and India. WHO came up with a defensive statement that "in certain ecological conditions eradication may be hampered by the dynamic complexity of malaria transmission." Later in 1969, it recognized the role played by socio-economic, financial, administrative, and operational factors as also the inadequacy of the basic health services in the failures. Thereafter came an honest admission that in "most African countries south of Sahara, and in some Asian countries, malaria eradication is not practicable at present" (WHO 1972), and the strategy reverted to control, but not until a colossal setback in the development of an integrated, comprehensive, and sustainable health services (in many developing countries) had taken place.

Tuberculosis Control

Tuberculosis (TB) Control Program began in 1961. There are four TB and eight segregation hospitals, 44 TB clinics at district level, and 21 district TB consultants, one at each district general hospital. One medical officer (MO) at thana health complex (THC) is available for TB-Control Program. The revised national tuberculosis program (directly observed treatment short course)—NTP(DOTS)—run by a project director, was jointly financed by the government, World Bank, and the Netherlands and was one of the largest of the Fourth Population and Health Projects 1992–98 (FPHP) with a budget of $17.2 million. According to the national guidelines, the objective and strategy of DOTS were:

- To break the chain of transmission of infection as early as possible and render infectious patients non-infectious by chemotherapy.
- By increasing cure rate of sputum smear positive cases from less than 40 percent to 85 percent and to increase case detection from existing 10 percent to over 70 percent of the estimated incidence.
- Case-finding and adequate chemotherapy that break the chain of transmission of tuberculosis improve the epidemiological situation. The guidelines reiterate, "case-finding and treatment to be one entity, because case-finding without effective treatment is pointless" (Tuberculosis Control Services 1995).

Case-detection is however hinged on the premise of alien experience of developed countries, namely: "case-finding in developing countries is usually passive, i.e., based on self-referral of symptomatic individuals who consult health institutions and who are diagnosed as tuberculosis cases." The problem of incomplete treatment is admittedly crucial, but prompt detection of cases in adequate numbers is of no less importance. Often, poorly functioning peripheral institutions which lack material, manpower, and drugs result in inadequate detection and incomplete treatment. Throughout their report on the tuberculosis epidemic, WHO highlighted the spectacular role of "multiple drug therapy" and of DOTS, based on self-referral of symptomatic individuals (WHO 1995). It demonstrated a cure rate "from 43 percent to nearly 80 percent in Tanzania pilot project; 54 percent (1986) to 78 percent (1992) in New York City and 52 percent (1980) to 91 percent (1994) in China." Case-coverage rate remained noticeably absent in the report. Strangely, nowhere in the report was the importance of case-detection emphasized, namely the necessity of active case-finding of poor TB patients living in remote villages, who due to inaccessibility (social, economic, and physical), cannot avail of treatment, and thereby continue to infect an average 10 to 15 people in a year's time (WHO 1995). Those who do eventually avail of services, mostly do so at an advanced stage. Learning lessons from China's success, the WHO report states, "A good health care system is crucial for implementing TB control strategies. The majority of work involved in control—such as case detection and treatment—is best accomplished at the primary health care level." Without undermining the role of adequate treatment by DOTS, it is difficult to comprehend what magic touch of the wand (of DOTS) would wake up our people from their socio-cultural milieu of veritable slumber and apathy and prompt them to avail treatment at rural health centers daily for six months, often traveling miles and leaving aside work that earns them their daily bread!

DOTS Performance in Bangladesh based on the Self-referral System Revised NTP with DOTS was introduced in four thanas in November 1993. It has progressively covered 363 thanas in 58 out of the 64 districts—43 districts by the government and 21 by non-governmental organizations (NGOs). The program had reached 78 percent of the population by November 1997. Nearly 150,000 people with tuberculosis had been diagnosed and treated since the program began, with the rate of success of treatment maintained at about 80 percent. Recent estimates suggest that 2.3 percent of the population of Bangladesh is infected with tuberculosis every year and annually, in about 300,000 people, the disease progresses. About half of these have infectious pulmonary tuberculosis and continue to spread the disease. In 1996, a total of 63,985 cases of tuberculosis were registered by NTP, representing 21 percent of the estimated incidence. Although, DOTS has been introduced in most thanas, intake of every dose of medication at the THCs is directly observed in less than half the patients (Government of Bangladesh 1997). According to Weyer's report,

> the most plausible model would suggest an incidence of smear-positive tuberculosis in 1996 of around 111 per 100,000 (range 89.134). This translates into approximately 358,950 cases of tuberculosis in Bangladesh in 1996, of which an estimated 161,669 were sputum positive. In the absence of recent epidemiological information on tuberculosis in Bangladesh, these estimates are considered to be very conservative (Weyer 1997).

Estimated smear sputum positive prevalence rate of 0.5 percent for 1964–66 and an estimated population of 123,700,000 for the year 1997 gives the estimated total number of sputum positive cases to be 618,500 (0.005 × 123,700,000). Applying the prevalence rates for 1980–87 (0.8 percent), this number rises to 989,600. In 1996, the total detection of cases of tuberculosis was 63,985 and the sputum positive pulmonary cases were 30,916. Seen against the total estimated cases of 618,500, it gives a 4.99 percent detection rate of the infectious cases from the pool of pulmonary tuberculosis cases. Against the estimated 989,600 cases, the detection rate further declines to 3.12 percent of the sputum positive cases. This is indeed a very poor performance. Weyer's conservative projection of existence of 161,669 sputum positive cases for 1996 comes to new smear sputum positive incident case detection rate of 18.50 percent (29,948/161,669 × 100) (Weyer 1997). In reality, sputum positive incident cases would be much more, and the detection rates far lower.

Despite Bangladesh's credible success in clinical cure rate of about 80 percent (which is twice as high as those in many developing countries), the bare truth is that with detection rate of 3.12 percent to 4.99 percent, 96.88 to 95 percent of sputum positive prevalent cases remain undetected, are either receiving inadequate treatment or no treatment at all, and are continuing to contribute to the huge infectious pool. Detection of 21 percent of the estimated incident cases of all forms, having a target of detection of "sputum smear positive tuberculosis... from present 10 percent to over 70 percent of estimated incidence cases...to break the chain of transmission of infection as early as possible, and render (infectious patients) non-infectious by chemotherapy, remains a far cry."

There exists no provision in the program for periodic assessment of the impact on the reduction of infectious case load and trend of annual rate of infection, the parameters most needed for success, nor of sputum culture and sensitivity-testing for monitoring of possible development of drug resistance. Further, the program is not based on any model projecting progressive reduction of various indices of epidemiological importance in terms of a time frame, as was done in Malaria Eradication Program.

If the present trend of meager case detection rate and the clinically-biased, market-oriented DOTS continues, then the program is apt to end up without any significant epidemiological impact on the incidence of tuberculosis despite the huge loan incurred. The coverage will remain poor in the absence of peripheral workers and unmodified passive detection of symptomatic individuals. According to international agencies, this is the primary task of the national health organization. Thus, the entire responsibility is conveniently shifted on to the national government as was done in the case of malaria eradication. Meanwhile, the debt trap of the World Bank continues to increase manifold. As understood, World Bank is now contemplating/recommending withdrawal of fieldworkers from domiciliary field visits and is emphasizing primary health care through static centers based on the self-referral system. This seems to be the groundwork that would eventually end up with the withering of the "old" public health approach of "greatest good for the greater number," (conveniently judged "dirty" like "control") and would make place for the "new public health" (NPH) of WHO.

Structural Adjustments in the Health Sector

Structural adjustments need not necessarily involve cuts in financial allocations. Its modus operandi may be in the form of shrinkage and/or poor investment in social infrastructure and in welfare sectors including health. For instance, there may not be an increase in the number of fieldworkers corresponding to increase in population or in workload, or vacant posts may not be filled. Although delivery of health services should not be a saleable, profit-making commodity, the failure of the public sector to perform its duties diligently has created a "big market" for the private sector. The latter is characterized by its greed for profits, substandard medical practice, negligence, and violation of medical ethics.

An examination of the total allocations of resources for health and family welfare over the years shows that investments have risen (see Table 16.7).

Table 16.7
Financial Allocations for the Health Sector in the Successive Five Year Plans

Plan	*Million Takas*
1973–78	2,000
Two-year plan (1978–80)	1,180
Second FYP (1980–85)	4,130 (at 1983/84 prices)
Third FYP (1985–90)	8,700 (at 1984/85 prices)
Fourth FYP (1990–95)	10,600 (at 1989/90 prices) (3.05 percent of total outlay)
Fifth FYP (1997–2002)	62,272.40 (at 1996–97prices)*

Source: The Five Year Plans, Planning Commission, Ministry of Finance and Planning, Government of Bangladesh, Dhaka.

*The Fifth FYP states "it is expected that private sector will come in a big way to supplement public sector efforts in health care. Total investment by private sector... in Fifth Plan period is expected to be at least 30 percent of the public sector investment, i.e. TK 18,682 million. Besides... their (other NGOs and voluntary organizations) contribution is expected to be 10 percent, i.e., TK 6,227 million. Investment by the private sector and NGOs is expected to be canalised for establishment of medical colleges, polyclinics, hospitals, nursing homes, pathological laboratories, X-ray clinics, etc."

However, there has been no corresponding increase in infrastructure. The experience of health services in Bangladesh reveals a series of adjustments in the planning process, right since 1971. These have been taking place despite the stated objectives of "Health for All."

These adjustments can be roughly grouped as those that precede the formal acceptance of World Bank (WB) policies and those that follow it.

The changes made in the seventies to eighties were:

- Shelving the program of opening 100 four-bedded rural dispensaries per year.
- Staggering the program of rural health centers with three subcenters.
- Detachment of MCH services from health services in 1976 and integrating it with family planning.
- Shelving the *palli chikitsak* program.
- No increase in number of fieldworkers despite increase in workload and in the population.
- Successive reduction of Expanded Program of Immunization (EPI) coverage target from 0–5 year age-group (in 1979) to 0–2 year age-group, to 0–1 year group by 1988.

The changes made over the nineties are:

- Shrinkage of service facilities by increasing coverage of rural health complexes from 50,000 to the population of the entire thana.
- Reducing the output of medical assistants.
- Introduction of user's fee for registration, with no corresponding increase in allocation or improvement in quality of services.
- Reduction in expenditure on primary health care from 39 percent (1990–91) to 33 percent (1993–94); increase in family planning expenditure, from Tk 6.67 per head (1983–84) to Tk 12.23 (1993–94); family planning is considered a top-priority program (Bayes 1998).
- Only 20 percent of the health allocation is spent on population in the rural area, while they constitute about 80 percent of the total population.
- Minimizing expenditure by not filling up vacant posts, often putting year-to-year embargo.
- On the recommendation of the World Bank, withdrawal of domiciliary visits at grass-roots level in preference to static services is under contemplation. Some NGOs have already abolished this component and retrenched their field-level workers. The Fifth FYP (Health and Population Sector Program 1998–2003 HPSP Part I) states "At the Community level, the service will be provided from a fixed center, namely community clinic. This is a significant

shift from the existing domiciliary-based service delivery system."
- Opening up sectors of public investment to the private sector.
- Subsidizing private sector grants from public sector.
- Experimenting with highly technocentric strategies with no regard for its epidemiological utility or for the socio-economic milieu that demands a holistic approach and comprehensive, cost-effective planning, such as conversion of "control" programs to expensive programs for "eradication."

These adjustments, of different types and at different times, are undermining the primary health care program. Inadequate integration and inclination towards re-verticalization of infrastructure and human resources have led to duplication and cost escalation, inefficiency, frustration, and confusion among the recipients.

Unlike the experience of other South Asian countries, structural adjustment in Bangladesh has had a harmful effect on quality and growth of health services. There has been no reduction in state allocations which, in any case, were abysmally low. Any meager increase has been offset by the spiraling inflation rate. The World Bank is using the leverage of money-lending and playing the role of a self-appointed guardian. It has openly taken responsibility for "planning, designing and organizing" of various sectors, including health. The views and recommendations of the World Health Organization, a seat of excellence and respected for its "know-how" on health seem to be often bypassed by the technocentric and expensive prescriptions of the WB.

Conclusion

The association between poverty on one hand, and poor health and disease on the other, is a well-established fact. When disease and ill health are deeply rooted in the socio-economic development of a society, health cannot be achieved in isolation from these related factors. A holistic approach is necessary for achieving sustainable results, as against a compartmentalized and highly technocentric approach, that ignores the multi-sectoral, socio-economic determinants of health. A sound, cost-effective, comprehensive, and integrated approach to health problems, the most desired model, is to be looked upon as an instrument to deal with community health problems. Different epidemiological situations call for different strategies. Due consideration to prevailing, indigenous expertise is also of utmost importance.

The concept of family planning has, of late, emerged as a health issue. Bulk of the family welfare services are an integral part of functioning health services. Yet, in Bangladesh, the dichotomy between health and family planning continues. Family welfare services through multipurpose health workers can be cost-effective and widely acceptable as the workers are in constant contact with people. Health services also act as catchment for family welfare.

A change in the administrative system is also essential. The highly centralized, bureaucratic, and inefficient system needs to be replaced by fewer tiers including an integrated secretariat and directorate, creating a simpler, democratic, efficient, and accountable system. There has to be optimal utilization of the limited resources. Of utmost importance is a pro-people health policy and a strong political will and commitment to implement it.

References

Bangladesh Bureau of Statistics (various years): *Statistical Pocketbook of Bangladesh*. Dhaka: Statistics Division, Ministry of Planning.

Bangladesh Observer (1998): Maternal Malnutrition: Alarming in Bangladesh. 25 April.

Bayes, A. (1998): *Shasth O Shikha Khate Sarkari Baye abong Shamajic Naye Bichar* (Public Expenditure and Social Justice on Health and Education Sector). *Bhorer Kagaz* (Bengali daily) 1 January.

Das, A.M. (1992): An Overview of Health and Population Problem and Issues in Bangladesh. Unpublished study report. Dhaka: WHO.

Directorate General of Health Services (DGHS) (1998): *Bangladesh Health Bulletin, 1996*. Dhaka: Ministry of Health and Family Welfare.

Government of Bangladesh (various years): Survey on Prevalence of Morbidity and Health Status. Dhaka: Bangladesh Bureau of Statistics, Statistical Division, Ministry of Planning.

——— (1980): *The Second Five Year Plan*. Dhaka: Planning Commission.

——— (1995a): Health and Demographic Survey, HDS-PUB-005, Findings in Brief 1994–1995. Dhaka: Bangladesh Bureau of Statistics, Statistical Division, Ministry of Planning.

——— (1995b): Selected Health and Social Statistics of Rural Bangladesh: 1994. Bangladesh Health and Demographic Survey, HDS-PUB-006. Dhaka: Bangladesh Bureau of Statistics, Statistical Division, Ministry of Planning.

——— (1997): Review of the National Tuberculosis Program, 16–28 November. Government of Bangladesh and WHO.

Hossain, S.M., and Begum, R. (1995): Women and Men in Bangladesh: Facts and Figures; 1981–95. Presented at the One-day Workshop on Gender Statistics Worldwide, September, Beijing. Bangladesh Health and Demographic Survey, HDS-PUB-008. Dhaka: Bangladesh Bureau of Statistics, Statistical Division, Ministry of Planning.

Human Development Centre (1998): *Human Development in South Asia: The Education Challenge*. Oxford: Oxford University Press.

——— (1999): *Human Development in South Asia: The Crisis of Governance*. Oxford: Oxford University Press.

Khan, A.Q. (1989): *Epidemiology and Disease Control* (first edition). Dhaka: A.Q. Khan.

Tuberculosis Control Services (1995): *National Guidelines for Tuberculosis Control* (second edition), Bangladesh.

United Nations Development Program (UNDP) (1999): *Human Development Report*. New York: Oxford University Press.

Weyer, K. (1997): Tuberculosis in Bangladesh, 1996. Report prepared as WHO consultant for Bangladesh Tuberculosis Review, November. Monograph for limited circulation.

World Health Organization (WHO) (1972): Malaria Eradication in 1971. *WHO Chronicle*, 26(11)(November): 485–96.

——— (1977): Natality-Mortality Survey and Survey of Selected Health Problems in Rural Bangladesh: A Joint Study of WHO Assisted Projects. Dhaka: WHO.

——— (1995): *Stop TB at the Source*. WHO Report on the Tuberculosis Epidemic. WHO/TB/95. 183. Geneva: WHO.

17

Structural Adjustment Programs and Health Care Services in Sri Lanka—An Overview

Dulitha N. Fernando

Health Care Services in Sri Lanka

Historical Background

Provision of health care service to the people of the country was an important activity undertaken by the ancient kings of Sri Lanka. The flourishing systems of environmental sanitation, hospitals, and other related services are well documented in the ancient chronicles (Uragoda 1987).

The Portugese, who colonized Sri Lanka in 1505, introduced the Western system of medical care in the island. Later, the Dutch established a few hospitals in the maritime provinces which came under their rule. The British expanded this system and established military and estate health services to provide health care services to those who served them. In 1859, the Civil Medical Department was established and in 1915, a sanitary branch of this department was set up to look after environmental sanitation and prevention of communicable diseases. In 1916, the "Hookworm campaign," a major public health program aimed at the control of ankylostomiasis, was implemented throughout the country. This campaign clearly demonstrated the positive economic impact of a preventive program aimed at disease control (Department of Medical and Sanitary Services 1949).

The establishment of the first "Health Unit" at Kalutara in 1926 is an important landmark in the development of the health care services in the country (Department of Medical and Sanitary Services 1949). It met many of the criteria which, in the present-day context, are considered important in the provision of primary health care services. It emphasized the provision of preventive and promotive health service at the community level by a medical officer and a team of health workers. During the next few decades, health units, with clearly defined functions, were established throughout the island and training programs were developed for the personnel required for the health units. This system of health units, with appropriate modifications, constitutes the mainstay of the preventive and promotive health services of the country even today.

Present-day Health Services

In present times, health services are provided by the state sector (through the Ministry of Health) and the private sector. They include the allopathic and traditional systems of medicine (specially the Ayurveda system) and other types of health care, such as homeopathy. The Ministry of Local Government is responsible for providing services in the larger local government bodies, i.e., municipal councils. The armed forces have their own system. There is limited involvement of non-governmental organizations; they are usually limited to specific areas, such as family planning and services to refugees in selected areas. In the past decade, there have been attempts to incorporate the practitioners of indigenous medicine in some of the programs, such as family planning and disaster management. The services provided by the state sector constitute the major component of the entire system of health services.

With the introduction of the 13th Amendment to the Constitution in 1987, the responsibility for the provision of health care services was given to the Provincial Council through the Ministry of Health. Each Provincial Council has a Provincial Director of Health Services at the provincial level and several deputy provincial directors for each district within the province. Further devolution of power by the end of 1992 led to the establishment of Divisional Directorates of Health Services (233 by 1996), which are responsible for the provision of comprehensive health care services to a defined population, with special emphasis on preventive and promotive health care. The levels at which the health care services have been organized coincide with the "levels" of the organization for other administrative activities, i.e., provincial, district, and divisional levels (Ministry of Health 1995).

The areas under the Divisional Director of Health Services (DDHS)/Medical Officer of Health (MOH), which are

Table 17.1
Number and Types of State-sector Health Care Institutions—1996

Type of Institution	*Number of Institutions*	*Bed Strength*
Teaching hospitals	15	11572
Provincial hospitals	05	5187
Base hospitals	29	2530
District hospitals	146	12377
Peripheral units	107	4401
Rural hospitals	125	3033
Central dispensaries & maternity homes	65	639
Other hospitals	16	4126
Total number of hospitals	511	2.9 beds per 1000 population
Central dispensaries	394	-
DDHS/MOH areas	233	-

Source: Ministry of Health 1996.

geographically defined and have a defined population, may be considered as the equivalent of the earlier health units. The health services are provided by a medical officer and several categories of field-level health personnel, mainly public health nursing sister, public health inspectors, and public health midwives. The focus of these services is mainly on the promotive and preventive aspects. Curative care services are provided through a range of health care institutions, ranging from central dispensaries at the lowest level to teaching hospitals and the National Hospital of Sri Lanka (NHSL) in the capital city of Colombo at the highest level.

Table 17.1 indicates the types and the total number of these institutions as of 1995. Distribution of hospital beds by district shows large inter-district variation in the availability of beds per 1,000 population: ranging from 4.2/1,000 in the Colombo district to less than 1/1,000 in Kilinochchi and Mullaitivu.

Private Sector

The main contribution of the private sector to the health care services is in the form of outpatient services/family care provided by "general/family practitioners." These practitioners, who work on a "fee for service" basis, make an important contribution as providers of curative care at the first contact level. Several studies have indicated the significant role played by the private sector allopathic practitioners as providers of outpatient care (Caldwell et al. 1989; Ministry of Health 1994).

Inpatient services in the private sector are much more limited than those in the state sector. They provide approximately 2,000 beds which are limited mainly to the urban areas. Approximately 70 percent of the facilities are in Colombo (Perera 1996).

The present private sector services have not developed in an organized manner, especially the general practitioner services. Hence it is not possible to make any accurate assessments related to the contribution made by the private sector.

In addition to the practitioners working full time in the private sector, medical officers employed in the government health services (specialists and non-specialist) are allowed to practice in the private sector outside their working hours. Although this has enhanced the quantity of services provided through the private sector, it has also led to a mix between the services available though the private and state sector health services.

Financing of Public Sector Health Care

The government's commitment to the international declaration of human rights and to the time-honored tradition of providing free health care in the public sector are the main premises on which the health development activities in Sri Lanka are based. In keeping with the above, the government has continued to be the main source of financing of health care services in the country. The overall development policy of the government is now being increasingly oriented toward the free-market mechanism, aiming at improving efficiency while trying to preserve the achievements in equity and justice (Ministry of Health 1995).

Provision of free health services and free education to the entire population are two important welfare measures that have been in existence in Sri Lanka since independence. Available data from 1970 to 1995 indicate that the state has spent an amount ranging from 3.2 percent to 6.5 percent of the total government expenditure on health, and the per capita expenditure has ranged from Rs 34 in 1977 to Rs 624 in 1996 (see Table 17.2). Distribution of the health expenditure for the year 1994 indicates that 61.9 percent of the total expenditure was on patient care services, while 12 and 24.7 percent were spent on community

Table 17.2
State-sector Expenditure on Health, 1977–96

Year	*Total Amount Spent on Health (in Million Rs)*	*As a Percent of the Total Govt. Expenditure*	*As a Percent of the GNP*	*Per Capita Expenditure in Rs*
1977	484	5.5	1.4	34
1979	752	3.7	1.5	51
1981	953	3.2	1.2	63
1983	2024	4.8	1.8	131
1985	2750	4.1	1.9	173
1987	3711	5.5	2.1	226
1989	5038	6.5	2.3	229
1991	5437	5.0	1.6	315
1993	7904	4.5	1.8	406
1994	8273	4.2	1.6	463
1995	10533	4.3	1.8	582
1996	n.a.	4.1	1.7	624

Source: Ministry of Health 1993, 1995, 1996.

health services and general administration, respectively. The amount spent on services related to indigenous medicine was only 1.4 percent.

Information on the investment/expenditure incurred by the private sector is not available, posing a major limitation in the assessment of expenditure on health.

The limited information available on the expenditure incurred by the users of the state-sector health services indicates major components of such expenditure to be transport costs, costs of drugs prescribed at the state health facility, and costs related to incidental expenses including those for accompanying persons (Galwaduge 1993; Jayatissa 1997).

Influence of Structural Adjustment Programs (SAPs) on Health Services

Structural Adjustment Programs were introduced in Sri Lanka in the late seventies. The Sri Lankan economy during the early seventies was inward looking and allowed an import substitution strategy. With the change of government in 1977, Sri Lanka began the process of economic liberalization. Two different phases in the restructuring of the economy could be identified. The first occurred during 1977–88 and the second commenced in 1989 and has continued since then, even with a change in the government in 1994 (Ariyabandu, Hidellage, and Wijesinghe 1995).

The policy reforms during the phase I included a substantial devaluation of the rupee by 46 percent, partial liberalization of the financial market, removal of price controls (for example, food subsidies were replaced by a food stamp scheme), and an incentive package to foreign direct investment. The main focus of the change implemented during this phase was in the area of trade, with adjustments in the exchange rates and tariff reductions. The activities undertaken during the phase II (1989 onward) included further liberalization to tilt the incentive structure in favor of tradables and a stabilization package to bring down the budget deficit: a high interest rate policy and a privatization program.

In broad terms, it could be stated that the introduction of SAPs can influence the health care services and health status of a population by influencing the financing of health care or its use, the two factors being interdependent to a large extent.

In Sri Lanka, the largest proportion of the cost of provision of health care has been borne by the government in keeping with the policy of providing free health services to the people. Training of human resources required for the provision of health services has continued to be a government responsibility; through the ministries of higher education and health, such training being provided free of charge to the trainee. The inputs into the other sectors contributing to health such as water and sanitation also need to be considered as investment in health. According to available information, such investments have not shown a decline so far and several funding agencies have supported such programs.

At the same time, the government has encouraged the private sector to invest in heath care, specially in faculties providing inpatient care, by extending the incentives given to other investors to those in the health care sector.

The approach used in this chapter to study the overall influence of the SAPs on the health care delivery and the health status at a macro (national) level is to relate the changes in the national-level health indicators to the introduction of the SAPs.

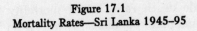

Figure 17.1
Mortality Rates—Sri Lanka 1945–95

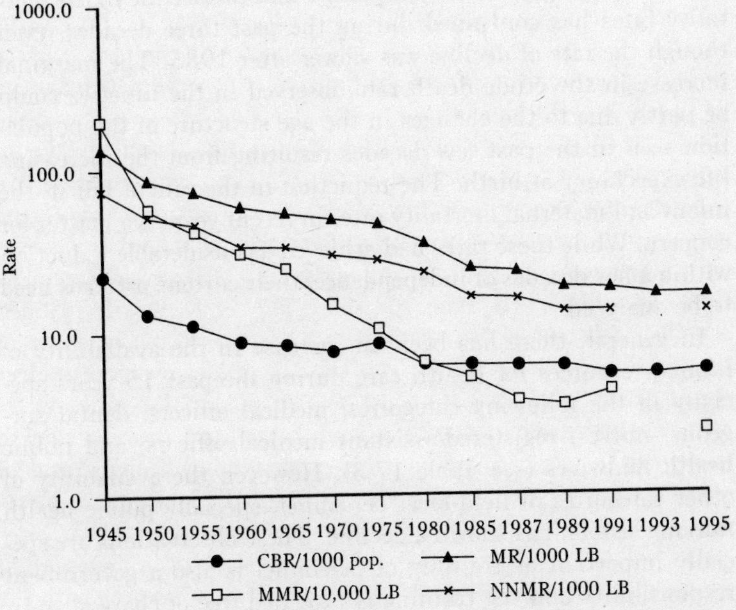

Several different indicators could be used making this assessment. They include indicators of:

- input availability of human resources, hospital beds, etc.;
- outcome: crude death rate, infant mortality rate (IMR), neonatal mortality rate (NNMR), maternal mortality rate (MMR);
- inputs in related sectors: availability of water and sanitation facilities;
- use of curative services: OPD attendance, inpatient attendance; and
- use of preventive services: contraceptive use, immunization coverage.

In making these assessments, it is necessary to use routinely collected data even though there are several inherent limitations in the use of such data. However, these comparisons are aimed at studying trends more than the absolute value; hence use of such data could be justified.

Data on crude death rate, infant mortality rate, neonatal mortality rate, and maternal mortality rate, from 1950 to 1992, are shown in Figure 17.1. They show that the decline in the mortality rates has continued during the past three decades, even though the rate of decline was slower after 1985. The marginal increase in the crude death rate observed in the nineties could be partly due to the changes in the age structure of the population seen in the past few decades resulting from the increasing life expectancy at birth. The reduction in the rate of fall in the infant and maternal mortality rates in recent years is a matter for concern. While these rates had achieved a considerable reduction within a few decades of independence, their current patterns need to be analyzed.

In general, there has been an increase in the availability of human resources for health care during the past 15 years specially in the following categories: medical officers, dental surgeons, nurses, registered/assistant medical officers, and public health midwives (see Table 17.3). However, the availability of other categories of field-level personnel, specially public health nursing sisters, has shown a decline. These observations are specially important as training of personnel is also a government responsibility and the training is provided free of charge.

In keeping with the government policy of providing inpatient care at government hospitals (free of charge), the availability of beds per 1,000 population has been maintained at approximately three per 1,000 in spite of the introduction of SAPs in the late seventies (see Table 17.4). This table also indicates that the utilization of the state-sector health services (both inpatient and outpatient services) has not shown any major changes from 1965 to 1996.

The preventive and promotive health services, which form an important component of the comprehensive health services provided by the state sector, have not been influenced by the introduction of the SAPs. Information related to the use of such services, i.e., to contraceptive use and immunization coverage is presented in Tables 17.5 and 17.6.

The improvements in the contraceptive prevalence (as shown by repeated surveys) and the increase in the percentage immunization coverage indicate that the preventive and promotive health services which are mainly provided through the state sector have continued to show an increase in the level of acceptance.

Table 17.3
Availability of Key Health Personnel per 100,000 Population, 1980–95

Year	*MO*	*Dental Surgeon*	*RMO/AMO#*	*Nurses*	*PHNS****	*PHIs***	*PHMWs**
1980	13.9	1.5	6.9	41.5	1.4	6.2	12.3
1982	13.4	1.8	6.0	45.6	1.6	6.3	15.1
1984	12.5	1.8	6.3	47.4	1.3	5.9	19.2
1986	13.7	2.0	6.5	49.7	1.2	6.0	19.2
1988	14.0	2.1	6.6	50.1	0.9	5.7	19.3
1990	15.5	2.0	6.8	57.1	0.9	5.6	20.2
1992	19.2	2.2	7.2	57.6	0.6	5.0	23.6
1993	21.1	2.2	7.4	67.1	0.6	5.0	24.8
1994	22.7	2.2	7.6	73.1	0.7	5.2	24.6
1995	25.5	2.3	7.6	73.1	1.0	5.2	24.6
1996	27.9	2.5	7.6	74.0	1.0	5.0	23.8

Source: Ministry of Health 1996.
Registered medical officer/Assistant medical officer
*** Public health nursing sister
** Public health inspector
* Public health midwife

Table 17.4
Availability of Hospital Beds and Inpatient and Outpatient Attendance

Item	*1970*	*1975*	*1980*	*1985*	*1990**	*1995***	*1996***
Number of beds	39173	4076	43389	44861	42079	47665	51866
Beds per 1000 population	(3.1)	(3.0)	(2.9)	(2.8)	(2.9)	(2.9)	(2.9)
Number of inpatients (in '000)	2054	2146	2335	2494	2533	2953	3339
Number of inpatients per 1000 population	(164.1)	(159.0)	(158.3)	(157.4)	(174.6)	(179.3)	(184.5)
Outpatient attendance (in '000)	2054	2146	2334	2494	2533	2953	35348
Rate per 1000 population	(164.1)	(159.0)	(158.3)	(157.4)	(174.6)	(1793)	(1953)

Source: Ministry of Health 1996.
Note: *excludes Northern and Eastern Provinces
**figures are provisional

Table 17.5
Contraceptive Use: Result of Surveys 1974–93

Contraceptive	*Percentage Currently Using Method*			
	SLWFS (1994)	*SLCPS (1982)*	*SLDHS (1989)*	*SLDHS (1993)*
All modern temporary methods	9.9	9.9	10.8	16.5
All sterilizations	10.6	22.0	29.8	27.2
All traditional methods	14.2	26.0	21.1	22.4
All methods	34.4	57.8	61.7	66.1

Source: Ministry of Health 1995.
Note: SLWFS: Sri Lanka World Fertility Survey
SLCPS: Sri Lanka Contraceptive Prevalence Survey
SLDHS: Sri Lanka Demographic and Health Survey

Table 17.6
Immunization Coverage—Percent of Children Immunized: Sri Lanka 1982–96

Year	*BCG*	*OPV (4 dose)*	*TV (3 dose)*	*Measles*
1982	63.8	55.5	56.0	-
1984	66.8	65.4	66.4	2.8
1986	73.8	74.7	74.9	45.3
1988	80.7	84.7	82.9	68.0
1990	84.4	86.2	86.0	79.7
1992	88.5	89.5	89.8	82.9
1993	87.9	89.3	90.2	85.9
1994	86.0	88.5	88.2	83.9
1995	90.1	92.4	93.0	87.5
1996	89.1	91.7	91.7	89.5

Source: Ministry of Health 1982, 1984, 1986, 1988, 1990 and 1992.
Note: BCG - Bacillus Calmette Guerin
OPV - Oral Polio Vaccine
TV - Tetanus Vaccine

Investment in health-related fields, especially those aimed at improving access to safe water and improvement of sanitation facilities could be considered as having a major contribution toward improving health status. Available data indicate that such investments have continued and the facilities have shown an improvement between 1981 and 1994 (see Table 17.7).

Table 17.7
Availability of Water Supply and Sanitation Facilities: 1981 and 1994

Facility	*1981*[1]	*1994*[2]
Water supply		
Main line	17.7	19.4
Tube-well	-	5.1
Protected well	52.2	43.9
Unprotected well	20.6	22.9
River/tank, etc.	-	4.7
Not stated	2.5	-
Toilet facilities		
Water seal	4.8	37.8
Pour flush	24.2	25.6
Pit latrines	32.3	22.2
Other	2.1	0.9
Not available	36.6	13.5

Source: Ministry of Health 1996.
Note: [1]Census of Population and Housing 1981.
[2] Colombo: Bureau of Statistics, Government of Sri Lanka.
Sri Lanka Demographic and Health Survey 1993. Colombo: Council of Population and Development, Government of Sri Lanka.
*Excludes Northern and Eastern provinces

It is likely that changes in the health care delivery system and other relevant sectors will lead to changes in the morbidity pattern. Due to several reasons, no attempt has been made in this presentation to study the changes in the mortality pattern. On the one hand, routinely available morbidity data are limited to the inpatient morbidity pattern in the state-sector institutions. On the other hand, there have been no major changes made in the organization and provision of health care services. Hence, any influence that such changes may have had on the morbidity pattern is unlikely to be observed in a relatively short period of time. However, the data on nutritional status available from a special survey were studied as nutritional status is influenced by health-related factors as well as those related to the socio-economic status of the community.

Data from the nutritional status survey carried out by the Ministry of Plan Implementation indicated that 21 percent of the children in the age group 3–6 months were stunted and 12 percent were wasted (Ministry of Plan Implementation 1994). Among the adults, 35 percent of the females and 42 percent of the males had a BMI of less than 18 and this proportion was the lowest for the highest income quartile and vice versa. The reported prevalence of stunting and wasting of children aged 6–72 months in a national-level study done in 1976 were 34.6 percent and 6.6 percent respectively. Even though the two studies are not strictly comparable due to methodological differences, there are indications that the nutritional status has not shown a significant improvement during the 18-year period.

Discussion

Sri Lanka is often quoted as a low-income country with relatively good health indicators (Morris 1979). Many attribute these achievements to the welfare measures implemented by successive governments, which included state-sector free health services and provision of free education. Even though SAPs have been introduced in Sri Lanka in late seventies, so far there have been no major changes in the financing or in the organization of the health services in Sri Lanka.

The mortality indicators continued to decline even though their decline has been slower in the late eighties and early nineties compared to the sixties and the seventies. To some extent, the changes in the crude death rate could have been influenced by the alterations in the age structure of the population with the increasing life expectancy. In drawing any conclusions regarding the pattern observed in IMR, NNMR, and MMR, it will be necessary to study the current status of the mortality indicator, i.e., actual value, important causes related to the same, and the services available to reduce the relevant causes. Even though such a detailed analysis is outside the scope of this chapter, it is necessary to focus on the need to closely monitor the changes in these rates in relation to the relevant inputs.

The approach used in this chapter was to study the trends in selected indicators at a macro level. It is necessary to consider whether such an approach is sensitive enough to detect changes resulting from the introduction of SAPs, specially changes related to the quality of care. The objective of this chapter is to present an overview of the health care system in Sri Lanka with a view to identifying the impact, if any, that introduction of SAPs may have had on the health care system and/or the health status of the population of Sri Lanka. Though subject to some limitations, making macro-level assessments was the most feasible approach that could be used in this study. Encouragement given to the private sector in recent years, to invest in the provision of inpatient services has so far not shown a significant influence on the use of state-sector services. Continued availability of state-sector services, the greater "confidence" that the community has on the state-sector services, and the inability to afford the private-sector services by a large proportion of the population may have contributed to this observation. However, close monitoring of the utilization patterns of the private and state-sector services is necessary to study any impact.

The observations made in this chapter could be interpreted in several ways. In Sri Lanka where introduction of SAPs did not lead to a major alteration in the financing or in the organization of health care services, it may be that SAPs did not have an influence on the health-related indicators at the national level. It is also possible that the macro-level indicators used are not sensitive enough to detect any influences or such influences could manifest after a longer time period. It is also important to note that the indicators have been considered only at the national level while subnational level differences could be important considerations. This may be so, especially when quality of care is considered.

Even though many of the indicators related to health care services and outcomes do not seem to be influenced by the introduction of SAPs, the nutritional-status indicator has remained unsatisfactory during the past two decades. As nutritional status is influenced by factors related to health care services, socio-economic, and environmental factors, the lack of improvement in the nutritional status may be an indication of the influence of socio-economic changes which could have been influenced by the SAPs.

The *World Development Report 1993* published by the World Bank suggests that the indicators used to assess the effectiveness of health services should include those related to the disease burden, disability adjusted life years, etc. (World Bank 1993). On the one hand, controversial views have been expressed on the applicability of such indicators in developing countries, while on the other, data required to assess disease burden, DALYs, etc., are not routinely available for Sri Lanka; hence such an assessment could not be attempted.

The influence of fiscal and other policy changes related to SAPs is likely to have a significant influence on the income levels and on income disparities in the population. Such changes could influence the use of the health care services whether in the private or the state sector. Access to micro-level data on utilization of services, specially those that would enable assessment of changes over a period of time, are very limited, thus limiting attempts for such studies.

There is no indication at present that Sri Lanka would make changes aimed at following the three-pronged approach suggested in the *World Development Report 1993—Investing in Health*, i.e., fostering an enabling environment for households to improve health, improve government spending by selecting cost-effective interventions for health, and promoting diversity and competition. Views expressed that the title of the document itself indicates the dehuman mechanistic market-place view of both health and health care, and that the three-pronged approach would have significant negative influences on provision of primary health care (Werner 1996), need to be taken into consideration before making any changes suggested in this report.

In keeping with the "trends" in many developing countries where SAPs have been introduced, concern has been expressed by the health policy-makers on the need for health sector reforms. Among the suggestions that have been considered are: the introduction of a "selective" user-fee system, introduction of a health insurance scheme as a long-term measure, and introduction of a "health tax." Emphasis has been placed on increasing the utilization of foreign donations and improving "internal" efficiency by linking the outputs of services to the costs and improving "external" efficiency by giving autonomy and financial responsibility to institutions and divisions. However, major changes in the state-sector health services have not been made so far.

At present, a Presidential Task Force is developing a "Health Policy Document" for Sri Lanka. It is expected that this activity will focus on areas, such as defining the role of the state sector in the provision of health care and increasing the efficiency of the state sector by improving managerial and organizational aspects of providing health care. The extent to which the changes to be proposed by the Presidential Task Force will be influenced by the SAPs and their influence on the provision and the use of services are important considerations for the future.

References

Ariyabandu, M.M., Hidellage, V., and **Wijesinghe, T.** (1995): Structural Adjustment—The Small Producers' Dilemma. *Economic Review,* Colombo: People's Bank (3) (January/ February): 15–30.

Caldwell, J., Gajanayake, I., Caldwell, P., and **Peiris, P.** (1989): Sensitization to Illness and the Risk of Death and Explanation for Sri Lanka's Approach to Good Health for All. *Social Science and Medicine,* 28(4): 365–79.

Department of Medical and Sanitary Services (1949): Administration Report of the Director of Medical and Sanitary Services for 1948. Ceylon.

Galwaduge, D.L.C. (1993): Financing of Maternal Health Activities at Primary Health Care Level. M.D. Thesis. Sri Lanka: Postgraduate Institute of Medicine, University of Colombo.

Jayatissa, K.L.R. (1997): An Analysis of Utilisation, Quality and Cost of Maternal and Child Welfare Clinic Service. M.D. Thesis. Sri Lanka: Postgraduate Institute of Medicine, University of Colombo.

Ministry of Health (1982): *Annual Health Bulletin.* Colombo: Ministry of Health.

——— (1984): *Annual Health Bulletin.* Colombo: Ministry of Health.

——— (1986): *Annual Health Bulletin.* Colombo: Ministry of Health.

——— (1988): *Annual Health Bulletin.* Colombo: Ministry of Health.

——— (1990): *Annual Health Bulletin.* Colombo: Ministry of Health.

——— (1992): *Annual Health Bulletin.* Colombo: Ministry of Health.

——— (1993): *Annual Health Bulletin.* Colombo: Ministry of Health.

——— (1994): Health Strategy and Financing Study. World Bank (unpublished document), Sri Lanka.

——— (1995): *Annual Health Bulletin.* Colombo: Ministry of Health.

——— (1996): *Annual Health Bulletin.* Colombo: Ministry of Health.

Ministry of Plan Implementation (1994): Report on the Nutritional Status Survey. Colombo: Ministry of Plan Implementation.

Morris, D. (1979): *Measuring the Condition of the World's Poor.* New York: Pergamon Press.

Perera, M.A. (1996): *Health Care Services in Sri Lanka—The Success Story of the Century.* Health for all—today? Faculty of Medicine. Colombo: A SIRHA Publication.

Uragoda, C.G.A. (1987): *History of Medicine in Sri Lanka.* Colombo: Sri Lanka Medical Association.

Werner, D. (1996): *Does Primary Health Care have a Future?* Health for all—today? Faculty of Medicine. Colombo: A SIRHA Publication.

World Bank (1993): *World Development Report: Investing in Health.* New York: Oxford University Press.

18

Evolution of India's Leprosy Program from Control to Elimination

B.R. Chatterjee

Introduction

After use of *chaulmoogra* oil[1] for centuries, leprosy control took a major turn in the early forties with the availability of the sulfone group of drugs. While the initial preparation was injectible, DDS (diamine diphenyl sulfone) could be administered orally. Leprosy treatment moved out of leprosy homes to the field, to the masses, and their communities. The National Leprosy Control Program (NLCP) was launched in 1954–55, wherein dapsone mono-therapy was dispensed from leprosy control clinics. The work was built around the survey, education, and treatment (SET) pattern, i.e., seek the cases out, educate the community, and deliver treatment. Treatment with dapsone for two to three years was soon replaced by treatment for five to ten years or for life for fear of relapse. This proved to be the undoing of the program, as discussed later.

Cases started to be non-responsive to dapsone after the initial few years, and it was "proved" that such cases had developed dapsone-resistant leprosy (Pearson 1981; Pearson, Haile, and

1 *Chaulmoogra* oil is a plant extract that had been used in leprosy treatment before the advent of sulfones when its use was gradually abandoned. Its real merit, if any, has not been properly evaluated and it deserves at least that much. Some practitioners have used it along with dapsone. Many old patients who were treated with it in the pre-sulfone days, still ask to be massaged by it, perhaps more for psychological re-assurance. Some clinics do oblige them. It was sufficiently effective to have been revered and idolized by leprosy workers; a large tree bearing the fruit still stands at the Leprosy Mission's Hospital at Purulia, West Bengal, India.

Rees 1977). To counter this perceived threat of a global epidemic of dapsone-resistant leprosy, multidrug therapy (MDT) was brought in almost as a panic response (Chatterjee 1982). Along with it came the World Health Organization (WHO) and many overseas voluntary organizations with money, material, and manpower. The shift from MDT to FDT (fixed duration therapy) may be said to be a quantum leap. How did it come about and what would be the end result of this truly gigantic intervention?

It is not clear whether she was moved by personal concern for the plight of the leprosy affected, but the late Indira Gandhi in her address to the World Health Assembly at Geneva, in 1980, made a fervent appeal to the advanced countries of the world to help India eradicate leprosy by the turn of the millennium (Gandhi 1981). She could be excused if she had conceived of the idea herself. But if she was briefed by her know-all bureaucrats and not-so-scientifically equipped technocrats, then one expects a national debate, involving competent professionals, to precede such decisions that commit the nation to something as absurdly unrealistic as leprosy eradication. That the term "eradication" has subsequently been scaled down to "elimination," thus conveying a qualitative difference in the goal to be achieved, hardly changes things. The difference is only of semantic interest; the outcome may not differ much. According to the World Health Organization, when leprosy prevalence comes down to less than 1 case per 10,000 population, the disease will greatly lose its transmission potential and will thus be considered to have been eliminated (Noordeen 1995). While one is not disputing the qualifying criterion, yet it still is not "elimination." It is only a linguistic veil to conceal the lack of thinking in the choice of the word "eradication." The so-called elimination level of prevalence, as cited above, should ideally be considered a level when we can say, the problem of leprosy has been contained.

The Problem of Leprosy

What is so unique about leprosy that makes it difficult to eradicate/eliminate? It is not very hard to understand or define. In a situation such as in India where chances of getting infected with the leprosy bacillus is universal, we all get infected. But only about five in a 1,000 population develop clinical leprosy after getting infected (Government of India 1982). This means that the majority of the population is capable of an immunological response. And amongst the five in a 1,000 that do develop clinical leprosy, only about five to 10 percent of this diseased population will develop the so-called infectious or multi-bacillary (MB) leprosy (Chatterjee 1993a). Proportionately more of the contacts of high grade MB leprosy have been seen to develop leprosy than those that are non-contacts or contacts of pauci-bacillary (PB) leprosy. This is why the high grade multi-bacillary or the lepromatous type patients, have been called infectious leprosy patients. However, chances of contacts of PB leprosy developing leprosy is about twofold for those who are non-contacts of leprosy patients. Since PB leprosy cases constitute about 80–90 percent of all cases, in reality a very large number of cases arise from amongst the contacts of the so-called non-infectious leprosy cases (Chatterjee 1993a). So, if one wishes to contain leprosy by chemotherapy, i.e., by killing the leprosy bacilli and thereby eliminating sources of transmission, the target should be to treat all cases, and to do so with equal vigor. However, in reality there is a difference in the approach to therapy of these two groups of leprosy cases. An appreciation and understanding of this is crucial if we have to design an effective elimination strategy. This will be touched upon later.

Flaws in the MB and PB Classification

The classification as MB or PB is based on a very superficial examination of skin smears from a few selected sites. If one could sample more sites, the chances of discovering or upgrading of the degree of positivity improves. If we had a way of sampling sites under the skin, we would almost certainly find that the nerves of a PB leprosy patient carry bacillary loads of multi-bacillary proportion. So, what is considered pauci-bacillary is very often multi-bacillary down under.

WHO has defined a PB case as one carrying a bacillary load of less than 1,000,000 (10^6) bacilli in their system. However, the basis or rationale behind this number is not clear, as it is based only on bacillary counts from skin smears. As the PB leprosy cases are thought to carry far lesser bacillary loads, it is assumed that they should do well with a lesser period of treatment, with a lesser number of drugs. So, they are prescribed a regimen for six months of daily dapsone (DDS) and a monthly dose/pulse of rifampicin, six in total. For reasons of immunological instability, more of PB cases downgrade toward multi-bacillarity. By the estimates of Government of India (GOI)/WHO, post-MDT there is ten-fold more relapse in PB leprosy of the WHO kind than amongst the MB patients. To understand why it should be so, we have to digress for a while into the domain of immuno-pathology of leprosy and immuno-pharmacology of anti-leprosy drugs.

Borderline tuberculoid (BT) types of leprosy are classified as pauci-bacillary, but these are potentially infectious cases downgrading toward multi-bacillarity. Denis Ridley, a highly experienced pathologist, a rare one to have followed leprosy from the very early stages through reactions, downgrading, and ending up as lepromatous leprosy, and who, along with Jopling introduced the clinico-histoimmunological spectral concept of classifying leprosy, has this to say about BT leprosy, the most unstable of the leprosy types:

> it was previously known that a majority of Hanson's Disease (HD) patients are BT at the time they first become classifiable, and that the proportion subsequently falls to about 20 percent as a result of downgrading towards lepromatous leprosy (LL). LL is the form of disease that develops after bacilli have been allowed to multiply, with all the secondary consequences that follow from this (Ridley 1993).

It should be obvious from this why our approach to the treatment of BT leprosy should not be a "strait-jacketed" affair, clubbed with all other groups of pauci-bacillary leprosy. BT leprosy is the forerunner of all cases that have a tendency to immunologically react with delayed type hypersensitivity (DTH) of inflammation. The latter is clinically called type I reaction. In the process such cases incrementally become multi-bacillary, with consequent loss of immune response of the kind that prevents bacillary multiplication and kills the bacilli. Note how emphatically Ridley asserts that most cases of leprosy are BT when they are clinically classifiable. One has to mention here that there are some very rare individuals who are wholly incapable of mobilizing an immune response of the kind that prevents bacillary multiplication from the very beginning of the infection. It is virtually impossible to detect such cases by clinical diagnosis for two reasons—(*i*) they are very rare, and (*ii*) because they do not react immunologically, there are no clinical signs that facilitate diagnosis, except for the very highly bacillated individuals, who show a very light wrinkling on the skin when viewed in daylight from a distance. This is easier said than done; I have seen only one such case with a BI (bacillary index) of six, who was diagnosed by a veteran para-medical supervisor. The lesson from what has just been said is that there will be no clinically diagnosable leprosy if the host does not immunologically react to his bacilli. Patients with low bacillarity (PB) may downgrade towards multi-bacillarity through suffering type I reaction. Patients with a heavy bacillary load may remain non-reactive due to (*i*) their bacillary lipids being immunosupressive; or (*ii*) the host being an immunological responder incapable of containing bacillary multiplication.

The problem with the regimen prescribed by the WHO is that little attention has been paid to this immunological dimension of the disease. The only aim of this regimen is to kill bacilli, literally with drugs that kill the bugs. However, a very important aspect of the pharmacology of anti-leprosy drugs in addition to bio-chemical pharmacology is immuno-pharmacology of the drugs. Namely, the effect that the drugs may exert on the host immune system. Two of the three currently used drugs have a profound effect on the immune system. DDS is a strong anti-oxidant and is pro-inflammatory, while clofazimine is pro-oxidant and anti-inflammatory (Chatterjee 1993b). This would put these two drugs at opposite poles in terms of their immumo-pharmacological effects. Dapsone has been known to provoke reactions in some patients and old-time leprologists used to build up the dose of dapsone incrementally hoping to avoid this unwanted reaction. Some British leprologists proved that dapsone was pro-reactive only when used in low doses and that at high doses (50 mg per day for an adult) there was no reaction. What these workers failed to appreciate was that the anti-oxidant dapsone could quench the toxic radicals of a type I reaction and thereby suppress the tissue damage that these radicals could cause. But the fact that the bactericidal action of these radicals would not take place because of their quenching by high dose dapsone has escaped their comprehension. Going by this blinkered view of dapsone's so-called anti-reaction properties, high dose dapsone was continued for years on end until dapsone became ineffective to control reactions/disease even at high doses; there was relapse/reactivation in many cases and these experts promptly branded such cases as suffering from dapsone-resistant leprosy. The MDT was conceived not because it was logical to use more than one drug for treating diseases with lot of bacillation, but because of the need to prevent the perceived global spread of dapsone-resistant leprosy. Again, dapsone is a common constituent of MDT for both PB and MB leprosy and relapse/reactivations are bound to occur—it is only a matter of time.

The Antagonism of the Drugs in the MDT Combination

The antagonism between DDS and clofazimine at the level of immuno-pharmacology has already been discussed. Another glaring antagonism is between DDS and rifampicin. The former is a bacteriostatic agent and the latter a very effective bactericidal agent. A bactericidal agent acts by blocking a vital metabolic pathway, which means that the bacterial cell must be metabolizing for the bactericide to be effective. Dapsone being a bacteriostatic agent (at least that is what we are told) does just the opposite—it stops bacterial metabolism. In a bacteriostatic–bactericidal combination, it is the bacteriostatic agent that takes the upper-hand and the monthly rifampicin doses are just wasted. At the working group meeting of the health ministry, we prescribed an initial daily dose of rifampicin for two to three weeks. This was based on the report that it takes at least three weeks for dapsone to become optimally effective. Thus the effect of rifampicin would not be countered by dapsone-induced bacteriostasis. This was promptly overruled by the WHO and GOI experts. And the rationale for a monthly dose being sufficient was that the generation time of *M. leprae* was two to three weeks, so why does one have to use it daily. Now, conceding that the generation time is two to three weeks, to believe that a monthly dose is enough means that the entire population of *M. leprae* in the system is dividing synchronously, which is absurd. If the generation time is taken to be two weeks, one has to contend with the fact that there will be 14 possible cohorts of *M. leprae* dividing from the first to the fourteenth day of this period. Which means that in a monthly pulse, rifampicin can hit only one of the possible 14 multiplying/metabolizing cohorts of *M. leprae*. One has also to contend with the fact that not every member of the bacillary population would be vigorously metabolizing.

Can this Combination Effect Relapse and Complication-free Recovery?

Reports of a ten-fold increase in relapse of PB leprosy have been referred to. This relapse, in absolute terms, is also very low if one goes by WHO and GOI reports. But these reports are collected virtually under coercion. A very good technician from my laboratory, who joined a leprosy service organization in Calcutta, found a 2+ BI positivity in a patient declared negative. Her supervisor and the medical officer would have nothing of it. Their argument was "how can we explain this to the WHO? We know this case is negative!" Such is the countdown to elimination by A.D. 2000! Our pay clinic at Jhalda is crowded with men and women who can afford to spend for their treatment. Almost all of them are MDT failures or dropped out ofter their condition did not change within a few months of initiation of treatment.

The so-called MB cases are also relapsing, but much later. Based on longitudinal findings, it has been suggested that it is necessary to evaluate treatment regimens in MB leprosy and to follow patients until 9 to 10 years after the end of treatment; the risk of relapse increases with time (Pattyn 1993). Whereas the opinion of WHO on post-MDT surveillance is that "there is no need to have long term active post-MDT surveillance of patients for the purpose of detecting relapse...leprosy workers need assurance that cure will not be followed by high risk of relapse in 20 years after completing treatment" (Daumerie and Pannikar 1995). I am coming across relapses in cases that were released from treatment in the late eighties and early nineties. These are not cases treated in our clinic, but are from a field project in the Singhbhum district that is run by an organization with impeccable credentials.

The refrain of the WHO–GOI now is to only consider "cases of consequence," i.e., cases that have a greater potential of disease transmission. To meet the deadline of elimination by A.D. 2000 they are introducing a three drug, all bactericidal, single dose therapy for all monolesion cases (WHO 1997). The term monolesion has not been clearly defined—a monolesion can cover the whole of one's back, buttock, thigh, or leg (from thigh down to the ankles) or hand (from shoulder to wrist). A fieldworker, whether or not doctor, will have to go by numbers. For MB leprosy, the WHO is shortly to recommend a 28 days-two bactericidal drug combination. Every one completing the one day (PB) or 28 days (MB) course of treatment is to be declared cured. No further questions, please! This is going to be the single largest therapeutic operation in history, where the facts will be "swept under the carpet." Those escaping this dragnet are just too unfortunate to be left behind as one of the 100,000 cases still to be shown remaining after the elimination target of less than one per 10,000 population will have been accomplished. If leprosy re-emerges, it is no fault of the planners and implementing agencies.

It needs to be borne in mind that leprosy is not a disease that can be settled by the "drugs and bugs" mind-set. It remains an immuno-biologist's curiosity even today. In some districts where MDT was started in the early eighties and where to my knowledge very good work was done, the new case detection rates remain constant. Which can only mean that this MDT intervention has failed to interrupt transmission. Even by the leprosy directorate's figures, 500,000 new cases are recorded annually (Government of India 1993). Although with the approaching tryst with elimination, there is a change in tone. There are muted assertions that a perceptible trend of decline in new case detection is being noted now. However, these claims have not convinced leprologists who see problems, both at the scientific and operational levels (Tare 1990). I believe that areas that have gone through MDT intevention still show two to five per 1,000 prevalence, which is 20 to 50 times the elimination level of 0.1 per 1,000 population or 1 per 10,000. Unless dapsone, which I consider to be the most destabilizing drug when used in the recommended 50 to 100 gm dosage, is not removed from our regimen, leprosy treatment will continue to be destabilizing for a significant fraction of the patients who do not tolerate dapsone. These patients will continue to be disease transmitters even ofter a full course of MDT will have been given and will always stand the risk of relapse/reactivation.

How does this Anti-leprosy Treatment, Aimed at Elimination/Eradication Fit in Here?

In the first place, one needs to appreciate the fact that leprosy is an infectious disease with a variable course from infection to clinical cure. Hence, like any infectious disease, the natural history of leprosy is also governed by both host and environmental factors. It is necessary to repeat, *ad nauseam*, that *M. leprae* is a rather harmless pathogen. It is not *M. leprae,* but the response of our immunogenic cells to different constituents of *M. leprae* that cause the symptoms that enable us to diagnose a case as leprosy. And the nature of this immunogenic response depends in a good measure on the HLA/MHC (major histocompatibility complex—class II antigens) haplotype constitution of the host. Some of the HLA haplotypes predispose an individual to excessive DTH response on antigen recognition. These DTH responses bring on a type I reaction, as seen in borderline tuberculoid (BT) leprosy. These DTH responses or type I reactions are highly damaging to tissues and therfore are destabilizing and downgrading. Also, at the site undergoing a type I reaction, the tissue oxygen concentration (pO2) and pH are reduced. These are conditions that favor *M. leprae* multiplication. We all know that the bacillary index (BI) in a BT patient increases during and after a type I reaction. Occurrence of repeated type I reactions pushes the patient toward multi-bacillarity, with all the secondary consequences that follow from this. What are these consequences?

1. BT leprosy becomes BL–LL (borderline lepromatous leprosy). Only, it is not really polar, it stays subpolar and is revivable (immunologically restorable), and increases bacillation. The lipids of the bacilli continuously act as immuno-suppressants, preventing both immune recovery and scavenging of the bacilli that proper chemotherapy may be killing.
2. The bacilli remain an intrinsic source of relapse/reactivation and a source of disease transmission in the community.

Coming back to the natural history of leprosy and for that matter any infectious disease, the requirement for the epidemic/endemic to decline has to be a saturation and elimination of the susceptibles by infection and cure or by death. Quicker and wider the transmission, the quicker will the endemic wane. Leprosy that was very prevalent in Europe up to the fifteenth to sixteenth centuries disappeared quickly by the seventeenth century. And not by good food, nutrition, and hygiene as is commonly believed.

Leprosy disappeared because with growth of industry, towns, cities, and roads facilitated communication. Groups of people could come in contact, marital relationships were established beyond the immediate confines of the village/parish, thereby avoiding consanguineous marriages so that newer gene pools were introduced (Chatterjee 1993a). This kind of change at the population level started to be perceived in India after independence and by the sixties and seventies there has been a distinct change in the profile of leprosy. There is loss of lepromatous disease, less of bacillarity amongst the cases, and a decline in rates of deformity and disfigurement. While the prevalence has been growing due to increased chance of communication and transmission, the majority of cases are of the pauci-bacillary type (Guinto 1978). Most of the MB type of leprosy cases seen now are those that downgrade from PB. I do not give much credit to the MDT programs for this change for the better. It is a natural process. Rather, the compulsory force-feeding of dapsone to patients who do not tolerate dapsone is adding to the number of BL–LL cases through downgrading. The need of the hour is the immediate withdrawal of the strict edict, "reaction or no reaction, DDS must be given in full dosage." Together with this, immunotherapy must be introduced without any more delay to dampen the type I reactions that precipitate tissue damage, bacillation, neuritis, and deformity. The normal practice of administering steroids to treat these dapsone-induced reactions add not only to the downgrading, it brings on complications, like diabetes, cataract, and hyperacidity/peptic ulcers. Once patients experience the magical effect of steroids on their reactions, neuritis, and pain, they cannot be weaned out of it. They will buy it themselves to get relief from their pains.

Lastly, it needs to be emphasized that the government is producing or generating the kind of data that it wants. Much of the data and conclusions therefrom are not based on the true situation. An unbiased epidemiological survey in any area showing a dramatic decline of prevalence rates as per official estimates will reveal that new case rates have gone up by two- to fourfold that of the official figures.

Leprosy will go ultimately, MDT or no MDT. But surely individual sufferings, both medical, physical, socio-economic, and psychological can be greatly reduced, and a great deal of confidence in the patient, his/her family, and community can be restored with good treatment, which is available. We are just not using our competence and conscience, but have surrendered them to the dictates of the WHO that behaves like some sort of a "multinational" operating in a banana republic. Its leadership commands that

> until directed otherwise by its memberhip, the ILA (International Leprosy Association) must not announce a policy on how best to eliminate leprosy, nor may it oppose the policy announced by the WHO...the multidrug regimen proposed by the study group on chemotherapy of leprosy for control programs is virtually 100 percent effective in preventing relapse of multibacillary leprosy. I believe this presages the elimination of leprosy as a public health problem by the year 2000 (Levy 1995: 8010).

Levy is angry with correspondences and short notes lately appearing in *The International Journal of Leprosy*, critical of the WHO regimen.

That this MDT has failed to interrupt transmission is evident from the steady rate of new case detection. The tearing haste to remove patients from the case registers and not asking any questions or looking back to consider what may have happened to the patients consuming the drugs can at best create the illusion that the target has been met and that leprosy has been eliminated!

References

Chatterjee, B.R. (1982): Drug Resistance and Multi-drug Therapy in Leprosy. *Leprosy India* (Editorial) 54: 402–11.

——— (1993a): Epidemiology of Leprosy. In B.R. Chatterjee (ed.). *Leprosy: Etiobiology of Manifestations, Treatment and Control*. Jhalda, W. Bengal: Leprosy Field Research Unit.

——— (1993b): Treatment of Leprosy. In B.R. Chatterjee (ed.). *Leprosy: Etiobiology of Manifestations, Treatment and Control*. Jhalda, W. Bengal: Leprosy Field Research Unit.

Daumerie, D., and **Pannikar, V.** (1995): Issues in Evaluating Information on Relapse in Leprosy. *Indian Journal of Leprosy*, 67: 27–33.

Gandhi, I. (1981): Address by Mrs. Indira Gandhi to the 34th World Health Assembly. 6 May, Geneva: WHO.

Government of India (1982): Report of the Working Group on the Eradication of Leprosy. New Delhi: Ministry of Health and Family Welfare.

——— (1993): Health Information of India. New Delhi: Central Bureau of Health Intelligence, Directorate General of Health Services, Ministry of Health and Family Welfare.

Guinto, R.S. (1978): Epidemiology of Leprosy: Current Views, Concepts and Problems. In B.R. Chatterjee (ed.). *A Window on Leprosy*. Jhalda-Wardha: Gandhi Memorial Leprosy Foundation.

Levy, L. (1995): The ILA and Elimination of Leprosy: In Defence of the Establishment. *ILA Forum*, 2: 8010.

Noordeen, S.K. (1995): Elimination of Leprosy as a Public Health Problem—Is the Optimism Justified? *World Health Forum*, 17(2): 109–18.

Pattyn, S.R. (1993): Search for Effective Short-Course Regimens for the Treatment of Leprosy. *International Journal of Leprosy*, 61: 76–81.

Pearson, J.M.H. (1981): The Problem of Dapsone-resistant Leprosy. *International Journal of Leprosy*, 49: 417–30.

Pearson, J.M.H., Haile, G.S., and **Rees, R.J.W.** (1977): Primary Dapsone-resistant Leprosy. *Leprosy Review*, 48: 129–32.

Ridley, D.S. (1986): The Classification of Hanson's Disease: Origins and Outcome. *The Star*, (March–April): 8–10.

——— (1993): The R-J Classification. Reviewed in B.R. Chatterjee (ed.). *Leprosy: Etiobiology of Manifestation, Treatment and Control*. Jhalda, Bengal: Leprosy Field Research Unit. p. 296.

Tare, S.P. (1990): How Far the Goal of Leprosy Eradication by 2000 A.D. is Achievable? *Swasth Hind*, 34(1)(January): 14.

WHO (1997): Single Lesion Multicentric Trial Group, Efficiency of Single-Dose Multi-drug Therapy for the Treatment of Single Lesion Paucibacillary Leprosy. *Indian Journal of Leprosy*, 69: 121–37.

19

Tuberculosis Program in India: Current Operational Issues

A.K. Chakraborty

National Tuberculosis Program

The National Tuberculosis Program (NTP) was introduced in India in 1962 with the aim of systematic reduction of tuberculosis in the community within the available resources and within a reasonable time (Banerjee and Andersen 1963; Nagpaul 1967; NTI 1994). Its operational objectives were:

1. To detect maximum number of tuberculosis cases in the community and to treat them efficiently and in doing so, to give priority to sputum positive patients.
2. To provide case-finding and treatment facilities through as many general health institutions as was operationally feasible.

The epidemiological dimensions were quantified by undertaking a countrywide sample survey. It was realized that the most cost-effective way to deal with the tuberculosis (TB) problem would be to have a widespread service network for integrated case-finding activity—coupled with the facility for treatment of the cases found—as near to their homes as possible. Simplification of technology and its appropriateness were to be the cornerstone of success. The most notable aspect of the NTP, even 35 years later, is its attempts to operate the service-network through the existing general medical and public health institutions.

The author is grateful to Mr Umesh Jangan, Mr Sanjay Juvekar (Foundation for Research in Community Health, Pune branch office), and Mrs Nandita Chandavarkar of Bangalore, for assistance in processing this chapter.

Figure 19.1
Organizational Scheme of the NTP

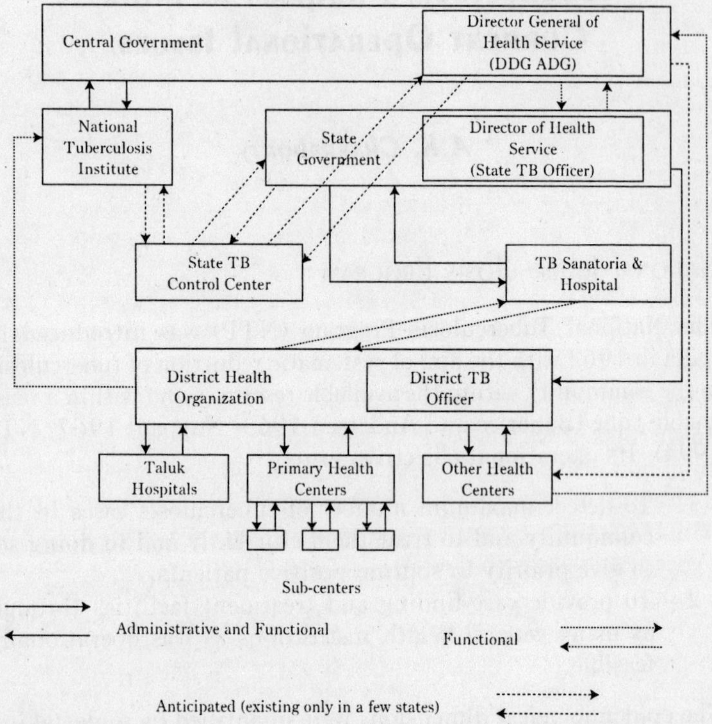

Source: Nagpaul 1967.

Figure 19.1 depicts the organizational framework and interactions between different program levels under the NTP (Nagpaul 1967).

District TB Program

The District TB Program (DTP) is the functional unit of the NTP, with case-finding and treatment as the principal technical activities (NTI 1994). These are done through general peripheral health institutions (PHI) in the district as well as through clinics run by the district TB centre (DTC). Cases of tuberculosis are detected in the DTP among the chest symptomatics voluntarily attending the PHIs and DTCs. Mostly, sputum smear examination is the only diagnostic tool available at the PHIs. At the DTC, outpatients with chest symptoms are selected for sputum test by direct smear microscopy and X-ray examination.

Both, at the DTC and the PHIs, treatment to all the patients diagnosed to have TB is offered free of cost. Treatment of sputum positive patients is accorded priority over sputum negative and extra pulmonary TB patients. When patients, as identified from the treatment cards sorted out for collection on the due day, fail to collect drugs, defaulter action is taken. Priority in defaulter action is accorded to sputum positive patients. Failure due to drug resistance and relapse cases are referred to the district TB officer (DTO) for advice. Patients on treatment are required to be followed up as per a given schedule.

Some Critical Observations on NTP

In the first place, the NTP suffered from lack of funding and also from non-utilization of budgetary allocations, both at the national as well as at the state level (Chaudhury 1991; Krishnamurthy 1994; ICORCI 1988). Of the central plan outlay, only between 2 percent (1982–83) and 1.7 percent (1990–91) were allocated for health. Of this, only 0.8 percent and 1.3 percent respectively were for NTP (Krishnamurthy 1994). Utilization of even this meager allotment was poor, symptomatic of the deeper malaise that had, over the years, crept into the general health services (GHS) administration in this country. Even with regard to its priority amongst the infectious diseases, TB has always been occupying a substantially relegated position (see Figure 19.2).

There was an overall lack of direction in integration with the GHS, especially in respect of fitting it into the newer infrastructure brought into place under the Minimum Needs Program (MNP). The kind of supervision and management support, required to get the best of services in a methodical way from the GHS workers, could not be organized within the framework of the existing NTP. Considering that integration of the NTP is a key element in the success of NTP, the national planners had sought to achieve it, but without a proper planning, preparation, and operations research (ICORCI 1988). The confusion in this regard has been detrimental both to the development of an integrated health services in general, and to that of NTP in

Figure 19.2
Allocation of Budget to Centrally Sponsored Programs 1992–93
(in Crore)

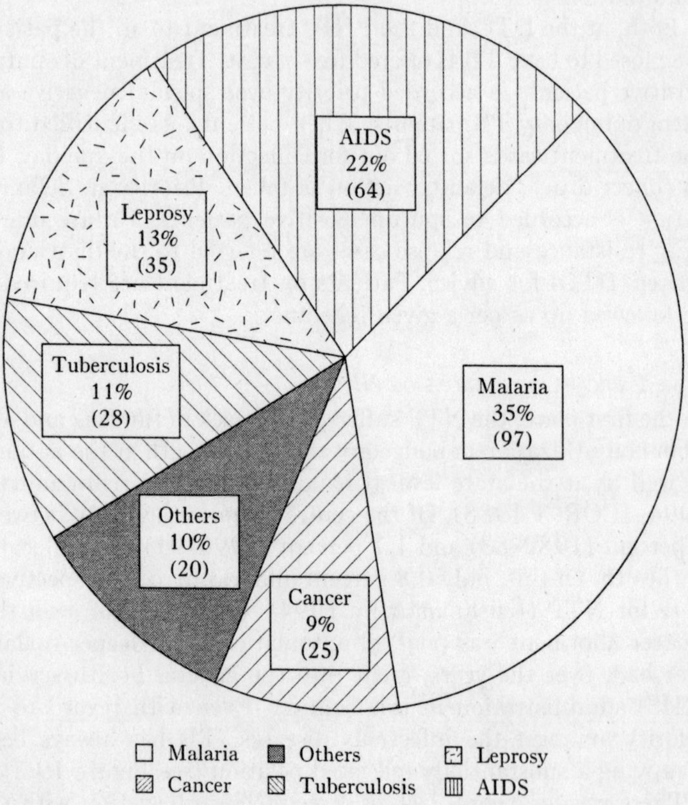

Source: Krishnamurthy 1994.

particular. A set of recommendations from a report by an investigating agency—Institute of Communications, Operations Research, and Community Involvement (ICORCI), Bangalore—which was commissioned by the GOI in 1987–88 to review the NTP, had highlighted the status of integration and how best it could be achieved under the Indian health services situation (ICORCI 1988). The recommendations were never acted upon.

Table 19.1
Performance of an Average DTP

1. **Case detection**

	Potential (No.)	*Expectation (No.)*	*Achievement*	
			No.	*%*
DTC	500	500	390	78
PHIs	2,000	1,120	445	40
DTP	2,500	1,620	835	52

2. **Treatment**

	Potential	*Expectation*	*Achievement*
SR: (percent of patients completing 12 or more collections)	80.0	73.0	33.0
SCC: (percent of patients on Regimen "B" making 75% or more collections)	88.0	NA	56.0

Source: Chaudhury 1991.

Table 19.2
Tuberculosis Patients Diagnosed under DTP (1992)

Program/ Institution	*Pulmonary TB Patients*	*Smear Positive Cases*	*Extra-pulmonary Cases*
DTP	14,68,530	3,23,149 (22)*	91,088
DTC	7,46,160	1,56,796 (21)*	56,693
PHIs	7,22,370	1,66,353 (23)*	34,395

Source: Krishnamurthy 1994.
* percent in bracket.

Progress under NTP

There had been efforts to expand NTP to as many districts as possible. However, it was realized in the course of a few decades, that the dream was not so easy to fulfill, in terms of expectations on case-finding and treatment as well as for organizing the distribution network of the program at as many PHIs as possible (see Tables 19.1 and 19.2) (Chaudhury 1991; Krishnamurthy 1994).

To an extent, it also suffered from a lack of focus with regard to treatment-priority for the transmitters. In course of time, the number of sputum negative cases treated under NTP had gone up to three to four times the number of sputum positive transmitters. This posed serious problems for drug-supply, defaulter-retrieval activities, and compounded the load on the NTP-organization many times over (see Table 19.2).

There is no doubt that the NTP did need a serious review with follow-up action in tune with the above considerations. There was also international pressure to bring it in line with the World Health Organization (WHO) policy. Therefore, the Government of India, in association with the WHO and the Swedish International Development Agency (SIDA) undertook a review of NTP in 1992 (WHO 1992).

Revised National TB Control Program (RNTCP)

The government undertook to revise the NTP as per the recommendations of the review after conducting pilot projects in phases I and II. Based on these experiences, the RNTCP was to be extended to other areas in the country in phase III (Anon 1996). Under the RNTCP, broad strategies were developed for implementation of directly observed therapy—short course (DOTS) (Mukherjee 1995; Sarin and Dey 1995).

Through the ongoing operational analysis it was proposed to:

1. Improve the implementation of RNTCP at the designated sites in terms of case-finding (70 percent case-detection) and treatment (85 percent cure rate).
2. Implement research results into RNTCP in India.
3. Aid scaling up of projects from pilot areas to state level.

Long-term Objectives of RNTCP Reviewed

In view of the long, continued, and slow nature of the epidemic and the rather crippling socio-economic implications it has for a community, TB has long ceased to be a concern of the medical scientists alone. However, after everything is said and done, TB still remains an infectious disease. One would therefore expect a TB program to be devoted to a systematic reduction in the problem of TB, if nothing else. Of course adequate and appropriate technology has to be available in the first place to "control" the disease. Moreover there has to be a clear definition as to what the term "control" in fact means. Unfortunately, however, "TB control" is yet to be defined, both in epidemiologic as well as operational terms (see section on epidemiological perspective) (Chakraborty 1993).

Socio-economic Benefits of DOTS

Whereas the sociological dimensions of introduction of RNTCP in India are yet to be understood, an economic analysis carried out by the Indian Institute of Management, Ahmedabad, shows the investments to be viable (Dholakia and Almeida 1997).

For the calculation of the economic benefit, future benefits are discounted to the extent of the consumption rate of interest. The hypothetical discounting rates, called the social time preference rate (STPR), as imputed to the calculations, are between 5 and 16 percent. The STPR is preferred by Dholakia over the other index used by the World Bank, i.e., the DALY Index. Even when the discounted values are considered at as high a figure as 16 percent, the DOTS is found to be of high economic benefit. The future potential economic benefits of DOTS to the Indian economy turn out to be at least 3.8 percent GDP in 1993–94, or about Rs 266 billion (US $8.3 billion). Dholakia argues that so long as a lesser amount than this is spent to make DOTS work and succeed, a handsome return of 16 percent or thereabout could be expected. Since the budget and other managerial inputs required to successfully implement DOTS under RNTCP in the entire country must be far less than 3.8 percent of GNP, DOTS would represent a very cost-effective strategy of health intervention.

Coverage and Efficiency of DTP

Presently, the RNTCP, as being implemented in the pilot phase, appears to have a self-inflicted bias toward the achievement of only the treatment results without regard to the coverage of cases in the community or even those reporting on their own to the GHS for relief. Table 19.3 presents the results from the pilot sites. These need to be looked at in the light of the coverage attained and the total efficiency required of a tuberculosis program, i.e., District TB Program Efficiency (DTPE) (DTPE = case-finding efficiency × treatment efficiency). The latter could be regarded as the key index of achievement of a TB program devoted to reduction of problem, as shown in a mathematical

Table 19.3
Cure Rates for New Smear Positive Patients under RNTCP in Pilot Areas (1993–94)#

Project Area	*Population Covered (Million)*	*Year*	*Quarter*	*Diagnosis Expected from the Area Annually (CFP)**	*Actually Put on DOTS (No.)*	*Cured (No.)*	*CFE>* (%)	*TE*** (%)	*DTPE@* (%)
(1)	(2)	(3)	(4)	(5)	(6)	(7)	(8)	(9)	(10)
Bangalore	0.25	1995	1 & 4	340	14	9	8.2	66.7	5.2
Gulabi Bagh (Delhi)	1.00	1994	4	1,360	31	30	9.2	96.8	8.9
Calcutta	0.30	1994	4	408	44	32	43.1	72.7	31.3
Gujarat (rural)	0.45	1994	1,2,3,4	612	197	122	32.2	61.9	19.9

Source: Directorate General of Health Services, New Delhi (regional data unpublished).
Hypothesis used in Chakraborty 1996.

Performance (with regard to TE) only at the two ends of the spectrum, and that from an average performing center only presented.

*CFP—Case Finding Potential ($\frac{CFP}{4}$ = The average number during a quarter).

$$CFP = \frac{\text{Av. no. of sm '+' expected to be diag. in a distt (2584)} \times \text{Col. 2}}{\text{Population of average district in India (1.9 million)}}$$

>CFE—Case Finding Efficiency = $\frac{\text{Col. } 6 \times 100}{CFP}$

**TE—Treatment Efficiency = $\frac{\text{Col. } 7 \times 100}{\text{Col. } 6}$

@DTPE—District TB Program Efficiency = CFE × TE (Col. 8 × Col. 9) model (Chakraborty et al. 1992). Merely obtaining high treatment results in a small number of cases is no indication of a public health achievement. It was shown that nearly 2,500 smear positive cases could be diagnosed in an average DTP with 1.9 million population in the district (potential of case-finding) (see Table 19.1) (Chakraborty 1996). Based on the findings of a recent field study, Jagota et al. had worked out the potential to be 2,240, when 42 health institutions were implemented in the district for TB activity, more or less corroborating the basis of the estimate on potential shown above (Jagota et al. 1998). As against the above potential estimated by Chakraborty, the performance in case-finding activity under the pilot phase had ranged only between 9.2 percent (Delhi during the fourth quarter of 1993) and 43 percent (Calcutta during the fourth quarter of 1994) (see Table 19.3). The efficiency of treatment (TE), on the other hand, as seen from sputum negativity at six/seven months, had ranged between 96.8 percent in Delhi and 51.5 percent in Gujarat (first quarter of 1994), and 61.9 percent in the latter for 1994 as a whole. The total effect of DTP, i.e., DTPE, could be calculated to be between 8.9 percent in 1993 (Delhi the fourth quarter) and 31.3 percent (Calcutta the fourth quarter of 1994) (see Table 19.3). The rather high figure shown in Table 19.3 as DTPE for Calcutta city appears to be due more to the method of estimating the DTPE followed here than anything else. It could be attributed to the extrapolation of the national average of prevalence rate of cases as four per thousand in calculating the "potential," when it could be nearer to the rate of 50 per thousand, as reported for Calcutta city slums under the National Sample Survey of the ICMR. One can derive one's own conclusions regarding the DTPE in Calcutta, if the latter rates were used for estimating the "potential" in order to work out the "efficiency." These figures are quoted to show variable efficiency, even of treatment activity, from time to time and region to region. RNTCP apologists could argue that in the pilot phase, only the achievement of high treatment results were attempted without emphasis on coverage of patients. In a recent editorial, Nagpaul has rightly observed, "waiting to make one component efficient first, before attending to the other, would not be wise" and has underlined the need for "efficient case-finding, going hand in hand with efficient treatment effort" (Nagpaul 1998).

Thus, it is evident that the DTPE needs to be considerably raised under RNTCP in the days to come, primarily by extending services both for diagnosing and treating smear positive cases successfully. How this scaling-up operations could be achieved remains the foremost challenge for operations research (OR). It is suggested that the coverage of cases and thereby higher efficiency of the RNTCP could be attempted by:

1. increasing the number of microscopy centers from 1 per 100,000 population as recommended now, to say one per PHC (or, one per alternative PHC); the actual distribution depending on results of OR; and
2. discontinuing the discrimination as currently practiced under RNTCP in placing patients on RNTCP regimens in favor of only those smear positive cases, which tend to fulfill certain criteria, on the basis of investigation by the field staff and merely on the inclination and antecedents of these cases towards treatment-compliance.

However, as to why DTPE was not the objective of the pilot study defies all logic. It is symptomatic of the lack of awareness among those involved in designing the pilot study and those accepting the design for investigations on operational issues confronting an Indian program.

Treatment Efficiency (TE) under RNTCP

While analyzing the field data in search of an index for a prior identification of the ultimate defaulters under the NTP, Jagota, Sreenivas, and Parimala observed that the "first time defaulters of the first month" could constitute a high-risk group for non-adherence to treatment. It is this group that accounted for the maximum incidence of defaults, when patients on diagnosis were placed on a routine self-administered SCC regimen under NTP (Jagota, Sreenivas, and Parimala 1996). In monitoring the TE under RNTCP, as in Table 19.3, what has in fact been done is that this high-risk group has been cleverly eliminated from the denominator in order to achieve a higher treatment result. This would appear to be a dubious output from the system, achieved not by removing, reducing, or correcting the chances and reasons of default—through counseling, etc.—but by removing the likely highest risk group of defaulters, from those covered under

RNTCP. If such a statistical exercise is carried out for SCC regimen under NTP, the results will not differ from that under DOTS.

Inherent Social Discrimination under the Program

There is a certain kind of a covert discrimination, as outlined in this paragraph, which should be a matter of concern for those interested in equity as an issue under health care dispensation. As per the current practice, on diagnosis of a patient under RNTCP, he/she is visited by the RNTCP field staff (health visitors, etc.), at his/her home. Many of the patients, especially in the urban conglomerations, live in temporary accommodation with no semblance of an address. They happen to be the poorest of the poor among the TB patients and are precisely the ones who get omitted under DOTS, under RNTCP as practiced today. As is the general practice, a careful analysis is made on the spot by the supervisory field staff on the possibility of a particular patient to be able to complete the DOTS. Patients, assessed as unlikely compliers of DOTS regimen, are carefully excluded from it and put on an alternative NTP regimen. It is another matter that the coverage of cases put on treatment is reduced in this manner. It is also possible that a significant number of patients are not placed on the best possible treatment options (unlike some others) merely on the basis of a doubtful socio-economic exercise, purportedly on the possibility of "compliance". Socio-economic bias in such an operation no doubt remains a key issue, since it is possible that during the course of these operations, the economically underprivileged segment of patients do not stand to be covered under the RNTCP. There is even a hint of gender-gap in the cases treated under RNTCP; as many as between three and four times the number of smear positive cases are male, as compared to the females. This requires investigation before further comments.

Shift in Health Policy?

It is argued that with the introduction of RNTCP, there has been a major shift in the direction the NTP was representing. This is so not only for TB control, but for health care as such in the overall context. The NTP was designed to be developing on the lines of integration of health services. Improvements in its functioning should have logically been made to guide it along that course in a rational manner as per suggestions made by the ICORCI (ICORCI 1988). A strong group of health scientists, spearheaded by the doyen among social scientists in India, see in the RNTCP the very negation of the principle of health care for all and a turnaround from the conceptual progress made in that direction (Banerjee 1997). Other intellectuals resent the centralized impositions made in a bureaucratic manner on the instruments of local self-governance, e.g., panchayati raj, especially when these are at the behest of international agencies (Antia 1993). Voluntary health groups like the Voluntary Health Association of India (VHAI) and the Tuberculosis Association of India (TAI) are astir, and harbor major reservations on the directional change RNTCP represents, especially in the context of this country. Considering the continued intransigence, nay failure, of the Indian government to bring about necessary corrections/revisions in the NTP in time and in accordance with the monitoring/evaluation reports, one would find it hard to accept the summary changes made in its principles and functioning in the garb of RNTCP. It appears that the revolutionary sociological concepts and the principles of management of the program on the basis of continued OR, as embodied in the NTP framework, have been rejected by the government and the RNTCP is being introduced at the behest of foreign agencies. Considering this background, one would like to adapt what the Latin American poet Guillen had said of Che Guevara, and recite an ode to the NTP thus: "No poque hayas caido, the luz es menos alta..." (Not because you have fallen, is your light less high...).

Private Sector Involvement

More than half the TB patients are currently being serviced by this seemingly omnipresent sector and RNTCP/NTP cannot really proceed toward its objective without the involvement of this largely unorganized sector. The GOI, the state governments, and other policy-makers are not helping matters through their gingerly attitude in involving the private sector and other important stakeholders, e.g., VHAI/TAI, in making policy decisions. There is no doubt that the threat-perceptions of the government functionaries from these players represent an appropriate analysis of the situation. But what is strange and baffling in this regard is the fact that the government does not seem to have a plan to take care of the denouement when it would unfold. Operations research followed by a strong socio-economic analysis of the Indian situation is one of the tools, which should be employed in building the rationale for the RNTCP activities.

National Institutes and RNTCP

It is argued that the central unit had sidelined the path-finding technical institutions, like the National Tuberculosis Institute (NTI), Bangalore, and Tuberculosis Research Center (TRC), Chennai, in RNTCP development. In the process, the central unit must have lost considerable amount of credibility for the RNTCP, at least in the initial years. In designing the revisions of the program, considerable input has been received from some of the foreign institutions, e.g., the WHO and World Bank. However, the work experience and OR results developed at the national institutions of TB research in India were not relied upon or drawn from even when much of the information and experience has been in the operational sector of running a program in India. The mind-set against the indigenously acquired and documented national experience could, in fact, be evident through the *TB Program Review* published by the WHO SEARO (WHO 1992). The same mind-set could also have led the RNTCP authorities to probably consider the foremost TB institutions in the country, specializing solely in OR, i.e., NTI Bangalore and the TRC Chennai, as mere custodians of some fungoid parchments, as it were, and to grant them the sinecures in perpetuity! It is possible that these national-level institutions were considered by the authorities to be too entrenched in a technical legacy of their own, which could, as per their assessment, come in the way of the proposed revisions of the national program! It has been made to appear as if the NTI, marinated for decades in the cliched principles of the NTP, should not be involved in the development of the so-called "revolutionary concept" of the RNTCP. It is certainly nobody's case that the NTP is scripted in unalterable terms or that it should remain steeped in an irrelevant orthodoxy. However, the truth of the matter remains that the NTI has always striven for changes in NTP, within the OR framework, applied to the Indian reality. As brought out earlier, it has been one of the earliest of the health programs to be OR-based. For that matter, even the RNTCP should cease to be an uncriticized ideology (unfortunately it appears to be so at present), with a remit to direct the behavior pattern of a whole set of people, from the health-seekers down to the providers themselves.

When objectively considered, however, OR should be carried out at all levels of the program implementation and monitoring, with the active involvement of the national-level TB institutions, e.g., NTI Bangalore and TRC Chennai. The bureaucratic command structure of the Ministry of Health could have gained immensely from the expertise available at these institutions and used these to work for all-round efficiency. In fact, these institutions should be further developed in order to meet the new challenges of revising the program operations, especially since they have been functioning under tremendous resource constraints.

RNTCP and State Health Services

Though health is a state subject and implementation and management of the health-related activities fall within the states' domain, the Government of India (GOI) assumes the responsibility of providing advice, direction, guidance, as well as resources for some of the identified health issues of national importance. Nevertheless, the states cannot remain entirely dependent on the center for central assistance, even for these programs. It is also important to realize that the states will go along as long as they are sure that they have a stake in the RNTCP, not if they feel that they are to function as mere galley-slaves on a ship circling around a whirlpool.

A Few Impedance-variables of RNTCP

As the RNTCP is to be implemented all over the country in stages during the ensuing decade or so, it is destined to face similar hurdles as the NTP that it seeks to replace. The hurdles in the realm of policy, resources, and implementation are highlighted in the points below:

1. Need for acceptance of RNTCP by the states through continued dialogue with the center—sometimes the states are not willing to implement the program as it is conceived.

Recent examples are: Tamil Nadu wanted to have DOTS for the entire six-month period instead of the first two, Maharashtra did not want a phased implementation in districts, and Gujarat took up case-finding on a house-to-house basis to start with. These are resolved for the present. However, such problems could continue to recur.

2. The most important operational consideration coming in the way of RNTCP could be the implementation of DOTS in the vast expanse of rural India. It is not being recognized by the concerned authorities that the GHS throughout the country are in shambles. They may not be ready to shoulder the task however well-meaning the prescription could be, unless far-reaching changes are brought about and integration attempted somewhat on the lines suggested by the ICORCI Report.
3. Budget is often a bugbear. In the NTP, it was not only the mere lack of finances, but also the inability of the system to channelize and utilize the same, when provided.
4. RNTCP is yet to be evaluated with respect to its overall efficiency in curtailing infection transmission achieved through the conversion of a sufficient number of smear positive cases in the community and this does not mean achievement of TE alone. It appears, however, from the annotated bibliography produced by the WHO Geneva for the use of DOTS workers, that sufficient awareness among the program strategists is lacking on the operational issues confronting a program (GTB and SEARO 1997). For some obscure reason, no papers on TB program operations and their problems/solutions are listed even though a wealth of Indian research material is available on this. The insensitivity thus betrayed by the DOTS strategists towards the socio-economic issues involved in designing the NTP or the lack of awareness with regard to problems involved in operationalizing a program in a country like India raises serious doubts on the manner the RNTCP would actually be run and its ultimate success as a long-term grass-roots program in this country.
5. The non-involvement of the voluntary organizations/private practitioners, etc., in TB control activities is a serious constraint and needs to be overcome.

These are just some problems which could be conveniently listed at present. The problems need to be continuously identified and addressed through an ongoing process if RNTCP has to strike roots in this country.

RNTCP in India in the Epidemiological Perspective

Global Situation: What does Problem Reduction Mean for the Respective Regions?

The countries in the world could be seen to form themselves into two broad groups in terms of the hypothesis made by Wade Hampton Frost way back in 1940. Those in whom the "tubercle bacilli is losing ground," so that a given number of sputum positive transmitters "do not succeed in establishing an equivalent number to carry on the succession," and the others, in whom "no such prospect is in sight" in the conceivable future (Frost 1937). It is another matter that these two groups also enjoy an equivalent economic grouping (i.e., the industrialized and the developing nations). Apart from these two major groups, there are other countries, positioned intermediately, in whom the tuberculosis situation may not be at these two extremes. It could therefore be convenient to consider the countries in the world into, say, four epidemiologic groups, given their current trend and future prospects (Styblo 1989).

Though Frost had talked of an "eventual eradication," the "goal" of anti-tuberculosis measures could obviously be less optimistic. Instead of "eradication" or "control," the pragmatists, on the basis of actual observation of the situation in the past and projecting it to a conceivable future in respect of the Netherlands, would like to see the "goal" defined in more precise terms as: "Elimination," "Virtual Elimination," and "Close to Elimination." Table 19.4 gives the definitions used and Table 19.5 the classification of the countries, going by these definitions (Styblo 1989).

The epidemiological trend of tuberculosis, in the best possible scenario, and that in the worst, is depicted in Figure 19.3 by the respective risk of infection in these countries (Styblo 1990). Table 19.6 shows that in respect of the Annual Risk of Infection (ARI), there is an exponential decline in the countries with the best possible scenario, such as the Netherlands (up to 14 percent

Table 19.4
Global Tuberculosis Situation—1 (Suggested Definition of Goal)

Eradication (E)

↑

Elimination (El)

↑

Virtually identical with El
Incidence of smear positive cases:
Below 1 per 10 million
(Prevalence of infection:
General population 0.1%)

↑

Close to El
Incidence of smear positive cases:
1 per million population
(Prevalence of infection below 1%)

Source: Styblo 1989.

Table 19.5
Global Tuberculosis Situation—2 (Grouping of Countries)

Annual Risk of Infection	*Annual Decline*	*Group*
0.1–0.01%	≥ 10%	Group I Industrialized countries (the Netherlands, Norway, etc.)
0.5–1.5%	5–10%	Group II Middle income countries (Latin America, West & North Africa, etc.)
1–2.5%	≤ 5%	Group II B Middle income countries (East & South East Asia, etc.)
1–2.5%	0–3%	Group III (Sub-Saharan Africa and Indian subcontinent, etc.)

Source: Styblo 1989.

annually: some 5 percent of it is natural and the rest is attributed to anti-tuberculosis measures in specific). For the worst, on the other hand (example, Lesotho), there is nil or minimal decline of between 1 and 1.4 percent annually. In the former, the

Figure 19.3
The Annual Risk of Tuberculosis Infection in the Netherlands (1950–77), Uganda (1950–79), and Lesotho (1958–65)

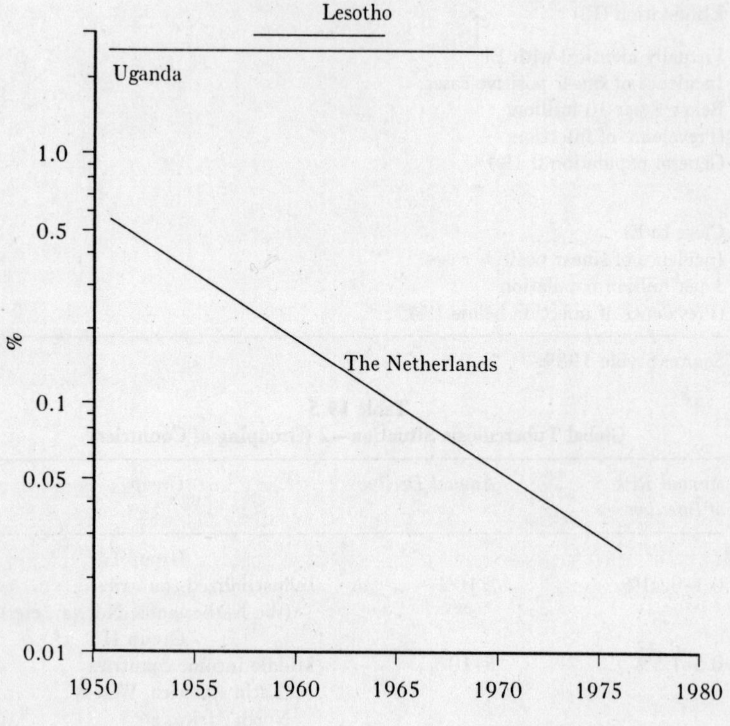

Source: Styblo 1990.

problem is likely to be halved in five years without any such prospect for the latter. Table 19.6 gives what these would mean in terms of the comparative incidence of smear positive cases in India and group I countries, at present and when the goal of close to elimination is to be addressed (Chakraborty 1993). In terms of cases, the annual incidence of 12–15, as at present, remains to be reduced to 1.2 for 1.5 million population in the group I countries, in order to achieve close to elimination status by the year 2025. For India this would mean the present incidence of smear positive cases of about 750 annually in the same population (i.e., equivalent to an Indian district), requiring to be

Table 19.6
Indian Situation set against that in the Epidemiologically Advanced Countries Heading toward the Goal of "Elimination"

Country	*Epidemiological Situation*			
	Present		*Qualification for "Close to Elimination" Status*	
	Incidence of Smear Positive Cases per Million/Year	*Prevalence of Infection All Ages (%)*	*Incidence of Smear Positive Cases per Million/Year*	*Prevalence of Infection All Ages (%)*
Most advanced*	12–15	15	1.0	1.0
India**	500 (750)	40	(1.2)	

Source: Chakraborty 1993.
*Norway, the Netherlands, etc.: (ARI 0.1 to 0.01%, 10% Annual Decline, "Close to Elimination" status projected to be achieved by A.D. 2025).
**Figures based on NTI Survey (NTI 1994). Calculated for 1.5 million population, i.e., an average Indian district.

brought down to 1–2 by that date (Chakraborty 1993). This should lead Indian program strategists to rethink seriously on the objective and goal and on the use of "control" in renaming the NTP as RNTCP. Both the expression and the concept behind its use require a revision. In order that a certain degree of laissez-faire is avoided, only measurable objectives and realistic goals need to be set up under the NTP.

Epidemic Curve in India: The Task of Achieving Problem Reduction

Over comparatively shorter periods of observation of the natural dynamics in the NTI longitudinal survey or the TRC study, tuberculosis appears to have a steady state in India (Chakraborty 1993, 1997). Evidence is available to permit one to hypothesize that the situation in India is probably on a slow downward curve of the epidemic (Chakraborty 1993). Such evidences could be as follows: declining mortality and case fatality rates due to TB, decline in meningeal and miliary forms of the disease, relatively high prevalence of cases in higher ages with a low rate of positive cases in children, relative concentration of cases in higher ages, higher prevalence of cases in the males, especially adult males, and equal prevalence rates across the urban-rural divide.

It should however be understood that even if on a downward limb of the epidemic curve, the decline in TB situation at present could only be minimal, as seen from direct measurement of ARI. It could be observed from the data from various infection surveys carried out in India that the ARI had varied from area to area and was in the range between 1.0 and 1.2 percent per year (Chakraborty 1997). It could be concluded that India has the epidemiological trend in common with the countries of the sub-Saharan region, which have an ARI between 1 and 3 percent and an annual decline in it varying between 0 and 3 percent. Only when high efficiency intervention, both in case-finding and treatment is carried out, would a decline of between 7 and 10 percent result. For this to materialize, a mere treatment adherence of 85–90 percent would not suffice. A sufficiently high case-finding would be required to be achieved, say of the order of about 70–80 percent with all sputum positive cases on short-course chemotherapy (Chakraborty et al. 1992). With the given state of development of GHS in the country, it is anybody's guess whether the twin program objectives could be achieved in a foreseeable future.

It is strange that no provision for an epidemiological assessment/surveillance in the nature of periodical effect-evaluation is built into the RNTCP-framework, even though reduction of transmission remains its proclaimed goal. Even as the RNTCP is in its fourth year, since its pilot phase, no baseline ARI studies were conducted even for the pilot/OR areas. It is suggested that suitable ARI studies are designed to obtain a trend in the tuberculosis situation, subject to various levels of the intervention-efficiencies under the RNTCP. Small population sizes, as required for infection surveys, make it possible to conduct such studies and they could yield valuable information (Chakraborty 1997).

Conclusion

Now that considerable infrastructure has been created in all the states as part of the NTP, the time has come to make it functional and to ensure delivery of an effective program. To make it functional as per the scientific parameters of the the term "cure," the requirements are: careful planning, implementation, training, and monitoring, supported by effective logistics and supply.

References

Anonymous (1996): Contemporary Issues: Revised NTP: Current Status of Pilot Project. *Indian Journal of Tuberculosis*, 43: 169.

Antia, N.H. (1993): World Bank and India's Health. *Economic and Political Weekly*, 28(52): 2883–87.

Banerjee, D. (1997): Serious Implications of the Proposed RNTCP for India. New Delhi: Nucleus for Health Policies and Programmes and Voluntary Health Association of India.

Banerjee, D., and **Andersen, S.** (1963): A Sociological Study of Awareness of Symptoms Among Persons with Pulmonary TB. *Bulletin of World Health Organization*, 29: 665–83.

Chakraborty, A.K. (1993): TB Situation in India: Measuring it through Time. *Indian Journal of Tuberculosis*, 40: 215–25.

——— (1996): Tuberculosis Programme at Cross-roads: Issues Towards Mid-course Correction within the System. Proceedings of International CME on TB. 27–28 Sept., MGIMS Sevagram, Wardha.

Chakraborty, A.K. (1997): Prevalence and Incidence of Tuberculosis Infection and Disease in India, a Comprehensive Review. *WHO Technical Report* Series No. WHO/TB/97.231, Geneva: WHO.

Chakraborty, A.K., Balasangameshwara, V.H., Jagota, P., Sreenivas, T.R., and **Chaudhuri, K.** (1992): Short Course Chemotherapy and Efficiency Variables in NTP—A Model. *Indian Journal of Tuberculosis*, 39: 9–20.

Chaudhury, K. (1991): District Tuberculosis Programme—Key Issues in Management, *NTI News Letter*, 27: 62–73.

Dholakia, R.H., and **Almeida, J.** (eds.) (1997): The Potential Economic Benefits of DOTS Strategy in India. Global TB Programme. Geneva: WHO, 1–46.

Frost, W.H. (1937): How Much Control of Tuberculosis? *American Journal of Public Health*, 27: 759–66.

GTB and SEARO (1997): *Tuberculosis Control: The DOTS Strategy. An Annotated Bibliography*. Geneva: WHO.

Institute of Communications, Operations Research, and Community Involvement (ICORCI) (1988): Indepth study of NTP of India. Bangalore: ICORCI.

Jagota, P., Sreenivas, T.R., and **Parimala, N.** (1996): Improving Treatment Compliance by Observing Differences in Treatment Irregularity. *Indian Journal of Tuberculosis*, 43: 75–80.

Jagota, P., Mahadev, B., Srikantaramu, N., Balasangameshwara, V.H., and **Sreenivas, T.R.** (1998): Case-finding in DTP: Potential and Performance. *Indian Journal of Tuberculosis*, 45: 39–46.

Krishnamurthy, V.V. (1994): National Tuberculosis Programme in India 1992–93. Bangalore: NTI.

Mukherjee, A.K. (1995): Tuberculosis Control Programme in India: Progress and Prospects. *Indian Journal of Tuberculosis*, 42: 75.

Nagpaul, D.R. (1967): District Tuberculosis Programme in Concept and Outline. *Indian Journal of Tuberculosis*, 14: 186–98.

——— (1998): Whither Case-finding? *Indian Journal of Tuberculosis* (Editorial), 45: 1–2.

National TB Institute (NTI) (1994): *Introduction Manual: DTP*, 4th edition. Bangalore: NTI.

Sarin, R., and **Dey, L.B.S.** (1995): Indian NTP: Revised Strategy. *Indian Journal of Tuberculosis*, 42: 95.

Styblo, K. (1989): Overview and Epidemiologic Assessment of the Current Global Tuberculosis Situation with an Emphasis on Control in Developing Countries. *Review of Infectious Diseases*, 2(Suppl 2): S 339–46.

——— (1990): The Estimate of Tuberculosis in the Netherlands. *Bulletin of International Union of Tuberculosis and Lung Diseases*, 65(23): 49.

World Health Organisation–SEARO (1992): *Tuberculosis Programme Review, India*. New Delhi: WHO–SEARO.

Part IV

Decentralization in Health Care

The recent trend of decentralization in governance has raised issues about its ideological underpinnings. Although essentially a political process for giving power to the people, it is being advocated as a component of the reform package, in which only managerial and technical issues are highlighted. Even privatization and transfer of responsibilities to NGOs are conceptually considered as a form of decentralization. It is this form of decentralization that is being offered as a panacea for increasing the efficiency and quality of public services. It needs to be distinguished from the political process of decentralization, in which autonomy is achieved at the lower levels in resource control, policy formulation, implementation, etc.

The important issues regarding decentralization that need to be addressed are: the viability of a truncated approach, the spaces available to people for positive action even within such state sponsorship, issues and conflicts emerging out of the interplay of technical and popular domains, the impact on health and health services, and the possibility of a culturally acceptable alternative paradigm of health care through a community-based approach linked to people's movements. The chapters in this section try to do this by highlighting different experiences in some of the South Asian countries such as Sri Lanka and India.

Anwar Jafri, in his chapter states that the new Panchayati Raj bills enacted in the states have generated high expectations amongst those communities that were hitherto marginalized in the political processes. By focusing on the panchayats in the Malwa region of the state of Madhya Pradesh in India, the chapter reveals that the changes in the functioning and constitution of panchayats have not resolved some basic conflicts that involve the poorer sections. K.R. Nayar, in his chapter argues that the experience of decentralization in other countries has not been encouraging, largely because of the type of decentralization and the political context and social domain in which it was implemented. The chapter analyzes the unique experience of people's planning in the state of Kerala, wherein the state made an effort to give power and resources to the people in order to enable them to collectively participate in shaping their future by identifying problems and evolving programs according to local needs.

Binayak Sen demonstrates that community-based approaches linked to people's movements provide an alternative framework for addressing contemporary health issues in the absence of genuine state provisions. The chapter analyzes the experience of an innovative trade union in Dalli Rajhara that attempted to provide health care to the workers by focusing on demystification of technology, rational therapeutics, and people-friendly ways of hospital management. Nimal Attanayake, in his chapter argues that decentralization in the country was largely truncated, with a narrow political objective of containing the ethnic conflict. In health, it largely represented a non-purposive direction of change, in which neither central level administrators nor politicians had the motivation to accelerate the process of decentralization.

20

Politics of Decentralization: Lessons from Kerala

K.R. Nayar

Decentralization is usually understood as a process in which resources, functions, and authority are transferred from the center to the periphery, with decision-making largely vested with the people at the latter level. Conceptually, there have been several types of decentralization (Mills et al. 1990).

1. De-concentration involves shifting of workload from the center to the periphery, without decentralizing the decision-making powers.
2. Delegation refers to transferring functions and responsibility to para-state organizations for the purpose of achieving some degree of efficiency.
3. In some cases, as in privatization, responsibility is transferred by the center to private and non-governmental organi- zations. This is currently being practiced as part of the Structural Adjustment Programs.
4. Devolution in a stricter sense is closest to the ideal form of decentralization, in which autonomy is achieved by the lower levels, with respect to resource control, policy formulation, implementation, etc.

Decentralization was often misused to transfer the burden of financial responsibilities to the lower levels, leading to adverse impacts on the poorer sections (Standing 1997). In the name of "decentralization," where along with authority responsibility for finances was also decentralized, the process often resulted in the transfer of power from the center to regional elite, resulting in intra-regional inequity. The recent approach to decentralization, as espoused by Structural Adjustment Programs and the reform package, has also introduced conceptual ambiguity by reducing it, on the one hand, into a mechanical process within a managerial paradigm, and on the other, into a corollary to the package of privatization.

The main objective of this chapter is to examine the present process of decentralization and the dynamics of people's planning in India. We take the case of Kerala in order to identify positive features, issues, and conflicts in the state, especially with regard to health services decentralization. This chapter will also examine whether this initiative can redeem the health services system from the present crisis, arising as a result of SAP and health sector reforms (HSR).

Country Experiences with Decentralization

Decentralization in health care was attempted in several countries, including China and Brazil, with mixed results. The Chinese decentralization had led to a market orientation and a new ethos within the health services, in which health facility managers generate revenue, invest the surplus in new equipment, and pay bonuses to employees. Individuals and institutions now give priority to earning money. This form of decentralization was successful in the penetration of the market into the health service system while maintaining it as a non-political entity (Bloom and Xingyuan 1997). In Brazil, decentralization became an official policy after the fall of the military regime of 1964–85. Yet a gap was observed between the type of decentralization called for in the national constitution and the de-concentration actually implemented. This gap is explained by Brazil's centralist tradition, resistance at the national level, and the weaknesses of local governments (Araujo and Luiz 1997).

In Zambia, inter-regional inequalities increased during the decentralization process, when wealthier districts and hospitals in those districts could raise more funds and were able to draw key staff away from the less wealthy areas by offering them better terms and conditions (Standing 1997). In Senegal, where high levels of political, financial, and managerial devolution to community health committees were achieved, the cost of prenatal checks and the cost of maternal deliveries increased. As a result, health services utilization substantially reduced among mothers and infants (Standing 1997). A number of other constraints have been observed in the decentralized health delivery system in Latin America and in African countries such as Kenya, Sudan, and Tanzania (Collins and Green 1994). These include inadequate number of trained staff, inadequate financial resources, and poor local administrative capacities.

In the United Kingdom, competition and private markets were allowed into the state-run National Health Services as a part of the decentralization strategy, without recourse to a direct process of privatization (Collins and Green 1994). The reform package in Croatia included privatization and rationalization of expenditure based on economic principles. Several basic features of post-war welfare health systems, such as cost-containment policy, role of market economy, decentralization, privatization, quality of services, type of health insurance, and health education formed the background of the reform package. Devolution and delegation in the Croatian health system were thus part of the rationalization strategy as determined by the privatization package (Oreskovic 1995).

In the USA, the present era of decentralization—new federalism—led to medicare cuts and massive restructuring of health care by the private market (Estes and Linkins 1997). It led to a debate on whether devolution reform could achieve national goals other than those related to a reduced federal role in domestic health and social policy. It has been pointed out that the dominant structural, economic, and political interests operating at the federal level are not likely to be challenged by the fragmented and diverse interest groups of the poor at the state and local level. With decentralized policy-making, those who are well-off, best-funded, and best-organized corner most of the benefits. Given limited taxing capacity and fiscal resources of the states and localities, social services could face severe stress and therefore, problems of access to care would become more acute.

These experiences of participatory models are not very encouraging in various contexts and may not serve as universal solutions. However, this is largely due to the type of decentralization, the political contexts, and the social domain in which they are implemented, rather than any inherent weakness of the principles of decentralization. Largely, this could also be attributed to the limitations of state-initiated process of decentralization, in which the main approach was shifting of workload, transfer of certain functions, and privatization, without any devolution of powers and resources.

The Indian Experience with Decentralization

The Indian experience with decentralization is much more complex. Although implemented during the SAP period, it did not primarily emerge as a response to reform package, but as a part of the political expedience felt by the ruling classes since independence. Therefore, the objective of decentralization was more political than managerial. The 73rd and the 74th Amendments to the Indian Constitution in 1993 and the enactment of Panchayati Raj Acts as a consequence herald a new era in decentralized governance in the states. Elections to panchayati raj institutions have been made mandatory and state governments have been prevented from superseding these institutions for indefinite periods. Under the new Act, a set of items would be entrusted with the local self-governments or the PRIs. This includes health and sanitation and covers hospitals, primary health centers and dispensaries, family welfare, housing, drinking water, etc. (Government of India 1993). PRIs will also receive adequate funds to carry out these functions; this includes grants from the state governments and a share of certain taxes. This would be in addition to the revenue that the councils are allowed to raise and retain with them. Notwithstanding the legislation to facilitate decision-making at lower levels, the degree of political commitment will determine whether or not such institutions can become effective levels of governance with enlarged participation of the local communities (Satishchandran 1994).

The process of decentralization in several states in India throws up a number of issues. The Karnataka experience shows transitional difficulties with regard to rural health care. There was considerable misunderstanding and confusion among different segments of the government regarding personnel issues such as transfers, disciplinary control, and their administrative boundaries. Also, the government was ambivalent towards the process of decentralization (Satishchandran 1993). The Maharashtra experience shows increasing groupism on the basis of parochial considerations, failure of panchayats to harness new resources, overdependence on the government funds, etc. (Rao 1994).

The West Bengal experience has been lauded for its effective implementation of some of the centrally sponsored programs (Rao 1994). Although administratively some form of routine culture has set in, nevertheless it has helped in generating social and political awareness among the people and in facilitating new leadership, thereby strengthening the roots of democracy. The major problem in West Bengal was with regard to allocation of funds. For schemes executed by the PRIs, funds are received in numerous unpredictable installments throughout the year, making rational implementation difficult (Mukherjee and Bandhopadhyay 1994). The experiences in other states are limited as the process has not yet taken off concretely.

Decentralization in Kerala

The developmental experience of Kerala has been considered as an alternative model against the domination of the international capitalism. In fact, the model has attracted the attention of a number of scholars, who perhaps have dissected it from different dimensions (Panikkar and Soman 1984). The present initiative for decentralization in the state has emerged from an international congress convened specifically for re-examining the experience (Thomas and Tharakan 1995). Realizing that the present macro-economic scenario has led to serious developmental crisis, the planners in Kerala are now groping for avenues within the existing institutional framework. The constitutional amendments ushering in the new system of governance are considered one of the avenues for realizing this objective. The Planning Board considers decentralized planning as an approach to resolve not only the earlier contradictions in developmental planning, but also as a remedy for the present crises in the economy of the state as well. The government had also appointed a committee (Sen Committee) to consider the recommendations and criticisms of various elected representatives at different levels and to suggest changes in the laws and in the process of implementation (Government of Kerala 1997). The report of this committee has been accepted recently by the government. An important feature pointed out by this committee as well as several other expert committees is that there should be complete autonomy with regard to financial matters at the lower levels. It is assumed that a regional approach to program development would be suitable for a state like Kerala where there exists geographical and resource diversity.

The unique feature of Kerala's decentralization is that it is an effort to move forward from merely holding panchayat and municipal elections and merely implementing centrally sponsored schemes. The endeavor is to give power and resources to the people, especially at the lower levels in order to enable them to collectively participate in shaping their own future. This is achieved by the people themselves identifying their problems and formulating programs according to local needs. Decentralization is considered an integrated program to foster high degree of interaction between the government and the ordinary people (Franke and Chasin 1997). It is also assumed that local self-sufficiency would provide a buffer against the negative elements of Structural Adjustment Programs. It is less likely to lead to extreme forms of inequality than the one created by the market-led initiatives.

The Process of Decentralization and People's Planning

A brief examination of the process of decentralization attempted in Kerala would enable us to understand how through a series of programs an effort is made to ensure democratic, participatory, and justice-oriented development in the emerging world order (Frank and Chasin 1997). This understanding is essential for distinguishing this process from other forms of decentralization.

The planning board intended to implement the integrated people's planning in four stages:

1. In stage one, resource maps were to be prepared in order to understand water and other resources in each plot of land. This task was to be undertaken by voluntary workers and local-level experts.
2. In this stage, studies on socio-economic status, problems in the village, institutions, and history were to be attempted, to provide a human dimension to development programs.
3. In the third stage, programs were to be evolved using the data from resource maps and socio-economic survey. Two

types of programs were to be identified: those that could be implemented with the available data sources, and those that required further studies.

4. In the last stage, the development programs were to be given the final shape. It was to be also ensured that these programs would be sustainable and could be carried out with continuous participation of the people. It was also hoped that along with the need-based programs, the schemes that had been handed over to the panchayats and municipalities would also be successfully implemented through this process.

The entire process of implementation was to include activities such as meetings of panchayats and municipal wards, developmental seminars, formation of working groups for assessing developmental programs evolved by this process, state-level working groups, and training at different levels.

Health in the Context of Decentralization

When there is a major shift, in part or whole, in the pattern of governance and when health is a major component of that process, what happens to the health care delivery system? Issues of quality and accessibility of health services have to be kept in mind in the process of decentralization.

In order to understand this, it is necessary to examine the health profile of Kerala. Although the health status of Kerala has been acclaimed world over, recent reports suggest that it stands on a weak base (Ekbal and Ramankutty 1996). According to the report, the public health system in the state has collapsed and the government hospitals have lost their credibility. This could be attributed to the declining investments in health and the new agenda that facilitates the entry of private sector into health (Nayar 1998). About 60 percent of the hospitals and health workers including doctors are in the private sector, which is inaccessible to 30–40 percent of the people. It is in this context that the implementation of people's planning has been considered as a panacea for overcoming the collapse of the health service system and to counter the new agenda in public health.

The health status in Kerala is a major conundrum which has received considerable attention from a number of scholars

Table 20.1
Disease Profile in Kerala 1988–93

Disease	*1988*	*1989*	*1990*	*1991*	*1992*	*1993*
ARI	812,836	1,530,859	1,894,788	2,328,262	2,327,967	2,870,610
Pneumonia	9,959	9,363	8,661	11,159	11,315	16,735
Viral hepatitis	7,592	8,036	9,010	7,584	7,573	10,387
T.B.	70,176	62,139	49,288	46,250	38,716	40,406
Cholera	424	139	174	294	44	36
Malaria	5,146	6,126	6,411	6,758	8,255	9,277
Enteric fever	7,448	5,217	6,092	9,483	8,707	11,598

Source: Government of India 1988–94.

Table 20.2
Disease Profile in India 1988–93

Diseases	*1988*	*1989*	*1990*	*1991*	*1992*	*1993*
ARI	4,322,801	7,388,715	8,929,103	10,126,044	11,058,759	12,373,146
Pneumonia	312,014	499,296	434,065	403,337	434,439	488,261
Viral hepatitis	145,903	134,948	124,531	93,497	98,047	117,789
T.B.	1,075,226	1,040,772	1,131,743	898,047	942,254	1,111,100
Cholera	8,957	5,044	3,704	7,088	6,911	9,437
Malaria	1,854,830	2,017,823	2,018,783	2,117,472	2,125,826	2,203,545
Enteric fever	323,572	321,694	370,863	354,143	352,980	357,452

Source: Government of India 1988–94.

Table 20.3
Infant Mortality Rate in Some Selected States in India 1985–95

States	*1985*	*1986*	*1987*	*1988*	*1989*	*1990*	*1991*	*1992*	*1993*	*1994*	*1995*
Bihar	106	101	101	97	91	75	69	73	70	67	73
Orissa	132	123	126	122	121	122	124	115	110	103	103
M.P.	122	118	120	121	117	111	117	104	106	98	99
U.P.	142	132	127	124	118	99	97	98	94	88	86
Rajasthan	108	107	102	103	96	84	79	90	82	84	86
Kerala	31	27	28	28	21	17	16	17	13	16	15
T.N.	81	80	76	74	68	59	57	58	56	59	54
Punjab	71	68	62	62	64	61	53	56	55	53	54
Karnataka	69	73	75	74	80	70	77	73	67	67	62

Source: Government of India 1997.

(Kannan et al. 1991). It is often mentioned that despite an epidemiological transition, there exists a paradox of low mortality and high morbidity. Many of the diseases are showing a rising trend. The pattern of communicable diseases is also largely similar to that of India (see Tables 20.1 and 20.2). Diarrheal diseases, pneumonia, acute respiratory infections (ARIs), etc. are some of the diseases which are noticeable. Apart from these, diseases such as Japanese encephalitis have also surfaced in 1995–96. The Infant Mortality Rate (IMR) is also showing a rising trend after a sharp fall in the pre-reform period (see Table 20.3). This pattern is also broadly similar to that seen in some other states, where a rise or stagnation in IMR is observed. This means that the underlying epidemiological processes are more complex than are usually assumed and that we need to incorporate shifts due to SAP in our epidemiological analysis. The second issue, therefore, is that in any decentralized health care delivery system, there is a need to recognize and resolve such complexities.

Given the fact that all the PRIs have identified the problems and suggested projects in several areas including health, it is now possible to provide a preliminary analysis of the health components of the need-based programs. For this purpose, we examined the development reports of about eight panchayats, six from Pathanamthitta district and one each from Trivandrum and Kollam district (Government of Kerala 1996).

An analysis of the themes identified by the panchayats for evolving projects in health shows that they fall into a number of categories. A number of panchayats have identified programs on sanitation, expansion of indigenous systems of medicine, such as Ayurveda and Unani, removal of garbage and waste, upgradation of services at the primary health center, health education, and health camps, etc. (see Table 20.4). That is, preventive aspects have been largely identified as important. This means that the delivery of health services including curative services and those related to communicable diseases would remain unchanged as they still fall within the ambit of a centralized structure. Whether this reflects a class bias of those who have identified the programs needs to be explored further. It needs to be mentioned here that the crises in the health service system in Kerala is largely in relation to the delivery of communicable disease control programs, the supply of drugs, and

Table 20.4
Panchayats and their Need-based Programs

Programs	*Panchayats*							
	1	*2*	*3*	*4*	*5*	*6*	*7*	*8*
PHC building—other facilities	+						+	+
Subcenters	+	+						+
Sanitation	+	+	+	+	+	+	+	+
Garbage, waste disposal, and related problems	+	+	+		+	+	+	
Appointment of staff	+						+	+
Upgradation of services	+	+	+	+			+	+
Indigenous systems	+	+	+		+		+	+
Committee for supervision	+							
Nutrition				+		+		
Immunization		+						
Health education/Health camps	+	+	+	+	+			
Drugs/Laboratory, etc.			+			+	+	+
Water supply			+			+		
Communicable disease control	+		+					

Source: Government of Kerala 1996.

the quality of curative care. It appears that in the initial phases of people's planning these aspects would not be covered. On the other hand, some of the preventive programs identified by the people would not get sufficient attention of the health services as they fall outside their ambit or because of the costs in implementing some of these programs. However, the kind of social mobilization that has taken place and the process by which people were engaged in understanding different dimensions of development, especially health, could be carried forward with adequate understanding of conflicts and gaps that are discussed in the following section (Brown 1997).

Future Concerns

Notwithstanding the considerable advantages of people's planning, it is possible to say that resource constraints and multiple authorities would continue to plague the effectiveness of the programs identified. Second, the type of programs which do not intervene into the core area of health and health services would result in the continued supremacy of medical bureaucracy in the villages. To some extent, the type of programs identified by the people involve de-mystification of health. But, at the same time it is also necessary to think in terms of making the health service system more efficient to achieve effective delivery of primary health care.

The question as to whether people's planning could lead to a more vibrant and responsive health service system is still open as a number of conflicts and gaps which are discernible at present could pose constraints on the effective implementation of a much appreciated legislation.

1. An understanding of gaps between the need-based programs identified and actual felt need on the one hand, and those between need-based programs and the epidemiological need would further help in consolidating the effectiveness of this initiative. This is essential for taking forward the process of democratization of health services and the forgotten concept of primary health care.
2. The second level of conflict is between the professional and the political leadership at the village level. The existing health personnel do not participate at the policy-planning

stage. Nor do they participate at the project-preparatory stage. They are also largely excluded during the participatory training programs. In short, doctors and other health workers are supposed to implement the programs formulated without their participation. Thus, the total exclusion of health service system raises the issue of new conflicts in the villages.

3. One can also identify a number of conflicts between the panchayats and the state government. The state government evolves the major chunk of the programs that are handed down to the panchayats for implementation. With regard to health services, a number of areas where conflicts can surface could be identified. These include: (*i*) drug supply which is controlled by the state; (*ii*) recruitment of staff, service matters including leave, etc.; and (*iii*) allocation and proportion of funds for need-based and other programs.
4. Another area of possible conflict is between centrally sponsored schemes and the programs evolved by the state. It needs to be pointed out that the centrally sponsored schemes remain as they are and the responsibility for implementing them is with the panchayats. In effect, the negative features of the vertical programs would continue to affect health in spite of elaborately prepared need-based programs.
5. As with other earlier initiatives on devolution of political and financial powers to the lower levels, Kerala has also witnessed some resistance at the upper levels, especially from the state-level political leaders and bureaucrats. The government has not paid due attention to overhaul the panchayat and municipal laws to make the devolution more effective.
6. Another level of conflict arises within the health service system. This is in the form of preventive and curative programs. While most of the programs evolved are preventive programs, there is total confusion regarding the role of health services in this process.

The process of decentralization in Kerala may be considered as an expression of democratic rights of the people in the face of the onslaught of globalization and centralization of governance.

However, if this process is to be made effective, there is a need to understand the complexities of health services, the epidemiological undercurrents, and the conflicts at several levels of governance. While enactment of laws would facilitate the process of social transformation to some extent, the Kerala example could be used to highlight the social and the technical dimensions of such processes. As more states in India and other countries begin to experiment with decentralization, these experiences could offer valuable lessons if not serve as a "model."

References

Araujo Jr, J., and **Luiz, A.C.** (1997): Attempts to Decentralize in Recent Brazilian Health Policy: Issues and Problems, 1988–1994. *International Journal of Health Services,* 27(1): 109–24.

Bloom, G., and **Xingyuan, G.** (1997): Health Sector Reforms: Lessons from China. *Social Science and Medicine,* 45(3): 351–60.

Brown, P. (1997): Popular Epidemiology Revisited. *Current Sociology,* 45(3): 138–56.

Collins, C., and **Green, A.** (1994): Decentralization and Primary Health Care: Some Negative Implications in Developing Countries. *International Journal of Health Services,* 24(3): 459–75.

Ekbal, B., and **Ramankutty, K.** (1996): *Health-Handbook for Workers.* Trivandrum: Kerala Sastra Sahitya Parishad.

Estes, C.L., and **Linkins, K.W.** (1997): Devolution and Aging Policy: Racing to the Bottom in Long-term Care. *International Journal of Health Services,* 27(3): 427–42.

Franke, R.W., and **Chasin, B.H.** (1997): Power to the Malayalee People. *Economic and Political Weekly,* 32: 3061–68.

Government of India (1993): *The Gazette of India Extra Ordinary.* New Delhi: Ministry of Law, Justice and Company Affairs.

——— (1988–94): Health Information of India. New Delhi: Director General of Health Services.

——— (1997): *Sample Registration Bulletin,* 31: 6. Office of the Registrar-General, Vital Statistics Division, Ministry of Health, New Delhi.

Government of Kerala (1996): Development Reports of Six Panchayats. Trivandrum: The Planning Board.

——— (1997): People's Planning. Trivandrum: The Planning Board.

Kannan, K.P., **Thankappan, K.R.**, **Raman Kutty, V.**, and **Aravindan, K.P.** (1991): *Health and Development in Rural Kerala.* Trivandrum: Kerala Sastra Sahitya Parishad.

Mills, A., **Vaughan, J.P.**, **Smith, D.L.**, and **Tabibzadeth, I.** (1990): *Health System Decentralisation: Concepts, Issues and Country Experiences.* Geneva: WHO.

Mukherjee, N., and **Bandopadhyay, D.** (1994): New Horizons for West Bengal Panchayats. In A. Mukherji (ed.). *Decentralisation: Panchayats in the Nineties.* New Delhi: Vikas.

Nayar, K.R. (1998): Old Priorities and New Agenda of Public Health in India: Is There a Mismatch? *Croatian Medical Journal,* 39(3): 308–15.

Oreskovic, S. (1995): Health System Reorganization in Croatia in the Light of Major Reform Tendencies in OECD Countries. *Croatian Medical Journal,* 36(1): 47–54.

Panikkar, P.G.K., and **Soman, C.R.** (1984): *Health Status of Kerala: The Paradox of Economic Backwardness and Health Development.* Trivandrum: Centre for Development Studies.

Rao, S. (ed.) (1994): Panchayati Raj and Health. Proceedings of the Seminar, 9–10 April, Bombay: FRCH.

Satishchandran, T.R. (1993): Panchayat Raj and Health Care: The Karnataka Experience. In N.H. Antia and K. Bhatia (eds.). *People's Health in People's Hands: A Model for Panchayati Raj.* Bombay: FRCH.

——— (1994): Inter-tier Allocation of Functions. In A. Mukherji (ed.). *Decentralisation : Panchayats in the Nineties.* New Delhi: Vikas.

Standing, H. (1997): Gender and Equity in Health Sector Reform Programs: A Review. *Health Policy and Planning,* 12(1): 1–18.

Thomas, T.M.I., and **Tharakan, M.P.K.** (1995): Kerala: Towards a New Agenda. *Economic and Political Weekly,* 30(31–32): 2004.

21

Promises and Problems of Panchayati Raj: Experiences from Madhya Pradesh

Anwar Jafri

Introduction

Panchayati Raj is a system of governance through local self-government that seeks to involve people at the grass-roots level in the affairs affecting them.

Soon after independence the development planning that was adopted gave center space to community development programs. People's participation in the planning and execution of the program was considered a vital aspect of community development. The program, however, failed to involve the people in its planning and implementation (Dubey 1990). In 1957, the Central Council of Local Self Government resolved that "village panchayats should be given as large a role as possible in the development programs of the village, including land reforms." Such and other steps accelerated the pace of constituting Panchayati Raj Institutions (PRIs) in all the states. The states were allowed to evolve PRIs suited to the local conditions. By 1959, all the states had passed Panchayat Acts and by the mid-sixties, panchayats had reached all parts of the country. There was much enthusiasm in rural India as people felt they had a say in the affairs affecting their daily lives (Jena 1995; Mathew 1994).

Eklavya is a voluntary organization in Bhopal, M.P., working in the areas of education and development. The study described here was the result of teamwork by members of Eklavya. A key role in data collection was played by Shri Sundar Singh, Shri R.N. Syag, and others, who provided many insights into panchayat dynamics. This study and our earlier work with panchayats was supported in part by UNICEF, M.P.

Unfortunately, the performance of PRIs in most states, with the exception of Gujarat and Maharashtra, was dismal to say the least. The Ashoka Mehta Committee on Panchayati Raj Institutions was appointed by the Government of India in December 1977 to enquire into the "working of PRIs, and to suggest measures to strengthen them, so as to enable a decentralized system of planning and development to be effective." In a broad survey of the various phases through which Panchayati Raj has passed since its introduction in 1959, the committee has observed that "the story of Panchayati Raj has been a story of ups and downs." Its three phases have been those of ascendancy, stagnation and decline (Shukla 1990). Of the several factors which seem to have contributed to this weakening, mention has been made about their structural inadequacies, role of bureaucracy, weakening of political will, lack of conceptual clarity, as also the dominance of the economically or socially privileged sections of the society in the PRIs, thereby depriving the weaker sections of the benefits which could have legitimately reached them through these institutions. Apart from these, other factors, such as factionalism, corruption, inefficiency, political interference, parochial loyalties, power concentration, and motivated actions, severely limited the utility of Panchayati Raj for the average villager. Lack of resources, irregular elections, indiscriminate dissolution/supersession have been other factors.

In keeping with its approach that panchayats should be regarded as political rather than mere developmental institutions, this committee made the first official recommendation for including Panchayati Raj in the Constitution, thus making it a statutory requirement (Mathew 1994). In the eighties, there was a resurgence and renewed interest in the revitalization of local bodies. West Bengal, Karnataka, Andhra Pradesh, and Jammu and Kashmir reformulated their Panchayat Acts and took steps to implement them accordingly. This renewed interest, in a way, culminated in the 1992 Constitution (Seventy–third) Amendment Act. The Amendment seeks to address the problems that have been identified in earlier years in the functioning of the panchayati raj system. It has introduced some fundamental changes in the membership and working of the system.

1. It has given constitutional status and backing to all local government institutions, thus making it obligatory for the

states to introduce local self-government at the village and district levels. The necessary powers and framework have been provided to the states to make suitable legislation so that the new legislation is in line with the mandatory provisions.

Subsequently, all state governments with Madhya Pradesh taking the lead in 1994 have ratified the Amendment and accordingly enacted the state Acts. This has led to a three-tier structure of local government, with the village panchayat at the grass-roots, the block-level panchayats in the middle, and the district panchayats at the top. The Act also establishes a gram sabha (a general body of all the adults in the village panchayat area) for the enhancement of people's participation in an institutionalized form.

2. The new Act ensures reservation of one-third of all seats for women and reservation for scheduled castes and scheduled tribes in proportion to their population in all positions in the three tiers.
3. The new Act includes provisions for periodic elections.
4. The other important feature is the provision for setting up a state finance commission to find ways and means of raising adequate finances for the local bodies.

In view of the important role assigned to the state governments, important questions arise regarding how the Act has been made operational in different states, to what extent the provisions of the Act have been diluted, and to what extent the states have incorporated the key elements of the 73rd Constitutional Amendment. These will determine to what extent the local bodies/ institutions will succeed in becoming self governing.

Background and Objectives

This study focuses on panchayats in the Malwa region of Madhya Pradesh. Elections to village panchayats in this state were held under a non-party system, where parties could not directly canvass support for a candidate, nor could a candidate declare open allegiance to any political party.

This study was preceded by Eklavya's participation in a UNICEF-supported panchayat training program for six months, through which we covered about 180 panchayats in three blocks.

It was the interaction with panchayat members during this program, which included one or more women and SC/ST members from each panchayat, which brought out the need for a more detailed interaction and study, especially in the context of the changing village politics. At the time that this study was undertaken, the panchayats had already been functioning for two years. The panchayat members had gained sufficient time to settle down to whatever extent this was at all possible.

Initial euphoria amongst the recent entrants to panchayats, especially the women and scheduled caste and scheduled tribe candidates, seemed to have given way to a certain realism and even to a fair degree of despair, since they found themselves unable to convert the promises of this Act into actual gains. The women, especially, having been elected for the first time to panchayats, found themselves at a disadvantage on a number of planes. First, they found it difficult to cope with the paperwork and legalities of the panchayat system. Second, the poor and the landless found their numerical advantage in the panchayats being lost to their better organized and wily adversaries from the upper castes and classes.

In an effort to resolve these problems, the Madhya Pradesh government with support from other organizations, including a large number of non-governmental organizations (NGOs), had taken up training in a big way to enhance the functioning skills of panchayat members. Efforts had been made to develop relevant training and orientation modules for panchayat members. However, in our experience with such activities, it became clear rather early that orientations and training can at best play a limited and supportive role in strengthening panchayat functioning. A major problem also seemed to be the lack of participation of the gram sabha members. Further, effective strategies as well as policy initiatives may be needed to evolve an atmosphere where panchayat and gram sabha members share responsibilities and work together.

The field study reported here is meant to help develop a better understanding of the dynamics and problems which panchayat members, especially women and those belonging to th SC and ST, face during their work. This could, in turn, lead to more meaningful interaction and orientation modules for strengthening panchayats and gram sabhas that go beyond the elementary orientation courses normally organized by the government or NGOs.

Methodology and Selection of Panchayats Our strategy was to use the case-study method for an in-depth understanding of real life situation which could then be analyzed for insights and possibly used for further large-scale studies.

Information about panchayat functioning and the village situation was collected mainly during discussions with the village community as well as panchayat members. We ensured that interaction took place with members of different communities and groups to cross-check the information gathered. Each panchayat required a number of visits by the survey team. Where possible, discussions were also held with the village patwari to ascertain the overall accuracy of the information on landholdings, although land records have not been referred to.

Initially, we selected 10 panchayats in Dewas and Hoshangabad districts for the study. These were within a radius of approximately 50 km to enable continued visits to the team members. Since we were interested in observing the performance of panchayat leaders belonging to the backward and reserved sections, we selected eight panchayats in this category, three with women sarpanches (heads of the panchayat) and five belonging to the SC/ST category. All except for one had won their election against the reserved quota of seats. Two other panchayats with sarpanches from the influential class (there was no reservation for these seats) weref selected to enable some comparisons in performance between various categories.

We formed two teams to conduct the survey work and selected two clusters of five panchayats, one each in Harda and Khategaon blocks in Hoshangabad and Dewas districts, respectively. Data and information from other villages and panchayats, available from some earlier program activity, were also used. Initially, it was decided to collect general data about the villages, which would give the profile as well as an idea of the influential communities and what sort of hold they have in the village. This formed the background for studying village dynamics and panchayat functioning.

A broad assessment of the performance of the sarpanches and the functioning of the panchayats was carried out keeping the following criteria in mind:

1. style of functioning, including ability to follow and enforce the panchayat institutional mechanisms, such as holding

the stipulated number of panchayat meetings, following correct accounting procedures, participation of members in decision-making, and organizing gram sabha meetings;
2. quality of implementation in the schemes taken up by the panchayat, knowledge and understanding of the various schemes for the benefit of the local communities; and
3. ability to interact with and to hold one's own with different segments in the panchayat and regional community, including the influential groups and government functionaries.

What follows is an outline of the initial study as it developed and some of the information collected. The main body of the work is still evolving and we cannot claim comprehensiveness in perspective. But the case studies provide a number of insights which could help give direction and improve working methods in panchayat-related programs. As an example of the approach followed, we give here the case study of one panchayat. On the basis of this and a number of other case studies that we carried out, we have tried to observe some patterns pertaining to alignments and strengths of the communities involved.

Working of the Panchayats

Some patterns about who controls the strings of power in the village, and how this is related to the landholdings and community influence, started emerging at the initial stage of the study. Questions arose about why one section of a village was neglected by the panchayat and another favored. Was it related to group or caste politics or was it related to the backward condition of the community and their low educational levels? An interesting question which was raised in this context was "what is it that decides the *haisiyat* or status of a person in the community and village?" This is an important question and it must be answered in the case of new panchayat members who have traditionally not been members of the *haisiyat* group, but are now trying to gain that status.

In the context of the performance of panchayat members, some general patterns were emerging. In case the sarpanch belonged to a traditionally influential group and was educated and motivated (read ambitious and well-off), he would try and organize some "constructive" activities, normally in the areas which he percieved as his support base. This seemed the case at Sirali in Khidkiya block and at Magardha in Harda block. Both these sarpanches who had won on non-reserved seats belonged to traditionally influential families nursing political ambitions. The Integrated Rural Development Program (IRDP), providing limited support to local developmental schemes such as minor road construction, earth filling, and other such works, as well as the Indira Awas Yojna (a scheme to support housing for the poor) were reported to have been well implemented in these panchayats. However, there were complaints that these schemes were implemented only in colonies known to have supported the sarpanch.

In cases where the new sarpanch had been elected from a non-traditional group, i.e., a woman from a backward community or a male SC/ST and was not a proxy candidate, all the traditional forces in the village would be out to disrupt any efforts at positive or independent work. This could be seen in the panchayats of Kolhipura, Uda, Kailanpur, or Padwa. It was almost as if the entrenched groups hated and feared any possible success on the part of a sarpanch from a non-traditional group.

We came across distinct cases, where strong and potentially effective women sarpanches had been thrown out using no-confidence motions or were prevented from functioning by adopting a combination of manipulation and brute power (Kolhipura and Kailanpur). However, there were still exceptions to these rules, where the concerned person had survived or even fought back. Ayodhya Bai, the spirited young lady sarpanch of Kailanpur belonging to the Balaai caste (a scheduled caste working mainly as field laborers) succeeded in getting re-elected after having been thrown out through a no-confidence motion by panchayat members. There were individuals, both men and women, who had defied the old logic of tradition and power through some magical combination of education, caste, personal abilities, and politics. Later on in this chapter, we have elaborated upon the leadership styles of some sarpanches. What are the factors which help such people to survive? Will they be able to move on from individual survival to community mobilization? These are some of the questions we wished to answer.

Socio-economic Dynamics of Panchayat Functioning

Our case study of Kolhipura panchayat showed that this panchayat was somewhat unusual in that, Kolhipura and Kunjargaon, the two villages making up this panchayat presented rather contrasting profiles, which complicated the relationship between their inhabitants. The village Kolhipura, which was the larger of the two (with 121 families), had a proportionally stronger presence of upper castes and other backward castes (OBCs). There were also 35 families of Korku tribals, but this community, encouraged to settle here and work as laborers, was submissive like most recent migrants. Kunjargaon (with 78 families in all) had a larger proportion of SCs and STs. Most of them owned 10 to 20 acres of land.

The people of Kolhipura panchayat had elected Bhavar Bai, a *Charmkar* by caste, as sarpanch, to a seat reserved for women. In the elections, Bhavar Bai had defeated a Jat woman, the wife of the former sarpanch. The former sarpanch himself had to be content with the post of the *up-sarpanch* in the new set-up. Bhavar Bai, who had about 15 acres of land in Kunjargaon, had often traveled to Bombay with her husband for trade. She exhibited strong personality traits and confidence, emanating from economic and social independence. It was for these reasons that her community requested her to contest.

Her divide from the Jat *up-sarpanch* was complete. They lived in different villages, belonged to opposing castes, and were supporters of different political parties (she supported the Congress while he was a staunch member of the Bhartiya Janata Party, which was reason enough for discord). And if all this was not enough, she was *the woman* who had defeated his wife in the elections. Although the *up-sarpanch* was too sophisticated to say this himself, other members of his community were more forthcoming. "How can we ever attend a panchayat meeting, where we will have to occupy a position below that of a chamar woman? We will never accept her as our sarpanch."

To her great credit, the totally illiterate Bhavar Bai continued fighting the battle with the upper castes, never cowering before them. Bhavar Bai's disadvantage, however, was her lack of political exposure and absence of a clear political agenda. She had not been able to mobilize wider support of even the SC/ST groups in her favor. Not being literate and unable to win over the panchayat secretary, proper accounts had not been maintained. In this situation, she had become isolated even from her own community members by relying excessively on bravado and by adopting an aggressive stance.

Landholding Pattern

Tables 21.1 and 21.2 show the community-wise landholdings in Kolhipura panchayat. To simplify our analysis we have combined the figures for the two villages, Kolhipura and Kunjargaon, which make up this panchayat. We have also grouped castes into two main groups. The division into just two caste groups was used to obtain a sharper picture of village politics. The OBCs, consisting of castes such as the various artisans, i.e., *Lohar, Sutar, Kumhar,* etc., and the castes servicing the upper castes, i.e., the *Maali, Naai, Yadavas,* etc., have been grouped together with the upper castes, such as, the *Brahmins, Jats, Rajputs,* and *Banias*. Although in economic terms the poorer OBCs may be closer to the SCs and STs, in village politics and in their caste outlook we find them closely aligned to the upper castes. A *Sutar,* i.e., the carpenter, would share his well water with an upper caste (even a *Brahmin*) but would not let a "lower caste" do so. And the village *Naai* (barber) would refuse to visit a *Balaai's* house to give him a haircut. Such alignments seem to carry over to village elections and politics as well.

Another reason for grouping the OBCs with the upper castes was that some of the OBCs, such as the *Gujjars* and *Yadavas,* are defined as backward possibly due to the political clout they wield in state politics. A more impartial assessment would place them with the upper castes. To be sure, the poorest castes amongst the OBCs, i.e., the *Katias* (weavers), or *Kachis* (vegetable growers), are considered very lowly by the upper castes. However, in the context of any political alliance they still tend to side with the privileged.

Community-wise Landholdings in Kolhipura Panchayat

An analysis of Tables 21.1 and 21.2 shows that the overall average size of the landholdings per family for the general castes and OBCs is 11 acres. However, if we consider only the upper castes in this group then their average goes up to 18 acres per family.

Table 21.1
General Castes and OBCs* (Landholdings in acres)

Caste	*No. of Families*	*Over 50*	*50–20*	*20–10*	*10–2*	*Landless*	*Avg/Family*
Brahman	2	-	1	1	-	-	25
Jat	24	-	7	7	10	-	17
Bishnoi	7	-	4	3	-	-	26
Rajput	10	-	2	4	4	-	15
Kachi	20	-	-	5	13	2	7
Khati	12	-	-	-	7	5	3
Katia	15	-	-	3	5	7	5
Maali	3	-	-	1	2	-	8
Naai	6	-	-	-	4	2	3
Total	99	-	14	24	45	16	11

Note: *The data for the table have been collected during the surveys that were conducted during the study.

Table 21.2
Scheduled Castes and Tribes in Kolhipura

Korku Thakur	50	-	1	9	25	15	6
Balaai	22	-	1	6	11	4	8
Charmkar	16	-	-	4	5	7	5
Total	88	-	2	19	41	26	6

Note: The data for the table have been collected during the surveys that were conducted during the study.

Table 21.3
Caste and Gender Composition of Kolhipura Panchayat

Caste	*No. of Members*	*No. of Women*	*Literate*
General Castes and OBCs			
Jat	1	-	1
Naai	1	1	-
Maali	1	1	-
Kachi	1	-	1
Total	4	2	2(2m*)
SC/ST			
Korku	3	1	2(1m+1f*)
Balaai	1	1	-
Charmkar	4	1	1(1m)
Total	8	3	3(2m+1f)
Grand total	12	5	5(4m+1f)

Note: The data for the table have been collected during the surveys that were conducted during the study.
m*—males
f*—females

This can be contrasted to the 6 acres per family, which is the average holding amongst the SC/ST group (see Table 21.2).

The overall economic condition of the SCs/STs in Kolhipura panchayat was not too bad. Their average landholding, in comparison to caste-mates elsewhere, was on the higher side. Second, due to the proximity of the Tawa irrigation canal, most of their lands were irrigated. The presence of irrigation also helped the landless in that they found employment through the year within their own village and did not have to migrate to other regions in search of labor.

Caste Composition of Kolhipura

In addition to understanding patterns of landholdings we also tried to understand the functioning of the panchayat in terms of the background and caste of its members.

Some interesting features of the Kolhipura panchayat evident from Table 21.3 are:

- The SC/ST members outnumbered the others by two to one.
- Among the SC/ST members themselves the *Charmkars* outnumbered other communities in the panchayat, whereas their population was less than that of the others, namely the *Balaai* and the *Korkus.*
- The only literate woman belonged to the SC/ST group.

In spite of a majority of panchayat members belonging to the SC/ST group, the sarpanch, Bhavar Bai, was unable to function effectively. Most members of the panchayat including the SC/ST members along with the panchayat secretary supported the *up-sarpanch.* The *up-sarpanch* complained that Bhavar Bai did not work cooperatively with the other members and hence he did not support her. Bhavar Bai complained that the environment had been made hostile and unmanageble. Panchayat meetings were held late at night, when it was impossible for her to attend. The panchayat secretary did not show her the accounts books. With the connivance of the panchayat secretary, the *up-sarpanch* called the shots; he managed the panchayat register and the accounts, and fixed the meetings.

A move was initiated by the *up-sarpanch* to pass a no-confidence motion against Bhavar Bai. The motion would have been passed, but it was stalled by the tehsil revenue officials who, it seems, wanted to avoid the embarrassment of having a woman sarpanch of the SC/ST group removed, an act which would have attracted undesirable attention. Due to her outspoken nature, Bhavar Bai may be considered a bit of a celebrity amongst women sarpanches of the district; they even invited her once to address a public gathering of panchayat sarpanches in the presence of the collector.

Bhavar Bai's inability to mobilize members of her caste and class needs to be understood in the context of the social and economic conditions prevalent in the region. It was revealing to observe the behavior of her caste members in the panchayat. Her panchayat consisted of two villages and members of her caste belonging to her village supported her, while those from the other village had voted against her. They sided with the assistant headman who also hailed from their village. This act can be understood by the fact that the assistant headman was an influential landowner and the panchayat members needed to retain his patronage. In other words, even comparatively better off SC/ST panchayat members were unable to assert themselves due to their lower social and economic status, thus in a way retaining a political process which worked against their long-term interests.

Fall-out of the Reservation Policy

Intra-caste Divisions—Loss of Vital Advantage

A broadly similar trend, as in the case study above, seems to be present in the panchayat dynamics of the whole region. SC/ST and women's votes within the panchayats were split along village-level loyalties and pressures. Thus, the advantages expected to flow from the "reservation policy" to the poorest groups were partially lost due to intra-caste divisions. *Charmkars* being most vocal and economically more independent could be in a position to provide leadership to the other SC/ST groups. Their numerical strength in the panchayats of Hoshangabad district exceeded their proportional strength in the community. However, the caste prejudices against them within the SC/ST groups are very strong at present, preventing acceptance of their leadership and thereby preventing alignment across castes.

Women-advantage Poor

Women of low caste and of the poor communities are amongst the most deprived and illiterate. It was surprising, therefore, to discover that women amongst the SC/ST seemed to be a potential source of substantial advantage for their own communities in comparison to the upper caste groups.

The reason for this is not difficult to fathom. Because of economic and cultural factors, women from the poorest communities are capable of functioning in public and community life on an equal footing with their men. In rural areas, women from the upper and middle castes are usually kept behind the scenes and prevented from participating in public activities, such as the panchayat.

The case studies in over half a dozen instances showed that women sarpanches from the SC/ST groups had been "selected" by their communities for individual qualities of leadership and confidence, rather than being the husband's or family's choice. Often they had defeated the wife of some influential person, such as a former sarpanch, who could not stand for elections himself due to the seat being declared reserved for women. On the other hand, women panchayat members from the upper castes had mostly been put up as proxies by influential husbands or relatives. After the elections, such women were normally relegated to the background by their active relative.

In Khategaon we met two women sarpanches from the scheduled castes. In each of the cases, both the husband and wife talked to us. They seemed to be working together as a team, and claimed to play an active role as and when demanded by the situation. When asked what the major gain was, they replied that so far there may not have been any direct economic or political gain, but what they considered important was that by being in the panchayat they could observe first hand and begin to understand how political games were "played" by influential groups from behind the scenes.

The Democratization of Corruption

Since a certain percentage (about 7 percent in Madhya Pradesh) of rural development funds now go directly to the panchayats and since decisions regarding the beneficiaries of various government schemes are meant to be taken at this level, there is, perforce, more transparency about these dealings. As information about these funds is now locally available, it means that the village community can now observe the deals, honest or otherwise, at first hand. It is hoped that this would lead to greater public awareness and control.

Corruption and democratic practices seem to be inversely related. An interesting pattern which seems to emerge is that even in cases where the sarpanch and the panchayat seem to be functioning effectively, the democratic functions and structures are usually given the go by, with scant respect for accountability to the gram sabha. The concept of participation as an important part of the process of panchayati raj is rarely seen in practice. In fact, in retrospect, it seems inevitable that community participation would be looked upon with hostility by persons of influence. One reason for this could be that even where the sarpanches concerned were motivated and effective, they usually did not operate totally above board. A number of expenses had to be taken care of/borne by them including those for travel and food in addition to local hospitality to visitors, etc., which could not be claimed as working expenses. These were then adjusted against other expense categories with the help of the panchayat secretary and possibly the connivance of some other panches. Transparency and participatory functioning obstructed such a style of functioning.

However, other causes leading to corruption seem more problematic. Elected representatives may consider it their right to compensate for the expenses incurred in contesting elections and these may be more significant at the janpad and zila levels. In addition, the many functions of the zila and janpad chairperson as well as those of the village sarpanch are in the nature of a full-time occupation. A small farmer or laborer cannot afford this type of attention or involvement without jeopardizing his livelihood. Elected representatives who do so often start expecting more than purely social or political returns.

The issues of mobilization of the gram sabha and imparting institutional status to access to information and transparent functioning seem to be of critical importance for the existing situation to change. However, these should extend beyond any particular panchayat body.

Styles of Functioning of Panchayat Leaders

There exist two sharply contrasting groups of performance in the arena of panchayats: one is the group of traditionally influential and entrenched representatives and the other is that of the new entrants. Therefore, a focus on and a close scrutiny of the latter's performance was natural. Another question that arose was, "How is the performance and effectiveness of sarpanches and panchayat members related to their class and caste background?"

In this context, one thing that emerged quite clearly was the great variety in styles of leadership provided by the new persons in power. Although, in retrospect, this variety seems natural, at the time we began our study there was an underlying expectation that the SC/ST sarpanches would be largely weaklings and proxies. As far as our limited samples of panchayats go, this fear has proved to be largely misplaced.

From amongst our case studies, it may be worthwhile to recount some categories of leadership styles amongst the SC group that were notable in their own ways.

The Stubborn Crusaders

Although illiterate, Sarpanch Bhavar Bai was a tough and intellectually independent woman, but lacking in "statecraft." Therefore, both she and her husband had spent considerable energy in continuous conflict with the *up-sarpanch* as well as the panchayat secretary. However, they had not been able to muster support from other members of the panchayat or from the gram sabha.

In contrast to Bhavar Bai, Ayodhya Bai, the sarpanch of Kailanpur, determined in her own way, had the social background and skills to mobilize support in the face of stiff opposition. This young and educated woman from the laboring *Balaai* caste fell out with her mentors when they realized that she would not play second fiddle to them. In a short time, she was ousted by a no-confidence vote in the panchayat. In contrast to most other cases that we observed, she was able to mobilize support from her community and other poorer sections and was re-elected sarpanch after a confident win in the re-elections.

The Diplomat

Sarpanch Asha Ram Dilare, belonging to the *Charmkar* community of Ranhai panchayat, had completed school. From an early age he had been active in *bhajan mandalis* and cultural programs through which he had gained entry and exposure to the upper caste culture of his area. Relatively young, in his late twenties, he was active in the rawhide trade as a flayer and also traveled to Bombay to trade in old shoes. He came across as a suave man with a clear strategy for survival in a potentially hostile atmosphere. Elected sarpanch to a reserved seat in a village whose patel was one of the largest landowners and a former member of the legislative assembly (MLA) of the region, Asha Ram knew that he could not succeed in a direct conflict with the powerful. He stated emphatically that by accepting the patronage of the patel's son, who was the present *up-sarpanch,* he was able to continue functioning and be a source of support to the poor. Asha Ram is said to have organized an effective literacy campaign amongst the SC/ST community in his village.

The Bouncer

Gyaras, the sarpanch of Baranga panchayat, also belonged to the *Charmkar* or flayer community. He was illiterate, with no landholdings and yet when he held forth at the gram sabha meetings, no one dared to intervene. He was known not to call any panchayat meetings but his proposals were passed while he stayed home. Gyaras was described alternately as a *rangdar* (equivalent to a *dada*) and a *ghutnebaaz,* meaning a person who would use his knees rather than his head. We learnt that over 20 years ago, Gyaras used to be one of the more notorious members of a gang of local raiders. His companions included members of the Jat caste and other landowning families. Gyaras was not known to give up easily and followed his proposals for the village needy to the block or tehsil office, threatening dharna if not heeded. His confident demeanor and the aura of his adventurous past were known to bring results. He declared his resolve to solve the problems of the poor and needy in romantic tones. But his was the style of the lone ranger, probably retiring into oblivion without leaving any followers.

The Cowherd

The sarpanch of Abgaonkala fitted the traditional picture of the meek and submissive. He was said to be a bonded laborer at the *up-sarpanch*'s house and in the candid words of this influencial Jat, was duly ordered off to herd cattle during a panchayat meeting. He was later asked to sign on the dotted line.

Discussion

This qualitative exploration of "panchayat dynamics" reveals two key aspects that would ultimately decide the success of the panchayats. These are as follows:

- How will the struggles and efforts for survival by the new panchayat leaders ultimately transfer into the community's conscious efforts at upgrading and improving their status?
- How can the diverse lowest caste groups rise above traditional antagonisms to work together for their common long-term interests?

Though we do not have a macro-picture yet, our data provide some crucial insights.

Through the reservation policy, the 73rd Amendment attempts to bring about changes in the composition of the panchayats. It seeks to alter not only the gender balance, but also the socio-economic profile, as often women who win belong to the SC/ST. However, this positive outcome is negated by the existence of unchanged land-ownership patterns which force the poor and landless SC/STs to vote and support their landed patrons. In other words, the increasing numbers of the poor and lower castes are not able to break the barriers created by caste and economic dependence.

Panchayat raj faces a crisis of trust. It has raised enormous expectations amongst the new entrants and their support base, which is not easy to fulfill in the short run. The run-up to the recent changes in panchayati raj has not been a process of demand through mass struggle. Rather it has come as a gift, bestowed upon the people by leaders "in their wisdom." Both sides in this transaction have been found wanting in their preparations. They were not adequately equipped to take forward the logic of this rather momentous decision. In the meanwhile, the image of panchayati raj runs the risk of suffering. However, many proponents of panchayati raj assert that preparation itself can be made only by being cast into this whirlpool of practice and struggle.

Coming to the issue of devolution of power to panchayats, we find that in the case of Madhya Pradesh, in spite of the consistent and strong expression of support from the state government, the panchayats continue to be at the receiving end of a double-edged hostility. On the one hand, this comes from the district bureaucracy which fears loss of its power and influence as the zila and block-level panchayat representatives strive to exercise control over planning and development activities. On the other hand, members of the state legislature as well as those of the national parliament tend to see the panchayat representatives as competitors in their local political arena.

In part due to this hostility and in part due to the present inadequate governance and managerial skills and abilities of panchayat members, a lack of faith is often cited by state-level officials while taking decisions about the channelization of community and developmental programs and funds. Panchayats often are the losers in this. Two recent examples of such programs, in both of which the panchayats were bypassed, are the Literacy Campaigns and the Watershed Development Programs. In both cases, the panchayats were seen by the state as systems where planning skills were missing, and proper monitoring and accounting procedures were yet to be established and hence accountability could not be ascertained.

We could consider panchayati raj to have come of age as an institution of local self government only when the panchayats possess both the institutional mechanisms as well as the political influence to be able to demand and handle such responsibilities. The latter, however, is a function of multiple factors among which unfinished land reforms remains a major constraint. The present effort at decentralization through panchayats has to function within these given limits.

References

Dubey, S.N. (1990): Organizational Analysis of *Panchayati Raj* Institutions in India. In S.L. Verma (ed.). *Panchayati Raj, Gram Swaraj and Federal Polity.* Jaipur: Rawat Publications.

Jena, A.C. (1995): Panchayati Raj and Development: Analysis of Structural Features of Gujarat, West Bengal, Karnataka and Andhra Pradesh. *VIKALP*, 4(2): 29.

Mathew, G. (1994): Introduction. In *Status of Panchayati Raj in the States of India 1994.* New Delhi: Institute of Social Sciences.

Shukla, K.B. (1990): Panchayati Raj Revisited. In S.L. Verma (ed.). *Panchayati Raj, Gram Swaraj and Federal Polity.* Jaipur: Rawat Publications.

22

An Assessment of the Effectiveness of Decentralization of Health Services in Sri Lanka

Nimal Attanayake

Introduction

Decentralization policies are one form of "structural adjustment" advocated by international and bilateral donors and have become an integral component of health sector reform packages (Cassels 1995; Zwi and Mills 1995). However, decentralization is still a new policy measure for the South Asian region; only Sri Lanka has implemented decentralization as a national policy. This chapter examines the experience of decentralization in the health sector in Sri Lanka. It begins with a description of the implementation of decentralization and then examines changes in health care service, financing, and provision, before and after implementation of decentralization. Thereafter, it assesses the effectiveness of decentralization on the basis of well-accepted HSR objectives, with particular emphasis on accessibility and equity.

Decentralization—Policy Content

In Sri Lanka the present system of decentralization of management and administration of public health services was initiated in 1987 following the 13th Amendment to the Constitution. This Amendment devolved responsibility for a set of functions including health to elected provincial councils

The author thanks Steven Russell of the Health Policy Unit, London School of Hygiene and Tropical Medicine, for his valuable comments on an earlier draft of this chapter.

(PCs). According to the Ninth Schedule of the Amendment, Provincial Ministries of Health were to have the following roles:

1. establishment and maintenance of hospitals and dispensaries other than teaching and specialist hospitals (e.g., cancer hospital);
2. provision of public health services, health education, nutrition, family health, maternal and child health services, food and food sanitation, and environmental health;
3. formulation and implementation of health development plans and the annual health plan for the province;
4. provision of supplies, except procurement of drugs, for all medical facilities managed by the PCs; and
5. awarding post-graduate scholarships to the personnel attached to the medical facilities under the PCs. These personnel would be employed within the country (Government of Sri Lanka 1987).

A second round of decentralization in 1992 transferred administrative functions of the government downward from the district to the subdistrict (divisional) level (i.e., deconcentration). All public services including health, education, etc., were brought under divisional secretariats and the administration and management of provincial health services, both curative and preventive, were assigned to Divisional Directors of Health Services (DDHS). Vertical programs such as the Anti-Malaria Campaign were abolished in the late eighties and were brought under DDHSs. All the DDHSs in a district were made directly accountable to the Deputy Provincial Director of Health Services (DPDHS), the chief authoritative officer at the district level. The Provincial Director of Health Services (PDHS) overlooks all activities in the province.

The content of decentralization therefore took two forms: (*i*) devolution of power to PCs and in theory, to PDHSs; (*ii*) deconcentration of administration within the provinces to DDHSs. The 10-year span for which these processes have been operational is time enough to assess how far devolution and deconcentration have been able to achieve their prime objectives.

Roots of Decentralization

The roots of decentralization in Sri Lanka go back to two decades. In 1974, a decentralized budgeting (DB) system was introduced along with the setting up of district political authorities (DPA) in 1973. A well accepted aim of decentralization, namely, to bring the government nearer to the people and to encourage community involvement (Mills 1994) was invoked, mainly by politicians to justify those policy measures. In practice, however, both DB and DPAs became political instruments of the governing party, with one of its Members of Parliament (MP) heading the DPA. With the change in government in 1977, DPAs were replaced by district development councils (DDC), with the appointment of a district minister to each of them by the President. In the health sector, 13 functions were deconcentrated to DDCs. Similar to DPA, DDCs too became center-governed apparatuses. Only a very few functions were handed over to the DDCs. Most of the district-level administrators including those in the health sector functioned under direct control of the respective line ministries. Cassels has pointed that as a component of HSR, decentralization can be placed within a framework of fundamental and purposive changes designed to achieve broad health policy objectives (Cassels 1995). Clearly, that was not the case in the earlier period of decentralization in Sri Lanka. Those attempts were largely focused on strengthening the center's hold at the district level (Russel et al. 1996).

In the present context, decentralization is largely a political maneuver under external pressure to devolve power to the provinces as a remedial measure to the ethnic conflict, rather than a deliberate attempt to reform the organizational structure of public services (Russel et al. 1996). The 13th Amendment can be viewed as an attempt to formulate a new social contract for power sharing between the Sinhalese majority and Tamil minority and for greater power sharing between the center and periphery (Coomaraswamy 1994). Irrespective of the organizational and management system introduced under the decentralization policy, its main objectives were clearly political and not economic or managerial.

Decentralization in Practice: Emerging Organizational Arrangements

The success of the implementation of decentralization critically depends on improving planning, management, and organizational systems and of skills at provincial level and within other deconcentrated bodies such as DPDHSs and DDHSs. Mills has brought up this issue in highlighting practical difficulties of decentralization: the need for management skills in a large number of small units; new roles and skill requirements at the center and the difficulties of interacting with a large number of local units, and difficulties in organizing services that can be provided efficiently only for a reasonably large population (Mills 1994). Setting up of such a complex administrative framework would naturally lead to increase administrative costs at provincial levels. However, this may be outweighted by greater service efficiency resulting from improved planning, monitoring, and management systems within a decentralized structure.

With respect to the question of capacity at subnational levels, interviews with a few PDHSs revealed that annual planning at provincial levels is undertaken as a routine exercise. No provincial health department (PHD) has an approved cadre for a medically qualified planning officer. The planning officers recruited from the planning service are normally engaged in routine data collection. District plans are based on the routinely prepared requests made by DDHSs and the provincial plan normally takes the form of an aggregation of district plans. In fact, the PHDs do not seem to have human resources to follow up basic steps of planning, such as situation analysis, need assessment, and appraisal in formulating their annual plans. The responsibility of planning as well as improving capacity of planning are still in the hands of the line ministry. With such poor planning practices and capacities, PCs seem to be far away from achieving other objectives of decentralization such as responsiveness to users, accountability, and equity.

At the divisional level, DDHSs appear to lack not only the skills of annual planning, but also staff for general administrative tasks transferred to them. For instance, there was a great reluctance from some of the DDHSs in the central province to undertake salary payments for the employees of the division.

This was largely due to the lack of staff to handle such payments. Thus, the PDHS was forced to get that responsibility back to the PDH—a centralization process within the province. Such a tendency can be observed for tender procedures as well. Some PDH officials are reluctant to transfer responsibility for selecting contractors for certain services such as raw-food provision to hospitals. Even if the actual values of some contracts are within the limit of DPDHSs, tender decisions are taken at the provincial level by making the estimated cost of the contract a little above the limit of DPDHSs (Russel and Attanayake 1997). In other words, officially deconcentrated functions are actually becoming more concentrated at the provincial level. According to the views of provincial level officials, lack of capacity at subprovincial levels and therefore their reluctance in transferring responsibilities to those officials are the underlying reasons for this tendency.

Whilst lack of skills in planning, management, and organization has hindered achievement of the objectives of a typical decentralized system, transference of authority to the subnational units before they had the capacity to perform new tasks has been detrimental to the implementation of the decentralization process and to some extent has encouraged counter-reaction of re-centralization towards the national Ministry of Health (MoH). With these weaknesses in general, health sector decentralization in Sri Lanka has taken a form which looks more like a deconcentrated structure than a devolved one (Russel et al. 1996). Moving further, the authors make a comparison between an ideal system of devolved power with the actual situation in Sri Lanka (see Figure 22.1). Even though some authority should be given to provincial authorities for health policy development, in practice, no such authority has been given. Similarly PCs are given only limited authority for human resource management, whereas an ideal type would have extensive authority for that function.

PCs have not been given any authority for capital budgeting. On the other hand, to carry out the functions of annual planning and resource allocation, mid-term planning, and recurrent budgeting more effectively, most of the PCs have been given some authority. At the DDHS levels, no authority is given for any of

Table 22.1
Degrees of Decentralization to Different Bodies according to Health Management Functions

Function	*Level of Authority Given to:*			
	Devolved Provincial Department of Health		*Deconcentrated Divisional Directorate of Health Services*	
	Ideal type	*In practice*	*Ideal type*	*In practice*
Health policy development	++	0	0	0
Human resource management (power to hire and fire)	+++	+	+	0
Annual planning & resource allocation	+++	++	++	+
Mid-term planning	+++	++	+	0
Recurrent expenditure	+++	++	++	0
Capital expenditure	+++	0	+	0
Inter-sectoral collaboration	++++	++++	+++	++
Staff and facility supervision and monitoring	+++	+++	+++	+++

Source: Russell et al. 1996.

Key: ++++ full authority; +++ extensive authority; ++ some authority; + limited authority; 0 no authority.

these functions except limited authority for annual planning and resource allocation.

Effectiveness: Equity and Quality

In principle, the potential benefits of decentralization include greater management authority and flexibility to respond to local needs and weaknesses, greater responsiveness to service users, and therefore more efficient and accountable use of resources (Mills et al. 1990). Some indicators that reflect improvements in efficiency, responsiveness, accountability, quality, and equity could therefore be the analytical tools in assessing the effectiveness of decentralization. However, the critical question in the Sri Lankan context is the scarcity of data and reliable indicators. This section will attempt to address some of these issues given these limitations. Further, a question arises as to whether it is reasonable to assess effectiveness of the decentralized health sector in Sri Lanka, which was clearly a politically motivated one, on the basis of technical criteria such as efficiency and equity? But that should not necessarily hinder an analysis of the decentralization process from an economic point of view since it could identify factors which obstructed successful implementation of decentralization.

With this background and limited decentralization in practice, this section will begin with examining whether there was any improvement in equity with respect to the allocation of resources across provinces. To some extent, availability of resources indicates the level of quality as well. Therefore, the second half of this section, for illustrative purpose, sets out the trends of some indicators related to the provision of services across provinces with particular emphasis on primary health care.

As noted above, whilst capital budgeting is done by the MoH in consultation with the Finance and Planning Ministry, the Finance Commission makes allocations for recurrent expenditure. A large part of those recurrent allocations are based on a criterion which reflects socio-economic status and infrastructural facilities in the respective province. Matching grants are based on revenue generation within the province, and a relatively small

Table 22.2
Resource Allocation Patterns on Health across Provinces in 1995 (in Rs)

Province	*Provincial Health Expenditure*		*Provincial Health Expenditure and Recurrent Expenditure of the Hospitals Handled by the Line Ministry*	
	Total (in million)	*Per capita*	*Total (in million)*	*Per capita*
North-Central	467	439	467	439
Uva	336	298	336	298
North-Western	554	263	554	263
Central	513	217	890	377
Southern	461	199	690	299
North-Eastern	466	177	645	245
Western	687	148	2,695	579
Total	3,484	214 (avg.)	6,277	386 (avg.)

Source: Finance Commission, Offices of the Provincial Directors of Health Services, Ministry of Health, Colombo. Quest 1996.

grant called "block grant" is allocated on the basis of identified specific needs of the province.

In 1995, the North-Central Province received the highest per capita allocation of Rs 439 (Quest 1996).[1] Once recurrent expenditure of the hospitals managed by the MoH are added to provincial totals,[2] except Central and North-Central provinces, others received substantially low per capita allocations, i.e., Rs 579, compared to the Western Province—the most urbanized province where the capital city is located. Western Province absorbed almost 43 percent of the total resources. Compared to Western Province, whilst per capita allocation to Uwa and Southern Provinces was

[1] The highest allocation to the North-Central Province is primarily due to the large amounts of additional inputs to its provincial hospital (Anuradhapura), which serves injured army personnel as it is the closest tertiary-level public hospital to the war zone. In 1995, total recurrent expenditure of this hospital stood at about Rs 135 million which was indeed the highest for any hospital outside the Western Province (Quest 1996).

[2] No data are readily available on provincial distribution of capital expenditure handled by the MoH.

almost a half, both North-Eastern and North-Western Provinces received even less than a half[3] (see Table 22.2).

Provincial disparities can be further examined with respect to the availability of and hence access to and quality of services. Three indicators were used for this comparison and are presented in Table 22.3. Whilst the first indicator—number of MOs per 10,000 population (MOPOP)—indicates the availability and quality of general health services, the other two indicators—number of AMOs[4] per 10,000 population (AMOPOP) and number of public health midwives per 3,000 population (PHMPOP)—indicate the same for primary health care. Since there was a tendency to concentrate most of the resources in Western Province, for the first indicator an alternative measurement of dispersion was estimated in which the central point of dispersion was taken as its value for the Western Province, rather than the national average—an indicator of the level of variation of the ratio from the most urbanized province.

First, the indicator of doctors has increased marginally in its value from 1.18 in 1982 to 1.19 in 1987; the coefficient of variation (CV) with respect to the national average as well as the dispersion from Western Province has substantially increased. During this pre-decentralization period only three provinces (i.e., Western, Southern, and North-West) have recorded positive growth rates of MOPOP ratio. During the first 10 years of decentralization, however, this ratio had more than doubled by moving up to 2.44. Compared to the growth rate of 0.2 from 1982–87, during the decentralization period it recorded a substantially

[3] With the available data, no comparison can be made with the pre-decentralization period, in which MoH followed a planning programing budgeting system. Allocations as well as actual expenditure were classified by programs, projects and categories. For instance, all district hospitals were classified as one project. But no reclassification was done by district. Under decentralization, although allocations and actual expenditure records are available for provinces only for the past few years, no attempt has so far been successfully made to classify them by programs and projects. Total expenditure is classified into categories, such as wages and salaries, and drugs. This hinders any analysis of allocation pattern with respect to service components, such as curative and preventive care. Lack of capacity at provincial level, namely shortages of trained staff, is the main reason for this poor system of recording of expenditure.

[4] AMOs are not medical graduates. But they have a formal training in medicine, especially for primary-level care.

Table 22.3

Some Indicators of Variations in the Distribution of Medical/Assistant Medical Officers and Public Health Midwives with respect to Populations across Provinces from 1982 to 1996

Province/ Districts	*MOPOP*					*AMOPOP*					*PIIMPOP*				
	1982	*1987*	*1996*	*GRI*	*GRII*	*1982*	*1987*	*1996*	*GRI*	*GRII*	*1982*	*1987*	*1996*	*GRI*	*GRII*
Western	1.99	2.27	4.56	2.7	11.2	0.37	0.39	0.52	1.1	3.9	0.39	0.50	0.56	5.8	1.5
Central	1.36	1.27	3.09	–1.2	15.8	0.44	0.68	0.96	11.0	4.6	0.47	0.55	0.69	3.4	2.6
Southern	0.59	0.84	1.96	8.4	14.9	0.52	0.51	0.72	–0.4	4.6	0.50	0.56	0.96	2.0	8.1
North-East	1.05	0.80	0.99	–4.6	2.7	0.76	0.91	0.86	3.9	–1.6	0.38	0.37	0.39	–0.2	0.5
North-West	0.68	0.64	1.56	1.1	15.8	0.76	0.73	1.05	–0.7	1.9	0.57	0.66	0.72	3.3	1.0
North-Central	1.11	0.69	1.76	–7.6	17.4	1.16	0.79	0.85	–6.3	3.6	0.44	0.81	1.03	16.6	3.0
Uwa	0.79	0.60	1.18	–4.8	10.9	0.66	0.81	0.81	4.4	0.6	0.34	0.66	0.94	18.8	4.7
Sabaragamuwa	0.86	0.70	1.40	–3.8	11.3	0.56	0.57	1.00	0.2	4.8	0.64	0.69	0.92	1.1	3.8
Matale & Polonnaruwa	0.57	0.73	1.77	5.5	15.8	0.67	0.72	1.00	1.5	4.4	0.36	0.68	0.93	18.0	4.1
Average	1.18	1.19	2.44	0.2	11.7	0.58	0.62	0.76	1.6	2.4	0.45	0.56	0.71	4.8	3.0

(Contd.)

(Contd.)

Province/ Districts	*MOPOP*					*AMOPOP*					*PHMPOP*				
	1982	*1987*	*1996*	*GRI*	*GRII*	*1982*	*1987*	*1996*	*GRI*	*GRII*	*1982*	*1987*	*1996*	*GRI*	*GRII*
Standard deviation	0.43	0.50	1.06			0.22	0.15	0.15			0.10	0.12	0.20		
Coefficient of variation	0.36	0.42	0.43			0.38	0.25	0.20			0.21	0.22	0.28		
Standard deviation from Western Province	1.08	1.41	2.74												

Source: *Annual Helath Bulletin*, Medical Statistics Unit, Ministry of Health Colombo.
MOPOP = number of medical officers per 10,000 population.
AMOPOP = number of assistant medical officers per 10,000 population.
PHMPOP = number of public health midwives per 3,000 population.
GRI = annual average growth rate, 1982–87.
GRII = annual average growth rate, 1987–96.

high rate of 11.7. All provinces have recorded positive growth rates: five provinces and the two combined districts have experienced growth rates substantially higher than the Western Province. For instance, growth rate of North-Central Province (17.4) is higher than the Western Province by more than 50 percent (11.2). Whilst CV has marginally increased up to 0.43, the relatively high increase in the standard deviation from Western Province up to 2.74 indeed does not indicate a worsening of disparities but inequality in relatively high growth rates across provinces.

The scenario of public health midwives (PHMs) is very much different in that the number of PHMs per 3,000 population (PHMPOP) has recorded annual average growth rates of 4.8 and 3.0 for the periods before and after decentralization, respectively. This ratio has sharply increased from 0.36 in 1982 to 0.68 and 0.93 in 1987 and 1996, respectively. By 1996, whilst North-Central Province has reached the standard norm of the availability of PHMs, some others have moved much closer to it, i.e., Southern (0.96), Uwa (0.94), and Sabaragamuwa (0.92). The observed increases in the CV and standard deviation in this ratio could be due to a lack of any uniformity in its growth rates across provinces. For instance, whilst North-East and Sabaragamuwa Provinces have recorded average annual growth rate, 1982–87 (GRIs) of just –0.2 and 1.1, respectively, it was 18.8 for the Uwa Province. Similar differences can be observed for annual average growth rate, 1987–96 (GRII) as well. Yet the movement of this indicator to the standard norm in many provinces has traded off those low growth rates extensively. In general, these appreciably high growth rates of the accessibility to primary health workers in almost all provinces both before and after decentralization indicate the firm commitment of the health sector in reaching the targets of primary health care. The slow growth rates of the PHMPOP ratio after decentralization could be due to the organizational and management constraints encountered in moving more closer to the standard norm.

Similar trends can be observed for the changes in the ratios of the number of AMOs per 10,000 population as well. Its national level average has continuously increased in both periods. But the ratio as well as growth rates have recorded with relatively high values during the decentralization period. AMOPOP was

0.58 in 1982 and 0.62 and 0.76 in 1987 and 1996 respectively; GRI was 1.6 and GRII was 2.4. On the other hand, although three provinces have reported negative growth rates before decentralization, only the war-affected North-East Province has such a setback after 1987. Similarly CV has continuously moved down from 0.38 in 1982 to 0.25 and 0.20 in 1987 and 1996, respectively. Quite clearly, all provinces including North-East have recorded relatively high ratios of AMOPOP throughout the period. This indicates once again a substantial increase in the accessibility to primary care particularly in well-deserved provinces.

Concluding Remarks

The decentralization process in Sri Lanka can be largely considered a political maneuver under external pressure, rather than a deliberate attempt to reform the organizational structure of public services. It was a sudden reaction to external pressure. In the health sector, just like in any other public service, changes in the organizational structure of the MoH were imposed from elsewhere. No adequate attempt was made before implementation to assess its technical, management, and organizational feasibility. Even after a decade, it can be clearly observed to be partially implemented. Neither central-level administrators nor politicians had the motivation to accelerate the decentralization process. In fact, the MoH appeared to be quite resistant to such changes (Russel et al. 1996). For example, allocation as well as administration of some vital inputs such as capital resources and manpower are still in the hands of central agencies. Delegation and devolution have not been implemented to an adequate level for the subnational agencies to carry out their functions smoothly. No concrete measures have so far been taken to delegate responsibility for defined functions to relatively autonomous organizations. At the divisional level, political and administrative bodies are still apart, which makes an assessment of the effectiveness of decentralization extremely difficult. On the other hand, as a result of the partial implementation of decentralization, a tendency has developed among provincial authorities to put more pressure on central authorities for more autonomy. Thus, undertaking measures towards proper implementation of decentralization itself has become a necessity and a formidable challenge to the national government.

Implementation of decentralization is further aggravated due to the lack of capacity at all subnational units to carry out devolved functions. The MoH too appears to be lacking capacity to effectively play its role under the new system. A hidden tendency towards centralization seems to be taking place at the MoH level. All provincial hospitals, except two are now directly handled by the MoH. Two provincial hospitals were absorbed by the line ministry very recently, making them marginally involved in teaching activities. Interference by the center, for political motives, on peripheral level activities was very common in the recent past; in that, several lower-level hospitals were upgraded to the next grade without providing necessary additional resources including manpower. On the other hand, due to lack of capacity at divisional and secondary hospital levels, there seems to be a centralization tendency at the provincial level as well. Even though the provinces have displayed some improvements in upgrading their capacities with the assistance of the center, particularly in planning and management, they still have a long way to go in successfully carrying out their devolved functions.

Decentralization appears to be responsible for easing out provincial disparities in resource allocation, access to care and quality of care, etc., particularly with respect to primary health care package. Even though a similar tendency could be observed before 1987 especially for PHMs due to the country's firm commitment to primary health care approach, this tendency appears to have accelerated during the decentralization period. In fact, easing out of provincial disparities with respect to the distribution of the manpower directly involved in primary health care was much higher than the other manpower categories and medical inputs (Attanayake 1997).

Gradual restructuring of the whole health system, with due recognition given to provincial autonomy and formulation and implementation of a strategy for strengthening capacity at provincial, divisional, institutional, and program levels, are critical issues for the success of decentralization. This raises the critical question of the capacity of the MoH too to perform its role as the central agency of improving managerial, organizational, and planning skills of all subnational bodies.

Finally, decentralization in Sri Lanka largely represents a non-purposive direction of change in the provision of health services as a result of a broader political process. Only now is some discussion taking place in policy forums (e.g., presidential task for the implementation of national health policy) to relaunch the decentralization process in the form of a purposive and fundamental change in the organizational and management system of the health sector.

References

Attanayake, N. (1997): Sri Lankan Health Sector: Policy Perspectives and Reforms. *Economic Review*, 23(3): 2–6.

Cassels, A. (1995): Health Sector Reform: Key Issues in Less Developed Countries. *Journal of International Development*, 7(3): 329–48.

Coomaraswamy, R. (1994): Devolution, the Law, and Judicial Construction. In S. Bastian (ed.). *Devolution and Development in Sri Lanka*. International Centre for Ethnic Studies, Colombo. Delhi: Konark Publishers.

Government of Sri Lanka (1987): *Thirteenth Amendment to the Constitution*. Colombo: Government Press.

Mills, A. (1994): Decentralization and Accountability in the Health Sector from an International Perspective: What are the Choices? *Public Administration and Development*, 14: 281–92.

Mills, A., Vaughan, J.P., Smith, D.L., and **Tabibazadeh, I.** (1990): *Health System Decentralisation: Concepts, Issues and Country Experience*. Geneva: WHO.

Quest, U. (1996): A Study on Financing of Social Services Project, Sri Lanka: Health & Population Sector. Study undertaken for the Asian Development Bank, Manila.

Russell, S., and **Attanayake, N.** (1997): *Sri Lanka—Reforming the Health Sector: Does Government have the Capacity? The Role of Government in Adjusting Economies*. Paper 14, Development Administration Group, The University of Birmingham.

Russell, S., Wijeratne, K., Abayaselera, G., and **Perera, M.A.L.R.** (1996): *Sri Lanka: Decentralization and Health Systems Change*. Ministry of Health, Sri Lanka. Division of Strengthening of Health Services, Geneva: WHO.

Zwi, A.B., and **Mills, A.** (1995): Health Policy in Less Developed Countries: Past Trends and Future Directions. *Journal of International Development*, 7(3): 299–328.

23

People's Health Care Initiatives in Chhattisgarh District, Madhya Pradesh

Binayak Sen

Most attempts to address the problem of health care within the context of globalization seem to take for granted the legitimacy of the state as an agent of welfare. Such attempts mostly have either an analytical or an exhortatory character. In other words, they either tell us where we are or where we should be, but very little about how to get there. This is only natural because in our view, there are insurmountable structural constraints to state intervention in health. On the other hand, we certainly do not advocate any form of privatization as a solution.

Community-based approaches, which are linked to people's movements to control livelihoods, have access to natural resources, open up important cultural and political spaces and provide an alternative approach by which this problem can be addressed.

A series of health care initiatives has been effected over the last 15 years in the context of the Chhattisgarh People's Movement. This is the most significant example of sustained activity in the field of health that has been initiated and carried out by a people's organization. As such it holds important lessons for the future of a community-based health care approach.

The Dalli Rajhara Experience

In 1977, the Chhattisgarh Mines Shramik Sangh (CMSS) was formed in Dalli Rajhara among the mine workers working in a very large iron-ore mine in Durg district, in eastern Madhya Pradesh. This area is also called Chhattisgarh and its people are known Chhattisgarhis. These people have a long history of oppression and resistance. Under the leadership of Shankar Guha Niyogi, the CMSS undertook a long and heroic struggle against social and cultural oppression in the workplace in the existing trade unions as well as in their homes. Their just demands for fair wages and working conditions were met with severe state repression, including police firing.

Niyogi was a political worker with a long experience of participation in people's struggles in Chhattisgarh. In the course of his work he had developed certain definite ideas about the mutually supportive interaction between people's struggles and community-based development activity. The objective conditions in Dalli Rajhara also favored such a conjunction. The Chhattisgarhi workers lived in distinct colonies called *dafais* which had no infrastructural or health facilities. This was in marked contrast to the infinitely better favored colonies of the regular workers of the Bhilai Steel Plant (BSP), which owned the mines. The struggles at the workplace found their logical extension in organized efforts to improve life in the *dafais*. These efforts included campaigns against alcohol, for primary education, and a health program.

The immediate impetus for initiating the health program was the death of Kusumbai, one of the popular leaders of the movement, at childbirth. Public sentiment was therefore committed to building an appropriate clinical facility that people would find accessible and friendly. The Shaheed Hospital began to take shape around 1981 and today has 80 beds, with a medical laboratory, an operation theatre, and an X-ray machine. The entire unit has been financed by the organization.

In the first few years, hospital assets were acquired from contributions made by the mine workers. Although the fee structure was kept extremely modest to enable poor people to access its services, still there was enough money left over to finance a steady train of asset acquisition.

Since many of the activities that could be classified under preventive and promotive health care—such as the struggle for safe drinking water, the campaign against liquor sales, and alcohol abuse—were being directly undertaken by the organization, my medical colleagues and I were able to concentrate on building an alternative, culturally acceptable paradigm of clinical care. The operative details of this paradigm were:

1. An overall emphasis on rational practices in health care, with special efforts at making the rational basis of our practice accessible to all users.

2. Demystification of technology, with maximum possible decentralization of all technical procedures.
3. Constant attempts to minimize the distinction between mental and manual labor.
4. Democratization of all decision-making processes.

These points are elaborated upon below.

1. *Accessible rationality*

We tried very hard to subject all our practices to rational scrutiny. We also tried our best to involve patients and their relatives in sharing our perceptions of the scientific and rational contents of our efforts. Significant time was devoted to explaining procedures and therapies. This was more than an attempt to rid health technology of its magical trappings. Proletarians need dignity before they need bread and this was an attempt to bring about an atmosphere in which people could become the subjects and not the objects of a healing enterprise.

2. *Decentralization of technology*

From the beginning, Shaheed Hospital was fortunate to have a group of health volunteers from among the mine workers who while continuing their work in the mines, devoted three to four hours every evening to the hospital and participated in its management. While initially they were very apprehensive about their capabilities, over time they became highly skilled at nursing, dressing, and operation-theatre work. Gradually, they also took over the entire range of management functions in the hospital including accounts. All the para-medical and nursing workers have been trained in the hospital itself. Some of them have had very little formal education.

3. *Minimizing the distinction between mental and manual labor*

From the beginning, we believed that the emphasis in modern medicine on esoteric knowledge serves as the ideological justification for an enormous stratification of position and rewards, both within the profession and with reference to society at large. In Shaheed Hospital, we tried to incorporate a model of science in which manual and mental skills were given equal importance and in which the entire range of workers was able to participate. Differentials in financial rewards were kept as low as possible.

4. *Democratic decision-making*

Management decisions were taken at the Shaheed Hospital at weekly meetings attended by the entire staff. Decisions were taken by consensus after discussions. Policy issues were referred to the parent organization.

Extension of the Dalli Work

The experience gained at Dalli Rajhara served as the basis for a series of health initiatives. Health exhibitions at local fairs and at public meetings of the organization, which had by now evolved into the Chhattisgarh Mukti Morcha (CMM), became a regular feature. These exhibitions incorporated poster displays, an extremely attractive "magic show" designed to promote rational thinking on matters of health and disease, and songs and skits. A series of pamphlets on basic health issues, produced by Shaheed Hospital and sold at a nominal price, became extremely popular. Topics covered in this series included: fevers, blood transfusions, injections versus tablets, the dangers of pitocin injections at delivery, and rational drug therapy.

With the extension of the political work of the CMM to adjacent districts, satellite units of the Shaheed Hospital were established in Bhilai, Kumhari, and Urla. Initially, these were run by people from Dalli Rajhara. The Urla unit is now in the process of developing into an independent health program.

However, the largely clinic-based services, developed as part of the Shaheed Hospital initiative, were not able to surmount an inherent limitation. A decentralized, community-based primary health care program could not be established due to the dominance of the clinical component of the service. For the same reason, the model was never able to overcome its dependence on a small group of highly skilled, motivated, and selfless technical personnel. It remained necessary to make further efforts to broaden the base and democratize the initiative.

The experiences of "development" of the CMM gave rise to a slogan "Sangharsh ke liye Nirman, Nirman ke liye Sangharsh" (Struggle to further development, and development to further the struggle). Rupantar, a non-governmental organization which began work in Raipur in 1989, tried to extend this philosophy to areas outside the ambit of the trade union-based parent organization. The health programs of Rupantar are carried out in the Nagri Sihawa block in the southern part of Raipur district. This area has a long history of struggle amongst the people displaced by the dams in the upper Mahanadi catchment area. Health services of any kind were practically non-existent until Rupantar began work in the area.

Rupantar's work has consisted of allying with existing organizations, training, deploying, and monitoring the work of community health workers in 20 villages, and providing referral back-up services for these workers. Rupantar has set up a basic medical laboratory with a full-time lab technician, which can be accessed by the health workers. The senior health workers who have been with the program for about five years function at an extremely high level of competence. Routine cases include *falciparum* malaria, sputum positive tuberculosis, lower respiratory tract infections in young children, diarrhea, malnutrition, and antenatal care. Through these means, Rupantar has tried to extend the Shaheed Hospital experience in terms of decentralized access and control and shift the locus of technological and social control from the hospital directly into the community.

There are some other dimensions to the community activities of Rupantar in this sector. The Nagri Sihawa area is covered under the Sixth Schedule of the Constitution and the "Extension of Panchayati Raj to Scheduled Areas Act" came into effect here from December 1997. These constitutional changes that have been brought about over the last few years give decision-making powers with regard to service activities and the management of certain natural resources to the general body of adult village residents, namely the gram sabha. Future development in health services will have to take account of structures and processes within this new dispensation. We believe that Rupantar's approach opens up significant possibilities in this regard. Rupantar's activities so far have been mediated through external resource inputs. We are actively searching for ways whereby political decentralization can come together with economic decentralization and this work can be financed through surpluses generated through community-based production.

People's movements do not substantially alter the social metabolism of capital. However, they do create a space within which, however temporarily or partially, the constitutive cells of a socialist hegemonic alternative can be created. Recent technological developments in health care and information technology, leading to the possibility of the application of decentralized algorithms and technical tools and skill application modules make it possible to create scientifically relevant, epidemiologically sound, and culturally challenging alternatives in this area.

Part V

Perspectives of Clinicians

The recent influx of new technology and new approaches in medicine may not represent a paradigm shift based on substantive clinical evidence but may be an ideological imposition grounded in a particular economic thinking. These include the recent changes in the strategy of tuberculosis control, the use of new drugs in the treatment of malaria, or the dumping of irrational drugs in the market. On the other hand, clinicians are also recognizing the linkage between recent societal changes and the resurgence of diseases. This forces them to underline the strength of classical ways of dealing with disease. At the same time, while searching for alternative ways of public health practice, practitioners could become increasingly vulnerable to the new strategies being propagated. This section includes the reflections and opinions of clinicians and practitioners as they encounter the changes in technology or the fading away of established forms of primary health care delivery systems. This represents the meeting point of medical knowledge and society. The chapters included in this section serve as a caveat to those who have unbridled faith in the new technologies.

Anurag Bhargav, in his chapter, discusses issues related to the implementation of the program in terms of the contradiction between patient-centered and program-centered strategies. The chapter states that patients are not given central importance in the program. Anand Zachariah argues that the resurgence of specific diseases is related to social, economic, political, demographic, and ecological changes. By examining the experience with malaria and cholera, the chapter illustrates that the epidemiology of these two diseases has changed in the post-Structural Adjustment Period due to widening socio-economic differences, unplanned urbanization, and lack of investment in the basic infrastructure, such as safe water supply and sanitation. Yogesh Jain, in his chapter, questions the cafeteria approach to antimalarial therapy. The chapter states that given the inadequate understanding of chloroquine and quinine resistance in the country, the introduction of new drugs such as mefloquine and artemisinin in the open market is irrational. Anant R. Phadke contradicts the assumptions regarding the efficiency of the private sector with respect to pharmaceuticals. A study conducted in Satara district of the state of Maharashtra in India shows that the use of medicines in the private sector was more irrational and more wasteful. Shyam Ashtekar's chapter emphasizes the need to develop a rational curative package in the PHC system, which so far has been neglected due to an inherent bias against less trained healers. It proposes an alternative community health worker scheme, operationally managed by the people, who will also make a small financial contribution, but supported largely by the state.

24

Prescribing Practices: A Comparison of Public and Private Sectors

Anant R. Phadke

One of the assumptions of the Structural Adjustment Program is that the private sector is more efficient than the public sector. There is also a widespread feeling that the existing resource-development is quite inadequate to meet even the basic needs of the Indian population and hence there is no alternative (TINA–syndrome) to a sea-change in the developmental strategy. The findings of our study of "supply and use of pharmaceuticals in the Satara district," Maharashtra, contradict these assumptions in case of the pharmaceuticals.

Poorer Prescriptions, More Wastage in the Private Sector

In this study, our pharmacist investigators sat with the doctors for a day and noted down the symptoms/diagnosis and the prescription for each patient. A representative sample of 3,882 prescriptions from 30 public and 19 private outpatient clinics from different parts of the Satara district was collected by visiting these clinics thrice a year (once each in summer, monsoon, and winter). With the help of specially prepared prescription analysis guidelines and scoring system, these prescriptions of doctors with varying educational qualifications were analyzed and given marks. As seen in Table 24.1, the performance of doctors in the private sector was worse than that of public sector doctors with respect to all parameters of drug use (Phadke 1996).

We found that the use of medicines in the private sector is more irrational and more wasteful. To study this wastage, we took a 10 percent systematic random subsample of prescriptions from

Table 24.1
Prescription Analysis of Doctors in Satara District

Level of Rationality of Prescriptions
Sector-wise and Area-wise Comparison

Sector	*No. of Visits to Clinics*	*Total Cases*	*Grading of Prescriptions*			*Avg. Score (per out of 30)*
			Rational ®	*Semi-rational* (S)	*Irrational* (I)	
Total sector (%)	121	3,582(100)	651(18.2)	1,327(37.0)	1,604(44.8)	14.22(47.3)
Total public sector (%)	59	1,944(100)	424(21.8)	752(38.7)	768(39.5)	16.14(53.8)
Rural public (%)	40	1,234(1,000)	264(21.4)	476(38.6)	494(40.0)	16.22(54.07)
Urban public (%)	7	271(100)	86(31.7)	108(39.9)	77(28.4)	16.34(54.47)
Small towns (%)	12	439(100)	74(16.9)	168(38.3)	197(44.91)	15.76(52.53)
Total private sector (%)	62	1,638(100)	227(13.85)	575(35.10)	836(51)	12.52(45.06)
Rural private (%)	14	371(100)	56(15.1)	138(37.2)	177(47.70)	14.42(48.07)
Urban private (%)	27	726(100)	94(12.9)	256(35.3)	376(51.8)	12.55(41.83)
Small town (%)	21	541(100)	77(14.2)	181(33.5)	283(52.3)	11.36(37.87)

Source: Phadke et al. 1995. All figures in this chapter are from this report.

Table 24.2
Monetary Wastage due to Irrational Prescriptions

Sr. No.	*Private*	*Public*	*Total*
1. No. of prescriptions	68	84	152
2. Cost of doctors' prescriptions per day (in Rs)	467.62	315.67	783.29
3. Cost as per standard prescriptions per day (Rs)	144.09	140.82	284.91
4. Wastage due to irrational prescriptions per day (row 3 minus 1)	323.53	174.85	498.38
5. Wastage as %age of money spent by the patient (row no. 4/2 × 100)	69.19	55.39	63.63
6. Wastage per prescription per day (Rs) (row no. 4/1)	4.76	2.08	3.28

our collection of prescriptions during the summer of 1993. This subsample was subjected to cost-analysis by comparing the cost of these prescriptions with that of the standard prescriptions for these particular ailments. As seen in Table 24.2, the financial wastage due to irrational prescriptions was more in the private sector (Phadke et al. 1995).

Given the lower quality of and higher wastage due to prescriptions in the private sector, a strategy of further privatization as per the SAP would not increase the efficiency of resource-use; on the contrary it would increase the wastage.

Do we Need Rapid Increase in Drug Production?

To find out whether the existing drug supply to Satara district was adequate for primary health care needs, we first estimated the drug supply to this district. From reliable sources (audited accounts of the wholesale suppliers), we estimated the supply to the private sector during 1991–92 to be a minimum of Rs 21.28 crore. In the public sector, it was a mere Rs 0.56 crore as per official data. Thus, the total supply of drugs to Satara district during 1991–92 was Rs 21.84 crore.

As against this actual supply, the estimated total drug need of Satara district during 1991–92 for primary health care was as follows:

1. Drugs for curative/symptomatic care to outpatient level (based on total morbidity load for acute diseases and average standard drug cost for adequate rational medical treatment for each patient excluding tuberculosis and leprosy) : Rs 15.17 crore
2. For all estimated cases of TB and leprosy : Rs 2.97 crore
3. For all indoor cases : Rs 1.78 crore
4. For 100 percent coverage for preventive medication in MCA program for pregnant and

Table 24.3
Availability of Drugs at nine PHCs and three Rural Hospitals in Satara District (1990–92)

Sr. No	*Type of Availability*	*PHCs*		*RHs*	
		No. of Drugs	*Total No. of Drugs (%)*	*No. of Drugs*	*Total No. of Drugs (%)*
1.	AA—always available	0	0	2	1.25%
2.	R—regular (available 76 to 99% of days)	4	2.68%	18	11.32%
3.	I—irregular (available 51 to 75% of days)	10	6.71%	26	16.35%
4.	VI—very irregular (available 25 to 49% of days)	.45	30.02%	60	37.73%
5.	EN—effectively not available (available 1 to 25% of days)	81	54.36%	51	32.07%
6.	NA—not available through the year	9	6.04%	2	1.25%
	Total	149	100.00%	159	100.00%

Note: The data exclude anti-TB drugs and very marginal supplies.

lactating women and children under five years (immunization, iron, calcium, etc.)	Rs 0.67 crore

Total estimated drug cost for primary health care: Rs 20.59 crore.

This exercise shows that the drug supply to Satara district was adequate for primary health care in 1991–92 provided all drugs were to be used rationally. Hence, the argument that we need a very rapid increase in drug production to meet even the basic drug needs, is questionable.

Gross Shortages in the Public Sector

This drug supply study also showed that the drug supply to the public sector is grossly inadequate at the primary health center and rural hospital level as seen from Table 24.3.

Hence any further cutback in the budget on health/medical care at PHC-level as part of SAP would further erode whatever credibility PHCs have as centers for curative/symptomatic care and thereby reduce the people's response to the preventive programs. On the contrary, what is needed is an increase in the drug supply to the public sector. We estimated that the drug supply to the representative sample of nine out 69 PHCs in Satara district was an average of Rs 39,496 during 1991–92, whereas the average drug needs of these PHCs, if they were to rationally and adequately cater to all the patients coming to the PHCs, was Rs 67,660 per PHC.

Thus, there was a shortfall of Rs 30,526 per PHC, which was only 8.41 percent of the annual recurring expenditure per PHC during 1991–92. With this increase in drug expenditure for PHCs, at least all patients coming to PHCs can be adequately treated.

The results of our study contradict the rationale of privatization of medical care, from the viewpoint of adequate, rational drug treatment of the population.

References

Phadke, A.R. (1996): The Quality of Prescribing in an Indian District. *The National Medical Journal of India*, 9(2): 60–65.

Phadke, A.R., Fernandes, A., Sharda, L., Mane, P., and **Jesani, A.** (1995): *A Study of Supply and Use of Pharmaceuticals in Satara District*. Pune: Foundation for Research in Community Health.

25

Revisiting the Community Health Worker

Shyam Ashtekar

Some years back I met a community health worker (CHW) in a remote Himalayan village. When asked about the CHW scheme, he narrated the woes of the scheme that the government was quietly winding up. Whatever may be the difficulties of the government in continuing it, it was a dire need for the villagers. In this Himalayan village at least, villagers argued with this man to continue giving them medicines, for which they paid him. It made life easier for them. If CHWs had engaged in activities like bringing down the birth rate, the authorities in Delhi would have continued to support the scheme. For the simple and down-to-earth villagers, the CHW was a person who could give them some medicines and somebody they could approach even at midnight. It was the barest people could have without government support; anything else was a bonus.

However, the CHW could satisfy neither the community which banked on him/her nor the state that wanted the CHW to fulfill its own agenda. As a result, the CHW survives merely as a budget item and amongst non-governmental organizations (NGOs), for whom the CHW runs errands, performing tasks as varied as health work to developmental activities to small savings. The CHW scheme is nobody's baby in the nineties.

If India still needs a CHW program, and it does, a better version will have to replace the old one. What is more, we will have to let people rather than the state take the initiative. Otherwise, the CHW will soon be a part of history and we would have lost a potent option for the primary health care needs of lakhs of villages. In the Indian context, primary health care is inseparably linked with the issue of village health workers. This is so because much of the population lives in villages, of which only a small proportion have resident health services—government or private. The recent effort to revamp the CHW scheme in a large state like Madhya Pradesh is evidence of its indispensable nature.

The Entry and Exit of CHW

Mahatma Gandhi was the first to think of doctors for villages, in the forties. He even thought about training courses for village healers; one such was to start in Wardha, when he was assassinated. This was decades before the advent of the concept of barefoot doctor in China. The latter concept, along with the Alma-Ata Conference stimulated the Indian government to institute village-based health workers. While Gandhi and the Chinese administrators preferred to call their versions of healers as doctors, although with some limiting adjectives, our health policy-makers always referred to them as workers, guides, volunteers—anything but doctors. This points to an inborn bias, something that was to undo the program later. Due credit has never been given to the essential role of the CHW as healer. CHW has been an apology of a healer and this is always writ large on any CHW program in India, be it in the state or in the voluntary sector.

Whatever the defects of the CHW scheme of 1978, it was a departure from the earlier model of services. However, the program had nearly died out by the mid-eighties. Changing names, departments, and budget heads, cutting off medicine supplies, paltry honoraria, poor training, and overall apathy were responsible for the CHW program not gaining foothold on the Indian soil. These are features that are characteristic of the general services too.

The services offered by the subcenter health staff (male and female para-medical) are nowhere near comprehensive. They mostly include immunizations, distribution of contraceptives, and some medicines for select illnesses like malaria and diarrhea. Access/outreach problems make even these scant services barring immunization available only to a third of the subcenter population. The mobile staff of subcenters can barely serve the daily needs of villagers. Home deliveries by untrained hands or neighbors still top the maternity statistics despite decades of midwifery program. On the one hand, international agencies continue to fund newer and newer programs on safe childbirth services, such as

Child Survival and Safe Motherhood (CSSM) and reproductive health programs; on the other, village people continue to depend on the poor old dai (birth attendant) and neighbors at childbirth and in times of difficulty. Dismal is the word for primary-level care as well as for most other infrastructure facilities, be it primary education, water supply, roads, or communication.

The CHW program did not fail for technical reasons, although this part of the program was quite weak. The failure arose from the way the government handled its investment policies and programs. A major cause of this failure is in the rural–urban dichotomies. Government hospitals in the cities function, albeit badly, as there is some public pressure in cities which is absent in rural hospitals. Rural hospitals are largely dysfunctional. Primary-level health care services in villages are afflicted by a problem, which is of a different order. Over half the para-medical staff does not stay in allotted villages for reasons genuine and not so genuine. The fact that the government collects taxes and pays salaries to the staff is not enough to force them to stay and work in the villages. Unauthorized collection of money is a rule rather than exception, making free service only a theoretical possibility. Increasing allocations does not cure this problem. High costs, wastage, insensitivity, and non-performance are inescapable facts, at least in the present Indian context.

Neglect of Curative Services

An unfortunate aspect of infrastructure development for primary health care is that, unlike in urban areas, in the rural areas the curative component was treated as largely unnecessary. So the need to develop a rational curative package based on the felt needs of the people was, and is always, met with derision. The neglect of curative services has led to a rise in the number of quacks in village clusters, so much so that they occupy the central place in the arena of rural health services. This is so even in the so-called advanced states like Maharashtra. Over three-fourths of sickness episodes are served by private medical practitioners, the majority of whom know little about the illnesses and medicines they are handling everyday. This fact is conveniently ignored by Indian health policy-makers, who advance the argument that curative services in addition to that offered by the national programs are unnecessary or even a luxury. They do not take into account the inadequacy of these services.

Resurrecting CHW

The situation calls for a lateral thinking—expanding the services without increasing government apparatus. CHW scheme was an attempt in this direction. An alternative CHW program has to be based on the following principles:

- Better technical content—curative, preventive, and promotive—which is sensitive to issues of acceptability, availability, and accessibility for all sections of the village community.
- Primarily operated by people's groups—panchayat, *mahila mandals* (women's clubs), youth clubs, cooperatives, etc., or even self-motivated individuals—under the guidance of technical bodies.
- An open school mechanism to train health workers in a step-ladder manner, with all essential elements like qualifying tests, and continuing education.
- A definite role for the CHWs in defining courses, institutional requirements, list of medicines, and procedures as well as in determining supply sources, etc.
- Technical inputs of the best quality must be available for CHWs who would provide basic services in the village. In turn they will be remunerated, either by individual users or the village body. The state should support the training and some of the recurrent costs. Even in the absence of any initiative by the state, it is possible to provide for the very basic needs by a well-thought-out scheme run by the community.
- The technical content of the scheme will depend upon the role that is assigned to the CHWs. Schematically, the role of CHW can be defined by the intersection of two circles, one comprising what people need and want as health services—preventive as well as a dependable element of curative. The second circle is what CHWs can be trained and supported to do. The more we try to match the two circles, the more relevant the CHWs will be. To be more specific, we

need to have good diagnostics, a good bag of cures—modern and traditional—and all reasonable elements of preventive health strategies. Specifying the details is equivalent to naming a book or syllabus. We have made an effort in Maharashtra (Ashtekar 1992); it is an open-ended issue and more can always come into it. For instance, why should we not include the WHO–SEARO list (WHO 1992) of primary health care medicines (35–40 medicines) in the bag of CHWs?

- Let village people run the program rather than the state thrusting it on them. The social management and partial financial support must be entrusted to village communities even if some genuine minds feel guilty about asking people to bear the cost of even such a humble program. The panchayats could play an active role in running the scheme.

Financing CHWs

At present, people are spending sizable amounts of money on sickness episodes. It is usual to carry at least Rs 50 to 100 as expected expenses for average medical encounters. In addition, there are travel (access) costs for at least two persons—the sick and the attendant. These costs can be reduced to one-third at least, if a rational village-based service is available. For example, in this scheme the average episode—say of malaria—will cost people about Rs 10 to 15. If government supplies the antimalarial as part of the NMEP, it will cost still less (only service charges). Other than medicines, however, there are recurring expenses, such as cost of materials, procedures, and remuneration for the personnel, which need to be mobilized. In addition, training of CHWs, supervision, and technical support are also required. These constitute the capital costs. Materials and procedures are thus the remaining recurring costs. Whether the program is to be financed from a common pool or on an individual basis could be decided democratically. If there are some people who are in no position to pay in either manner, then the panchayat or state will have to extend support. Experience from Maharashtra shows that the apprehension that CHWs will exploit the people is needless, as people simply do not pay them as much as they pay doctors. Currently, the real worry in CHW projects is that people are not paying them enough. The remedies will depend upon the reasons for the inability to pay. Poverty, poor quality of services, or social class differentials will need to be tackled differently. The way the scheme was initially conceptualized, health work was a part-time activity for the CHW. However, in the present situation, where jobs are scarce, it will become a job. If CHWs cannot get better than the locally prevalent wage rates for farm labor, there is no way we can prevent their shifting to more gainful enterprises. In a poor region, one cannot ask for voluntarism. In areas with high levels of poverty some people may continue to have problems in paying even a small amount as fees. Yet, for those who are willing to pay, CHW will cost less than what they pay presently for accessing medical care.

At present there are a number of national health programs, such as tuberculosis control, CSSM, and malaria control, which for want of proper infrastructure are ineffective at the village level. The approach proposed in this chapter can serve these initiatives, provided the government is keen to ensure supplies and service charges. Through CHWs, the community can consider alternative ways of supporting and reinforcing the state-run programs, such as national health progams, health education, and school health. In this context we have much to learn from the Chinese experience, where a variety of options have been explored (Ashtekar 1999; Kan 1992). Let us view changes positively; with time they may mature into viable alternatives.

Institutional Support

A rejuvenated program involves tasks, such as designing books, courses, tests, identifying institutes, providing registration facilities, ensuring access to medicine supplies/purchases, and evolving monitoring systems. The technical and managerial control of such a program must be as distanced from the state machinery as is possible. Medical councils loathe the very idea of lesser people practicing health care. But open universities can come forward to help in this matter. There can be an accreditation facility for CHW institutes. The health courses run by some open schools do not enjoy medical council approval and these courses simply advance non-drug interventions as the panacea. Little can be achieved by these courses in terms of creating health personnel. There is a need to foster regional institutes for whom primary-level health care is the principal concern and not a peripheral business. We have made concrete suggestions to the Maharashtra state government regarding this program.

It is unrealistic to expect too many things from the CHW. Some projects even went to the extent of putting CHWs in areas of poverty-eradication, agriculture, and savings. While a discussion regarding these issues is beyond the scope of this chapter, even health tasks need to be optimized if they are to be effective in providing primary-level care. It is necessary to work out a consensus of what is possible through CHWs rather than bring in all that must be done to improve overall health. This is the only way to promote at least some health for the villages through the CHW, if not all. This is not to say that other levels and aspects of health care are irrelevant. The dual structure of people and state-supported primary-level care and national health programs can mutually support each other.

An important component of the program is to educate people about the role and scope of CHWs, the costs of services, and methods of control. This is crucial for ensuring two things: first, to keep the program from taking an entirely pills-for-ills way, and second, to promote community control over quality aspects.

Recently, the Madhya Pradesh state government has launched an ambitious scheme which is somewhat similar to the one proposed in this chapter. It is known as the 1995–96 Jana Swasthya Rakshak scheme. The scheme trained village youth as health workers. They are expected to provide health care in their villages and earn remuneration from the user community. A sizable loan to start a clinic facility has been promised. The primary health centers have trained several candidates in each block for a period of six months. It is too early to make a structured evaluation of this important initiative, but anecdotal reports suggest that there are shortcomings.

Creating Legal Space

A program with better technical substance will need to use 35–40 medicines, as listed in the WHO–SEARO publication. Under the existing Indian laws (the Medical Practitioners Act of each state), this can be done only if the government is willing to act positively. For Ayurvedic medicines a separate law already exists. Legally, it requires nothing short of registering training courses and the institutions that run them and allowing the candidates who qualify to use basic drugs in their practice as CHWs. Without such legal safeguards the implications for the CHW would be serious. The central government health apparatus ignores this necessity. It also ignores the possibility of certificate courses in the present State Acts, which have a small loophole to allow them. There seems to be no political will to use even this small provision.

CHW Scheme in Health Policy

As mentioned earlier the state is unwilling to promote such cost-effective, epidemiologically relevant primary health care strategies. It is increasingly turning to donor-driven agendas, in which hospital care finds a prominent place, and so, the issue of financing high-cost health care also assumes importance. The prescribed policies in hospital care—sophistication, user-fees, insurance, etc.—come from donor agencies. It also comes from a hidden agenda of looking for markets for health technology.

The realities of village-based PHC systems are vastly different and bear no parallels to these prescriptions, although on the face of it they may look similar. For instance, when I say user fees for user-felt needs, it is not the same as that for hospital care. The costs involved in the former are just a fraction of the latter and will cost even less than commuting costs that people already incur for reaching health care facilities. The CHW also reinforces the national health programs which are necessary and the costs of these must come from the state.

Thus, there are visible contradictions between policy trends and people's needs. At the policy level, it needs to be acknowledged that a CHW-like program is essential to primary health care efforts in the context of village-dominated countries like India. And if the people need such a program, a technically viable model must be allowed to develop and grow. If the government has failed to finance and run it, people must be given a chance to try and collectively manage it. Supported by the people, village health workers may be able to match at least some of their felt needs and professionally at that.

The ground realities tell us that in the face of all-pervading inefficiency and corruption and the indifference of the state health services, people do mobilize even out of their meager resources something for the CHWs, who are their only hope at times. Can this self-supported first level of care be shaped into an alternative, where communities and CHWs begin to influence and participate in the effective implementation of health care?

References

Ashtekar, S. (1992): *Bharat Vaidyaka (A Manual for Health Workers)* (Marathi). Dindori: Bharat Vaidyaka Sanstha.

——— (1999): China: Reforms and Health Care. *Economic and Political Weekly*, 34(41) (9 Oct., 1999): 2908–11.

WHO (1992): *Essential Drugs for Primary Health Care*. New Delhi: WHO–SEARO.

Kan, Xugei (1992): The Current Situation of Village Health Worker Programmes in China. In S. Frankel (ed.). *The Community Health Worker*. Oxford: Oxford University Press.

26

Disturbing Trends in the Treatment of Malaria

Yogesh Jain

I work as a pediatrician in a teaching hospital in Delhi and am keenly interested in public health. Problems faced in clinical practice may not often seem to be of public health importance. I wish to share a few observations in the changing pattern of treatment of malaria which disturb me. These changes seem to arise out of the new economic visions and are likely to have lasting and harmful impact on the disease pattern of malaria.

Technology needs to be carefully handled at the community level with due considerations of epidemiological, economic, and social issues. However, what is happening at present is that a blind faith is being placed on technology packages. Transplant medicine or coronary bypass surgery are useful for an/some individual(s); but its sponsorship by the state diverts resources away from some more important problems. Let me state the case of malaria. In the case of malaria, drugs are one important technology. The manner in which the drugs are used affects not only the individual but the pattern of resistance, and the costs of therapy for the individual and society as well.

There are various problems in malaria control which arise from clinical issues. First, the diagnosis of malaria is a problem. Often, microscopy is either not available or is substandard; the results are available only after a substantial gap and the diagnosis is often on clinical grounds alone. The National Malaria Eradication Program (NMEP) recommends presumptive antimalarial therapy with chloroquine for any fever, which leads to over-treatment. Selection of resistant malaria due to drug pressure is a key factor in the development of drug resistance (Wernsdorfer 1994). The treatment guidelines set by NMEP,

Table 26.1
Drug Cost of a Complete Course of Treatment of Severe *Falciparum* Malaria

Drug	*10 kg Child*	*60 kg Adult*
Quinine	Rs 45.00	Rs 241.00
Mefloquin	Not recommended in severe malaria	
Artemisinin	Rs 280.00	Rs 1,700.00

by textbooks, and by professional bodies differ, adding to the confusion.

Over the last year and a half, two new anti-malarial drugs, Mefloquin and Artemisinin have been allowed entry into the open market in India. Ostensibly, they have been introduced on demand by the medical fraternity because of the perceived increasing resistance of malaria to chloroquine and quinine. Mefloquin is a drug similar to quinine and is useful for uncomplicated resistant malaria. It is given orally in a single dose. Side effects like nausea, vomiting, and dizziness are common. One out of every 1,500 patients who receives this medicine for treatment of malaria can develop acute neuro-psychiatric reactions (Weinke, Trautman, and Held 1991). This drug has many drawbacks:

1. It does not work in severe malaria because it acts slowly and only through the oral route.
2. It does not prevent reappearance of the infection.
3. It leads to development of resistance if used widely. This is of serious concern because we might lose a future resource.
4. It is very expensive and therefore not feasible for widespread use. Four tablets of this drug cost Rs 180.

Artemisinin compounds are a group of drugs of Chinese herbal origin with proven efficacy in severe malaria. They are very efficacious, not more toxic than quinine, and act quickly in all grades of severity. However, they are very expensive and resistance to them is likely to develop. They are no more efficacious than quinine in those cases of malaria which are quinine responsive (Hensbrock et al. 1996; Hien et al. 1996). Therefore, this drug would be useful in the event of quinine resistance, a phenomenon which is very uncommon at the present juncture.

Table 26.1 shows the comparative cost of drugs for treatment of malaria with quinine, mefloquin, and artemisinin compounds.

We do not have detailed information about chloroquine and quinine resistance for our country. In such a situation, allowing a cafeteria approach in anti-malarial therapy is hazardous. A preliminary understanding of infectious diseases warns us of the serious risk of developing resistance to a drug when its use is irrational or excessive. By allowing use of mefloquin and artemisinin, not only are we being irrational (using a more expensive, less efficacious drug such as mefloquin or a more expensive one such as artemisinin), we are also depriving the future generations of a resource which would be required when the parasites become resistant to the presently used drugs. We have found quinine to be safe and efficacious, a view endorsed by carefully conducted research studies too (Hensbrock et al. 1996; Hien et al. 1996).

It seems that drugs which should have been used with extreme caution are being made available in the open market without epidemiological assessment of the extent of quinine resistance in serious cases of malaria. This laxity in rational action is a matter of concern as it reflects a gap between the requirements of a scientific approach and actual practice.

References

Hensbrock, M.B., Onyiorah, E., Jaffer, S., Schneider, G., Palmer, A., Frenker, J., Enwere, G., Forck, S., Nusmeijer, Bennett, S., Greenwood, B., and **Kwiatkowski, D.** (1996): A Trial of Artemether or Quinine in Children with Cerebral Malaria. *New England Journal of Medicine*, 335: 69–75.

Hien, T.T., Day, N.P.J., Phu, N.H., Mai, N.T.H., Chau, T.T.H., Loc, P.P., Sinh, D.X., Chuong, L.V., Vinh, H., Waller., D., Peto, D.T.H., and **White, N.J.** (1996): A Controlled Trial of Artemether or Quinine in Vietnamese Adults with Severe *Falciparum* Malaria. *New England Journal of Medicine*, 335: 76–83.

Weinke, T., Trautman, M., and **Held, T.** (1991): Neuropsychiatric Effects after Use of Mefloquin. *American Journal of Tropical Medicine and Hygiene*, 45: 86–91.

Wernsdorfer, W.H. (1994): Epidemiology of Drug Resistance in Malaria. *Acta Tropica*, 56: 143–56.

27

Public Health in Vellore: Experiences with Malaria and Cholera

Anand Zachariah

The appearance of HIV/AIDS and its opportunistic infections and of several multi-resistant pathogens following an era where infectious diseases had been controlled in the West, rekindled an interest in these diseases in the late eighties. This interest was heightened by the outbreak of Ebola virus in Africa and plague in India, which were seen as dangers posed by the developing world to the developed world. Two streams of opinions emerged out of the ensuing debates. One that emphasized the emergence of new diseases and the need to conquer and control them. The other was that some of the emerging infectious diseases have been with us all through and are being discovered now with the availability of better diagnostic facilities. And that they may be contributing very little in quantum to the overall problem of infectious diseases. In other words, they focused on understanding reasons for the re-emergence of infectious diseases.

It is against this background that I look at the experience of a team from Christian Medical College and Hospital, Vellore, in dealing with the problems of malaria and cholera in the town. An attempt is also made to locate these happenings in the larger context of changes in the health and welfare sector.

Re-emergence of Infectious Diseases

Kala-azar and malaria, which were under control in the early seventies, are now steadily worsening as public health problems. Outbreaks of dengue are increasing in frequency and magnitude; the eighth pandemic of cholera is continuing. Plague, which was thought to be under control, has come back. The HIV epidemic is progressing and with it the problem of tuberculosis is likely to become more life-threatening. There is a widespread perception that this resurgence is related to social, economic, political, demographic, and ecological changes that are taking place in our society. The connections between economic policies and infectious diseases in the Indian context have been recorded by researchers. Zurbrigg has looked at the links between wheat prices, infectious diseases, and famine mortality in the latter part of the last and early part of this century. She has demonstrated how the institution of famine relief in 1908 led to reduction in malaria mortality in Punjab (Zurbrigg 1992). It has been suggested that economic liberalization policies in the pre-independence period precipitated the West Bengal famine in 1943 (Greenough 1982). In recent times, Shah has looked at the occurrence of plague in Surat in the context of urbanization and its impact (Shah 1997).

In Vellore, the epidemiology of cholera and malaria has changed in the post-Structural Adjustment Period. Our study indicates that these changes are closely linked to socio-economic processes and to failures in town-planning in terms of providing basic public services. They are not just because of the absence of adequate medical care.

Vellore is a small city, about 130 km from Madras in the southern state of Tamil Nadu. The important industries in the region are household beedi-making and the leather-tanning industry. A large part of the economy of the town runs on the Christian Medical College and Hospital (CMCH). The population of the town and its suburbs in 1991 was 3.2 lakh, with a decadal growth rate of 14.2 percent, which is lower than the national and state average. However, the municipality estimates that along with the mobile population, the figure is between four to five lakhs. Nearly the entire growth of the population of the town in the last 15 years has been in the suburbs. Although the suburbs constitute 44 percent of the town population, this area is not provided with basic public amenities as it is outside the municipal limits.

The curative health services are dominated by the private sector. There are about 150 private practitioners and 16 nursing homes. The district hospital provides the main public curative services, apart from municipal doctors. Most of the town people have access to these services. The CMCH is a referral and teaching institution in the private sector, with about 1,200 beds. About 2,600 outpatients are examined daily. Less than 10 percent of these patients are local and about one-third from outside the state. These figures have grown by more than 60 percent over the last 15 years. A large proportion of these patients come from the east and north-east parts of our country. It is estimated that at least 10,000 patients and their relatives enter the hospital everyday.

To cope with this large patient influx the hotel industry has rapidly expanded. There are about 85 lodges in Vellore town, which house approximately 6,000–8,000 people everyday. Ninety percent of these are patients and their relatives. The number of lodges has increased by about 25 in the last five years. There are a large number of eating places and it is estimated that about 50,000 people eat here.

All the vaccine-preventable diseases of childhood have been controlled. However, the infectious diseases of adulthood that are not vaccine-preventable have remained remarkably stationary.

The municipal water supply comes from the Palar river basin, which is a dry river adjoining the town and supplies about 100 lakh liters of water a day. Most of the town receives water only on alternate days and usually there is severe water scarcity in summer. The suburbs do not have access to this supply. Other water sources include a number of borewells located in the town. The town sewage system consists of nine separate open sewers that drain into a sewage farm on the banks of the Palar, a short distance upstream from where the water supply is drawn. In 1993, the municipal health budget was stated to be Rs 16 million. The cost of the renovation of the sewage system alone is estimated to be Rs 277 million.

Malaria

Our country is the largest focus of malaria outside Africa. In 1953, there were 75 million cases and 8 lakh deaths (Park 1994). In 1991, there were 2.1 million cases (Government of India 1992), while the National Malaria Eradication Program (NMEP) reported 3 million cases in 1995 (Government of India 1995). The important features of its changing epidemiology are: focal outbreaks with malarial deaths as occurred in Rajasthan in 1994; increasing urban malaria and countrywide spread of *falciparum* malaria, especially chloroquine-resistant *falciparum*. In Tamil Nadu, urban malaria is a serious problem, with Madras city alone accounting for half of the cases in the state. Urban malaria is unique in several aspects. The vector, *Anopheles stephensi* is adapted to breeding in overhead tanks, small water-storage containers, and wells. High population density facilitates disease transmission. Immunity is highly variable, probably due to the non-homogenous and mobile population. Health services are readily available and breeding sites easily identifiable. The focus of the urban malaria scheme is on:

1. Identification of cases using fever surveys.
2. Weekly application of the larvicidal agent, abate, in wells.
3. The use of personal protection against mosquito bites.

Till about 1991, Vellore was a malaria free area. Whenever malaria was diagnosed, the person was shown to have had a history of travel outside Vellore. In 1992, there were increasing reports of malaria among those who had no history of travel outside Vellore. In 1993, the town was pronounced to be a malaria endemic area, which indicated that local transmission was taking place. Municipal records reveal that the annual parasite index (API) varied from 1.22 to 3.41 between 1977 and 1992. In 1993, the API shot up to 9.41 and reached an all-time high of 12.01 in 1995.

Ward-wise analysis showed that the API was maximum in the overcrowded central parts surrounding the hospital. Another worrisome aspect is the rising rates of *falciparum* malaria in Vellore town. In 1993, local transmission of chloroquine resistant *falciparum* malaria was demonstrated. The district health information service also showed a rise of cases in the districts surrounding Vellore in the same period of time.

Studies conducted by the community health department on the operational efficacy of the malaria control program showed that people were aware of the malaria problem; they quickly sought treatment from the municipal dispensary. The time from case-detection to radical treatment was short; contact tracing and focal spraying of affected households was regular. However, most people did not use personal protection against mosquito bites. At the time of the study, larvicide was being applied regularly once a week. In 1997, it was found that abate had not been applied for several months. It is not known whether this was due to inadequate staff or due to the shortage of abate. An entomological survey conducted by the zonal entomology team in August 1995 showed breeding of *Anopheles stephensi* even in wells where abate was being applied. However the most common site of breeding was in small water containers, up to 50 percent of which had mosquito larvae. Due to the acute water scarcity in summer, people were forced to store water in small containers and this was the main cause of mosquito breeding.

Another clue to the increasing malaria problem came from a case study in 1996. To cope with the increasing load and expanding infrastructure, the hospital had been converting existing buildings into multistorey complexes. For this, it had engaged the services of a large construction company from outside the town. In March 1996, a group of construction workers from rural Orissa and Andhra Pradesh fell ill with malaria soon after coming to Vellore. They had been housed in makeshift huts on the periphery of the town at the banks of the Palar. Their working and wage conditions differed from those of the local workers. They were brought for medical aid two weeks after arrival, when they could not work any longer. Of 48 people in this group, 41 were found to be smear positive for malaria and 62 percent of these were positive for *falciparum* malaria. Most of them were anemic, half had palpable spleens, all age groups were affected, and several were very sick. Based on the clinical features presumptive treatment was initiated. When we went to the campsite to complete the treatment we found that the group had been sent back to their native place. Their company indicated that they were employed by a subcontractor and had no knowledge of these workers; neither had the district authorities been informed. Therefore, radical treatment could not be given and some members of the group had not received the most appropriate treatment.

After the migrants left, a mass survey conducted by the government team at the campsite showed that of 108 workers, 32 were positive for malaria, of which 13 cases were of *Plasmodium falciparum.* The place of origin and travel history of these workers was not known. The campsite was an ideal breeding ground for mosquitoes and was located near that locality of the town, which had a high API. It is possible that the group studied was the source of infection for the others at the campsite. The urban malaria scheme data showed an increase in the number of cases of *falciparum* in the town in the period immediately following the migrant malaria episode. The total number of cases in 1996 was 172 compared to 131 in 1995 excluding the migrant cases. It is possible that some of this increase could have been due to the reservoir of infection among the migrants. Since the workers were from an area of the country where *falciparum* malaria is endemic, it is also possible that some of these cases could have been chloroquine resistant *P. falciparum*.

This case study provides a clue to the worsening situation of malaria in Vellore town. Of the patients entering the hospital, 8.6 percent are from malaria endemic zones. Malaria among them may never be recognized unless screened for. They could be the reservoir of malaria infection. While the town has seen an increase in permanent residents in the suburbs, so far malaria has not been much of a problem in these areas. Therefore, temporary migration is possibly the main contributing factor.

The possible economic reasons for the worsening malaria situation in Vellore could be the various economic factors that led to increased migration into the town. The migrants were poor people coming from a backward part of the country and the reason for their migration was economic hardship. The large construction company in a small town facilitated their migration.

The expansion of our hospital services has occurred concomitant to the rapid privatization of the country's curative health care. Patients from far flung parts of the country come to this hospital for different reasons: such as, absence of good local health facilities, lesser cost of care at our hospital, and availability of money in a certain section to spend on tertiary health care. All these have contributed to the increasing influx of patients from malaria endemic areas.

The lack of adequate investment in local public amenities and in the public health system is another factor. Acute water scarcity is due to inadequate investment in water supply, unplanned urbanization, and shortage of water resources. Inadequate manpower to apply abate and the larvicide are again due to financial cuts in public-sector health services.

Yet another aspect that our study revealed was the denial of economic rights to migrant workers, i.e., to minimum wages, basic living conditions, health facilities, and freedom of movement. The malaria control program advocates spraying of settlements and use of bed-nets for the control of migrant malaria. When the migrants are not in a position to demand any of the above rights, how can they ensure that any of these measures are implemented?

The World Bank loan for malaria control focuses on impregnated bed-nets and larvicidal agents. Bed-nets have been shown to be variably useful in our country, but are hardly likely to be effective where people do not have beds. Larvicidal agents are obviously important. None of these technological measures address the problems of worsening socio-economic inequalities, increasing privatization of services, unplanned urbanization, and lack of investment in basic public infrastructure, which are at the root of the malaria problem. Recent Structural Adjustment Policies are likely to worsen the factors that lead to the malaria problem.

Cholera

Cholera epidemics in the earlier part of this century were due to the classical strain of *Vibrio cholera 01*. In 1961, the *Vibrio cholera EL T-or* strain started spreading and soon replaced the classical strain all over the world. In the latter part of 1992, a new strain of non-01, later named *Vibrio cholera 0139 Bengal*, was simultaneously identified from Vellore, Madurai, and Madras as the cause of epidemic cholera. This strain differed from the *EL T-or* strain in a single antigen on its surface, but in all other respects behaved in the same fashion, producing a clinically indistinguishable illness. By 1993, it had spread to different parts of India and Bangladesh and hence to the rest of Asia, Europe, and America. It is not known whether this is a strain variant of *EL T-or*, a non-pathogenic *vibrio* which has acquired pathogenic potential.

Vellore experiences cholera outbreaks once or twice a year, coinciding with the monsoons. Our hospital data show that from 1992 to 1994, *V. cholera 0139* predominated as the organism producing epidemics, with a basal level of the *EL T-or* strain. In 1995 and 1996, *0139* was hardly isolated, except towards the end of 1996 and early part of 1997, when both strains contributed to the epidemic.

In July 1994, an epidemic of *V. cholera 0139* was found to be due to the failure of chlorination of the town water supply. This organism was isolated from one well, the main overhead tank of the town, and from four taps of houses affected by cholera. This is the first time that *V. cholera* was found to grow in drinking water. The epidemic abated soon after chlorination was restarted.

The large influx of people into the town is another cause for cholera. The rapid growth of the hotel industry has added to the pressure on the public amenities that were already scarce. Patients who visit the town during the epidemics are sometimes affected and occasionally develop complications such as acute renal failure. In a focal outbreak in one of the lodges, a drinking-water pipe crossing a sewage line was identified to be the cause. Another factor may be that visitors to the town are relatively non-immune.

In the 1997 outbreak, many patients and their relatives were affected, the casualty facilities overstretched, and some hospitals even ran out of intravenous fluids. Simultaneously, outbreaks were noted in Ambur, Vaniyambadi, and Melvisharam, the neighboring towns along the river bed of Palar. It was suggested that the river bed itself may be contaminated.

To evaluate this, the community health department made a study of the water supply of Vellore town. Two main wells on the Palar had high coliform counts, indicating gross fecal contamination. The wells were badly maintained and the river bed was being used as a public toilet. Perhaps, this was contributing to the contamination. One factor that was not considered was the effect of the outlet of the sewage farm which was a short distance upstream of the wells. Despite these, the water from the main overhead tank of the town was micro-biologically satisfactory, indicating that at least chlorination was effective.

Other factors contributing to the spread of cholera epidemics are the intermittent flow in the water pipes, which creates negative pressure columns that suck in sewage water through the gaps and faults. The problem is exacerbated by people using high pressure pumps to increase yield of water from a low pressure system. Poorer people have to resort to direct water tapping. When the open drains are flooded during the monsoons, the sewage cross-contamination increases.

The variation of strain seems to be an incidental event. The disease and the factors that cause it point toward inadequate planning for the increasing population of the town, where migrants are pouring in, in search of a livelihood. The water supply and sanitation facilities no longer suffice. The sewage drain that the river could earlier handle is today poisoning it; so are those who have no access to toilets. Inadequate investment in pipe maintenance, chlorination, and the failure to construct an underground sewage drainage system add to the problem.

The dialectics of the debate over who should finance improvements in public infrastructure is quite revealing. The hospital feels that cholera is a problem of the municipality. It focuses on managing the clinical problem and studying its biological aspects. Clearly, the municipality has problems in improving civic amenities. It therefore records cases of cholera as gastroenteritis. If at all it reports the problem, high profile steps, such as vaccination, are undertaken, which anyway are ineffective. While the public acknowledges the responsibility of the municipality, nevertheless it feels that the medical community should take more initiative. This dichotomy between medical care and public health services is only being enhanced by handing over medical care to the private sector, thereby undermining the comprehensive approach to infectious disease control.

Concluding Remarks

The experience with infectious-diseases problem in Vellore suggests that technological fixes, such as therapeutics and vaccination are necessary, but not sufficient. Where illnesses are the result of widening socio-economic differences, unplanned urbanization, and lack of investment in basic infrastructure for water supply and sanitation, these kind of solutions will be ineffective. Structural Adjustment Programs are likely to adversely affect the planned investments in these sectors and may, therefore, contribute to the resurgence of infectious diseases in India.

References

Government of India (1992): Health Information of India. New Delhi: Ministry of Health, 115.

——— (1995): National Malaria Eradication Programme. Operation Manual for Malaria Action Programme, New Delhi: Ministry of Health and Family Welfare.

Greenough, P.R. (1982): *Prosperity and Misery in Modern Bengal, The Famine of 1943–44*. Section: The Failure of Relief. New York: Oxford University Press.

Park, K. (1994): *Text Book of Preventive and Social Medicine*. Jabalpur: M/s Banarsidas Bhanot.

Shah, G. (1997): *Public Health and Urban Development: The Plague in Surat*. New Delhi: Sage Publications.

Zurbrigg, S. (1992): Hunger and Epidemic Malaria in Punjab 1868–1940. *Economic and Political Weekly*, 27(4): PE 2–25.

28

The Revised National Tuberculosis Control Program: A Critical Perspective

Anurag Bhargava

The Revised National Tuberculosis Control Program (RNTPC) represents the directly observed therapy–short course (DOTS) strategy of the WHO in India. According to this strategy, it has been projected that if a case-detection rate of 75 percent and a cure rate of 85 percent are achieved, a program can reduce the incidence of TB by 50 percent in 15 years (Kochi 1991). These objectives are laudable. However certain basic assumptions underlying its implementation in India need to be questioned. This chapter draws attention to some patient and program related issues in the NTP, neglect of which might once again jeopardize the fate of the program that has been launched at a critical point in the evolution of the TB epidemic in India.

The RNTCP has some positive features. Its main achievement has been that of putting TB back on the agenda of the decision-makers, albeit because of the influence of the WHO and the World Bank. In the general neglect of public health in the country, tuberculosis, the disease of the have-nots, has suffered even more. The budgetary allocation for TB had been grossly inadequate despite being increased to Rs 50 crore in 1995 from a mere Rs 2 crore in 1980–81 (Mukherjee 1995). These allocations were sufficient to treat only 30 percent of the patients completely. It should not be surprising then, that the cure rate of the previous NTP was around 30 percent. The previous National Tuberculosis Program had a sound sociological and epidemiological basis. However, it became a casualty to inadequate budgetary outlay, poor organizational set-up, poor quality microscopy, inconsistency in availability of good quality treatment and to apathy and poor functioning of the peripheral institutions. Short course therapy was available only in 56 percent of District Tuberculosis Programs as of 1993 (Suryanarayana et al. 1995). These were compounded by the lack of any accountability. In the RNTCP, the budgetary allocation has been increased following a $142 million loan from the World Bank, which should ensure that therapy would not fail for lack of resources and availability for drugs. The drug regimes have also been standardized and rationalized so that even patients with smear negative pulmonary tuberculosis and extra pulmonary tuberculosis, who are seriously ill, will have access to more effective regimes containing rifampicin. Cohort analysis of the cases treated would also be available. Greater attention to sputum microscopy, with greater accessibility to sputum microscopy centers is another positive step.

However, the RNTCP has certain provisions which can negate these gains. The program places overriding emphasis on directly observed treatment, with the insistence that every dose of the drug, at least in the intensive phase, be directly administered by a health worker. There is little doubt that direct observation of the therapy throughout the course of the therapy will result in superior outcomes compared to unsupervised therapy. What is in doubt is the operational feasibility of such a program under field conditions. This chapter raises some basic questions about the program and its implementation.

Program-related Issues

The RNTCP extrapolates results of studies which have been conducted in different epidemiological conditions and which used different interventions. There is no operational research to support its nationwide implementation in India. We are told of the success stories of the DOTS strategy in countries as diverse as Tanzania, Bangladesh, and the USA (predominantly New York City which is the epicenter of the TB epidemic in the US). The case-holding and cure rates reported are impressive. On closer analysis, it is evident that the epidemiological setting, the patient profile, the method used to ensure drug intake, and even the agency supervising the program vary. In Bangladesh, the success story reported is that of a TB program run by an NGO called the Bangladesh Rural Advancement Committee. The program involved village health workers who were paid a portion of the money deposited by the patients at the start of the therapy, as an incentive. The remainder was refunded to the patient on successful completion of therapy. Even in India, many NGOs have experience of similar success in their own TB programs. In rural areas of Tanzania and Malawi, patients were hospitalized during the intensive phase, whereas the continuation phase consisted of self-administered treatment (Kochi 1997). The DOTS strategy in India appears to mean only supervised ambulatory treatment. To describe these different interventions under the same rubric of DOTS is incorrect and misleading.

The choice of pilot areas and the pace of implementation were far from satisfactory. For example, in pilot phase I, which covered a population of only 2.35 million spread over six sites, there was only one rural site, namely, six taluks of Mehsana district. One would have expected an equal number of rural areas to be part of the pilot phase, since the main objection to the DOTS strategy is that of its operational feasibility, especially in rural areas. In pilot phase II, no new rural sites were added and there was only a small increase in the population covered in the urban areas. In pilot phase III, the program was to be extended to 102 districts in 15 states by the end of 1997, but only 16 districts had been covered (Kaul 1998). In light of this poor coverage, it is doubtful whether the target of covering a population of 130 million by 1998 and 240 million by 1999 from a coverage of 20 million in 1997 (Ministry of Health and Family Welfare 1997) was achieved. The same may be said regarding the target of detecting 70 percent of the cases.[1] It is to be remembered that the World Bank loan has to be eventually repaid.

The results of the pilot studies have been obtained in conditions that are difficult to replicate in the national program. The Mehsana study involving only six taluks of the district is a case in point. The program was supervised and intensively monitored by virtually all the key TB personnel of the state and national-level organizations. In spite of that, the cure rates fell to 50 percent when supervision was decreased to resemble field

[1] In the third WHO report on global TB control released in 1999, figures from India indicate that although treatment success rates are acceptable, case-detection rates remained low (case-detection rate under DOTS is less than 10 percent as against the target of 70 percent).

conditions and the government had to fall back on the services of a particular district tuberculosis officer known for his commitment and integrity, to salvage the program. Now the program is being run with the help of "link workers" who supervise the therapy instead of multipurpose workers and are paid Rs 175 per patient cured. Whether it was the Madras study, or the pilot studies of short-course chemotherapy in India, in each case the results obtained under field conditions were always inferior to those of the pilot studies.

There is a need for regular audit of the program. In a funded program, in which the funds will be repaid by the public, the community (including the public health professionals) has a right to know how the program is functioning. However, as of now, information sharing is inadequate, e.g., there is no mention of incentives in any document, which are otherwise being used in Mehsana.

The RNTCP is target driven. In the eagerness to pursue targets, undesirable practices may creep in, such as, leaving out patients who are not likely to come regularly to the DOT center. This has been observed in the Delhi pilot area (Kaul 1998). There is little sense in achieving a cure rate of 85 percent in some patients at the cost of leaving out many others. Similarly, setting a target for sputum positivity rates is an invitation for cooking up results.

The RNTCP has still not defined the role of the private sector and NGOs, which treat around two-thirds of the TB patients. No program can truly be a national program if it cannot access these patients.

The RNTCP appears too centralized in its decision-making. It is important to ensure flexibility and the ability to adapt the intervention according to local needs, the ground realities, and the resources available in a particular area. If it has to succeed, the program has to be more decentralized in its functioning so that only drug procurement, monitoring of performance, and fund raising is handled at a central level and the rest is left to the state and district level officers to decide. The proponents of the DOTS strategy themselves feel that "Programs of directly observed therapy are not simple or easy to conduct. They require an energetic administration, creativity and flexibility" (Iseman, Iseman, Cohn, and Sbarboro 1993).

Patient-related Issues

The universal requirement for direct observation of therapy presumes universal patient non-compliance. The DOTS strategy has been employed in other countries including China and some African countries. The factors predisposing to non-adherence to treatment differ in different settings. A study showed that in spite of having the correct knowledge and initially taking the correct action, patients were forced by the service providers—public as well as private—to become non-adherent (Juvekar et al. 1995). In a study conducted by the National Tuberculosis Institute, the reasons for loss of treatment were mainly due to referral to a hospital or medical advice given to stop the treatment (Jagota, Gupta, and Channabasaviah 1994). Yet Indian patients continue to be blamed for their ignorance and self-destructive behavior. It is clear from the foregoing discussion that a large part of the non-compliance attributed to the patients was caused/reinforced by the operational weaknesses of the NTP including the erratic drug supply and variable performance and commitment of the staff involved.

Even in places like New York City, only 40 percent of TB patients receive therapy in the form of DOT. It is recommended for non-compliant patients and those likely to be non-compliant (Bradford et al. 1996). On the other hand, in some pilot areas under DOTS, a patient is enrolled for chemotherapy only if he/she is thought likely to be compliant (Kaul 1998).

Consideration of the Patient's Convenience and Problems

Convenience to the patient is essential for the success of any program in solving intermittent chemotherapy. Even the best available regimen will have a low success rate as long as treatment services are not focused on the cooperation of the patient (Toman 1979). Unfortunately, the insistence on regular clinic attendance, lack of active participation, constraints regarding travel costs and time, and total dependence on health workers negatively affect the program. It leaves no option for the patients to self-administer therapy and to decide the time and place of drug delivery. The option to administer therapy oneself does not officially exist as per RNTCP guidelines, although workers in some pilot areas are unofficially allowing the patients to do so (Kaul 1998).

The Issue of Patient's Rights and Autonomy

Some public health scholars have questioned the intrusion into the patient's privacy and autonomy by the process of DOT (Bayer and Dubler 1993). A study in South Africa comparing direct observation with self-supervision, in which patients on the same drug regimen are not observed taking their pills, found that self-supervision achieved outcomes equivalent to DOT, although neither reached international levels (Zwarenstein et al. 1998). In re-treatment self-supervision achieved high rates of successful treatment. The researchers felt that the surveillance of pill swallowing can be alienating and authoritarian. Surveillance can detract from the ability of the caregiver to provide support, can decrease responsibility for self-care, and increase stress on the caregiver by transferring to him/her the responsibility for successful completion of therapy. In contrast, the active part played by self-supervised patients in their own care may encourage staff to engage them in a positive and supportive way. Self-supervision, even though in the ad hoc form, offered more promise for improved rates of success in treatment, apart from the advantages gained from respecting the autonomy of the patients.

In Many Government Health Institutions Services are Not Free

Doctors indulge in private practice by legal and illegal means, using the services provided by the government. It is to be seen how the existing corrupt practices within the health services interfere with the quality of the RNTCP. At one district TB center in my own knowledge, short-course regimes were being made available only on payment of a certain sum. Second, a program which demands such a high level of commitment from the patient should also ensure prompt punitive action against a defaulting DOT worker on the recommendation of the patient. Every patient needs to be informed clearly about whom to contact in case of non-administration of drugs.

Improved IEC activities is one of the aims of the RNTCP. Yet, there is still no properly designed leaflet giving facts about the disease and its treatment. Recognition of the patient's right to information and providing him/her information and instructions are an essential part of the management of TB. However, this is not done properly under the NTP or even outside it. It is common experience to find patients being confused about the number of tablets to be taken as well as the duration of therapy. Patients are frequently unaware that rifampicin is responsible for the orange discoloration of their urine. Often we come across patients who have been treated by private practitioners to be unaware of being treated for tuberculosis! Often patients stop treatment when they develop even minor hemoptysis because they incorrectly believe it to be a side-effect of the drugs. The other issue about which patients are not informed is the possibility of persistence of chest symptoms, in the event of extensive lung involvement or a co-existing respiratory disease (e.g., related to smoking). In a study, 30 percent of the patients who had completed standard chemotherapy and 19.8 percent of those who had completed short-course chemotherapy still had chest symptoms, most commonly cough (Jagota, Gupta, and Channabasaviah 1994). The figures were higher in those who were lost to treatment. It is possible that persistence of symptoms could result in dissatisfaction with therapy and default, since cure to a patient means total relief from symptoms. Bacteriological cure has little meaning for him/her.

Finally, patients have the right to be treated with respect, kindness, and consideration. I will not dwell on this, but being treated shabbily by health providers in the public sector is an important (albeit hidden) cause of dissatisfaction amongst patients.

References

Bayer, R., and **Dubler, N.N.** (1993): The Dual Epidemics of Tuberculosis and AIDS: Ethical and Policy Issues in Screening and Treatment. *American Journal of Public Health*, 83: 649.

Bradford, W.Z., Martin, J.N., Reingold, A.L., Schecter, G.F., Hopewell, P.C., and **Small, P.M.** (1996): The Changing Epidemiology of Acquired Drug Resistant Tuberculosis in San Francisco, USA. *Lancet*, 347: 318–21.

Iseman, M.D., Cohn, D.L., and **Sbarboro, J.A.** (1993): Directly Observed Therapy. *New England Journal of Medicine*, 328: 576–78.

Jagota, P., Gupta, E.V.V., and **Channabasaviah, R.** (1994): Fate of Smear Positive Patients of Pulmonary Tuberculosis at an Urban District Tuberculosis Centre Five Years after Treatment. *Indian Journal of Tuberculosis*, 41: 223–31.

Juvekar, S.K., Morankar, S.N., Dalal, D.B., Rangan, S.G., Khanvilkar, S.S., Vadair, A.S., Uplekar, M.W., and **Deshpande, A.** (1995): Social and Operational Determinants of Patient Behaviour in Lung Tuberculosis. *Indian Journal of Tuberculosis*, 42: 87–94.

Kaul, Sunil (1998): An Observation Study of DOTS in Three Districts. New Delhi: Voluntary Health Association of India.

Kochi, A. (1991): The Global Tuberculosis Situation and the New Control Strategy of the World Health Organization. *Tubercle*, 72: 1.

——— (1997): Tuberculosis Control—Is DOTS the Health Breakthrough of the 1990s? *World Health Forum*, 18: 225.

Ministry of Health and Family Welfare (1997): RNTCP Information Brochure. New Delhi: Central TB Division, Directorate of Health Services.

Mukherjee, A.K. (1995): Tuberculosis Control Programme in India: Progress and Prospects. *Indian Journal of Tuberculosis*, 42: 75–85.

Suryanarayana, L., Vembu, K., Rajalakshmi, R., and **Satyanarayana, C.** (1995): Performance of National Tuberculosis Program in 1993: An Appraisal. *Indian Journal of Tuberculosis*, 42: 101–15.

Toman, K. (1979): Tuberculosis Case Finding and Chemotherapy: Questions and Answers. Geneva: World Health Organisation.

Zwarenstein, M., Schoemanm, J.H., Vundule, C., Lombard, C.J., and **Tatley, M.** (1998): Randomised Controlled Trial of Self-supervised and Directly Observed Treatment of Tuberculosis. *Lancet*, 352: 1340–43.

PART VI

EXPERIENCES AT THE MICRO-LEVEL

The imposition of a packaged set of SAP on regions that are distinctly varied is as devoid of wisdom as the strategy that makes the poor bear the burden of reforms everywhere. South Asia is particularly vulnerable, given its colonial background and uneven development dominated by the interests of small but powerful elite. The post-independence development in these counties was characterized by a pattern of growth that was extremely skewed leading to a growing schism between the privileged and the working classes. This section highlights the vulnerabilities of the people of the region to shifts in policy that make their insecure lives even more precarious. Focusing on India, this section explores the lives of the poor and their dilemmas. It perhaps reflects the future of the region and underscores the urgency of putting a halt to the dismantling of the public sector.

The first two chapters discuss non-metropolitan urban settlements. Ghanshyam Shah studies the 1994 plague in Surat—the Indian city of the diamond trade—and points out the dangers of undermining public sector health care provision and monitoring systems. He argues that propositions like the private sector being an "equal partner in development" and "efficiency through market mechanisms" are clichés as private capital did not come forward to invest in infrastructure. K.S. Sebastian narrates the experience of yet another Indian town, Alleppey, in Kerala, which is experiencing the impact of SAP-generated cuts in subsidies and the commercialization of its agriculture and fisheries. These measures have aggravated the problems of the city's working class population in terms of food availability, civic facilities, and re-emergence of communicable diseases.

The next three chapters focus on the lives of Indian women and their experience of existing health services. Meena Gopal's study of the organization of female labor in the beedi industry of

Tirunelveli district of Tamil Nadu reveals the double edge of patriarchy and its links with liberalization. While women's economic contributions are treated as secondary and marginal, patriarchal values help maximize exploitation of their labor and the denial of social security or dignity of labor. The rapidly growing population of the slums in Delhi is the subject of Alpana Sagar's chapter. She vividly brings out the social dynamics of women's health and their awareness and efforts to deal with the causes of ill health. The health care system, bound by its narrow vision, is unable to perceive the women's dilemmas and remains indifferent. Mohan Rao illustrates the danger of handing over research to individuals and open markets, where neither its objectives nor its methodologies can be regulated. He focuses on the clandestine use of quinacrine as a contraceptive for Indian women to illustrate the indifference and callousness of the existing monitoring systems and the health market to the needs of women.

29

The Plague, the Poor, and Health Services

Ghanshyam Shah

The outbreak of pneumonic plague in Surat in September–October 1994, created worldwide panic. India's exports suffered a setback for nearly three weeks. Some countries stopped flights to and from India and imposed restrictions on the entry of Indians. In the city, production of fabric and diamond polishing worth about Rs 500 crore was affected. The municipal government lost an income of around Rs 8 crore.

Though the total number of deaths by the plague may be considered not very high and the epidemic was controlled within a week, the gravity of the problem still remains in more ways than one. The plague in Surat was an outcome of conditions that epitomize the state of the public health system and nature of urban growth in the country. Such outbreaks of one or other disease are a regular occurrence not only in Surat, but in other cities of the country as well. In mid-1988, gastroenteritis killed 350 persons and affected 11,000 lives in Ahmedabad; in Calcutta, daily, at least 50 patients with the disease are admitted to hospitals. In Bombay, 85 persons died of infectious hepatitis in 1993; 869 and 2,290 persons died in the country of kala-azar and Japanese encephalitis respectively in 1991; malaria took toll of 5,527 lives in Rajasthan in 1993; and recently in 1996, more than 250 persons died of dengue in less than a month's time in Delhi. In Surat, over the last 10 years, more than a 100 persons have been dying each year, especially during August and September, of malaria. A number of diseases have become endemic.

This chapter focuses on the nature of urban development in Surat city, the profile of the affected people, the health services, and the response to and management of the epidemic. It concludes by highlighting some of the lessons that may be drawn from the plague epidemic for the public health system, particularly in the context of the Structural Adjustment Program, which has been in operation since the early nineties.

Surat City: Urban Growth, Social Decay

Surat is a major city of Gujarat, one of the most industrialized states of India. It is one of the fastest growing cities of the country; it was the 19th largest city in the country in 1971; it is now the 12th largest. The population has increased more than four times in the last three decades, from 3.71 lakh in 1961 to 14.91 lakh in 1991; at present it is estimated to be around 2 million. There is also a floating population, on an average, of about 1.5 lakh. The growth rate of the population in the last decade was 4.8 percent per year. The density of the population is 13,483 per sq km (Shah 1997). In addition to internal growth and immigration, the population has also increased due to the expansion of the municipal limits of the city. Some of the surrounding villages, like Ved, Dabholi, and Tunki, and industrial pockets like Udhna and Pandesara became part of the city in the sixties and seventies.

Unprecedented growth of small-scale industries in the unorganized sector has significantly contributed to the rise in the city's population. This is the only city in the country where the manufacturing sector not only has the highest proportion of employed workers, but it has also consistently increased since 1971. The main industries are: power-loom and diamond cutting and polishing. Today, Surat is one of the largest centers in the world for the production of synthetic fiber fabrics, mainly nylon and polyester. The number of looms increased from 8,105 in 1960 to over two lakh in 1990. With the growth of power-looms, the textile processing industry developed. From eight units in 1961, the number rose to 250 in 1992. Surat is also one of the largest diamond cutting centers of the country with 13,000 units (Shah 1997).

Since the late eighties, a number of large-scale industries have also come up in Surat. Some of the major industries include the KRIBHCO, Hazira Fertilizer Company, Gas Authority of India, Larsen and Toubro, Reliance, Essar Steel, etc., with a total investment of about Rs 10,000 crore. They are capital intensive industries and their potential for employment is limited. So far they have provided employment to about 5,500 persons. The presence of these industries has pushed up prices of land, building, transport, and essential commodities (Shah 1997).

As is the trend in the small-scale sector in most parts of the country, in Surat too the workforce in the diamond, power-loom, *jari*, and embroidery industries is largely employed on temporary or casual basis. As much as 80 percent of the workforce is hired through the contract system (Shah 1997). Constant insecurity—the fear that the employer can throw them out at any time—haunts the workers. Barring about 10 percent, not all workers get work throughout the month. As the workers are piece-rated, there is a tendency, more so among the migrants, to work for more hours so that they can earn more. Though the wages in the diamond and power-loom sector have increased in the last two decades, they do not correspond with price rise. In fact, real wages have declined. Hence, there is no improvement in the conditions of the workers. Benefits such as paid holidays, medical allowances, provident fund, compensation, and fixed working hours are distant dreams for them. Labor laws are flouted with impunity. Labor officers and factory owners are hand in glove.

As more migrant laborers enter the market everyday, their bargaining power is non-existent. In the context of developing countries in general and Surat in particular, the working class is not just lowly paid, the workplaces and working conditions also make them vulnerable to all kinds of diseases. For instance, the workplace for diamond cutting is a small room of a 100 sq ft. Six to eight workers work there from morning to evening and at times during the night. The place does not have sufficient ventilation—owners avoid making windows for fear that the workers might throw out the diamonds, to be taken away later. The workers have to sit on the floor, in a bent position, for nearly eight to ten hours a day. Several workers who cannot even afford rented shelter, sleep at the workplace. Studies show that these workers are prone to tuberculosis and that their lifespan is reduced (South Gujarat University 1984).

Like all other fast-growing cities of the country, Surat too is a problem city as far as civic amenities are concerned. In the past it has been known as the city "floating on sewage water." Problems related to water, health and sanitation, and traffic are on the increase. The Surat Municipal Corporation (SMC) is unable to cope with the expanding needs of the population (Shah 1997). For instance, in 1991, the covered drainage system served only 13 percent of the area and 33 percent of the population. Now, 60 percent of the slums have no drainage system; which means that the used water from the houses flows around the house and fills up the ditches, beyond which it finds no outlet. Waterlogging is thus a common feature. The situation is at its worst during the monsoon. Storm-water drainage covers only 27 percent of the area.

Though the city is situated on the banks of the river Tapi, the SMC is unable to provide potable water to all the citizens. It supplies water to only 43 percent of the total area. The new areas do not get the municipal water. The groundwater and river-water have over the years become saline. They are open to contamination from open drains, leaching of garbage, and from industrial effluents. On the other hand, big factories, particularly textile-processing units, divert municipal supply wherever possible to their advantage. They also use water indiscriminately.

Delays in preparation and execution of town planning schemes have given rise to unplanned and haphazard growth of the city. A large number of unauthorized buildings have come up in many areas. The delays have been because of land-related politics, wherein interests of builders and factory owners play a significant role (Shah 1997).

The Plague Victims

Distribution of the Victims by Areas

The New Civil Hospital (NCH) admitted patients suspected to have plague from almost all parts of the city. The victims were those who, presumably, died of the plague, and those who were clinically diagnosed as the plague-affected patients. There were 85 deaths and 117 serologically positive cases.

As many as 73 percent of the victims were immigrants and most of them were from dry-land regions of Maharashtra and Saurashtra. The working class, irrespective of social status and place of origin, was the main target. As many as 80 percent of the plague patients in general and death cases in particular, were from this class.

The largest number of death and seropositive cases were from Ved Road, Tunki, Singanpor, and Katargam in the northern

Figure 29.1
Distribution of Plague Cases in Surat City

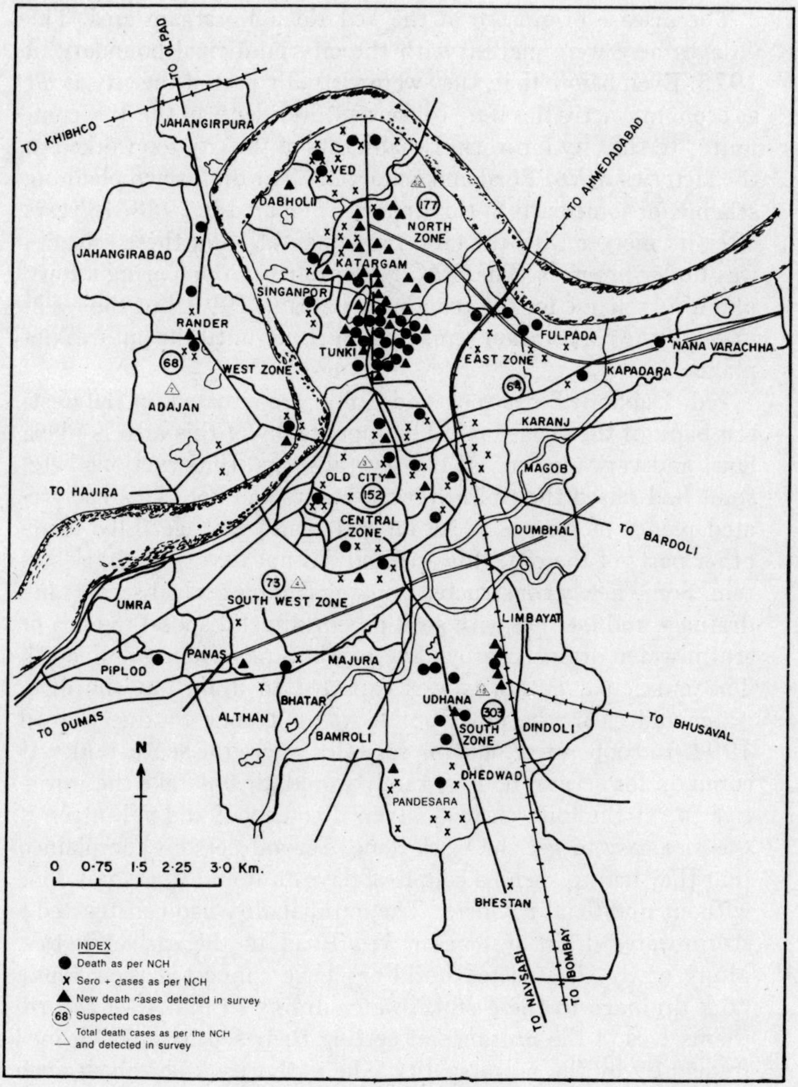

part. Udhana and Pandesara, in the southern part of the city, had the second largest number. Udhana had more of seropositive cases. Eight cases of death and 14 seropositive cases were also reported from the central zone, the most congested part of Surat (see Figure 29.1).

The disease originated at the Ved Road–Katargam area. The villages here were merged with the city municipal boundary in 1975. Even before that, they were virtually part of the city as far as economic activities were concerned. Residents of the area commuted to the city for work. Inhabitants of the city too worked in the factories in Ved Road and Katargam. The draft town planning scheme for some parts of this area was prepared in 1988, 13 years after its merger with the city. Implementation of these schemes was under progress. The SMC gave priority to preparing a town planning scheme for the remaining parts in 1991, but the resolution of the corporation remained on paper until the outbreak of plague.

Ved, Dabholi, Singanpor, and Tunki are situated on the western bank of the river Tapi. The topography of this area is like a bowl and very uneven. Of the several illegal constructions here, some had raised their plinth level, others had not. This had created plenty of storage space for water and garbage. Like many other parts of the city, this area too did not have a sewerage system. Some newly constructed housing complexes had septic tank drainage and latrines with soak pits or direct disposal to open or storm-water drains nearby. The septic tanks often got flooded. The municipal authority was expected to drain out the dirty water and clean the tank, but it was not done routinely, until 1994. In cooperative housing societies where the septic tank was common for several houses, rarely would anyone take the initiative to get the tank cleaned. Even if somebody did volunteer, it was not easy to get the work done. Several persons complained that they had to spend a couple of days on it and it was not done without unofficial payment. The municipality had constructed a storm-water drain system on Ved Road in the early nineties. Many newly constructed buildings have connected their septic tank drainage to these storm-water drains so that they can rid themselves of the nuisance of getting their septic tanks cleaned frequently by the municipality. The authority knew about such unauthorized connections but did not take action against the offenders. The storm-water drain had no velocity to flush sewage. Hence, it worked as a sedimentation pond of human excreta and garbage before the monsoon. Which is what happened in 1994.

The flood before the outbreak of the epidemic aggravated the condition.[1] There was a flood protection scheme that came into existence after the construction of the Ukai dam upstream, about 60 km from Surat. The scheme was designed to prevent flood waters from entering the city and at the same time stop the rain-water from the city from draining into the river. Unfortunately, the scheme was never completed, despite public petitioning (Desai 1995). In August–September 1994, the city was lashed by very heavy rain for three months. The water level in Ukai dam rose and reached a critical level, so it had to be released to protect the dam. That caused the city to flood. The maximum flood level of 10.1m was reached on 8 September. After four days, the water receded and returned to the normal level or lower. The flood waters gradually found a passage through three outlets and entered the north zone of Ved–Katargam. Garbage and sewage from the storm-water drain were distributed over vast areas at round RL of 12.0 or so. This water, while receding, left sewage, industrial waste, dead animals which came with the flood and garbage over a vast area. The water stored in the bowls of Tunki, etc., remained stagnant for a week or more (Desai 1995).

Udhana and Pandesara are industrial areas that were merged with the city municipal limit in 1986. Public amenities had not kept pace with industrial growth; there was no sewerage or potable

[1] Though plague is not a waterborne disease, rain and humid atmosphere do tend to cause pneumonia. Epidemiologists do not rule out the possibility that rodents or other animals carrying fleas may have been carried along with the floodwaters to the city. The National Institute of Communicable Diseases (NICD) observes, "Rodents trapped from Surat city by the present investigating team showed the presence of 'Y pestis' in microscopic examination of organ impression. This infection, of commensal rodents (and animals?), in all probability, was the result of spilling over of the infection from the wild rodents. The spilling was facilitated by the sudden environmental change in the area, due to floods in the catchment areas of Ukai reservoir and the subsequent flash flood in Surat city following the release of water from the said reservoir. When the floodwaters began receding, on 10-9-94, movement of people commenced, and cleaning operations, in the flood affected areas, mainly by the community members, went on for some days. In this process some people may have handled or come in contact with dead and infected rodents/animals and developed the disease." (Shah 1997: 275–76)

water system. Till that time, the SMC had not prepared town planning schemes for these areas. Hence, there was a good deal of haphazard construction of buildings. The textile printing and dyeing factories released their chemical wastes in the form of stinking colored water on to the roads. The roads were uneven with many holes. However, since this area was at a distance from the river, it was not as badly affected by floods as the northern part of the city.

Though the older parts of the city had better amenities than other parts of the city, still it did not escape the epidemic; neither could posh areas like Athawa lines, Nanpura, and Tamaliyawad. A notable feature was that an area like Varaccha Road, that adjoined Ved Road, and was more or less similar as far as civic amenities were concerned, had a negligible number of plague cases. So was the case with slum areas like Limbayat and Dumbhat in the eastern zone.

Housing Facilities of Victims

Fifty-eight percent of the suspected patients reported that they owned the house in which they lived. Needless to mention, all owners did not have equal space and amenities. Many lived in small houses without adequate ventilation. In Laxminagar, where the initial cases were detected, people lived in *zopadpatties*, namely, houses with mud or jute walls and a ceiling of bamboo held by plastic sheets, steel sheets, or country tiles, which often leaked in rain. Sanjay Nagar society in the southern part of Udhana and Bapunagar on the river bank in the west were clusters of dense *zopadpatties*. Flood and fire were routine calamities for the residents, experienced almost every year. Their shelters were hardly ten by ten feet wide, five to six feet in height. Public taps or a borewell handpump in or near the locality were their main sources of water for drinking and cooking. They cooked either in the open or in the corner of their hut and washed utensils and clothes in front of the shelter in a narrow lane. This was also their bathing space. The residents of Bapunagar used the river bank to respond to nature's call. But the people of Sanjay Nagar and Laxminagar had no such luxury—they used the road side or garbage tip as a toilet. Nearly one-fourth of the plague patients were reported to be residents of such slum areas.

Raman Nagar and Shiv Chhaya housing societies, where initial deaths occurred on 18 and 19 September, were somewhat better than many slums. They could be called lower middle-class localities. Most of the houses were small, generally one room or one room and a kitchen. Some were two-storied buildings. These houses had brick walls and a ceiling of cement-concrete and toilet facilities that were either exclusive to a single family or shared between two or three families. Food was cooked within the house in a corner or in the kitchen. Those who did not have a separate bathroom within the house, used this corner for bathing. An arrangement was made to drain out dirty water from the kitchen and bathroom either into the septic tank or into the open. A number of residents, as mentioned above, had joined the pipeline to the storm-water drainage. They complained that during the floods, water did not flush out from the toilets; on the contrary, drainage water, including excreta, entered their houses through the toilet tubes. It was unbearable, particularly for those who lived in single rooms. The plague patients from Udhana and Pandesara area were from similar housing complexes. Nearly half of the plague patients were from such localities (Shah 1997).

Class Distribution of the Victims

The working class was the main victim of the plague. Forty-seven percent of all the plague patients were factory workers or casual laborers. Among the dead, every second one belonged to this class. These figures to some extent underplay the magnitude of the attack on this class, thanks to the sizable number of "housewives," students and infants. If we look closely at the occupation of the head of households, the figure of the victims from this class rises sharply to 80 percent. The rich and middle class, however, did not completely escape from the calamity. Among all the plague patients, one out of 10 was from this class. Their proportion among the victims compared to their overall population in the city was small but not negligible. After all, they do not constitute a majority in the city. Had the plague not been controlled within a week, the equalizing effect of the infectious disease would have been greater than what the city did witness.

Health Care Services in the City

Like elsewhere in the country, the city has private and public health services. In terms of number and resources, the former is larger in size and coverage. The city has two government and eight municipal hospitals providing 1,161 beds. (There are 12 charitable hospitals dominated by private practitioners, providing 1,095 beds.) As against this, it has 288 private hospitals providing a total of 2,788 beds (Shah 1997).

In terms of facilities and sanitary conditions, the private polyclinics may be classified into two categories: old and new (those that came into existence in the eighties). The old hospitals were congested and badly maintained; sanitary conditions in these hospitals were hardly better than the government hospitals. The sweepers and ward boys were poorly paid and hospitals were understaffed. The operation theatres of many were not well-equipped and were badly maintained. Some of the polyclinics employed graduates trained in ayurveda or homeopathy as junior doctors. They were not trained to handle complicated cases. Some employed fresh graduates and allowed them to treat patients independently. They were cheaper than properly qualified and experienced doctors. Ironically, the employer doctors were not just critical but also looked down upon ayurvedic and homeopathic doctors as "quacks."

The new hospitals were of two types. A few were well equipped, relatively spacious, and well-maintained. They followed the Western model with tests, infrastructural facilities, and decor. They were expensive even for upper middle-class patients, and largely catered to business and industrial entrepreneurs and professionals. The other new hospitals were as congested and ill-equipped as the old ones.

Like other professionals, many medical practitioners too wanted to earn money in the least possible time. Money and power (influence) were their obsession. They provided "services" only when and where they were assured of such rewards. "After all we have invested a lot of money in our studies, this is not for public service. Why should not we earn?" argued a number of doctors. They invested their savings in the power-loom industry, shares, estates, and in medical shops. For many, practice was the mechanical application of their skills to earn profit. They routinely worked for 10 to 12 hours a day and hardly read professional journals. "We work from morning to evening and do not have time to read anything except newspapers," several doctors said. Whatever they learnt was through medical representatives who gave information on diseases and medicines. Though they were members of a professional organization, only a few doctors attended lectures and seminars (Shah 1997).

The total expenditure of the government hospital, the New Civil Hospital (NCH), in absolute terms had increased from Rs 16 million in 1981–82 to Rs 54 million in 1993–94. Nearly 50 percent of the total outlay was spent on staff salaries. Yet, a number of positions in various departments were vacant. One-third of the budget was spent on medicine and equipment, which were inadequate to meet requirements. Often medicines were out of stock and several equipment (such as the X-ray machine, and microscopes) remained unusable for days together. The hospital did not have its own laundry and electricity power supply, despite frequent power breaks. The overall maintenance of the hospital was neglected. The general hospital, run by the SMC, was in almost the same condition as the government hospital as regards equipment and maintenance (Shah 1997).

The response of the private hospitals, private consultants, and general practitioners to the epidemic was strikingly different from that of the government doctors and institutions. Though the disease was declared as plague on 20 September, some private practitioners including consultants treated these as cases suffering from a "mysterious" disease; they resulted in death in no time. Despite the statutory requirements, they did not inform the municipal government of these sudden deaths. Not only that, most of them were among the first to flee the city as soon as they came to know that it was plague. Among those who remained in the city, many kept their clinics, consulting rooms, and hospitals closed in the first week of the epidemic or referred most of the patients to the NCH without even a preliminary examination. Three leading consultants questioned the diagnosis of the NCH doctors. However, neither they nor the medical association reprimanded those of their colleagues who failed in their duty to inform the authorities of the mysterious and sudden deaths of their patients and those who fled from the city at the time of crises. On the other hand, the doctors of the NCH were on their toes and worked round the clock during the epidemic. While a few attended duty out of fear of suspension, many did so out of moral conviction and against many odds.

The lack of response to treatment and the sudden death of five patients with similar symptoms (three in the NCH and two in others) on 21 September made the doctors at the NCH concerned and vigilant. They immediately had a consultation to arrive at a diagnosis of the problem they were up against. By that evening they had arrived at a decision, namely, that it was plague.

The District Health Officer and the Deputy Commissioner (Health) of the SMC were immediately informed of the diagnosis. By midnight of 21 September, more than 25 new patients were admitted at the NCH. The number of patients steeply rose to 110 by the 22 September and to 156 on the 23 September. On 24 September, as many as 411 patients were suspected to have plague. The inflow of new patients continued thereafter but the rate declined from 26 September onwards. The number of deaths was the highest on 22 and 23 September. From 24 September onward, the death rate also declined.

The doctors of the medicine department formed an emergency team. The first requirement was that of prophylactic medicine for the patients as well as for the staff on duty. As the NCH did not have enough supplies, two of the doctors went to the market and bought the medicine. When they did not get the required quantity, they contacted some philanthropic individuals, who not only came to the hospital with money, but also immediately contacted friends in nearby cities to procure drugs. Whatever quantity of drug that was available in Navsari (the nearest town) was brought to Surat in a special vehicle. Thus on the first day the doctors had to fight at two fronts—looking after the patients as well as arranging for drugs. The young junior doctors, on individual basis, did everything to save the lives of the patients.

By the evening of the second day, the isolation ward was full. But the flow of patients continued. Immediately, a new ward was opened to accommodate more patients. Medicines were procured in the same manner as before. The stock of medicines from the state government not only reached the hospital after 48 hours; it was also inadequate.

Till 24 September, non-plague patients were also routinely admitted to the hospital. On 26 September, all suspected non-plague patients, except very serious ones, were discharged. The outpatients department (OPD), which on an average examines 600 patients, was closed. The NCH turned into the plague hospital and remained so till the third week of October. The number of patients increased beyond the capacity of the hospital as most of the doctors engaged in private practice had fled and those who remained had stopped treating even their regular patients.

Chemoprophylaxis was prescribed on 23 September by the medical superintendent as prophylaxis for the staff and their family members. However, a large number of staff members and accompanying relatives were not protected for the entire period of exposure. Protective clothing was not supplied to the doctors and the staff on time. More important, among the doctors and other medical staff, there was no concept of barrier nursing— meaning that all the gowns, masks, shoes, linen, and instruments used in the patients isolation room had to be changed before leaving the isolation area. No part of this was observed and there seemed to be lack of awareness about it (Government of Gujarat 1995).

Notwithstanding some irritant incidents and infrastructural limitations, the staff and the resident doctors of the medicine department worked as a team throughout the epidemic. The work of the doctors, especially of the medicine department and other staff of the hospital, was exemplary. Whereas, the private health sector, despite its very large size and resources, collapsed and failed to meet the challenge. Their burden was shifted to the public health system. Yet, there has been no discussion on the efficiency and responsibility of the private health sector.

Lessons to be Drawn

At the outset it should be mentioned that in India the private health services dominate the public health sector. This domination has continuously increased since the mid-seventies. The SAPs of the nineties have accelerated the process. Over the years, the state has not been spending more than 3.5 percent of its resources on the health sector. In fact, the allocation has declined in the nineties with the introduction of SAPs. It was 2.63 percent in 1994–95 and remained more or less the same in subsequent years. Analysis of data by the National Institute of Public Finance and Policy reveals that the share of central grants for public health declined from 27.92 percent in 1984–85 to 17.17 in 1992–93 and for disease programs from 41.47 in 1984–85 to 18.50 percent in 1992–93. In 1994–95, Gujarat, one of the states leading in industrial development, allocated merely 2.16 percent of its total expenditure for health. Its expenditure on national disease programs declined sharply from 24.37 percent in 1975–76 to 13.76 percent in 1994–95 (Duggal 1996).

With the weakening of the public health system, monitoring and surveillance of communicable diseases has been severely fractured. According to some, it has been "systematically demolished." The plague in Surat is a case in point. Early signals of the possibility of a resurgence of plague in the country were ignored. The plague surveillance departments were made either defunct or virtually closed down. The surveillance system in Gujarat and Surat failed to report the deaths due to the "mysterious disease" in the third week of September.

To quote from the report of the Technical Advisory Committee on Plague, set up by the Government of India in October 1994:

> Surveillance of plague is weak in India and needs to be considerably strengthened and expanded.... A certain amount of lopsidedness in the development of Public Health Laboratory services is evident. While there is expertise for study of microbes at the sub-cellular and molecular levels, diagnostic capability for the isolation and characterization of common infectious agents at the peripheral levels of the health-care system is weak. As a result a vulnerability in India's health care system, relating to rapid diagnosis of infectious diseases, exists... (Shah 1997: 294).

Despite these and many more problems associated with the public health system, we see that in Surat it was the doctors of the government hospitals who rose to the occasion and performed their duty against all odds. Whereas, the private practitioners failed to even diagnose the problem. They actually ran away under the threat of an epidemic. In a sense, the doctors of the public hospitals were far more "efficient" and "committed."

This assumes importance in view of the fact that the people most affected by such epidemics cannot afford the expensive treatment offered by the private doctors. It points to the urgent need to maintain, restructure and strengthen, and efficiently run, the public health system. Surat belies the notion that privatization will automatically lead to efficient and better services. Privatization, as envisaged by SAPs, is therefore not going to bring about efficiency or equity. On the contrary, it has encouraged establishment of five-star hospitals sponsored by and meant for the rich. It has already excluded a large section of the society from its purview.

While "privatization" is being offered as the panacea for all the problems of the public services, yet we see, as in Surat, that so far private capital has not come forward to invest in infrastructure projects like water, and sewage. This is so, possibly because of low profits in this sector. Owners of small and large scale industries who have multiplied their profits several times during the last three decades and who grab public resources indiscriminately, are unwilling to invest in promotive health services like potable water, sewage collection and disposal of garbage, and reducing air and water pollution. They create more garbage and pollution and use larger quantities of water and energy for domestic and industrial purposes than a common citizen. But they do not wish to own responsibility for the mess that they create. More than 80 percent of the entrepreneurs asserted that as industrialists they had no responsibility. "We pay taxes to the corporation and to the government, it is their responsibility to keep the city clean and provide infrastructure facilities to the people," is their attitude. "We have no time to do anything for the city, it has to be done by the government," a factory owner said. It may be noted that effluents from his factory were flowing outside his factory. The president of the South Gujarat Chamber of Commerce argued that industrialists were already overburdened by taxes. According to him "privatization" of public services was the only answer to the problem, as it would improve efficiency of the services.

The assumption of "economic reform" is that the market is perfect and governed by rational action of individuals and provides equal freedom to capitalists and workers, dominant classes, and vulnerable sections. Through market forces, the reforms expect to bring about "the transformation of vulnerable and marginalized groups into productive self-reliant partners in the social and economic development of their countries. It rests on the capacity to strengthen vulnerable groups in such a way that they themselves become responsible for promoting and improving their health status and quality of life as well as their economic productivity" (WHO 1992).

This is, indeed, a laudable objective. The objective of "strengthening vulnerable groups" is shared by everyone. In fact, this is the main concern of the critics of SAPs. Can market forces attain that objective? Theoretically it is not possible, as there is no perfect market and labor and capital are on an unequal footing. Workers in India have no real choice to assert their rights to work and wages. The condition of the workers in Surat is a glaring example of their vulnerability. They are organizationally weak and socially fragmented and do not have strong bargaining power against capital. In such a situation to expect them to be "self-reliant partners in social and economic development" is nothing but a cliché to perpetuate illusions among the masses. And what would they do till they became "equal partners?" The strategies to evolve the "safety nets" in the form of "social investment funds" has so far not worked with desirable results in the countries which have followed the SAPs since the seventies (Roy 1997). Evidences from the studies on poverty alleviation programs suggest that to become a partner in socio-economic development, vulnerable sections need to have access to assets, like land in the rural areas and employment opportunities in the urban sector. This has to be accompanied by access to education, potable water, shelter, and health care. These are prerequisites for their empowerment. There are no short cuts. The situation calls for fresh thinking and approach to evolve ways and means to increase productivity as well as attain equity so as to make society truly healthy.

References

Desai, M.D. (1995): *Engineering Aspects of So Called Plague in Surat*. Centre for Social Studies, Surat. Mimeo.

Duggal, R. (1996): *The Private Health Sector in India: Nature, Trends and a Critique*. CEHAT, Bombay. Mimeo.

Government of Gujarat (1995): Report of the Expert Committee Appointed to Investigate Suspected Plague Epidemic in Surat during September–October 1994. Gandhinagar.

Roy, S. (1997): Globalisation, Structural Change and Poverty: Some Conceptual and Policy Issues, *Economic and Political Weekly*, 32(33–34):
Shah, G. (1997): *Public Health and Urban Development: The Plague in Surat*. New Delhi: Sage Publications.
South Gujarat University (1984): Working and Living Conditions of the Surat Textile Workers: A Survey, Gujarat University, Surat.
World Health Organization (WHO) (1992): *Health Dimensions of Economic Reform*. Geneva: WHO.

30

Public Health Issues of Small Towns: The Case of Alleppey

K.S. Sebastian

Studies on issues relating to urbanization in the developing countries are often limited to the problems of metropolitan and mega-cities. The developmental and public health issues of the large number of intermediate cities and small towns have not got sufficient attention. These urbanized areas have a long catalog of problems, such as shortage of land, housing, and water; over-utilization of service systems; and meager resources to meet civic needs. Few studies examine the causes of uneven development across regions, which results in regional inequalities and urban primacy, in terms of centralization of political and economic power. It is also to be pointed out that in the specific context of public health, too much emphasis is being laid on health problems, such as AIDS, which is perceived by the developed countries as the biggest menace in the urban centers of South-Asia. Chemical agents in air are perceived as more serious health hazards than biological agents in water, food, air, and soil, which cause diarrhea, dysentery, and other intestinal problems. Due attention is not given to diseases such as malaria, dengue, filariasis, and Japanese encephalitis, which are re-emerging as health hazards in developing countries.

This chapter attempts to place the health issues of Alleppey town (Kerala) in a broader perspective that goes beyond bio-medical factors. Production, availability, and utilization of food within a society as well as within households are important determinants of health. The chapter examines the changes in food production and availability in Alleppey over the years. It also presents the ecological features of the town that make the people vulnerable to certain diseases. The chapter argues that given their nature, Structural Adjustment Programs will only worsen the existing trends which were set in motion since the colonial times.

This chapter is based on fieldwork conducted at different periods between 1994 and 1997. Alleppey town has 36 wards, of which five wards were selected for survey of households regarding their health problems, health status, and health-related actions. The wards were shortlisted after studying the various characteristics such as location, population density, literacy levels, and presence of various caste/class groups, obtained through field visits and through studying the urban primary census abstract of the town. After purposively selecting five wards, 50 households were chosen from the electoral voters list of the municipality using random sampling method. However, the present chapter is not burdened with the large chunk of data collected through this survey. Many of the observations that appear in this chapter are based on records of the health department of the Alleppey Municipality, archival documents, interviews with experts, and from relevant secondary sources. It needs to be pointed out that the "time series data" on epidemics in Alleppey town are only indicative of certain trends during the Structural Adjustment Program period and are not sufficient to empirically establish that they are the result of the programs.

Alleppey's Spatial and Social Contours

Once a flourishing port, established in 1762 during the zenith of European expansion into the Malabar coast, Alleppey is now a sleepy town with a population of more than 200,000. The town's geography is largely defined by its proximity to the Arabian Sea and the presence of numerous rivers, and small canals, both within the town and in the adjacent Kuttanadu region which forms part of Alleppey's hinterland. The western part of the town is bordered by the Arabian Sea and the eastern side by the Vembanadu Lake which is 84 km long and about 3.1 km wide. To ensure smooth passage of forest products and for public transport, several canals were dug in and around Alleppey. These canals had water flowing through them in the earlier days, but the water system has now stagnated due to various developmental activities, enumerated in later sections.

The British East India Company was successful in persuading the erstwhile king of Travancore to join "British India Free Trade

Zone" in 1865. The establishment of a free trade zone witnessed unprecedented expansion of commercial activities in Alleppey. These were related to the demand for pepper as a preservative for beef, for teak wood to construct battleships as oak wood was in short supply in Britain, and for coir yarns to substitute for jute as packing material. The above products were extracted from the hinterlands of Alleppey and processed in the town. The coming of a modern port at Cochin just 60 km away, reduced the importance of Alleppey. The traditional industries such as coir, coconut oil, and spices trade, for which Alleppey was well-known, have also declined over time.

The social composition of Alleppey is largely similar to a decayed, erstwhile industrial town, in which majority of the people belong to the working class. The main occupations in the town are: services, trade and commerce, manufacturing, agriculture, and fishing, and livestock. Fisher-people form a substantial part of Alleppey's population. Nearly 14 percent of the marine fishermen and 27 percent of inland fishermen of Kerala live in Alleppey district. People also work in limestone mines in the Vembanadu Lake. Alleppey district has a large number of workers in the household manufacturing sector as compared to the entire state. This is because of the concentration of the coir and umbrella making industries in the household sector. Leading umbrella exporters of the country give out their work to home-based workers. There are many workers in the organized sector industries too, such as Scooters Kerala Limited, Kerala State Drugs and Pharmaceuticals Limited, and Foam Mattings. There are a lot of women workers in the coir, fisheries, and agricultural sectors in the hinterlands of Alleppey. Female work participation is higher for the district than for the state. There are nearly 30,000 women working in about 250 fish-processing units in Alleppey district. Alleppey town also has fish-processing units. Census data indicate that the number of unemployed is very high for Kerala state and even higher for the town (see Table 30.1).

Main workers are "those who had worked for the major part of the year preceding the enumeration." Marginal workers are "those who have worked any time at all during the year preceding the enumeration, but have not worked for the major part of the year."

Table 30.1
Percentage of Workers and Non-workers

Category of Workers		*Kerala State*	*Alleppey District*	*Alleppey Municipality*
Main workers	Total - T	28	30	28
	Male - M	45	43	44
	Female - F	13	17	12
Marginal	T	3	4	2
	M	3	3	2
	F	3	4	2
Non-workers	T	68	66	70
	M	52	53	54
	F	84	78	86

Source: Sebastian 1998: 172.

Health Supporting Systems in Alleppey—An Analysis of Food Production and Consumption

Changes in Agriculture

In 1860 (before joining the British India Free Trade Zone), Travancore was a net exporter of rice, which is the staple food of the local population. Today, the State of Kerala imports 16 lakh tonnes of rice from other states, the state's own total production being 11 lakh tonnes (Umadevi 1994). The cause of decline of paddy cultivation to about two lakh hectares and of vegetable farms can be traced to various domestic and global factors.

In the later part of the nineteenth and early part of twentieth century, there were famines followed by epidemics in Alleppey. The occurrence of such famines was associated with commercialization of farming and government's policy of non-interference in private grain trade. Laws were enacted to hand over large tracts of land to European planters on very favorable and easy terms to facilitate large-scale cash crop cultivation (mainly of coconut, rubber, coffee, and tea) by British agro-entrepreneurs (Black 1992). This liberal and free trade, initiated by the mercantile capitalism during the colonial period, may be considered as a precursor to today's structural adjustment regimes.

Promotion of cash crops continued in the post-independence period. In the seventies, there was aggressive promotion of cocoa plantations by the multinational Cadbury-Schweppes. The company's withdrawal in the eighties caused severe hardship to the farmers. In the same period, there began a similar promotion of rubber plantations. In 1996–97, when the central government put rubber and rubber products in the import list as part of the liberalization policies, prices of rubber fell. Small-scale rubber farmers were once again in the same plight as the former cocoa cultivators. Some of them even took the extreme step, that of suicide.

The local farmer's reasons for cash crop cultivation ranged from the increasing cost of inputs such as labor and fertilizers to the comparative non-profitability of paddy cultivation. The high literacy and unionization of labor resulted in high wages (Anthony 1994), and landowners looked for less labor absorbing crops. Cultivation of cash crops was less labor consuming than paddy cultivation, and much more profitable. The growth of

Table 30.2
Landholding Pattern in Alleppey Town

Quantity	*Percent Households*
Less than 1 hectare	84.78
1–2 hectares	8.9
2–4 hectares	5.44
more than 4 hectares	0.86

Source: Sebastian 1998: 108.

Table 30.3
Area under Various Crops in Alleppey Town

Crop	*Percent Area*
Paddy	18.05
Tapioca	1.104
Rubber	0.0
Pepper	1.8
Cashew	0.08
Coconut	78.7
Others	1.65

Source: Sebastian 1998.

trade, commerce, and the banking sector in the state also played a role in promotion of cash crop cultivation. Many farm owners were in need of doing one more job apart from farming in their small holdings and it was only natural that such farmers would take to cash crops, which do not need much attention and time (see Tables 30.2 and 30.3).

The introduction of measures under the Structural Adjustment Programs, such as withdrawal of subsidies for farming, and decontrol of fertilizer prices, have further aggravated the problems on the food front. There was a steep rise in fertilizer prices in 1991 (George 1994). After the decontrol of pricing and distribution of fertilizers in 1992, there was an alarming drop in the consumption of phosphate and potash, which are very important to the soil conditions of Kerala. Fertilizer consumption in the state declined from 0.225 million tonnes during 1991–92 to 0.201 million tonnes during 1992–93. Though fertilizers are scale neutral technically, they are not scale neutral in the special case of

Kerala and of Alleppey in particular, where small and marginal farmers find it difficult to invest in fertilizers with their little surplus. In the coming years, paddy cultivation may suffer serious setbacks.

The export orientation of Structural Adjustment Programs gave further impetus to the conversion of Alleppey's farms for purposes other than paddy cultivation and deprived people of their resources for survival. The demand for crabs, prawns, and lobsters in Western countries lured people to convert their rice fields into farms of the above aquatic organisms and to make quick money in the emerging export market. This also resulted in large-scale unemployment among agricultural workers, whose services were no longer required in the new lobster farms. When food prices went up, unemployed workers found it difficult to buy sufficient food and were forced to switch over to consumption of poor quality, high bulk, and low energy food.

Reduction in Fish Catch

Liberalization has opened up the coastal areas to mechanized fishing, with trawlers and "purse seines." These cause extensive damage to the seabed and hence to the entire ecosystem. They have also affected the livelihood of traditional fishermen.

Fish has become a rare and costly item for the poor, who used to eat fish in plenty in earlier times. First, some of their favorite fish, such as sardines, are now being exported. Second, there has been a reduction in fish catch from the ponds and backwater basin in Alleppey, partly due to "infrastructure development" projects in and around Alleppey. The construction of "salt water barriers," "spillways," and "highways" have obstructed free flow and killed the water system of Alleppey, causing reduction of a large number of aquatic organisms. Third, several types of chemicals from the paddy fields (where the Green Revolution promoted the increased use of fertilizers, pesticides, and insecticides) have spilled over into these stagnant water bodies. This has not only reduced the fish population, but has also made them unsuitable for human consumption (Sebastian 1998).

Public Distribution System to Ensure Food Security

Alleppey's public distribution system is part of a state-wide network established during the forties as a war-time emergency. During the Second World War, when Japan captured those countries which used to supply rice to India, Kerala was one of the most affected states in terms of food scarcity as it had already become dependent on import. Peasant organizations and trade unions of Alleppey took part in a state-wide agitation for compulsory procurement of food grains from landlords, and its distribution through fair price shops. People's food committees were set up to lead this struggle. War also led to a severe decline in export of coir products from the town and the situation of workers became particularly pathetic with famine and epidemic outbreaks. By 1943, the Travancore state brought the distribution of food under government control. The government passed an act in 1966 (Kerala Rationing Order) by which the state conferred on every individual the right to possess a ration card and to draw rations on it.

The utilization of public distribution services in Alleppey is very high. This may be related to the poor purchasing capacity of the people. The comparatively less income from Gulf remittances, absence of a highly remunerative cash crop like rubber in Alleppey, and growing unemployment levels could be the reasons for such poor purchasing power. The system, no doubt, provides food security to the poor and enables them to lead an active and comparatively healthier life. However, the public distribution system by itself is not a sufficient measure to ensure sustained food security as other forms of economic security are also important.

Changes in Food Consumption Patterns

Food consumption patterns also seem to have changed recently. Among the middle class and rich households, infiltration of "junk food culture" is apparent; 12 out of 250 households surveyed in the town admitted that they regularly used bottled mineral water and carbonated drinks. An analysis of the various items of food consumed by households revealed the gradual replacement of traditional items such as *dosa-sambar* with cornflakes, cookies, and many other refined, fiberless, easy-to-make items. The advent of preserved and junk food into daily diets at the cost of locally available nutritious items may have far-reaching consequences on the health of the young generation. The "demonstration effect" of such practices may soon affect the dietary habits of the poor households too.

Implications for Nutritional Status

The above developments have depleted the health supporting systems of the people. In order to plant cash crops, farmers stopped planting various tubers, such as cassava and tapioca, which were consumed in earlier years. This has eroded their "emergency food stocks" and made them dependent on imports. Seafood formed a major component of food; as delineated above, this inexpensive source of protein is now not easily available. There is malnutrition and chronic hunger among the poor, although there is no absolute poverty or starvation in present-day Alleppey. A UNICEF study in late eighties found out significant prevalence of malnutrition among the children (Gopalan et al. 1995). One can see similar trends in the subsequent years in the height/weight records maintained by *Anganwadi* workers and the records of the Community Development Society, a major non-governmental organization involved in development activities in the town.

Patterns of Disease

The public health scenario of Alleppey is very much related to the ecological characteristics, namely, stagnant water and filth in the canals criss-crossing the town, the marshy terrain, hot and humid weather, and proximity to Kuttanadu region where intensive paddy cultivation is undertaken with a heavy dose of chemical agents. The drainages of restaurants and public urinals open into the canals. All these characteristics, as also the roots of water hyacinths which fill the backwater basin, and the many coir processing units in the town, facilitate mosquito breeding and the town is full of mosquitoes, especially the waterlogged areas where the poor live.

Out of the 250 households interviewed in an attempt to understand their health problems, only eight households stated that they were not affected by any ailments in the previous three months. The most commonly reported ailments were fever and stomach disorders.

Lack of access to safe drinking water is a major problem here. People mainly use groundwater, collected either from their own wells, or supplied by the Kerala Water Authority. Studies such as Kuttanadu Water Balance Study have pointed out that the

Table 30.4
Data on Cholera and Diarrhea Cases in Alleppey Town

Year	*No. of Cholera Cases*	*No. of Diarrhea Cases*
1988–89	77	1,044
1989–90	31	8,282
1990–91	105	8,581
1991–92	27	4,597
1992–93	36	5,568
1993–94	40	5,609
1994–95	42	5,656
1995–96	46	5,801

Source: Sebastian 1998: 158.

groundwater in the town is unsuitable for human consumption due to the presence of unfavorable chemical components, such as nitrites, nitrates, ammonia, and iron, and of micro-organisms arising from fecal pollution. The physical characteristics of water, namely, pH, turbidity, and color are also not favorable. The rusted pipes often allow the sewage water to mix with "municipal water" supplied for drinking. Repair work has not been undertaken for many years due to scarcity of funds.

The incidence of *Vibrio cholera* is increasing. The disease is common among poor households, where poor sanitation and unsafe drinking water provide a fertile soil for bacteria to breed. Children under five constitute the majority of the victims. Table 30.4 shows that the incidence of water-borne diseases has been steadily increasing since 1991–92.

The above data do not provide figures on cholera mortality. According to newspaper reports, there were five, four, six, and seven cholera deaths during the years 1994, 1995, 1996, and till July 1997 respectively. Though it is widely known that cholera is a reportable disease, there is widespread reluctance by authorities to report cases because of possible repercussions on the economy. Deliberate under-reporting of cholera cases is common, as the municipality would like to make money through tourism and food exports.

Re-emergence of Vector-borne Epidemics

In the early nineties, WHO had pointed out that areas adjacent to intensive wheat cultivation may record high incidence of dengue,

Table 30.5
Data on Number of Recorded Cases of Epidemics other than Cholera, Jaundice, Dysentery, and Diarrhea in Alleppey Town

	Numbers per year							
	1988–89	*1989–90*	*1990–91*	*1991–92*	*1992–93*	*1993–94*	*1994–95*	*1995–96*
Alleppey municipality	303	658	1,374	685	862	860	901	972
Total of the four nearby municipalities of the district	951	946	943	941	1028	N.A	N.A	N.A

Source: Sebastian 1998: 160.

while rice-cultivated areas would record incidence of Japanese encephalitis. Despite this warning, the municipal authorities could not arrest an outbreak of Japanese encephalitis during April–June 1996, in which 300 cases were reported from the town. Physicians who were interviewed talked of fresh cases of malaria and filariasis every month. The health department does not keep separate records of these cases. However, the data on epidemics other than the water-borne ones may include such cases also (see Table 30.5). The table indicates an increasing trend in incidence of such diseases.

The health department of the municipality, with assistance from the district medical officer, undertakes various programs, ranging from organizing mosquito eradication to conducting health classes. Over the years, the functions of the municipality have increased. However, the resources at their disposal are meager and the municipality is currently considering options, such as privatizing activities like waste-disposal. A review of various activities undertaken by the municipality gives the impression that almost all the time the authorities were reacting in panic to an emergency situation, rather than anticipating the situation and taking measures to pre-empt such situations.

Concluding Remarks

Evidence from Alleppey suggests that SAP may not be a new invention, but the latest of the ongoing efforts to have access to the resources of the developing countries by powerful interests. In the early years, "free trade," followed by foreign investment in large-scale production activities and employment of extremely cheap labor led to the growth of Alleppey town as a principal manufacturing and exporting center on the Kerala coast. But the investor entrepreneurs deserted the town at a later stage, partly due to the growth of a politically active population in the town, which demanded more wages and rights. When the decline in industrial and food production front started depriving people of their "exchange entitlements" and "health resources," the government could contain the situation to a limited extent only, by providing subsidized health services and ensuring food supply through public distribution networks.

Unfortunately governments are forced by international institutions to withdraw from investing in "public goods" or in the so-called "soft sectors." In areas like Alleppey, which were producing food crops for local consumption, there is tremendous pressure on food security systems because of export orientation and extensive cash crop cultivation. Withdrawal of subsidies and credit facilities as part of Structural Adjustment Programs have further affected the food production levels and therefore nutritional standards of households in the regions have suffered.

Measures need to be taken at small town levels to tackle local issues such as mosquito eradication, provision of safe drinking water, and disposal of waste. However, such measures may remain ineffective in the face of onslaughts by powerful transnational business interests that are capable of re-articulating and redirecting urban planning debates and policy priorities in developing countries. The problems faced by small towns as well as cities in these countries are in fact problems emanating from poverty and lack of resources.

References

Anthony, B. (1994): Trends in Agricultural Wages in Kerala 1986–90. Paper Presented in the International Congress on Kerala Studies, 27–29 August, Trivandrum.

Black, P.E. (1992): Planters Lobby in late 19th century—Implications for Travancore. *Economic and Political Weekly*, 27(33): 1747–53.

George, M. (1994): Uncertain Fertiliser Price Policy for Uncertain Agriculture. Paper Presented in the International Congress on Kerala Studies, 27–29 August, Trivandrum.

Gopalan, S., Bhupathy, R., and **Raj, Hilda.** (1995): Appraisal of Success factors in Nutrition Relevant Programmes/Projects—A Case Study of the Alapuzha Community Based Nutrition Programme. Paper presented at the National Workshop on UBSP (Urban Basic Services for the Poor), 3–5 July, Trivandrum.

Sebastian, K.S. (1998): Public Health and Urban Processes: A Study of Alleppey Town. Doctoral dissertation. New Delhi: Center of Social Medicine and Community Health, Jawaharlal Nehru University.

Umadevi, S. (1994): Critical Comments of Kerala Model of Development. Paper Presented in the International Congress on Kerala Studies, 27–29 August, Trivandrum.

31

The Labor Process and its Impact on the Lives of Women Workers

Meena Gopal

Introduction

In the planning and formulation of public policy, increasingly more emphasis is being laid on issues affecting women's lives and specific interventions are being targeted at them. For instance, the *World Development Report 1993* with its theme of *Investing in Health*, stresses the issue of women's empowerment. It suggests that governments should pursue economic policies that promote growth and equity so that the poor and vulnerable can increase their incomes. At the same time, the thrust should be on fostering an environment that enables households to improve their health and enhances women's capacity to improve their health and that of their families (World Bank 1993).

One of the aspects it addresses, which is of interest to us, is that of health risks in the occupational environment within and outside the home. It lists the burden of illness arising from exposure to toxic chemicals, noise, stress, and physically debilitating work patterns and suggests remedies such as "safety education for workers and managers, use of appropriate equipment and technology, and sound management practices." Governments are urged to press through legislation, regulation, financial incentives, and invest in education, research, and development in these directions (World Bank 1993: 95–96). In other words, the emphasis is on technological interventions and has nothing to do with the economic and social environment. These technological as well as managerial interventions that are adopted to achieve women's empowerment do not touch upon the structural constraints in the day-to-day lives of women. Also, the larger processes leading to their disempowerment do not figure in these strategies.

The specific focus on enhancing women's capacities in the workforce takes no cognizance of the fact that women are increasingly being pushed into the unorganized sector or of their burden of caring for the family. Along with the latter, women are expected to take on the responsibilities left behind by a receding state, which rather than relieving them of their pressures, adds to the burden of their existence. We argue, that to offer better strategies of empowerment, the social processes which impinge upon women's lives and work have to be understood.

Around 90 percent of the workforce in our country is in the unorganized sector that characterizes production in bulk of the small industries. In the current phase of export-oriented production and multinational investment, leading to integration of the Indian economy into the world market, these sectors are being tapped for the "cheap and docile labor-force." Though the products span a wide range, from processed foods to garments to electronic and pharmaceutical goods, the lines of production are similar. While the organized sector is declining, the unorganized sector is expanding and vulnerable sections are pushed into this labor market (Bagchi 1994). In 1991, around 96 percent of the women workers were in the unorganized sector. This had increased, from around 94 percent in the seventies (Gopalan 1995). Not only is the proportion of women workers in the unorganized sector of the workforce large, it has also steadily increased over the years in terms of absolute numbers. This sector is characterized by low levels of technological inputs in production, maintains decentralized processes, and perpetuates exploitation under inhuman conditions of work. The workforce is scattered and dominated by migrant labor, with a large number of women and child workers. The system of contracting and subcontracting is the predominant mode of employment. Wage payment is often through the piece-rate system and the workers have no control over the terms and conditions of work. In such situations women workers fare badly as they are pushed into the worst forms of unorganized production processes (Kalpagam 1994; Singh and Kelles-Viitanen 1987).

The question that needs to be addressed is: "will Structural Adjustment Programs (SAP), that actually enhance the pace of exploitative processes, help improve the conditions of women's lives?" We attempt to look at women's place within the labor process in one such form of production in the unorganized sector: the home-based beedi industry. We observe the conditions of work generated and the transformation induced in women's lives and identity as workers in home-based work.

Methodology

The objective of the study was to understand the processes by which the home-based beedi industry:

- absorbs women into the labor force;
- uses social institutions to control their labor;
- denies them the many privileges of being a worker;
- influences their lives and perceptions of health; and
- hinders the growth of workers' consciousness among them.

The home-based beedi industry in Tirunelveli district has the largest number of women workers in Tamil Nadu and also produces maximum number of beedis. Tenkasi subdivision was selected, as it alone has nearly 400 of the 1,000 registered beedi establishments in the district (Government of Tamil Nadu 1990). Keelapavoor block, which was the area of the study, has a higher percentage of rural population and is also not excessively commercialized, unlike the other three blocks of Tenkasi taluk. Beedi workers form a significant proportion of the working population, employed by numerous shops spread out in the block.

The structure of the industry was studied through a 50 percent random sample of the villages. All the beedi establishments in the 10 villages were surveyed for data on: the type of shops, the number of workers employed, the size of business and production, nature of the linkages between the various players in the industry, and the problems faced by the managers. One of the 10 sampled villages was chosen for an in-depth qualitative study. A baseline survey, essentially focusing on demographic, economic, and social aspects of the families was carried out. This helped to gain an understanding of the village structure and in identifying the beedi-making households. Four categories of households could be identified with respect to the economic value of women's work (beedi-making):

- households that did not take up beedi-making formed 14 percent;
- *survival households* that depended primarily on women's work for sustenance formed 3.5 percent;
- *support households*, where beedi-making made a significant contribution to the family expenses, but was not primary, constituted 45.5 percent; and
- *accumulation households*, where women's earnings were additional and not essential for the household were 37 percent.

During the qualitative study, the effort was on collection of in-depth information on issues such as:

- The socio-economic and occupational life in the village.
- The structure of the beedi industry in Kalloorani village and the place of women within the labor process as well as the pressures imposed by the shops and the social institutions governing women's lives.
- Women's lives within the household and the adjustments they make with respect to their beedi work.
- Their perceptions of their lives and work and their interaction with the community.
- How their social status tends to merge with the social value of their work and gets linked to their health and their self-image.
- Shifts in priorities that take place with respect to education, health, marriage, and choice of work, with the advent of beedi incomes into the households.
- The views and opinions of men.
- Collective efforts at unionization.

This exploration revealed how women's lives as beedi workers took on different trajectories and the beedi industry was able to reap tremendous benefits by employing them as labor. It also raised certain significant issues concerning health, nutrition, landholdings, the economics of beedi work, and women's perception of their labor. One-third of the households selected for the baseline survey were chosen for a quantitative study.

Organization of Production

The growth of the beedi industry is linked to changes in the rural economy of Tirunelveli in the early part of the twentieth century. The peasants who benefited from the boom in agriculture during that period invested their surpluses in other enterprises, such as trading, or in small-scale production of consumer goods, like matches. These Indian entrepreneurs took over the space created by the haphazard nature of European commercial penetration (Baker 1984). Factory production was overshadowed by small-scale manufacturing activity in tanning, metal and woodwork, and beedi rolling. These were carried out in thousands of little workshops, doorsteps, and backrooms of poor households, courtyards, and stretches of pavement (Baker 1984). The skill of rolling beedis was taught to women agricultural laborers who were temporarily jobless, during the slack season or during a drought. Until the forties, local manufacturers dominated the beedi industry. But when the Ceylon government banned the import of beedis, competition intensified, as entrants from the neighboring states of Kerala and Karnataka came to Tirunelveli in the quest for profits and cheap labor.

The Penetration of the Beedi Industry

Various developments contributed to beedi industry replacing agriculture as the dominant employer of women in the village. Opportunities for women in the agricultural labor market were steadily decreasing, with lesser absorption of female labor in agriculture (Government of India 1961, 1971, 1981). Further, there was a slow loss of agricultural skills especially among the younger women. For the poorer households, there was no land for women to work on and poor health precluded them from venturing into the hard labor of agricultural work. In the well-off households, social pressures for women to work indoors were immense. It was felt that it provided them with the "convenience" of combining beedi rolling with household work. Also, the popular perception was that women's work generally tended to be light and that it was done during spare time as a leisure activity. Perceptions of women beedi workers regarding the preference of work indicates that though about 30 percent of the women expressed a preference for agricultural work, they had no choice but to be pushed into beedi work (Gopal 1997).

Majority of the women were engaged in beedi work, combining it with both general and agricultural labor. The predominant occupations of the menfolk were cultivation, small and big businesses, petty trading, services in government and private institutions, general and agricultural labor, and traditional caste jobs.

Beedi-manufacturing was organized through contractors and subcontractors. There were two types of shops: the company shops and the commission shops. In the first type contractors for the company holding the trademark issued passbooks in the name of home-based workers, gave them the raw materials, and collected the beedis after paying them the "wages" as well as all other benefits due to them. In the commission shops, the subcontractors, also called commission agents, obtained a commission ranging from Re 0.80 to Rs 1.20 per 1,000 beedis collected and sold to the principal company, under whose brand name they operate. They exercised arbitrary powers because of weak links with their principal companies and the informality governing their relations with workers. The company shops also indulged in arbitrary practices but they were comparatively lesser.

At the shop level, women were employed either as passbook holders or as "joint" workers along with the passbook holders or given raw material, that was noted in a little notebook called the *chittai*. All three types of workers worked side by side in both, the company and commission shops. Women's disparate presence in the production process presented a fertile area for their manipulation and exploitation. Their limitations were: basic lack of knowledge of the outside world, illiteracy, and feeling of lack of control of their worker status, and their relationships at the shop.

Exploitative Terms of Work

The employers employed practices by which they kept the workers divided. These practices were: recruitment of some women as "joint" workers and some as *chittai* workers, not accounting for extra bundles collected, not permitting workers to retain leftover raw material for long periods of time, issuing raw material as per quota, and sudden closures of the shops. On entry into the shop, the majority of the women workers were treated in such a manner that they felt obliged and indebted to the shop manager. Such practices that give the employers an upper hand and complete control over women's labor are only possible where there is no common site of work where workers congregate, where the hours of work are not fixed, and where remuneration is in terms of piece-rate work. And where, above all, workers are largely from the socially disadvantaged and weakest sections.

Coping with the Stress of Work

Despite losing out on many benefits, women chose to roll beedis for the commission shops due to the socio-economic position of their families. Beedi work was indispensable in their struggle for survival.

The organization of production in numerous phases gave rise to two phenomena:

1. Work was divided between the actual worker and other members of the household or even neighbors. The latter supported her in various ways, such as folding, cutting the leaves, and making bundles. Thus, many invisible workers were sucked into the beedi-making process.
2. As pressure was exerted by the shops regarding time of delivery, the quota of beedi rolled, and their quality, the women workers had a tension-ridden lifestyle. They adjusted beedi work with household demands and reduced their own leisure.

One means of survival in this stressful situation was to evolve different working relations with other women workers, such as borrowing and lending beedis as interest on loans, rolling for multiple shops with the help of assistance at home, and being members of beedi "chits" or pools (a beedi pool is one where each woman contributes a fixed number of beedis to the pool and the respective members can draw from it in times of need).

Efforts at unionization were another mechanism to cope with the demands of work. A small section of women joined efforts to unionize. However, given the extreme informality of the work process, the perception of women that beedi work was given to them more as a favor than right and the lack of support from menfolk made these efforts at unionization and improving their conditions of work ineffective.

While women sought to help one another through these mechanisms, unwittingly they also passed the terms of exploitation onto one another. These were the "joint" rolling on the same passbook, using younger girls as assistants and as proxy deliverers of the beedis at the shops, the *vatti* (interest) beedi and the sale of raw material. The adjustment and adaptive processes evolved by the women were at the cost of their bargaining power and unity against the employer.

Thus, within the beedi industry, where women were denied a common workplace and knowledge of the totality of the production process, marketing and sales, they were at a definite disadvantage. Not aware of the real reasons for which certain terms and conditions were imposed on them, they tried to compete with each other, whereas they were perpetually dependent on each other as well. The result was that their own labor process resulted in divisiveness.

The Domain of the Household

The household is the place where the working, social, as well as the personal lives, of the women take shape. It is here that the direct and indirect implications of the labor process for health are seen.

Beedi work spilled over into all of women's waking hours. Women were perpetually racing with time. The conditions of work led to a continuous adjustment process not only with their physical needs of food, rest, and sleep, but also leisure as well as household chores. One of the primary adjustments was made in cooking and eating habits. Girls and women delayed their meals on return from the shops, worked for long hours in the sitting position without rest, sustained themselves on coffee to ward off hunger, and sometimes worked into the late hours of night to meet the quota of beedi rolling. Table 31.1 shows how a greater proportion of women of poorer households articulated the stress of beedi work on their eating patterns and sufficiency of food (Gopal 1997). Almost every family had a radio transistor which for most women was a source of leisure as they engaged in beedi work. Viewing films during the weekends was another popular means of leisure for the women and girls in almost all the families. The various adjustments made by the women also affected other

Table 31.1
Perception of Sufficiency and the Number of Times Food is Cooked

Sufficiency of Meals with Times of Cooking Meals		*Household Categories*														
		NOBD			*ACC1*			*ACC2*			*SUPP*			*SURV*		
		Once	*Twice*	*Thrice*	*Once*	*Twice*	*Thrice*	*Once*	*Twice*	*Thrice*	*Once*	*Twice*	*Thrice*	*Once*	*Twice*	*Thrice*
Sufficient	N	6	14	6	14	22	-	13	9	-	44	12	-	3	-	-
	%	20.6	48.3	20.6	31.1	48.9	-	38.2	26.5	-	45.4	12.4	-	42.8	-	-
Preoccupation	N	1	1	-	3	-	-	8	2	-	29	1	-	2	2	-
with work and neglect of food	%	3.5	3.5	-	6.7	-	-	23.5	5.8	-	29.9	1.0	-	28.6	28.6	-
Habituated to	N	1	-	-	4	2	-	1	1	-	10	1	-	-	-	-
eating less	%	3.5	-	-	8.9	4.4	-	3.0	3.0	-	10.3	1.0	-	-	-	-
Grand total	N		29			45			34			97			7	
	%		100			100			100			100			100	

Source: Gopal 1997.
Note: NOBD: No beedi making
ACC: Accumulation
SUPP: Support
SURV: Survival

people, especially the vulnerable in the household. The very young children were neglected and left to play with the hazardous raw material.

Household relations demonstrated women's dependence on men and their own powerlessness. Within the household, there were demands from parents or husbands on the women's incomes for household expenses or for dowry or jewellery. As women managed both their household work and beedi rolling, their lives were held taut by a tension-filled routine. Some women opted out of this tension, but had to lose out on many benefits that the money from making beedi brought in. Women who appreciated the monetary benefits reasoned that beedi work was a permanent job unlike agricultural work, which was seasonal. They felt that it offered jobs for many more people than agricultural labor. Most of all, women considered beedi work profitable because the more one rolled, the more "wages" one earned. Girls in the well-off households became independent as they saved for their dowry.

The economic incentive was so powerful that beedi work overruled all other activities in their immediate value. This affected the priorities of the households. Educating girls was seen as of no immediate value, especially in the well-off households. While a partial interest in girls' education was observed in the support and survival households, the imminent economic vulnerability of women's lives made mothers initiate their daughters into beedi work. In at least a quarter of all households (survival households), beedi rolling was the sole source of income. Only for well-off households, beedi income was for spending on items of leisure and luxury, such as clothes, jewellery, and steel vessels, and savings for dowry. Interestingly, while women's beedi income contributed to household expenses and family savings, the management of finances did not solely rest in women's hands.

Subtle shifts in consumption patterns of the women were linked to the generation and circulation of money. The capacity to buy articles of accumulation and cash, as well as articles of consumption, such as clothes, flowers, cosmetics, trinkets, and gifts, tea and coffee, and snacks served to perpetuate the notion that beedi work had brought "nagareekam" (symbolic prosperity or being cultured). It glamorized their work and provided a gloss over women's drudgery, while simultaneously distracting them from their exploitation at the shop, where their clothes and jewellery were points of reference, and not standing by their fellow worker who may be arbitrarily penalized and discriminated against. The shopowners and traders promoted this trend by encouraging a culture of conspicuous consumption.

Women's perceptions about the effect of their work was varied. Older women said that beedi work had brought *nagareekam*; women could now look after themselves. The middle-aged and younger women, however, felt that "beedi work was hell; they could not go anywhere and life was full of tensions." Besides, they earned backaches, body aches, and illnesses. Apart from the physical stress, they became perpetual victims of worry because of fear of the shopowner. Thus, although beedi work was recognized by the community for its economic value, women did not gain any status or support as workers. A pervasive value was that the dignity of women and girls lies in remaining indoors.

The economic security that beedi work provided did not instill much self-confidence in the women. The low value attached to beedi work, the secondary status of women in households despite being full-fledged workers, their invisibility in the social sphere and its decision-making processes, and the legitimization of their exploitation by their own kin created a sense of inferiority and dependency among women. These factors undermined women's confidence in themselves as workers and increased their work insecurity. The combination of the physical strain and mental worry increased their chances of falling ill. Their low self-esteem not only made them put up with suffering, it also led to their denial to adequate treatment and rest when they most needed it. When ill they mostly resorted to self-medication or treatment from semi-qualified practitioners. This was more out of the need to save time in attending to beedi work and household responsibilities, rather than out of ignorance. However, for their children and their menfolk, they mostly sought allopathic treatment from government hospitals and private practitioners. The inability to organize against the shopowners' arbitrariness and substitute their worry with confidence as workers, can be traced to the inter-linkages between the low self-esteem of women and the dominant ideology of contempt for beedi work in the community.

The shaping of the attitudes towards women's beedi work has to be seen in the context of prevailing social norms that dominate women's lives within the household. Women's relations with other members, mostly men and older women created their self-image. Despite earning Rs 125 to 150 per week and contributing to the household, women had less authority than men in the household decision-making sphere. Beedi work was treated as incidental and secondary to men's earnings even in households where it was the primary source of income. Their economic productivity did not have any liberating effect. It kept women subordinate to men within household relations which bred insecurity in individual women. In case of households where there were no men, male relatives acquired the aura of "protectors" of the household by making nominal economic contributions to the household. Although it was the women who toiled to sustain the family, yet they were dependent on and obliged to these men.

Given the dominant social structure, the traditional roles of women were reinforced by certain rites and rituals. Deviations from the proscribed social roles were sought to be controlled by certain norms and codes of behavior. In general, women were considered ignorant and powerless and needing the protection of men. The mobility of girls was curtailed when they attained puberty. Through marriage and childbirth, their role as "nurturers" was reinforced. It was considered respectable for women to remain indoors. The prevailing social norm did not deem it necessary that their ignorance and lack of exposure to the outside world be replaced by confidence and an increased self-worth. Within such a normative structure, the desires and aspirations of women are curbed as reflected in women's self-denial, powerlessness, and poor self-esteem. These attributes were especially pronounced in the women of the poorest survival households.

The perception of women's beedi work as "work done in their spare time" also affected the women workers. They were not only unable to unite with the men workers at the shops, but they themselves were divided because of their ignorance of the dynamics of the industry and their inability to comprehend their collective exploitation of one another. This was compounded by jealousy, resentment, and competition between one another. Those women who were partially informed and aware of the exploitative terms of the work and were able to articulate it, received no social support in their nascent attempts at collective bargaining.

Men's attitudes to women's beedi work displayed an ambiguity that undermined women's self-respect and dignity as workers. While beedi work was referred to with contempt as "women's work," as work that women did as a pastime for bringing in additional income into the household, and not regarded as hard work, its economic benefit was tacitly and covertly appropriated. Men who had power in the public sphere did not come out against the exploitative terms of work at the beedi shops. Instead, they tacitly supported the employers.

Socio-economic institutions and cultural practices that appropriate the fruits of women's labor, thrive on home-based systems of production. Liquid cash flows have given rise to an economy of credit, with women settling all their accounts once they receive their weekly "wages." A host of institutions of credit, such as "chit fund" companies and money-lenders have emerged to take advantage of this monetization of the economy. The practice of saving in chit funds worked as a social pressure on the support and survival households, which were often forced to join in either to please or to save their jobs, as often the shopowners were the ones who operated the chit-fund companies. The money-lender was only too willing to double-up as the manager of the chit funds that enabled women to save money to buy a little gold jewellery for occasions that glamorized women's traditional roles, such as the puberty rite. The woman who saved in these chits was hardly aware of the fact that whatever money she earned was sucked out by these institutions, which thereby controlled her earnings. The money-lender had considerable power over women and willingly lent money to the women beedi workers. He knew that as women they would not risk public humiliation as defaulters by a man who did not belong to their village and that he could always approach her door on pay day to claim his dues. Religious institutions also controlled women's labor and appropriated their earnings. Women, especially of the survival households felt the economic burden of these payments as they had to spend large sums from their hard-earned incomes on donations to temples and religious celebrations.

Women are aware of the complexity of factors that affect their lives and health, such as their tension-filled work schedules, the constraints on their food intake, sleep, rest and leisure, and overwork. Many women recognize the drudgery of their work and the exploitation they face, but feel isolated and helpless as they are tied down by binding family and community structures.

However, given the exploitative social and workplace structure, and the self-image and attitudes towards work that it instills in women, there seems to be very little scope for women workers to acquire consciousness of their productive worth, to feel empowered, and assert themselves as workers.

Implications for Policy Measures

This study points to the links between women's health problems and the social conditions of their work, and reveals that women's perceptions of themselves and their labor is largely influenced by the social value of their work, and their status within their homes and society.

We see that these issues are not only not being addressed by the present policies, but the entire burden of adjustment is being put on the poorest sections, which includes women, by SAP and liberalization policies. Unless the ground realities raised above are taken into account, the strategies of international agencies for empowerment of women and improvement of their health will not even make a dent in their lives.

References

Bagchi, A.K. (1994): Making Sense of Government's Macro-economic Stabilisation Strategy. *Economic and Political Weekly*, 29(18): 1063–66.

Baker, C.J. (1984): *An Indian Rural Economy: 1880–1955. The Tamil Countryside.* New Delhi: Oxford University Press.

Gopal, M. (1997): Labour Process and its Impact on the Lives of Women Workers: A Study of the Beedi Industry in Keelapavoor Block, Tirunelveli District, Tamil Nadu. Doctoral dissertation, New Delhi: Center of Social Medicine and Community Health, Jawaharlal Nehru University.

Gopalan, S. (1995): *Women and Employment in India.* New Delhi: Har-Anand Publications.

Government of India (1961): *Census of India.* Tamil Nadu, District Census Handbook, Village and Townwise Primary Census Abstract, Tirunelveli. Madras: Office of the Registrar-General.

——— (1971): *Census of India.* Tamil Nadu, District Census Handbook, Village and Townwise Primary Census Abstract, Tirunelveli. Madras: Office of the Registrar-General.

Government of India (1981): *Census of India*. Tamil Nadu, District Census Handbook, Village and Townwise Primary Census Abstract, Tirunelveli. Madras: Office of the Registrar-General.

Government of Tamil Nadu (1990): List of Beedi Establishments Under the Jurisdiction of the Inspector of Labour. Tirunelveli: Office of the Inspector of Labour, Department of Labour.

Kalpagam, U. (1994): *Labour and Gender: Survival in Urban India*. New Delhi: Sage Publications.

Singh, A-M., and **Kelles-Viitanen, A.** (1987): *Invisible Hands: Women in Home-based Production. Women in Household in Asia*. Vol. I. New Delhi: Sage Publications.

World Bank (1993): *World Development Report: Investing in Health*. New York: Oxford University Press.

32

The Reproductive Health Package—A Chimera for Women's Health

Alpana Sagar

Introduction

In India the Child Survival and Safe Motherhood Program has been replaced by the Essential Reproductive and Child Health (RCH) Services Package, which was formulated in the era of the SAP. The RCH Package consists of (*i*) family planning, (*ii*) safe abortion, (*iii*) safe motherhood, (*iv*) prevention and management of reproductive tract and sexually transmitted infection, (*v*) child survival, (*vi*) health, sexuality, and gender information, and (*vii*) education and counseling, and referral services for all of the above (Meashan and Heaver 1996). It is claimed that this package will improve the health of poor women (Government of India 1994). This claim is as questionable as that of the WB and the IMF that SAP will usher in a golden era, both for the economy of the country and the health of the people (Antia 1994). The cutbacks in expenditure on the social welfare sector and the reduction in subsidies are surely not aimed at improving the quality of life of the poor people (Prabhu 1994). Similarly, the health care reforms, with its techno-centric bias, stress on privatization, resetting of priorities, and neglect of social considerations, would affect the existing health services and primary health care (Qadeer 1995) and may well have a negative impact on poor people's health, especially that of women (Duvurry 1994).

This chapter explores the relevance of the RCH Package for the health of poor women. It looks at the ground realities of poor women's lives and assesses how far their needs will be met by the RCH Package. It also highlights the links between maternal health and general illness and reveals the gaps in the perceptions of doctors and women regarding the needs of the latter. It is argued that the experiences of ill health by women cannot be ignored/negated as is done by the medical professionals and policy-makers.

Methodology

The sources of the poor health of women are traced by integrating data on maternal health and general illness of women, pregnancy outcomes, as well as perceptions and experiences of women regarding pregnancy, with their socio-economic background. We also look at the impact of this ill health upon the women and their babies. The data were obtained from a study carried out over a period of five years in a slum in Delhi that was located in the midst of extremely affluent colonies and huddled under the shadow of the august All India Institute of Medical Sciences. From about 3,000 households a 50 percent simple random sample was selected. Women from these selected households, who were three to five months pregnant at the time of selection, were enrolled initially and more women were added to the sample as they became pregnant. A total of 183 women were enrolled, including 17 women who delivered twice, leading to a total of 200 pregnancies.

A socio-economic survey of the sample households and detailed medical and sociological data on the pregnant women were collected through observation, obstetric history sheets, informal semi-structured interviews, and open-ended questionnaires. Time was spent in establishing rapport with the women to understand their lives through case studies, in-depth interviews, and group discussions. The records of a general outpatient and antenatal clinic which was run twice a week by the researcher for the women of this slum were also used for comparison with the field data on pregnant women. To ensure comparability of obstetric field data, only women who were seen in the fifth, sixth, seventh, eighth, and ninth months of pregnancy were assessed. This excluded those who went to the village, delivered prematurely, aborted, or left the slum. Thus, only 117 women were considered for clinical evaluation, but all 200 women were questioned for their experience of pregnancies.[1] By developing close associations with these women, it was possible to note their experiences and perceptions of pregnancy, of maternal morbidity and its causes, and the various kinds of health care sought.

The People of the Slum

The people in this slum were migrants (commonly first generation), mainly landless or marginally landed villagers, and belonging to the lower castes. They had come to the city in search of a means of livelihood. A majority of these migrants were from Uttar Pradesh, others had come from Tamil Nadu, Rajasthan, Bihar, West Bengal, etc. A majority of the slum dwellers were in an economic situation where any crisis—be it an illness, or the loss of a job—could threaten the very survival of the family. Though a heterogeneous lot, what they had in common was the poverty that kept them in this dirty and squalid slum. There were almost no facilities in the slum—the entire population of more than 3,000 households was serviced by only about 40 toilets. Eight taps supplied drinking water at prescribed times of the day and 25 handpumps supplied saline ground-water for general household use. The drains were open and had been dug by the residents of the slum. There was no proper system of garbage disposal.

The socio-economic profiles of the subsample and the total sample were similar. Amongst the households of pregnant women, about 85 percent were Hindus, 12 percent Muslims, and the rest were Christians. Of the Hindus, 56 percent belonged to scheduled castes, 35 percent to backward castes, and 10 percent belonged to the higher castes. Almost 73 percent of these women had never been to school and only 18 percent had studied in primary school, though most of them could not even read at present.

[1]Amongst these 200 pregnant women, only 10.5 percent were *primigravida*, though 25.5 percent of these women had no live issue; for 19.5 percent it was the second pregnancy, while 24 percent had one live child; for 17.5 percent it was the third pregnancy, while 18 percent had two live children; for 17 percent it was the fourth pregnancy, while 20 percent had three live children; and for 35.5 percent it was the fifth pregnancy, or more, whereas only 10.5 percent had more than four living children. In all, 27 percent of these women had lost children and only about 61 percent of the children had survived, indicating the high foetal wastage and child mortality rate.

Males were better educated, but almost 36 percent had never attended school, 41 percent had attended primary or elementary school, and 23 percent had studied beyond that.

Monthly family incomes at the time of the study (1991–95) were below Rs 1,000 for 31 percent, from Rs 1,000–2,000 for 67 percent, and more than Rs 2,000 for only 2 percent. The importance of income lay in the degree of its regularity or irregularity.[2] It was seen that the lowest-income category had the largest number of men working for (irregular) daily wages and the least numbers working in government or private jobs. In comparison, the mid-income group had much fewer men working for daily wages and a greater number holding government or private jobs. In the highest-income group, none of the men were working on daily wages or were unemployed and comparatively much larger numbers were in government or private jobs. This indicated that the poorer families had more irregular incomes, whilst the less poor households tended to have more regular incomes.

As against the men, amongst the pregnant women, 72 percent were housewives; 25 percent were domestic help in houses or offices, with a temporary but regular monthly income ranging between Rs 300 to Rs 900; 3 percent were unskilled daily wage workers or ragpickers, with an irregular income of Rs 30–40 per day; and 0.5 percent had government jobs, mainly as sweepers, with a permanent monthly income ranging from Rs 1,200 to Rs 1,800. The men were somewhat better situated, with 55 percent in private jobs, earning a temporary but regular monthly income of Rs 900–1,200; or self-employed petty or medium traders, with monthly earnings ranging from Rs 1,000 to Rs 2,500; 31 percent were unskilled and skilled daily wage workers or small time self-employed people, with an irregular income ranging from Rs 40 to Rs 80 per day; 11 percent were in government jobs, mainly as sweepers, earning Rs 1,200–1,800 per month; and the

A government job implies permanent income and leave with pay. For those with private jobs, the income is regular for long periods unless the worker changes jobs or is dismissed. Also, occasionally these workers can avail of a few days' leave without losing their pay or job. For daily wage earners, however, there is pay only when they work. Whilst during a "good season" they may earn almost everyday, during the slack period they may hardly earn enough to survive. As men usually earn the greater part of the income, the significance of such a large number of male irregular earners must not be underestimated. The monthly income in these families can range from Rs 2,000 to Rs 300–400.

rest were either unemployed or had gone away. There was a distinct difference not only in the educational status between the men and women, but also in the jobs available to them, as well as in their incomes. This was significant as it revealed these women's social value—not only in the household, but also outside it.

In 28 percent of the families both husband and wife were contributing to the family income. Interestingly, in households where the husbands had lower incomes, more women were found to be employed. Households with employed women, however, had overall higher incomes, thus illustrating that family incomes were often higher because of the women's contribution. In the higher-income households, only 25 percent women were housewives, whereas in the middle-income group 65 percent were housewives, and in the poorest families, as many as 90 percent were housewives. This also demonstrated quite clearly the importance of the women's contribution to family incomes. In the higher-income households, 75 percent of women who were earning were all working as domestic help and had regular incomes. In the middle-income group 31 percent of the women were domestic help, while 5 percent were daily wage workers with irregular incomes. In the poorest families, while only 8 percent were domestic help and none were employed as daily wage workers, 2 percent held government jobs (none of the women in the other two groups had government jobs). This revealed that where women had comparatively better placed jobs, their husbands tended to earn less, thus placing a greater burden on their wives. It also indicated that in the poorest families women were unable to earn either because they could not get a job, or because they were moving between the village and the slum due to family or economic stress. Seven percent of the women of the total households were in the village.

Compared to women in the general sample, the women with pregnancies (200) had 6 percent less employment. The greatest number of women stopping work was in the better-off households. Thus, the women who cut down on their workload were more often from families where the husbands had a better earning capacity—often women in lower-income households despite their poor health could not afford to stop working. It was also important that in this subsample of pregnant women, there was no household without any income, whereas there were about

2 percent such families in the larger sample. Pregnant women therefore seemed to be under compulsion to work when their husbands were unemployed or absent.

The Links between Maternal Health and General Illness

On comparing disease patterns of non-pregnant women coming to the clinic for medical care with the disease patterns of the pregnant women in the study, a striking similarity between the women's general diseases and their diseases during pregnancy was noted. For example, 16 percent of the non-pregnant women were seeking treatment for anemia, as were almost 27 percent of the pregnant women. Similarly, 5 percent of the non-pregnant women and 15 percent of the pregnant women complained of symptoms of hyperacidity, demonstrating that pre-existing health disorders were exacerbated during pregnancy. However, the incidence of infectious diseases was 47 percent in non-pregnant, and 26 percent in pregnant women (see Figure 32.1). It would not, therefore, be wrong to say that women bear a large burden of ill health before pregnancy and as the problems of anemia and hyperacidity revealed, their health during pregnancy was adversely affected by this pre-existing burden of ill health.

The field data on the pregnant women revealed a large range of pregnancy-related and infectious illness. Almost 95 percent of the women had at least two complaints of pregnancy-related illness. At each visit, 72 percent women had complained of tiredness and 25 percent of body pains. Sixty-two percent had clinically moderate anemia for at least two visits, and 18 percent had marked pedal edema at least once. About 62 percent had at least one episode of lower abdominal pain requiring medication, 45 percent had anorexia and nausea (sufficient to need medication) more than once, 9 percent had spotting, while 5 percent had aborted. Twenty-six percent had suffered at least one episode of infectious illness and 64 percent had complained at least once of pregnancy-related or infectious illness per visit for all five visits.

However, of the 95 percent of women who had complained of pregnancy-related ill health at least twice, 68 percent had sought care, while of the 26 percent with infective illness, only 13 percent

Figure 32.1
Similarities in Morbidity Patterns between Pregnant and Non-pregnant Women

Infections	Pregnant women	Non-pregnant women
Respiratory	10.60%	17.60%
Alimentary	5.20%	10.60%
PID	2.90%	10%
Skin	1.20%	3.40%
Fevers	5.30%	3.20%
Urinary	0.80%	2.40%
Total	26.00%	47.10%

Infections	Pregnant women	Non-pregnant women
Respiratory	10.6% (78)	17.6% (104)
Alimentary	5.2% (38)	10.6% (63)
PID	2.9% (21)	10% (59)
Skin	1.2% (9)	3.4% (20)
Fevers	5.3% (39)	3.2% (19)
Urinary	0.8% (6)	2.4% (14)
Total	26% (191 of 734 problems)	47.1% (279 of 592 problems)

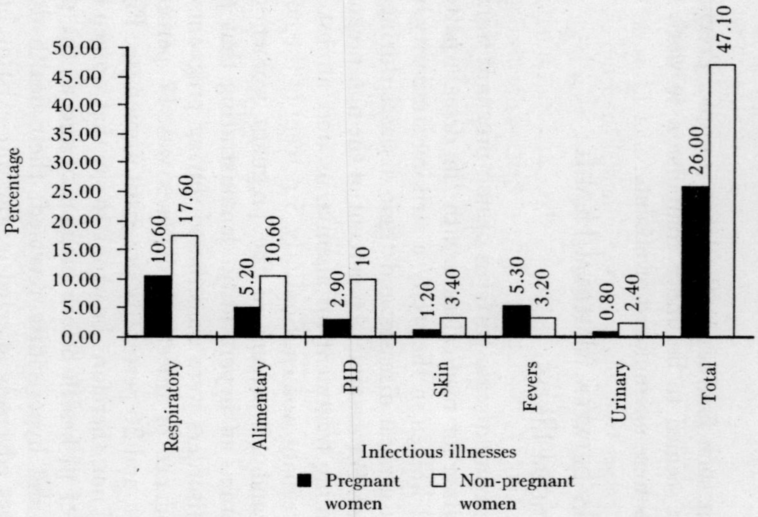

Note: Data for all the tables collected by the author through the surveys.

had sought care. It was also seen that women tended to visit the doctor only when they had more than one complaint of ill health.

Factors such as poverty, overwork, and social inequality accounted for the fact that these women's health had never been a priority. The foundations of their health had been laid in girlhood itself (Malobika 1993). Later, as wives and mothers, social roles had made them deprive themselves nutritionally and otherwise in favor of their family. An example of this was the custom of women eating after the household members had had their fill. In poor households, therefore, the women often did not get sufficient to eat and their health suffered (Harriss 1990). Along with this role as caretakers of the family was the burden of household and outside work as well as the toll reproduction took on their health.

The demands of managing a house, taking care of the husband and children, and going out to work to bring in extra money tended to place the women's own health quite low on the list of priorities. This was a social reality that they were resigned to accept—a manifestation of their lack of value in a patriarchal society. As one woman stated, "If I die, he (my husband) will bring a new wife who will hopefully take care of my children, but if he dies, our lives (mine and my children's) are ruined, for who will take care of us?" However, many women stated that it was pointless for them to waste their time talking and worrying about circumstances that needed to be changed, but which they had no power to change. Most of them had learned by bitter experience that there was precious little they could do about it, "it is best if one is not born if one is a girl." They knew there was nothing they could do about their financial constraints, household duties, or ill health. They realized that their socio-economic situation was to blame and many stated "rich women have better health during pregnancy and otherwise, for if one is rich then one can take care of one's health."

Most women could link their ill health during pregnancy to poverty, domestic tensions, excess workload, previous reproductive health problems, and previous ill health. For most women this wretched cycle of ill health and overwork was one they experienced throughout their lives as well as in every pregnancy. They agreed that they had more work than they could manage. Many felt they were unhealthy because of excess workload, while others felt they were unable to carry out their work because they were ill. In addition, they faced the problem of social negation of many of their illnesses that were attributed to their being "delicate," "neurotic or oversensitive" (Sagar 1994).

Morbidity was assessed by all women (whether pregnant or not) by its impact on their ability to carry out routine duties. Only when they could not manage their routine work did they think of seeking a doctor. A common refrain was, "since household duties have to be carried out by the woman, she may as well carry them out to the best of her ability without complaining." Therefore, when they were pregnant, these women tended to cut corners. Usually this mechanism helped them to keep up with the household work until about the sixth or seventh month of pregnancy, by which time their working capacity was markedly reduced. At this point in time, many employed women (those who could) began to cut down on their work.

Women had thus learned to live with a certain burden of chronic suffering and tolerated ill health until it crossed a certain threshold. Tiredness, weakness, and giddiness due to anemia were these poor women's companions throughout life, and were exacerbated during pregnancy. Problems like nausea, emesis, backache, a degree of abdominal pain were also accepted to a certain extent as a part of the discomfort associated with pregnancy. Infectious diseases too were recognized to occur during pregnancy as well as otherwise. However, since the pregnancy-related problems were chronic, after a point they tended to affect the women's work. Infectious diseases on the other hand often subsided in a few days. Only severe or chronic infections affected the women's functioning. Therefore, women sought care more often for obstetric problems than for infections and fevers. For many women (at least in this low-income population), pregnancy was not believed to be a disease which needed medical treatment by the doctor but a part of their life, and only the troublesome symptoms necessitated going for medical care.

A large number of the factors responsible for these poor women's ill health were not amenable to medical treatment. The women knew this, hence at bearable levels these problems were not sufficient reasons to seek health care. There was also the notion that medicines were "hot," and "were no substitute for food or rest."

Furthermore, even when women knew they were unwell and required treatment, their sickness needed to be legitimized by a figure of authority. These women lived in a social environment where their figures of authority—their husbands or mothers-in-law—tended to underplay their health needs, especially during pregnancy, when the burden of morbidity was negated merely because it was shared by all women. It was only when they were close to incapacitation that their ill health was socially accepted and became "real" and they could seek medical care.

Medical help was sought only when they were too ill to cope on their own, or when they felt that medicines would help them or their unborn child, or when they needed sanction for food or rest. For instance, women were told that tetanus toxoid injection prevents tetanus in the newborn and hence neonatal mortality. Therefore, a large number of women came for tetanus toxoid injections.

Validity of Women's Experiences of Ill Health

Given the correlation between the mother's health and the baby's birth-weight, the importance of the pregnant woman's experiential health was reaffirmed when it was used to assess the impact on the birth weight of the baby.[3] The data showed:

1. Almost 64 percent of women had at least one problem of ill health per field visit and suffered from ill health throughout their pregnancy. When compared with women who did not have a health problem at each visit, it was noticed that the former tended to have a comparatively greater percentage of babies of low birth weight (see Figure 32.2). This difference was statistically significant.
2. Infectious diseases had an impact on the birth weight of the baby. Of all women with any illness, those who had more than two episodes of infectious illness had a greater proportion of low birth weight babies compared to those who had one or no infectious episode (see Figure 32.3). This difference was also statistically significant. Whereas, 26 percent of pregnant women suffered from infectious illness, only 13 percent sought care, but many of those

[3] A birth weight of less than 2.5 kg was taken as low birth weight.

Figure 32.2
Relationship between Birth Weights of Term Babies and Pregnant Women's Subjective Ill Health

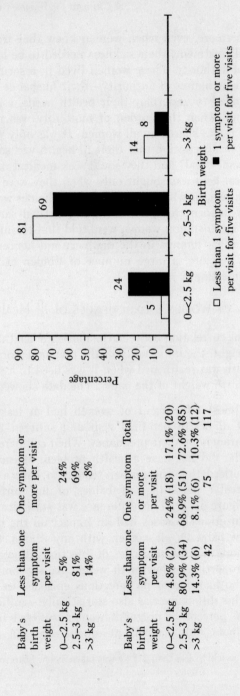

Baby's birth weight	Less than one symptom per visit	One symptom or more per visit
0–<2.5 kg	5%	24%
2.5–3 kg	81%	69%
>3 kg	14%	8%

Baby's birth weight	Less than one symptom per visit	One symptom or more per visit	Total
0–<2.5 kg	4.8% (2)	24% (18)	17.1% (20)
2.5–3 kg	80.9% (34)	68.9% (51)	72.6% (85)
>3 kg	14.3% (6)	8.1% (6)	10.3% (12)
	42	75	117

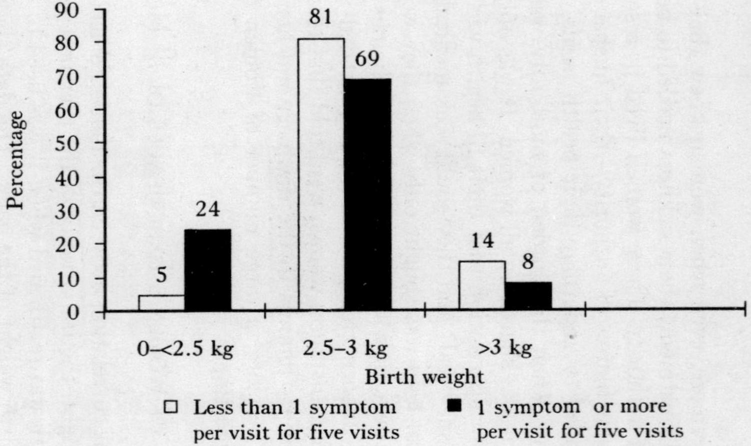

Figure 32.3

Relationship between Infectious Illness in Women during Pregnancy and Birth Weights of Term Babies

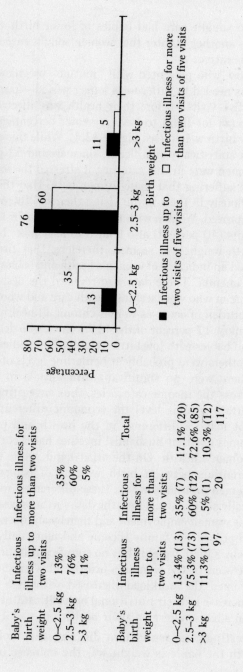

Baby's birth weight	Infectious illness up to two visits	Infectious illness for more than two visits
0–<2.5 kg	13%	35%
2.5–3 kg	76%	60%
>3 kg	11%	5%

Baby's birth weight	Infectious illness up to two visits	Infectious illness for more than two visits	Total
0–<2.5 kg	13.4% (13)	35% (7)	17.1% (20)
2.5–3 kg	75.3% (73)	60% (12)	72.6% (85)
>3 kg	11.3% (11)	5% (1)	10.3% (12)
	97	20	117

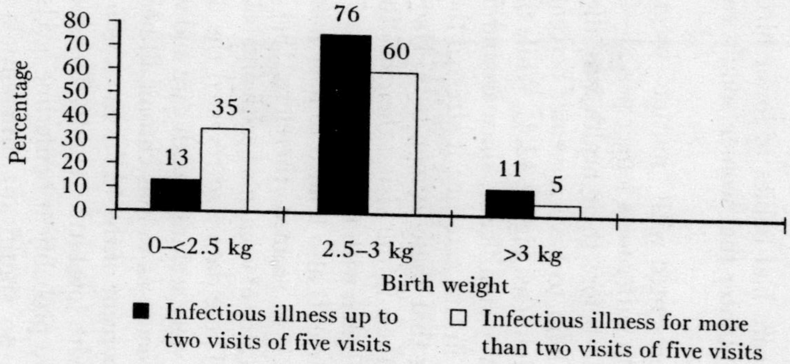

who sought care had babies of lower birth weights—this was another pointer that women sought care only as a last imperative.

3. Those who presented with "routine" pregnancy-related illness needed to suffer for a longer period—four or more, out of five visits—before their health was affected sufficiently enough for them to have a greater percentage of babies of low birth weight (see Figure 32.4). While this difference was not statistically significant, since around 52 percent of the women were in this category, it stressed the burden of chronic suffering that these women bore. Had they been taken seriously in their initial visits, their health could have been improved. Women with moderate anemia for four out of five visits (40 percent) also tended to have more babies of lower birth weights. It seemed, therefore, that tiredness was as good an indicator of women's health and babies' birth weights as anemia. These data also revealed the desperation of the women who were seeking health care and who were carrying a burden of acute as well as chronic ill health.
4. Almost 17 percent of the 117 women who delivered at term had babies with low birth weights. This indicated that these mothers were probably at borderline levels of malnutrition.
5. There were no significant differentials in birth weights across the income categories, thus suggesting that below a certain income level the economic differentials alone did not make a difference in the health and pregnancy outcomes nor that husbands' incomes had a correlation to the women's health. On the other hand, while there were differentials between birth weights of babies of employed women and housewives, these differences were not statistically significant. Thus, the data further revealed that giving the woman employment and thereby an independent income, improved the family income and marginally increased the baby's birth weight, but no significant improvement could be seen in the woman's health. This meant that for such women the workload increased without a commensurate increase in their nutritional or health status—and this had an adverse effect on their health.

Interestingly an aspect that did not seem to have a correlation with the babies's weight was the increase in the mothers'

Figure 32.4
Relationship between Extent of Obstetric Problems for Pregnant Women and Birth Weights of Term Babies

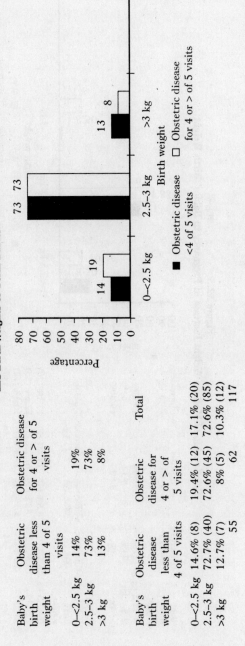

Baby's birth weight	Obstetric disease less than 4 of 5 visits	Obstetric disease for 4 or > of 5 visits
0–<2.5 kg	14%	19%
2.5–3 kg	73%	73%
>3 kg	13%	8%

Baby's birth weight	Obstetric disease less than 4 of 5 visits	Obstetric disease for 4 or > of 5 visits	Total
0–<2.5 kg	14.6% (8)	19.4% (12)	17.1% (20)
2.5–3 kg	72.7% (40)	72.6% (45)	72.6% (85)
>3 kg	12.7% (7)	8% (5)	10.3% (12)
	55	62	117

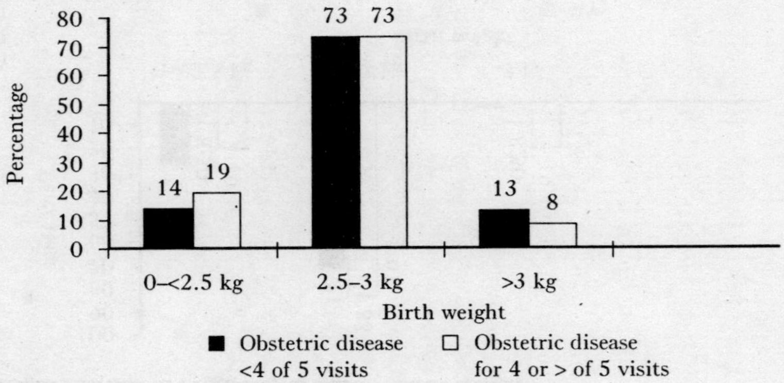

Figure 32.5
Relationship of Mothers Weight Increase in Pregnancy to Babies' Birth Weight

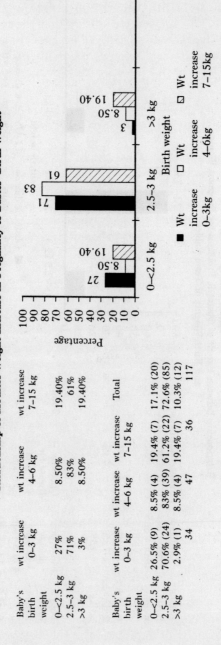

Baby's birth weight	wt increase 0–3 kg	wt increase 4–6 kg	wt increase 7–15 kg
0–<2.5 kg	27%	8.50%	19.40%
2.5–3 kg	71%	83%	61%
>3 kg	3%	8.50%	19.40%

Baby's birth weight	wt increase 0–3 kg	wt increase 4–6 kg	wt increase 7–15 kg	Total
0–<2.5 kg	26.5% (9)	8.5% (4)	19.4% (7)	17.1% (20)
2.5–3 kg	70.6% (24)	83% (39)	61.2% (22)	72.6% (85)
>3 kg	2.9% (1)	8.5% (4)	19.4% (7)	10.3% (12)
	34	47	36	117

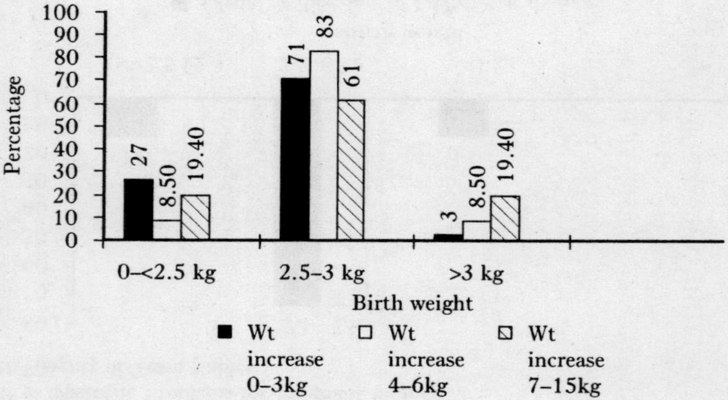

weight from the fifth month of pregnancy onward (see Figure 32.5). This seemed to indicate that the medical indicators for assessing women's health in pregnancy were not always infallible as was seen when merely the mothers' weight increase was viewed.

Antenatal Care—Schism between Women and Doctors

It is common knowledge that public hospitals are overloaded, leading to a poor doctor–patient relationship. Knowing this, the women therefore preferred not to go to hospitals for routine check-ups, but went for medical assistance when required. (In fact, 14 percent of the women visited the doctor because they had suffered problems in their previous pregnancy—this in medical language is termed as seeking preventive care—while only 4 percent of those who came for a check-up had no health problem.) Women working on daily wages lost work, others lost salaries for days off and some did not get leave; small children at home had to be left with someone responsible—these were just some of the obstacles in reaching medical care. After all this effort, the doctors who examined them were largely indifferent or not sympathetic and did not accept the women's subjective complaints. The women's burden of ill health was considered nonspecific, was not quantified, and thus ignored. While women sought health care only when their ill health crossed a limit, the doctors did not necessarily comprehend this desperate cry for help. Among recognized patterns of health and disease, subjective or experiential health of women finds no place; and unless its reality is accepted, it cannot be quantified.

On comparing morbidity in pregnant women in the field to those in the clinic a significant fact emerged. Sixty-four percent of women had had complaints of ill health (obstetric or infective) per visit in the field. But according to the clinic diagnosis of the women actively seeking medical care during pregnancy, only 15 percent had an illness and 85 percent were diagnosed as coming for "routine" antenatal care (incidentally, it was the same doctor who on the one hand collected such a wealth of detailed clinical and sociological information in the field and on the other gave such a paucity of information in the diagnosis of ill health in pregnancy).[4] The doctor in the antenatal clinic, like all other doctors, anticipated the "troublesome signs and symptoms of pregnancy," e.g., tiredness, nausea, and abdominal pain, and termed them "routine," unless they became floridly pathological, e.g., nausea became hyperemesis, anorexia was accompanied by weight loss, or tiredness was associated with marked pallor or pedal edema. Doctors therefore tend to miss a large load of morbidity, since much of women's ill health does not have obviously pathological manifestations, but is "merely" an experiential symptom. Thus many health disorders of these pregnant women are even denied existence (Sagar 1994).

Women's pregnancy and childbirth were traditionally managed by "wise-women" (*dais*), but over time, transformations in the concept and nature of medical care and intervention of the state have marginalized their role and pregnancy has been transformed into an essentially medical condition (Ehrenreich and English 1989; Mitchell and Oakley 1976). From a normal physiological phenomenon, pregnancy has been converted into a pathological process, potentially dangerous to the life of both mother and child. Antenatal care, as provided in modern hospitals, tends to focus only on the reproductive health aspect of women's lives, ignoring the fact that pregnancy is a part of their total lives. It constitutes an overall screening program with "efficient and constant supervision of the pregnant woman from the commencement of pregnancy, the correction of any dyscrasia [sic] whenever it occurs, and the transference to an institution of every patient who cannot be suitably treated and nursed in her own home" (Oakley 1986). Though stated in 1933, this statement still holds true. Another guiding principle of antenatal care is that women are ignorant and have no contribution to make toward their care during pregnancy and, therefore, need education and counseling about their pregnancy and that only recurrent routine visits to the doctor can help them in keeping the pregnancy "normal." The experiential health of women is ignored because medical practitioners have not attempted to assess their "subjective" health. This perpetuates the belief that if only women would come as prescribed by medical

[4] The diagnoses in the clinic register were cross-checked with the obstetric cards for the same visit. The obstetric card information tallied with the women's qualitative experience, whereas the diagnoses in the register did not.

technologists, their "dyscrasias" would be diagnosed and managed properly. It also tends to give rise to the medical opinion that women do not understand the significance or benefit of ANC.

Whilst the medical profession may believe that "dyscrasias" occurring during pregnancy are merely overt pathological manifestations of a subclinical illness (pregnancy), and as such are amenable to purely medical intervention, the women who undergo pregnancy usually know better. They are able to see the relationship between much of their ill health in pregnancy and their social existence.

As discussed above, it is seen that women's experiences of ill health are extremely valuable in assessing their morbidity and health status, more valuable in fact than the doctor's diagnosis. It also gives some idea of the burden of ill health on the women, a burden that they carry not only during pregnancy but throughout their lives. It is also obvious that many of their symptoms are interrelated and there are no technological quick-fixes for their situation.

If antenatal care would use women's experiences and perceptions along with the doctors' clinical data, it has the potential for supplying a very large amount of information about women's health and morbidity during pregnancy, which is a critical predictor for the outcome of pregnancy. Without needing to turn to sophisticated technology, a scheme for care during pregnancy and during a woman's life can be constructed, which instead of having a fragmented approach to her health would deal with it in its totality. However, at present, the women come seeking medical help and the doctors, expecting a certain amount of ill health in pregnancy, miss their distress. The doctors also do not realize the correlation between women's general disease burden and their disease burden during pregnancy. This schism in the views of the doctors and the patients is one of the factors leading to inability of this kind of medical care to significantly alter women's health, even during pregnancy.

Policy Issues—The Reproductive and Child Health Package

This study points to the importance of economic factors as well as of the issues of social status and traditions in the construction of women's health. It has been demonstrated that the social roles of women, their work, as well as their poverty are responsible for the heavy load of illness that they endure outside of pregnancy, as well as during it. It is also observed that improving the husband's income does not necessarily lead to a direct improvement in the woman's health, at least in the levels of incomes seen in the slum. On the other hand, the employed woman's income helps to some extent in improving her own health along with the general health of the family. This has been reflected in the positive changes seen *in utero* in the baby as demonstrated by the slight enhancement in birth weights. However, the increased workload on the employed woman prevents her from benefiting significantly from this marginally improved health. She suffers as much as her unemployed sister from tiredness, giddiness, etc. Additionally, in the long run the babies of these women have higher mortality rates. This has been documented by other researchers as well (Basu 1992). This confirms that factors other than financial are also responsible for the creation of women's health. It is within a scenario where their general health status is totally enmeshed within their social and economic reality that these women become pregnant and suffer from additional ill health, an exacerbation of their pre-existing morbidity.

SAPs will unfold in this picture of poverty and ill health. In 1978, the primary health care approach formulated at Alma-Ata had talked of inter-sectoral development to improve overall health. The health care reforms proposed by SAPs seem to be taking public health back once more to the bio-medical, technocentric and reductionist model, ignoring the social, cultural, economic, and political aspects of health. While technology- based, scientific medicine has its own place in medical care, to believe that this is the only tool to handle all health problems is being more than a little naive.

It is worthwhile to listen to the women who know that their ill health is rooted not in their reproductive system, but in the very rubric of their existence. This study has revealed the fallacy of the medical belief that "subjective" health of women has nothing to contribute to the doctor's "objective" assessment. The Reproductive Health Services Package at first glance seems to have a much broader base than earlier programs to improve maternal health. However, unlike the earlier Child Survival and Safe Motherhood

Program—which concentrated on childhood diseases, and antenatal care with folic acid, iron, tetanus toxoid injections, and obstetric referral units—this package is mainly a series of technical and medical services.

Such a Reproductive Health Package in tandem with the Structural Adjustment Programs that are known to worsen the economic burden of the poor can only add to the distortions that worsen the health of poor women.

References

Antia, N.H. (1994): The World Development Report 1993: A Prescription for Health Disaster. *Social Scientist*, 22(9–12): 147–51.

Basu, A. (1992): *Culture, the Status of Women and Demographic Behaviour*. Oxford: Clarendon Press.

Duvurry, N. (1994): Gender Implications of New Economic Policies and the Health Sector. *Social Scientist*, 22(9–12): 40–55.

Ehrenreich, B., and **English, D.** (1989): *For Her Own Good: 150 Years of the Experts' Advice to Women*. New York: Anchor Books, Doubleday.

Government of India (1994): *India Country Statement*. International Conference on Population and Development, Cairo 1994. New Delhi: Department Of Family Welfare.

Harriss, B. (1990): The Intrafamily Distribution of Hunger in South Asia. In J. Dreze and A. Sen (eds.). *The Political Economy of Hunger*. Oxford: Clarendon Press.

Malobika (1993): Girlhood in Rural Uttar Pradesh and its Implications for Health—A Study of Two Villages in Allahabad District. M. Phil dissertation, New Delhi: Centre of Social Medicine and Community Health, Jawaharlal Nehru University.

Meashan, A.R., and **Heaver, R.A.** (1996): *India's Family Welfare Programme: Moving to a Reproductive and Child Health Approach*. Washington D.C.: World Bank.

Mitchell, J., and **Oakley, A.** (1976): *The Rights and Wrongs of Women*. London: Penguin Books.

Oakley, A. (1986): *The Captured Womb: A History of the Medical Care of Pregnant Women*. Oxford: Basil Blackwell. p. 251.

Prabhu, K. Seeta (1994): World Development Report 1993: Structural Adjustment and the Health Sector in India. *Social Scientist*, 22(9–12): 89–97.

Qadeer, I. (1995): Primary Health Care: A Paradise Lost. *IASSI Quarterly*. 14(1&2): 1–21.

Sagar, A.D. (1994): *Health and the Social Environment*. Environmental Impact Assessment Review, 14(5/6): 359–77.

33

The Rhetoric of Reproductive Rights: Quinacrine Sterilization in India

Mohan Rao

The World Bank has since a long time made explicit its concern for the growing populations of the Third World. It considered rapid growth of population as "a major obstacle to social and economic development" and argued that "family planning programs are less costly than conventional development projects" (Mass 1974). Under its influence, family planning concerns came to contour the development of health services in developing countries as an integral part of the policy of reform. In India, the program was overhauled and considerably strengthened. The program strategy shifted from the clinic approach to the extension education approach to the intra-uterine contraceptive device (IUCD) approach and the vasectomy camp approach. When none of these bore positive results, thoughts among policy-makers turned toward the unthinkable, namely, compulsory sterilization. Over the same period, maternal and child health (MCH) services were separated from family planning in order to concentrate on the latter, while family planning itself was de-linked from health in a new and more powerful ministry. A host of other institutions, such as the Ford Foundation and the Population Council, joined the World Bank in shaping these twists in strategy and emphases.

All this took place despite the fact that the family planning approach to the problem of poverty had largely failed. In the process the need for a broad-based development approach had been highlighted. As Hodgson has noted:

> The failure of over a decade of family planning to substantially lower fertility in a number of societies raised questions among some sections about its effectiveness as a method of

> population control. Some of the disenchanted argued for more coercive forms of population control, while others called for redirecting development benefits to the impoverished to hasten their adoption of small family ideals (Hodgson 1988: 557).

The World Bank and the Population Council endorsed the "developmentalist" perspective. The echoes of such a shift were to reverberate in the country. Indeed, at the World Population Conference at Bucharest in 1974, the Indian minister of health and family planning stated that "development is the best contraceptive," as "we are quite clear that fertility levels can be effectively lowered only if family planning becomes an integral part of a broader strategy to deal with the problems of poverty and underdevelopment" (Singh 1976).

Both, as a desirable goal in itself and as a way to meet demographic objectives, Health For All through PHC was visualized as a major turning point. Indeed there was such a sense of optimism and hope accompanying the rallying cry of Health For All that there was talk of a new international economic order to arrest the continuing drain of resources from the countries of the Third World.

However, this sense of optimism was extremely short-lived. For a complex number of reasons, the long boom period of the post-war golden age of capitalism ground to a crisis. This saw the ascent of "ultra-liberal economic theologians" with the "ideological zeal of the old champions of individualism reinforced by the apparent failure of conventional economic policies" (Hobsbawn 1994). As the world of actually existing socialism turned upside down, the Keynesian world increasingly came under attack. In this new global environment, the importance of institutions like WHO shrank, while that of the World Bank relentlessly increased.

Third World countries, burdened with debt, were prescribed a package of macro-economic reforms under the rubric of SAPs. These reforms advocated the remorseless cutback of state intervention in the social sectors and gave rise to and dominance of the magic bullet approach to public health technology, accompanying what Raynaud describes as eliminating society from disease (Raynaud 1975).

As the prospects for Health For All through PHC receded, we saw the re-emergence of technology centered vertical programs. In the post-Cold War period, a variety of reasons such as simplistic concerns for the environment, paranoid fears of national security, racialist fears of rampant immigration from the South, and even genuine, if misplaced, concern for the health of women, saw the re-emergence of Neo-Malthusianism in a new avatar at the International Conference of Population and Development (ICPD) at Cairo in 1994.

Located strictly within the framework of SAPs, women's health was reduced to reproductive and child health (RCH), which became the new incarnation of the FP program. At the ICPD, they were together allocated $5 and $10.2 billion respectively, along with $1.3 million for HIV/AIDS and prevention of other STDs by the year 2000 (Bandarage 1997). The concept of women's rights was also co-opted; it was now restricted to only reproductive rights and the perspective of Third World women, which was rooted in their anti-colonial struggles was completely ignored. These transformations did not deflect from the Neo-Malthusian agenda and yet re-furbished the discredited Family Planning Programs.

It is, therefore, not surprising that the concerns of the ICPD have come under critical scrutiny by women's groups and public health scholars in India. In response to the government's country paper at the Fourth World Conference of Women at Beijing in 1995, seven all-India women's organizations prepared an alternative document, wherein the ICPD comes in for stringent criticism as "issues concerning third world women were left unaddressed." The alternative document notes that "women's health should not be subordinated to population goals nor restricted to reproductive matters" (Towards Beijing 1995).

This anxiety and unease, if not suspicion, with the concept of reproductive health, stems from several factors. An important one is that "debates being actively promoted today twist the very premises and values on which the women's movement had been based. Terms like empowerment, choice, reproductive freedom, etc., are being appropriated by forces inimical to the goals of the women's movement"(Agnihotri and Mazumdar 1995). Further, the agenda which marginalized issues of equitable and sustainable development of developing countries equally marginalized important health concerns. As the health implications of larger macro-economic changes were proving extremely deleterious to women's health, the technocentric focus on reproductive health seemed seriously misplaced. As Qadeer observed, "The ICPD converted women's health into issues of safe abortion and reproductive rights alone" (Qadeer 1995).

This marriage of structural adjustment with reproductive health care (RHC) has led to the birth of dangerous tendencies within a women-centered FP program. Achieving reproductive health through female sterilization with quinacrine is one such mutant offspring that I shall discuss in this chapter. The chapter is divided into two sections: the first is a brief outline of the story of quinacrine sterilization while the second attempts to raise issue for discussion.

I

Quinacrine, a synthetic anti-malarial belonging to the acridine group of drugs, was used in the treatment of malaria during the thirties and forties till it was replaced by better drugs such as chloroquine. It has also been used successfully in the treatment of giardiasis and systemic lupus erythematos.

Current interest in the drug stems from the novel use discovered for it about two decades back as a method for the chemical sterilization of women. However, issues of safety, efficacy, and ethics have trailed its "trials" around the globe. These trials have taken place in 19 Third World countries; currently all countries of South Asia are seats of this scandal.

The method was developed in Chile by Dr Jaime Zipper in the seventies. Dr Zipper had earlier experimented with chemicals such as formaldehyde and sulfuric acid to cauterize the fallopian tubes of laboratory animals. With the assistance of two American doctors, Dr Elton Kessel and Dr Stephen Mumford, who were to become the lions of the worldwide quinacrine sterilization movement, Dr Zipper tried out quinacrine sterilization in three public hospitals over the next decade and a half and involving more than a thousand women (Saheli 1997).

The procedure involves the transcervical introduction of pellets of quinacrine into the fundus of the uterus in the early proliferative phase of the menstrual cycle using a modified copper-t inserter.

While various schedules have been tried, the most common one currently used involves the insertion of seven pellets of quinacrine, each of 36 milligrams. This is performed either once or twice. It has been suggested that following insertion, the pellets dissolve in the uterus in about half an hour and then set up a local inflammatory reaction, specifically in the fallopian tubes. The fibrosis and scar tissue that ensue lead to tubal occlusion and, thus, sterilization. As it takes up to 12 weeks for tubal occlusion to be complete, an additional contraceptive is usually provided along with the first insertion of quinacrine. Typically, a long-acting injectible contraceptive such as the controversial Depo Provera is used.

The quinacrine sterilizations do not require anesthesia or trained personnel and can be performed in areas with no access to health facilities. While these are thought to be some of the method's operational advantages, given the nature of family planning programs and the poor development of public health facilities in many developing countries, it is precisely these factors which endow the method with a high potential for abuse. The fact that these are not merely Cassandra's fears is brought home in a documentary on the trials conducted in New Delhi. Entitled *The Yellow Haze*, this documentary, made by students of the mass communication department of the Jamia Milia Islamia University, features an interview with a woman who was sterilized with quinacrine when she had gone to a clinic for the insertion of copper-t.

Around the world these trials have been sponsored by Dr Elton Kessel and Dr Stephen Mumford. The former runs an NGO named International Federation for Family Health (IFFH), while the latter runs one evocatively named Center for Research on Population and Security (CRPS), both based in North Carolina, USA. Dr Kessel was the founder of the organization named Family Health International (FHI) which assisted Dr Zipper in his trials. It was involved with equally questionable trials with Norplant in Bangladesh (Rao 1997).

So far the largest trial has been carried out in Vietnam, where more than 31,000 women have been subjected to quinacrine sterilization between 1989 and 1993. The publication of a paper on these trials in the *Lancet* in 1993 provided them with a great deal of scientific legitimacy (Hieu et al. 1993). However, this publication raised a huge controversy and following recommendations of WHO, the Ministry of Health called off the trial. A retrospective study of this trial was carried out in 1994, but the report still awaits publication (Berer 1995).

In June 1994, the WHO Consultation on Female Sterilization Methods called for the conduct of four pre-clinical toxicology studies on quinacrine before approval of the drug for clinical testing. It categorically stated that human trials should be stopped forthwith pending outcome of these toxicological studies (WHO 1995).

Kessel's organization, FHI, undertook these toxicological studies with financial assistance from United States Agency for International Development (USAID). The rationale adduced was that resolving the scientific and ethical questions raised by the method was in public interest and that a safe and non-surgical method of sterilization would be cheaper than surgical sterilization.

The September 1995 issue of the FHI newsletter *Network* reported that three out of four studies on quinacrine were positive for mutagenicity. Mutagenicity is the capacity to induce somatic changes in cells, some of which can lead to cancer. While not all mutagenic substances are carcinogenic, nevertheless, further laboratory tests on animals are essential as per internationally accepted scientific norms in order to exclude carcinogenicity. Problems, however, arose with the next step involving trials on female rodents pertaining to the route of insertion, the dosage, the number of insertions, and above all, the heavy mortality load among the animals which had to be subject to repeated anesthesia during the course of the trials. FHI estimated that further studies would cost up to eight million dollars and would take at least eight years. In view of all these factors, USAID decided to stop the funding of these studies.

In Chile, meanwhile, there was an uproar following the receipt of a memo dated September 1994 from the CRPS, which stated that the Chilean government was considering replacing surgical sterilization with quinacrine sterilization in two of the most populous regions of the country. It jubilantly stated that the Chilean government's plans vindicated the efforts of the pioneers of the quinacrine method of sterilization in the face of WHO's "ridiculous" position. The memo turned out to be false; nonetheless it provided an impetus to activists to probe the conduct of these trials.

A broad-based coalition named Open Forum for Reproductive Health and Rights voiced four main concerns as they agitated for a halt to these trials. These were:

1. unresolved issues of safety, for in addition to possible toxicity (including carcinogenicity), side effects, and failure, quinacrine should also be assessed for embryotoxicity in the event of failure of the method;
2. the WHO recommendation that human clinical trials not be conducted till toxicology studies were satisfactorily conducted;
3. the need for informed consent procedures that had been completely lacking in these trials; and
4. the need for scrutiny of the trial documents by an ethics committee to assess both safety and ethical standards that had been followed.

The Chilean Ministry of Health withdrew its support in December 1994 and the public hospitals were asked to review their internal ethical procedures. However, Dr Zipper and his team are reportedly continuing their trials in private clinics with the financial support of CRPS.

In India, quinacrine sterilization is being carried out with "hundreds of doctors involved" according to Dr Biral Mullick, an early convert to the cause. Dr Mullick runs an NGO named Humanity Association in Calcutta. In a video-film made for the IFFH for promotion of quinacrine, he admits to having sterilized 10,000 women over the past two decades. He has also claimed to have trained over 200 village health workers from all over the country in quinacrine sterilization, even as he frankly admits that financial constraints prevent follow-up of his cases. Dr Mullick obtains his supplies from the CRPS and has published his findings along with Kessel and Mumford in international scientific journals.

In Bangalore, Dr Pravin Kini, Dr Sita Bhateja, and Dr B. Rajagopal completed trials on 600 women between July 1994 and July 1996. They have initiated a two-year project through a trust named Contraceptive and Health Innovations Project (CHIP) to sterilize 25,000 women. With supplies provided by IFFH, CHIP has mobilized about 300 doctors from all over Karnataka to carry out this project.

Other doctors and NGOs are also part of the Kessel-Mumford network. Among them are Dr Ajay Ghosh in Calcutta, Dr Ashi Sarin in Patiala, Dr Rohit Bhatt in Baroda, and Dr Maya Sood in New Delhi. Dr Maya Sood's involvement is perturbing; she is the head of the department of obstetrics and gynecology at the Lady Hardinge Medical College, one of the largest teaching hospitals in New Delhi. The "trial" conducted here was on a small number of women as part of a student's post-graduate research. It raises vital questions as to how the ethics committee of the hospital could have granted permission for the study without seeking the approval of the mandating authority in the country, the Drug Controller of India. This represents, as it were, the thin edge of the wedge with the involvement of doctors in the government sector hitherto immune from this malady. Dr Sood candidly states that she would carry out a much larger study should Dr Kessel provide her with the necessary resources.

Dr J.K. Jain, former Bharatiya Janata Party (BJP) member of the Rajya Sabha and the owner of Jain Studios and the Jain Medical Center in New Delhi, coordinated the supply of drugs and equipment in the country. Jain Studios has made a video-film promoting quinacrine sterilization, which is being distributed all over the world by Kessel and Mumford. Jain Medical Center, besides being a nursing home, is also the New Delhi address of the IFFH, of which Dr Jain has been the president over the last six years.

Kessel and Mumford obtain financial support from a host of private American foundations and individuals including the Leland Fikes Foundation and the Ted Turner Foundation, although the latter has now ceased to be a donor. They are linked to racist right-wing groups such as the Federation for American Immigration Reform and the Americans for Immigration Control. In a documentary telecast on BBC entitled "The Human Laboratory," they are on record that as patriotic Americans, they believe that the USA cannot have a free immigration policy lest she be swamped by immigrants who would turn the country into one more Third World nation. They also obtain funding from a section of the ecology movement, the eco-fascists, who believe that the growth of Third World populations constitutes the gravest threat to the global environment. Mumford, Kessel, and Mullick state in a paper that "not to be ignored is the most important role that sterilization must play in maintaining peace and security given the world's over-population" (cited in Rao 1998) The former two claim that they receive support from the highest echelons of the US security establishment in their endeavors.

There have, of course, been protests with several lead editorials in national newspapers calling a halt to these trials. In Calcutta, activists of the Ganatantrik Mahila Samiti forced the closure of Dr Mullick's clinic. The Government of West Bengal has since initiated an enquiry into Dr Mullick's practice. In Bangalore, demonstrations have been held by a broad coalition of women's groups and health activists outside the clinic of Dr Sita Bhateja and Dr Pravin Kini. In New Delhi, a demonstration by women's groups was held outside the Jain Clinic.

The Government of India denies granting approval to any of these trials. In reply to a question tabled in parliament, the minister of state in the department of legal affairs stated that the Government of India was aware that the WHO had specifically recommended that pending further studies, trials with quinacrine on human populations be stopped forthwith. He stated that the government had only permitted the Indian Council of Medical Research to carry out a study in 1992 but that the high failure rate early in the study compelled its termination. Subsequently, approval for clinical trials of quinacrine pellets had not been granted to any investigator by the Drugs Controller General of India. Further, the minister also stated that "no drug manufacturer has been granted licence to manufacture quinacrine and the drug is not imported" (Government of India 1997). However, in the same statement, the minister stated that the government was not aware that quinacrine sterilizations were being performed in the country.

Petitions from women's groups have also been presented to the minister of health calling for a ban on quinacrine sterilizations and punishment of the doctors who have been performing them in contravention of the laws of the land. Despite all these efforts, doctors in the private sector and some NGOs are continuing with these trials which defy all international norms for the conduct of clinical trials. It is in this context that the faculty of the Center of Social Medicine and Community Health, Jawaharlal Nehru University, New Delhi, along with the All India Democratic

Women's Association have filed a public interest litigation in the Supreme Court.

II

The quinacrine trials raise a host of issues regarding the safety of this method of sterilization as well as the methodology used to assess this. Above all, they raise issues regarding the conditions under which such a scientific scandal can be perpetrated with such apparent immunity.

One major criticism pertains to the issues of safety. The proponents of the method claim that risk-benefit assessment, the cornerstone of clinical trials, favored the use of quinacrine sterilizations in populations where maternal mortality is high and contraceptive prevalence low. Further, that toxicologists maintain that the dose and duration of exposure are the critical factors when humans are exposed to mutagenic or carcinogenic substances. Quinacrine has been used orally as an anti-malarial, in higher doses, over a longer period of time, on a larger population, with little deleterious effects.

These arguments miss out some salient points. First, they assume that maternal mortality is caused primarily by unwanted pregnancies, which contraception would avert. Whereas, a large proportion of maternal deaths occur among women with wanted pregnancies. Further, causes due to reproduction account for merely 2 percent of deaths among women in India. Even in the reproductive age group they account for 12 percent of deaths. In reality, a majority of the maternal deaths in developing countries are primarily due to diseases of poverty, under-nutrition, anemia, infectious diseases, and the lack of access to health care facilities in the event of complications of pregnancy. Contraception or sterilization alone would therefore have an extremely limited role to play in declines of maternal mortality. If this were indeed the case, countries such as Brazil and Indonesia—the latter marked by a particularly aggressive family planning program—which have witnessed remarkable declines in the birth rate, should also have experienced commensurate declines in the maternal mortality rate, which has not occurred.

The argument that quinacrine was used extensively as an anti-malarial and that quinacrine as a sterilizing agent is without danger, is equally specious. Quinacrine was used as an anti-malarial only till such time as better alternatives like chloroquine became available. Further, the extremely high mortality rate for malaria at that point in time far outweighed the risks due to quinacrine. Unlike the case with malaria in the past, there are alternative forms of terminal contraception available today, such as vasectomy for men and tubectomy for women.

The literature on quinacrine frequently argues that there were no deaths in the 40-day period following quinacrine sterilization in 100,000 women. There are however a number of problems with this facile presentation of data. Included in this huge number are presumably the 31,781 women sterilized in Vietnam which formed the basis of the *Lancet* publication. The New York based Association for Voluntary Surgical Sterilization (AVSC) found serious scientific flaws in this study (Carignan and Pollack 1994), such as:

- The data on side effects and failure rates were not derived from the full sample of women, but on varying subsets among them. The findings from these subsets were then extrapolated to the entire sample.
- It is not clear how the ectopic pregnancy rate was calculated: in one province two out of nine pregnancies were ectopic, which is a significant figure. Yet "this troubling finding is not mentioned in the analysis of ectopic pregnancies" (Carignan and Pollack 1994: 5).

AVSC therefore maintains that "it is not possible to conclude that quinacrine pellets are a safe and effective non-surgical method of sterilization" (Carignan and Pollack 1994: 6). We must also recall the huge failure rate that forced the premature discontinuation of the ICMR study.

Given the fact that multiple protocols of dosage, number of insertions, and adjuvants have been followed—a quaint methodology characteristic of all the trials in India also—it is not methodologically correct to compare the mortality rates obtained from such diverse and unspecified methods. The authenticity of the data is further undermined by the finding that three deaths known to have occurred due to quinacrine sterilization have not been reported.

The adoption of the cut-off date of 40 days that is normally used for determining mortality risks after surgery is also questionable. Potentially fatal ectopic pregnancies can occur as long as a woman sterilized with quinacrine is in the reproductive age group. The use of this cut-off date, therefore, does not constitute a long enough period to assess the mortality risks associated with this method. In fact, the complete lack of follow-up of the trials renders doubtful all the findings.

The frequently cited argument that approval for quinacrine for the treatment of other diseases precludes the need for a license to use it as an agent for female sterilization is completely false and misleading. Under the Drugs and Cosmetics Act of India, a new drug is defined to include "a drug already approved...which is now proposed...with new claims viz. indications, dosage form and route of administration."

The Drugs Controller of India has granted approval only for the oral use of quinacrine in tablet form for the treatment of malaria, giardiasis and amoebiasis. The drug is not approved for female sterilization. It has not received approval for this usage from any international authority either, including the United States. Recently, the US Food and Drug Administration issued a warning on the internet, on which quinacrine was being promoted as a method of self-sterilization. The warning states that the kit being advertised "uses pellets of quinacrine hydrochloride, an unapproved drug which can cause ectopic pregnancies, abnormal pregnancies and permanent damage to a woman's reproductive organs."

While it is necessary to critique the methodology of these trials, it is equally important to understand the context in which such experiments can be carried out so blatantly. They bring back memories of the grand eugenic experiments with chemical sterilization carried out in the Nazi concentration camps. The victims in that grand design were Jews, gypsies, communists, homosexuals, and all those deemed unfit by the "science" of eugenics. The women now being subject to this method of sterilization are poor women in the Third World, deemed to be the cause of every possible social problem by the science of demography. Among the concatenation of factors which have coalesced to make the quinacrine scandal possible is the assumption about the reproductive profligacy of the poor. There is such an overwhelming consensus about this among the elites in India that the only discussion in this respect is around "what to do about it." Often the solution is found in contraceptive technology directed at women irrespective of its hazards and impact on their health.

The use of contraceptives is made easy, given the euphoria created by the neo-liberal discourse in international circles on rights, including "reproductive rights" and "reproductive choice." What is elided in this discourse is that to talk of reproductive rights in absence of right to food, employment, water, access to education, health, and, indeed, even the survival of children—in short, all the accoutrements of a dignified existence—is to make a travesty of women's rights. The reification of such a concept of reproductive rights in the West makes it absolutely compatible with the violation of the rights of poor women in countries like India with quinacrine sterilization. There is, after all, nothing remarkably new about this. Women in Third World countries have often enough in the past paid the cost in health and well-being for the benefits by way of improved contraceptives, which have primarily accrued to women in the West. The low dose contraceptive pill, for instance, was refined after trials with extremely risky high dose combinations in Puerto Rico. In India itself we have had trials with Norplant and with the anti-fertility vaccine.

What is unique about the quinacrine trials is that, for the first time contraceptive trials on human populations have been undertaken in the country by private agencies and NGOs. None of the individuals and organizations conducting these trials have sought for or received permission from the statutory authority in the country, the Drugs Controller of India. Hitherto all institutions undertaking such research—and it is important to underline that they were institutions and not individuals—were accoun- table to the parliament and followed guidelines laid down by the Indian Council of Medical Research (ICMR) which broadly followed international guidelines in this regard. The quinacrine trials have completely bypassed all such agencies of monitoring and accounting. In other words, we have a completely unregulated and free market of human research at the command of dubious private institutions of the West, with poor women of the country forming the sample. The Drugs Controller of India has turned a

Nelson's eye to this abuse of quinacrine. It required the intervention of the Supreme Court to initiate a faltering and half-hearted action.

This would not be possible even in the countries where the free market supposedly is worshipped. In my opinion, what has made this extraordinary situation possible is the changes under the Structural Adjustment Program. The efforts at the "rolling back" of the state, which lie at the core of the program of globalization and liberalization, have led to the undermining of the public institutions of research and of monitoring and regulation of public health. In this case, ICMR has been reduced to issuing a few newspaper notices deprecating the trials. At the same time, under the rallying cry of privatization, what appears to have occurred is privatization of public health research, with NGOs and private individuals being encouraged by private institutions in the West to carry out research in the country. We have already seen the case of uveal tissue research, which was banned in the West, being carried out in a corporate sector hospital in Hyderabad until intervention by ICMR. A host of such research on reproductive morbidity, of dubious quality, is being carried out by NGOs around the country.

It is too often uncritically assumed that privatization is necessary and beneficial irrespective of the social costs incurred. However, the case of quinacrine sterilization reveals that the remedy being proposed by the doctors in the private and NGO sectors is worse than the ills to which they are supposedly responding. Whatever may be the limitations and the weaknesses of institutions in the public sector, they conducted systematic and scientific studies and accepted the findings. The private sector, on the other hand, flush with funds, continued with the flawed "trials" in disregard of the laws of the country.

Further, it shows that while the Indian state has withdrawn from its commitment to primary health care, there are no feasible alternatives in place. The World Bank has changed its perspective of intervention in the population sector from a broad-based "developmentalist" one to a more narrowly-based, technology-centered one based on a "minimum clinical package." This calls for the removal of "constraints on method availability, including excessively restrictive screening requirements and unnecessary or duplicative approval procedures" (World Bank 1993).

The commitments made at Cairo to enhance women's health and reproductive rights seem to be of no value or consequence. The impunity with which US-based NGOs are providing the lead in violation of human rights in Southern countries in conduct of such "trials," provides urgency to the need to monitor health systems that have been rendered vulnerable by the incorporation of the Indian economy in the global market. That this is not on anyone's agenda becomes evident from the Supreme Court's intervention in the matter of quinacrine sterilizations.

On 16 March 1998, the Drugs Controller of India made a written commitment to the Supreme Court that quinacrine sterilization in the country would be banned with immediate effect, by gazette notification. The Court on its part was happy to close the case at this. It paid no heed to the prayer of the petitioners for follow-up and compensation to the victims of this "trial," nor did it consider necessary strengthening institutions and mechanisms for the monitoring and regulation of public health research in the country. Women's health in India thus remains victim to the rhetoric of rights that emanate from the West, and are sought to be implemented by a weak health ministry and its research and monitoring institutions, and the legal system of the receding Indian State.

References

Agnihotri, I., and **Mazumdar, V.** (1995): Changing the Terms of Political Discourse: Women's Movement in India, 1970s–1990s. *Economic and Political Weekly*, 30(29): 1869–78.

Bandarage, A. (1997): *Women, Population and Global Crisis: A Political Economic Analysis*. London: Zed Books.

Berer, M. (1995): The Quinacrine Controversy Continues. *Reproductive Health Matters*, 6.

Carignan, C.S., and **Pollack, A.** (1994): The Quinacrine Method of Nonsurgical Sterilisation: Report of an Experts Meeting, AVSC Working Paper No. 6, July.

Government of India (1997): Unstarred Question No. 4045, 13 May. Rajya Sabha. New Delhi: Ministry of Health and Family Welfare.

Hieu, T., **Tan Tran, T.**, **Tan Do, N.**, **Nguyet Phan, T.**, **Than, P.**, and **Vin Dao, Q.** (1993): 31,781 Cases of Non-Surgical Sterilisation with Quinacrine Pellets in Vietnam. *Lancet*, 342(24 July): 213–17.

Hobsbawm, E.J. (1994): *Age of Extremes*. London: Viking.

Hodgson, D. (1988): Orthodoxy and Revisionism in American Demography. *Population and Development Review*, 14(4): 557.

Mass, B. (1974): An Historical Sketch of the American Population Control Movement. *International Journal of Health Services*, 4(4): 651–74.

Qadeer, I. (1995): Women and Health: A Third World Perspective. *Lokayan Bulletin*, 12(1–2): 111.

Rao, M. (1997): Surreptitious Sterilisations. *Health for the Millions*, 4(23): 26.

——— (1998): Quinacrine Sterilisation Trials: A Scientific Scandal? *Economic and Political Weekly*, 33(13) (28 March): 692–95.

Raynaud, M. (1975): On the Structural Constraints to State Intervention in Health. *International Journal of Health Services*, 5(4): 559–71.

Saheli (1997): *Quinacrine: The Sordid Story of Chemical Sterilisation of Women*. New Delhi: Saheli.

Singh, K. (1976): *National Population Policy*. New Delhi: National Institute of Health Administration and Education.

Towards Beijing: Crucial Issues of Concern (1995): *Lokayan Bulletin*, 12(1–2).

World Bank (1993): *World Development Report 1993: Investing in Health*. New York: Oxford University Press.

World Health Organisation (1995): *Progress in Human Reproduction*, No. 36.

Beyond Reforms: Postscript

Over the past three to four years, evidence has been accumulating from both developed and developing countries on the inherent contradictions and problems facing the current reform of the health and social sectors. There is growing evidence to suggest that at the conceptual level the basic premise of neo-classical economic theory is of questionable value in its application to health and social capital.

First and foremost, the experience of the past decade is beginning to reveal that the social costs in terms of equity have been considerable. An increasing amount of documentation shows that the vulnerable groups that were meant to benefit from reforms through targeting are actually worse off and further marginalized. Second, in purely economic terms the supposed benefits of cost-saving do not appear to have materialized. For example, the administrative costs of implementing reforms in particular have been high, where high cost of management has tended to increase the overall costs that are being transferred to patients. Containing demand—a primary aim—has simply reduced access to most who are unable to pay. Most significant is the growing awareness that competition—the core element of reforms—has been rather scarce. Instead there has been a surplus of mergers and monopolies among providers which has even caused alarm among users in the United States, where the principles of competition are normally much lauded (Fuchs 1997). Awareness of such fundamental deficiencies has led to doubt and discontent in the OECD countries as reflected at a recent WHO-sponsored meeting at Ljubljana (1996). The participants voiced serious concern about the efficacy of the reforms, and on the rate and pace of change imposed upon countries of Eastern Europe and their formerly socialized systems of health care (Mastilica 1996). The Ljubljana Declaration called for less haste and more caution in implementing changes for the greater use of markets and the private sector in the organization and delivery of health services.

The increasing disquiet in the OECD countries on the workings of the reform process has been paralleled by a rising crisis in the United States, where the paradigm of market supremacy emerged and was subsequently exported to Europe and the rest of the world. Here in its home ground, the notions of efficiency and competition are being challenged by the rise of monopolies and mergers which wholly undermine the basic principles of the rules of competition and choice. Instead there is evidence of rampant malpractice in the operations of the market-place, which all the powers of the federal and state governments have been unable to regulate. This has led some critics of the health care experience in the United States to conclude that the supremacy of the market in the delivery of health services cannot be feasible. "We can now be pretty sure that efficient competitive markets in health care do not and cannot exist. Their advocates are selling powdered unicorn horn. So why are they getting a hearing?" (Evans 1997).

Eminent professors of public health and health economics in the US—such as Reinhardt—have also begun to argue that the US experience based on a crude market model of health care delivery should not and cannot be compared to the socially oriented health systems prevailing in the European countries. He argues that the comparison of two very different systems of health services has been fundamentally erroneous: "...one cannot compare market driven health systems with government-run systems in terms of their relative efficiency. Although this point seems obvious to any thoughtful person, it is overlooked with distressing regularity in the debate on health policy..." (Reinhardt 1997).

Concerns about the fundamental premise of the reforms (efficiency, effectiveness) are now being increasingly reflected in Europe. Social policy analysts—such as Nickless—argue that the EC rules on competition to be shared by all member states overlook the fundamental issue of the vulnerability of patients. This is linked to the asymmetries of information that inevitably create a supplier-led health market (Nickless 1998). This leads Nickless, like many others, to question the very basis of applying the rules of competition to social good such as health care. He suggests that the rules of competition cannot be applied equally to commercial and social sectors since the latter is not and could never be the same as a grocer's shop or a car factory (Nickless 1998).

There is thus a visible trend in these countries where there are steps to revert to pre-reform welfare models and among others who are preparing to abandon wholesale, the core components of competition and the internal marketing of health care. The inadequacy and inappropriateness of the cost-benefit model of health care is further highlighted by the fact that despite pressures from global policy-making, many countries have begun to reverse their policies and return to the earlier social models. For example, New Zealand, which was a pioneering country to introduce competition in health services has reversed its agenda to return to the social-welfare model. Sweden and the United Kingdom are also reducing the competitive elements in their health service provision. The UK has altogether abolished internal markets at the level of primary care. It seems clear that for these countries greater caution is the order of the day due to the fact that the benefits of competition have not materialized. The importance of this changing scenario for the developing world is the need to acknowledge and learn quickly from the European experience since much of the welfare model being destroyed by the current reforms is fragile and an integral part of nascent welfare provision in this region and elsewhere.

Despite the visible deficiencies of market reforms in health services and the inadequacy and inappropriateness of the cost-benefit model, they continue to be advocated at the global level of policy. According to Koivusalo (in this volume), this can only mean that the main intention of the reforms had always been to provide greater opportunities for the private sector rather than improve in anyway the kind of services being provided to the population at large. The continued emphasis on the private sector and contracting out health and social care services is an agenda to appropriate from the poor of the world and one which can only add to the numbers of those dispossessed and burdened by debt.

Clearly, in this way, only the interests of the private sector and the multinational industry are guaranteed. It is evident that when issues of equity are concerned, health care should only be provided according to need and not according to the ability to pay. If the above background is the reality of experience in the developed countries, the appropriateness of applying an increasingly discredited and defunct model to the developing world is not only dubious but also highly questionable. This volume and the evidence that it provides from the South Asian region represent a major critique of the irrational and unjust policies being imposed upon the population at large and of the even greater need for challenge.

References

Evans, R. (1997): Who is Selling the Market and Why? *Journal of Public Health Medicine*, 19: 45–49.

Fuchs, V. (1997): Commentary. *Journal of the American Medical Association*, 277(11) (March): 921.

Mastilica, M. (1996): Health Care Reform in Croatia. In *Health Care Reforms in Central and Eastern European Countries*. Debrecen: European Public Health Association, Department of Social Medicine, University Medical School, Soros Foundation.

Nickless, J.A. (1998): Should the EC Rules on Competition be Applied to Social Health Care Providers? Annual Lecture 1997. Office of Health Economics, London.

Reinhardt, U.E. (1997): Accountable Health Care. Is it Compatible with Social Solidarity? *Eurohealth*, 4(2) (Spring): 16–19.

About the Contributors

Farida Akhter is the director of UBINIG in Bangladesh, an NGO involved in research, advocacy, and campaign work and she is also the editor of *Chinta*, a fortnightly Bengali magazine. She has been involved in action-oriented research work on health, women's issues, environment, and agriculture. Her specific focus in health is on accessibility of services for the poor, especially women, and linkages of health and social conditions.

Nimal Attanayake is a senior lecturer in economics and has nearly 15 years experience in health economics-related research in several developing countries. He is the founder and coordinator of the Health Economics Study Program (HESP) at the Department of Economics, University of Colombo.

Shyam Ashtekar is a medical doctor working with an action group on community health care in Maharashtra. He has been working on the issue of rural health services, training of community health workers, and lobbying for legal recognition of CHWs.

Debabar Banerji is Professor Emeritus at the CSMCH/JNU. He has played a seminal role in the formation of the center. A consistent critic of vertical national health programs and the recent global prescriptions for health, he has made pioneering efforts towards evolving an alternative framework for public health in India. He was part of a team at the NTI that formulated a people-oriented tuberculosis program for India.

Rama V. Baru is on the faculty of CSMCH/JNU in New Delhi. Trained as a medical social worker, she has experience of work with institutional and community-based programs. She is interested in the sociology of health care and her current area of research includes the privatization of health care in India and its implications for health services.

Jennifer Bennett heads the population and development unit at the Sustainable Development Policy Institute, Pakistan. Her areas of research include macro and policy-level health issues, globalization and its impact on social development, community development and peace, demilitarization of civil society, and ethno-religious and women's issues.

Anurag Bhargava is a postgraduate in medicine from the All India Institute of Medical Sciences, New Delhi. His interests include control of communicable diseases (especially tuberculosis, malaria, and HIV disease). He works as a community physician with the Jan Swasthya Sahyog (People's Health Support Group) in rural Bilaspur district.

Marc De Bruycker is an epidemiologist and public health practitioner and currently affiliated to the Directorate General for Development, European Commission, dealing with sectoral strategies for health and population. He has worked in Zaire on the organization of district health services and coordinated a project on health research with developing countries at the EC. Some of his areas of interest are social sector development, research and development, environment, equity, and justice.

A.K. Chakraborty is a public health expert, specializing in the epidemiology and management of tuberculosis. He also headed the National Tuberculosis Institute in Bangalore. He has a rich experience of work with various bodies at the national and international levels, including the World Health Organization.

Lalita Chakravarty is a Fellow of the Nehru Memorial Musuem and Library in Delhi and she teaches economics at the Indraprastha College for Women. Her areas of interest are economic development and labor circulation. She is also a member of the Association of Indian Labor Historians in Delhi.

B.R. Chatterjee is a public health expert working on the immunology, epidemiology, and control of leprosy since the early sixties. He has undertaken comprehensive laboratory and field-based study on leprosy in association with various universities in the U.S. and with the International Anti-Leprosy Federation. He is the principal investigator and director, Leprosy Field Research Unit of the Leprosy Mission in Purulia, West Bengal.

Dulitha N. Fernando is a professor of community medicine at the Department of Community Medicine in the University of Colombo and has over 25 years of teaching and research experience. She has undertaken evaluations of health service projects and served as advisor and consultant to several international organizations.

Meena Gopal has recently completed her doctoral research on the labor process and its impact on women workers. She is presently a faculty member at the Research Center for Women's Studies, SNDT Women's University, Mumbai. Her areas of interest include public health, labor studies and gender studies, with a focus on people's lives and struggles for dignity and justice.

Indira Hettiarachchi is the Director of Health and Women's Programs, Plantation Housing and Social Welfare Trust in Sri Lanka, where she handles programs for improving the status of women in the estates and for enhancing people's participation in social development programs. As a physician, her areas of interest include improving maternal and child health services and control of communicable and non-communicable diseases in the estates.

Anwar Jafri has been with the Eklavya Foundation in Bhopal since its inception in 1982 and is its director since 1991. His areas of interest are education and development and he has been working on issues relating to education, literacy, and rural technology. He is currently involved in training and capability-building activities for village panchayats in Madhya Pradesh.

Yogesh Jain works with a multidisciplinary team at evolving an appropriate community health program in rural India. He is looking at problems of malaria diagnosis and management at the village level and interaction on infectious diseases and nutritional status. He was involved in teaching and practice of rational child health care as a clinical pediatrician at the All India Institute of Medical Sciences, New Delhi.

A.Q. Khan is an epidemiologist and public health expert. He has been the director of the Malaria Institute and additional director general of health services in Bangladesh. He has worked extensively on malaria as well as problems of health services in Bangladesh. He has also taught epidemiology.

Meri Koivusalo is a Research Fellow in the Globalism and Social Policy Program in the National Research and Development Council for Welfare and Health, Finland. She has a background of active involvement in social movements. Her area of work covers international health, environmental epidemiology, population issues, and development policies.

V. Raman Kutty is the Director of Health Action by People, an NGO in Kerala working on health-related issues. Initially he taught pediatrics, then shifted to research on health policy issues and also became active in people's science movements. His areas of interest include health policy and its linkages with development issues, economics of health care and epidemiology of chronic diseases in developing countries.

K.R. Nayar, a social scientist, is an Associate Professor at the Center of Social Medicine and Community Health, Jawaharlal Nehru University. He has been extensively involved in studies related to environment and health. Presently, he is working on decentralized health care, health sector reforms, and cooperative medical services.

Anant R. Phadke is in charge of a project on VHW-based sustainable primary health care at CEHAT in Mumbai. His areas of interest include drug policy, rational therapeutics, and training of village health workers. He has carried out research work in these areas and is also actively associated with concerned organizations and people's science movements in Maharashtra.

K. Seeta Prabhu is a professor of development economics at the Department of Economics, University of Mumbai. Issues pertaining to social sectors and links between economic growth and development are her areas of specialization. She has been associated with various government and non-government bodies and is a member of a group of women economists working on methodological issues pertaining to the gender development index.

Ritu Priya is a medical doctor with training in public health and has been exploring the interlinkages between epidemiology, health culture, and health policies. At present she is on the faculty of CSMCH/JNU, where she has been specifically working on communicable diseases control programs and on health of the urban poor.

Imrana Qadeer is a professor at the Center of Social Medicine and Community Health, Jawaharlal Nehru University. A qualified doctor (M.B.B.S., M.D.), she works on issues at the interface of medicine and society. Her areas of interest include the organization of public health services, the political economy of health, the health of workers and women in India, and research methodology. Currently, Professor Qadeer is working on the health implications of structural reforms, and has also been involved with the planning efforts of both governmental and grass-roots organizations.

Mohan Rao is a public health specialist and teaches at CSMCH/JNU. His main contribution is in understanding the economic determinants of family size in rural

Karnataka. He has also worked extensively on public health, family planning, and the history and politics of health.

Alpana Sagar, a medical doctor, is on the faculty of Center of Social Medicine and Community Health, Jawaharlal Nehru University, New Delhi and works in the field of public health. Her recent doctoral research involved developing a multidisciplinary perspective of women's health, especially during pregnancy. She has been working in public health projects in different parts of the country.

K.S. Sebastian has recently completed his doctoral research on social science issues in environmental health and works in the Christian Medical Association of India. He is involved in educational campaigns on public health through the media. He is also the coordinator of Child Health Information Network, a partnership of five NGOs from India and U.K. and an editor of *Health Dialogue* and *Rational Drugs*, both published by CMAI.

Binayak Sen is a doctor interested in linking the organizational potential of public health and people's movements, especially in the context of globalization. He is actively associated with health care programs among the working people of Chhattisgarh in Madhya Pradesh, specifically with the Chhattisgarh Mukti Morcha, a mass organization and Rupantar, a social action group.

Kasturi Sen is a Senior Research Associate in the Department of Public Health, University of Cambridge. A social scientist, her main interest lies in the comparative analysis of welfare states with a focus on vulnerable populations. For the past ten years, she has been involved in issues related to demographic change and the political economy of health and development in India.

Ghanshyam Shah is an eminent political scientist who has worked extensively on caste, class, communalism, and social movements. His work on plague in Surat in 1994 has contributed to an understanding of the importance of public administration for public health. He has held many important academic positions and at present is a Professor at CSMCH/JNU in New Delhi.

Anand Zachariah teaches at the medicine department of the Christian Medical College and Hospital at Vellore. His research interests lie in multidisciplinary approaches to the study of clinical infectious diseases, especially HIV/AIDS and tuberculosis and of deliberate self-harm and organophosphate poisoning. He is also actively involved in development of innovative methods of medical education.

S. Akbar Zaidi was affiliated to the Applied Economics Research Center, University of Karachi. He now undertakes independent research assignments. His areas of interest are political economy, institutions in underdeveloped countries, issues of governance, decentralization and democratization, macro-economics, and public policy and the social sectors.

Sheila Zurbrigg is a doctor who has worked in rural Tamil Nadu and has developed a socio-political perspective for understanding the health services in this country. She is currently at the Department of International Development Studies of the Dalhousie University, Canada and has been working on hunger and epidemic mortality in history, especially on malaria mortality in Punjab. She was a visiting professor at CSMCH/JNU, New Delhi.